THE CHURCH OF ENGLAND IN THE TWENTIETH CENTURY

VOLUME II
(1919–1939)

By the same Author

THE CHURCH OF ENGLAND
IN THE TWENTIETH CENTURY

BY

ROGER LLOYD
(CANON OF WINCHESTER)

VOLUME II
(1919–1939)

LONGMANS, GREEN AND CO
LONDON · NEW YORK · TORONTO

LONGMANS, GREEN AND CO LTD
6 & 7 CLIFFORD STREET LONDON W 1

ALSO AT MELBOURNE AND CAPE TOWN

LONGMANS, GREEN AND CO INC
55 FIFTH AVENUE NEW YORK 3

LONGMANS, GREEN AND CO
215 VICTORIA STREET TORONTO 1

ORIENT LONGMANS LTD
BOMBAY CALCUTTA MADRAS

First published 1950

Printed in Great Britain
SPOTTISWOODE, BALLANTYNE & CO. LTD.
London & Colchester

TO
ROSEMARY
DEAR DAUGHTER AND FRIEND

PREFACE

With this volume I end the work I began ten years ago. The first volume covered the years 1900 to 1918; this one is concerned with the years between the wars, 1919 to 1939. I have not hesitated, however, to stray over these boundaries when a little trespassing seemed to make the narrative clearer. In this volume we come to within ten years of the immediate present, and it would therefore be absurd to pretend that it can in any way be regarded as a work of formal history. It is rather a series of pictures of a great Church at work, and variously expressing the faith by which it lives, during twenty years of peculiar difficulty. These pictures are selective samples, drawn here and there from a vast and crowded canvas of great complexity, and they make no claim to being exhaustive. The statement of the personal points of view and convictions of significance which govern the selection I have included in the text of the book, in the Prologue and the Epilogue, rather than in this preface. Only the pleasant duty of saying 'Thank you' now remains, and this is a task as embarrassing as it is joyful. It is embarrassing because to make it complete would stretch this preface to an inordinate length, for so many different people have helped me, and often at no little cost of their time. There has never been anyone who failed to do all he or she could when asked for help, and the writing of this book has made not a few new friendships and deepened old ones. But here are the names of some of those without whose help in the supplying of documents of various kinds which could not otherwise be got certain parts of the book must have remained unwritten: the Bishops of Newcastle and Southampton, the Deans of Canterbury and Chester, the Rev. Charles Jenkinson of Leeds, the Rev. Frank Bennett, Rector of Wigan, and the past and present clergy of Alton in Hampshire. To them and to all the others whom they represent I offer most sincere thanks. Embedded in Chapter Six are two or three paragraphs of a pamphlet of mine which S.P.C.K. published more than twenty years ago, and I am grateful to the Society for allowing me to reprint them here. I am very grateful, too, to Miss Hazel Galloway for her labour in typing an often rather illegible manuscript and for undertaking the index. As with the first volume so with this I owe more than I can say, because it must be even more than I know, to the Rev. Arthur Hopkinson, who has read nearly all the book chapter by chapter as it was being written, and whose criticisms and suggestions have much enriched it.

Winchester
June 1949.

ROGER LLOYD.

CONTENTS

PROLOGUE

I. *Disenchantment in the Nineteen-Twenties*

The Englishman who liked to choose his reading by his knowledge of his own mood and his sense of his country's occasion might well have reached for his Macaulay as the old year of 1918 died. Turning over the pages until he came to the review of Southey's edition of *Pilgrim's Progress* he would soon have come upon a single sentence, 'Very few and very weary are those who are in at the death of the Blatant Beast.' There maybe he would pause, reflecting that it was written in 1830, not long after the previous Greatest War in History, but struck still more deeply by the uncanny aptness with which Macaulay's phrase about the length of the *Faerie Queene* described his own mood and his country's spiritual situation. The blatant beast of aggressive tyranny had been killed—that at least seemed then to be true—and the necessary endurance, the heroism, the long national self-discipline had constituted not the least of the great achievements of English history. But the better part of a whole generation had been lost, and those who were left were far more tired than they knew, drained of the wells and reserves of spiritual quality and resource. Neither his reading nor his experience could allow him to comfort himself with the easy hope that pride of achievement would by itself be enough to replenish the emptying reservoirs of the nation's spirit. He remembered too well the lessons of English history that achievement is always disenchanting. 'How my achievements mock me,' said Troilus. It was not to be long before many Englishmen were mocking their own achievements, and even the very soldiers who had won them.

The victory had been won but the tide of disillusion had also come in flood. Of the negotiations proceeding at Versailles nothing was heard that was good. The General Election of 1918 was perhaps the most distasteful in our parliamentary annals, and it had resulted in a House of Commons of which no subsequent historian has ever found a good word to say. The air was soon thick with betrayals and rumours of betrayals of the fighting men and the cause for which they had offered their lives. Lawrence of Arabia was already writing his famous and bitter comment on the old men who had sent the young men to suffer and to die:

We were fond together, and there are here memories of the sweep of the open places, the taste of wide winds, the sunlight, and the hopes in which we worked. It felt like morning, and the freshness of the world-to-be

1 B

intoxicated us. We were wrought up with ideas inexpressible and vaporous, but to be fought for. We lived many lives in those whirling campaigns, never sparing ourselves any good or evil: yet when we achieved and the new world dawned, the old men came out again and took from us our victory, and re-made it in the likeness of the former world they knew. Youth could win, but had not learned to keep, and was pitiably weak against age. We stammered that we had worked for a new heaven and a new earth, and they thanked us kindly and made their peace. When we are their age, no doubt we shall serve our children so.[1]

Less often quoted was his still more bitter dedicatory poem, *To S.A.*, which stands at the beginning of *The Seven Pillars of Wisdom*.

> I loved you, so I drew these tides of men into my hands
> and wrote my will across the sky in the stars
> To earn you Freedom, the seven pillared worthy house,
> that your eyes might be shining for me
> When we came.
>
> Men prayed me that I set our work, the inviolate house,
> as a memory of you.
> But for fit monument I shattered it, unfinished: and now
> The little things creep out to patch themselves hovels
> in the marred shadow
> Of your gift.[2]

It is easy to say this bitterness was exaggerated and unfair: perhaps it was. Whether fair or unfair that was how many people were feeling. What Lawrence had written was just one drop in a vast flood of the literature of disenchantment which poured from the publishers for a dozen years or more, and it was significant that one of the most sensitive figures of his time, and one of the very few heroes of the war in whom no one descried feet of clay was driven to write it. Poets and novelists, essayists and historians all joined to chant the dirges of disillusion; and many of them had by their achievements, their sufferings, and their endurances in the war fully earned their right to a respectful hearing as they interpreted the nation's mood. But they were followed by a host of imitators whose credentials were less impressive.

A sadly large proportion of the nation believed dimly that it had been cheated—returning soldiers of houses and even of jobs, still serving soldiers and sailors of the security of the Service when it came under the economy axe of Sir Eric Geddes, the ardent and

---

[1] *The Letters of T. E. Lawrence*, edited by David Garnett (Cape, 1938), p. 262. It was part of the original preface to *The Seven Pillars of Wisdom*, and on the advice of Bernard Shaw, Lawrence suppressed it from the subscribers' edition. It was therefore some years before it was generally available to be read.
[2] T. E. Lawrence, *The Seven Pillars of Wisdom* (Cape, 1935), p. 5. The first stanza and the last are quoted.

generous of the better world they had been too glibly promised, the working man of improvements in his condition, the intellectuals of a faith to live by, and all alike of a settled and a pacified world in which to bring up their children. Everyone had given so much for so long that few were inclined to give any more. 'Of those who survived only a small proportion took to public life; the majority turned resolutely to private business and stayed there.'[1] But the many expected the few to produce at once and on the spot the new world of comfort and plenty with all its appurtenances.

How shallow (remarked one of H. G. Wells' most voluble characters) was our conception of Reconstruction! was every conception of Reconstruction I ever encountered! To most of the hopeful people of that time Reconstruction meant simply—all they wanted—at once. Labour, for example, demanded an immediate shortening of hours and a rise in wages, and was blind to any necessity for intermediate phases or auxiliary constructive effort. In England trade after trade struck vigorously and got its advances, its eight hour day, and crowded off at once to see the cinema and football matches, leaving the working out of the Millenium to anyone else who chose to bother. Nobody chose to bother.[2]

The millenium, therefore, showed no signs of arriving; far from that, England was a more uncomfortable and distressing place to live in during the first five of the twenty inter-war years than it had been for many generations. Widespread disenchantment passed into disillusion, and disillusion into resentment.

Among most ordinary people whose actions were determined more by instinct than by reasoning this resentment showed itself in a dark suspicion of all institutions with long traditions behind them, or which they could identify as belonging to that old world from which they had been promised (or were invincibly convinced they had been promised) an escape. From those who are ridden by a vague but haunting suspicion not much good can be had. In the universities the reaction from the war showed itself in a more studied and bizarre form of severance from the old world, and in the determination to make all life a repudiation of it. In Oxford, and especially among the undergraduates who had themselves fought in the war, the reaction

expresses itself in eccentricity, blaséness, and superficial pleasure. Coffee-coloured trousers of almost unmeasurable dimensions became the fashion of the day; the bell-bottomed trousers of naval ratings were reduced almost to spats in comparison. Freak behaviour, loud-coloured shirts and ties, neglect of the barber, suède shoes and studied nonchalance figured in the daily round of post-war life. Oxford challenged Chelsea in its reversion to

---

[1] John Buchan, *Memory Hold the Door* (Hodder & Stoughton, 1940), p. 183.
[2] *The World of William Clissold*, vol. ii, p. 334, quoted in *The Future of the Church*, edited by Sir James Marchant (Longmans, Green, 1926), p. 243.

Bohemianism, right up to 1924–25. Such was the difficult and unsettled state of Oxford after the war. It was an exaggerated microcosm of life in general.[1]

The fact that these sentences are mostly concerned with the clothes men wore does not make them trivial. Fashions in clothing often cloak and express spiritual attitudes which go deep, and much addiction to oddly cut trousers and magenta shirts spells a spirit of revolt. The political symbolism of shirts has been one of the less creditable discoveries of the twentieth century.

Among the articulate who guided and led public opinion through their writings revolt was just as evident, though they themselves were much more brittle than either the working man or the undergraduate. There was almost nothing against which they did not revolt— religion, the reticences of morality, the sense of greatness. Priests, moralists, and the great men and women of the past were all alike commonly regarded as figures to be repudiated and sneered at by the intellectuals, but, as John Buchan noticed, 'their voices would suddenly crack, and what began as a sneer would end as a sob.'[2] What they had revolted against they had lost, and their world was empty for lacking it.

The interpreting class, which Coleridge called the 'clerisy,' the people who should have influenced opinion ran round their cages in vigorous pursuit of their tails. If they were futile they were also arrogant, for they had no creed to preach . . . The interpreting class plumed themselves wearily on being hollow men living in a waste land.[3]

The social life of England was cursed by an ubiquity of suspicion, while the sense of disillusion, so constantly underlined by the consistently discouraging facts of the political and economic spheres, was a slow poison spreading through all veins and arteries. Two decades which saw the growing impotence of the League of Nations, the resurgence of totalitarian dictatorship, the constantly and evidently fumbling political leadership of the nation, the general strike, the economic crisis and the prolonged mass unemployment it caused, the abdication of Edward VIII, the Munich crisis, and at last the opening of another world war, were evidently overcrowded by disaster. No historian will ever be able to write happily about English history between 1919 and 1939, and it would be hard to find any other period of twenty years in which more people were unhappy, or more people also believed that their unhappiness was neither necessary, nor of their own making, but due to some betrayal of the powers-that-be, the custodians and vested interests of the old order, or to the indifference of God Himself. Thus it is that a weary

[1] E. Ian F. Thomson, *The Oxford Pastorate* (Canterbury Press, 1946), p. 92.
[2] *Memory Hold the Door*, p. 185.   [3] *Ibid.*, p. 183.

nation which is not given time to rest and recover after the long strain is bound to feel.

II. *Restlessness in the Church*

It was a difficult field for the Church of England to sow and reap in; and the Church, being composed of perfectly ordinary English folk, had to perform this husbandry while it was itself hampered by the presence of exactly the same weariness and tensions. The Church was not less embarrassed than the nation by the bitter quarrel between the revolutionaries and the traditionalists, and on the Church's leaders the rank and file both of clergy and laity often made the same bitter comment which Lawrence had made on the politicians, 'They thanked us kindly, and they made their peace.' The same suspicion, the same disillusion as was in the nation as a whole ran through the life of the Church. It was mercifully less disastrous, because in the Church there was always the parochial system, the service of which claimed the majority of clergy and laity, and where the parochial system is, there too is a ceaseless pressure of pastoral need hammering at the door day and night, which simply must be met however angry one is with the bishops. This fact it was which kept many clergy and laity going, and gradually laid to rest the bitterness which was in them. Of course it was true also that Christian people had another anchor of the soul in their belief in the God of Hope. But here again it was noticeable that the New Testament Doctrine of Predestination, in which this belief is defined, rather dropped out of circulation between the wars.

The very first meeting of the new Church Assembly (it was called the National Assembly of the Church of England in those days) on June 30, 1920, proved to be an occasion on which these tensions were exhibited. From the early days of the Life and Liberty Movement there had been a subterranean cleavage between those of its members who desired the Enabling Act because it would facilitate organisational reform and increase efficiency and those who believed it would revitalise the whole Church throughout the entire range of its life and witness.[1] As long as the Movement's purpose was to get the Enabling Act passed this cleavage remained hidden. When it had become law the cleavage came to the surface and in the first meeting of the new Assembly it was plainly seen.

It was an historic moment. 'It is a great hour in the history of the Church and the people of England,' declared the Archbishop of Canterbury. The Assembly might still be in the embryonic stage,

---

[1] See Dr. William Temple's essay in *The Church Assembly and the Church*, edited by Frank Partridge (Press and Publications Board, 1930).

but 'the actual pulsing life has already begun, and it is part of the constitution of England.' He then gave them a felicitous quotation:

> there is a day in spring
> When under all the earth the secret germs
> Begin to stir and flow before they bud.
> The wealth and festal pomp of midsummer
> Lie in the heart of that inglorious hour
> Which no man names with blessing: but its fruit
> Is blessed by all the world. Such hours there are

'and this,' he said, 'is one of them.' First of all they must shape and fashion the machinery of the Assembly, so they proceeded to appoint a secretary and a treasurer, and, after much argument about its numbers and about the nice meaning of the word Provisional, a Provisional Standing Committee. On this committee ten laymen were appointed to serve, and of these only two were without titles, Mrs. Creighton and Mr. T. W. H. Inskip, K.C. The comment made that 'the Old Gang had collected all the positions of influence' may have been over suspicious, but was not unnatural. After that there was some heat about the appointment of the Legislative Committee. The Archbishop of York said that the Lord Chancellor and the Speaker of the House of Commons had declined to appoint the Parliamentary Ecclesiastical Committee (though required to do so by law) until they had seen the character and membership of the Church Assembly Legislative Committee. So there was need of a very strong Legislative Committee, and, amid loud protests from the floor, it was agreed that the Provisional Standing Committee should choose and present the names.

This put the members of the Provisional Standing Committee in a very strong, even in an almost impregnable position, and very soon members began to protest that this was not what they had meant in their work for the Life and Liberty Movement. Miss Minna Gollock got up and said that if this sort of thing was all that the Assembly had been elected to do then she and many others would never have lifted a finger to bring it into being; and the Bishop of Southwell supported her by bearing witness to the new hope and enthusiasm created in the Church by the passing of the Enabling Act, which constituted a challenge to the new Church Assembly:

In every village, in every parish has come a wave of enthusiasm. Three weeks ago I received personally 279 churchwardens and spoke to them all. There was a perfectly different spirit. They see the chance now opening out of being able really to carry through work which they know is for the good and value of the Church.[1]

---

[1] *Report of Proceedings of Church Assembly* (S.P.C.K., 1921).

Too much can be made of just one meeting of the Church Assembly, and that the very first. But it was symptomatic of the deepest and most inward trouble of the Church in those years. It caused great disappointment, particularly to many of the leaders of the Life and Liberty Movement to whom it owed the fact that it existed at all. They had hoped for a New Deal for the Church. What it seemed as though they were to be offered was the Old Deal, made slightly more efficient.

The returning military chaplains have sometimes been described as bursting with optimism about the possibilities of reform in the Church, and carrying about with them the delusion that the country was ripe for a great spiritual revival. But the evidence is all the other way. Such as it is, it tells of spiritual fatigue and bewilderment. In January 1919 Archbishop Davidson toured France and Germany to hold conferences with the chaplains. He found an extraordinary mixture of suggestions, on the one hand for equalising clerical stipends and for covering the land with companies of mission priests, and on the other even for the organising of a general strike of chaplains who would refuse to come home until their demands for the radical reforms of the 'official elements' in the Church were met. Their mood was difficult and suspicious, and although Davidson's sympathy did much to allay their bitterness, they found it far from easy to come home to work again in the still unreformed ecclesiastical system and to fit contentedly into the old routines of parish life.[1] Their deepest loyalties had held them fast and at last brought them home through all the neuroses and complexes caused by their intense spiritual loneliness during the years of war. The treadings of many of them had well nigh slipped, and were not to be steady for some years. But what saved them from slipping completely were, under God, two things, the wonderful work done in Flanders by Toc H. under P. B. Clayton, and also the work, the friendship, and the love of B. K. Cunningham in the Chaplains' School at Blendecques. In two years, nine hundred chaplains had passed through it and 'recovered their sense of proportion . . . and their obsessions fell into place.[2] Without Clayton and Cunningham the situation would have been twenty times more difficult than it was when the war was over and the chaplains made the hard transition to peace, an embittered country and an archaically organised home Church.

Many plans were in the air to ease the situation. The reports of

---

[1] G. K. A. Bell, Bishop of Chichester, *Randall Davidson* (Oxford University Press, 1935), vol. ii, p. 943. (Hereafter cited as 'Bell.')

[2] John R. H. Moorman, *B. K. Cunningham, A Memoir* (S.C.M. Press, 1947), p. 92.

the Archbishop's several Committees of Enquiry after the National Mission had been published, and had done much to point out the ways in which the Church must go. The Church Assembly existed, and held out the hope that at least the grossest of the archaisms of organisation would be swept away. The setting up of the Knutsford Test School for Service Ordination Candidates promised a relief in due time to heavily over-driven incumbents. There were paper schemes for doing away at last with the age-old scandal of grinding clerical poverty and for some equalising of clerical incomes. The Lambeth Conference of 1920 served the Church magnificently in its Appeal for Unity, which stirred the imagination of Christendom at the moment when all Churches alike found imaginative enthusiasm the hardest of virtues. In the first years of the peace these things were promised, and the instruments for fulfilling their promise were in process of being fashioned. In the pages which follow we shall see how far all these promises came to fruition. Most of them did. But at that moment in the Church, as in the State, it was not easy to persuade men to believe much in promises; and everybody could see that time, much time, must pass before they could be fulfilled.

The spirit which specially characterised the rank and file clergy and laity of the Church throughout the period was perhaps most correctly suggested by the title of a celebrated book by a famous priest, Dick Sheppard, *The Impatience of a Parson*. It is true that there were more radically impatient sons among those who staffed and served the Church than there had been for many generations. Thus the air rang for year after year with criticisms of the Church uttered by those who were its members and of this denigration *The Impatience of a Parson* was a comparatively mild example. As the years passed it almost seemed as though some Anglicans had been born with a spiritual muck-rake in their hands, and were never tired of proclaiming how dead and stinking the Anglican Church was, and of accusing it of every sort of betrayal of its Master. Yet they rarely left it. They carried on their campaigns of vituperative denigration at the tops of their voices, and though it was all very unseemly, yet they did it because there was a fire burning within them. But the more they spat and nagged, the less they solved the problem which tormented them. They found no peace that way. Theirs was a very strained churchmanship, as probably it ought to have been, both for them, and for the less vociferous majority who felt as they did, but so much more tepidly, the truth for which they so eloquently contended. It is, in fact, a strain to belong to the Anglican Church, and loyalty both to it and to Christianity in general must involve some degree of tension. For ours is an adult Church, but we are the citizens of a raw and loutish age. We belong to a generation which fears freedom, but also to a Church which demands freedom from its members, and we walk erect only by somewhat difficult gymnastic feats. For some passionately loyal Anglican souls the tension was more than they could bear; and feeling acutely uncomfortable, they lashed out at the nearest and handiest target. It was inconceivable that they should criticise our Lord, and they did not care (or dare?) to criticise the twentieth century. So they denounced ceaselessly the Church of their Baptism. It was much too easy; but also very understandable—the rebellion of an immature mind against its membership of a profoundly mature society. If the account they gave of the Church was even approximately correct, then either it ought to have died or they ought to have left it, and neither has happened. They dimly perceived some greatness, some mission; but they disqualified themselves from coming to grips with it because of their chronic ill-temper, and their perpetual state of irritation blinded them. It is no doubt always true that there is a horrible contrast between the splendour of Jesus and the actual behaviour of the Body of Christ on earth, but to make the abuse of His Body the Church testify to the reality of one's loyalty to our Lord was to disqualify oneself from understanding wherein the greatness of the Church lies. They had all their knowledge about our Lord, about prayer, worship, and sacraments, at the hands of the Church they abused so wildly and incessantly: and the best of them acknowledged it.

In the generalisation that the Church of England in the twentieth century is the spectacle of an essentially mature Church struggling to shepherd and to redeem the citizens and institutions of an essentially adolescent and raw era, we come near to baring the heart of the tension. It was a strain to be a citizen and a churchman. It was no less a strain to be a priest and a citizen. This strain was at its intensest in the years between the wars. Since 1939 it has eased in various subtle ways. All through the period the phenomenon called Anglicanism has steadily asserted itself as having, under God, the first claim on the loyalty of churchpeople. It has asserted itself, for example, as over against the intensity of loyalty which in the period before 1919 was largely given to the Anglo-Catholic and Protestant parties in the Church. Between 1919 and to-day Anglicanism has so developed as to cut the ground from beneath the feet of the older party distortions of itself. Considered as organised parties both Anglo-Catholicism and Protestantism have shot their bolts, and in so far as they are still partisan there is nothing to be had from them and no virtue is left in them. The real obscurantists now are the people who are still singing the old Anglo-Catholic party choruses and shouting the old Protestant slogans of the early days of the century. As it gradually became apparent that Anglicanism was a

B*

far bigger thing than either of them, and that this Anglicanism was for good or ill expressed in the traditions and systems of the Church of England, there was (as there was bound to be) a period of doubt and even bitterness while those who had been trained to be loyal to a party were struggling to find their feet again in loyalty to a very great Church which accepted all that a party could do to enrich it, and then transcended the party. They had to learn that the Anglican Church claimed from them not humour and mockery but love and loyalty if they would serve her, and they were not accustomed so to express themselves. It was the reverse and the hard side of the truth that the Catholic Church in every part, and not least the Anglican part, is immortal with the eternity of the Body of Christ; and the leading achievement of the Anglican Church in this period is that it has steadily imposed this view of itself upon its members, and transcended every party view less wide than that of Anglicanism itself.[1] This process was certainly necessary, but it was not without pains and tensions for many.

Here, again, was seen the enormous power to steady those temporarily uncertain of their moorings and assailed by bitterness of spirit possessed by a Church with a strongly marked pastoral tradition. It may be exemplified in the ecclesiastical odyssey of one of the greatest of her children, Evelyn Underhill, as her letters reveal it.

She did not care a straw about ecclesiastical statesmanship, and she repudiated most of its methods of expression,[2] but she had to make up her mind about Anglicanism and its value to herself. Her published letters show how the problem perplexed her, how her views on it changed and matured, and what the value of her membership of the Church of England was for her. In May 1907 she was, perhaps, just a little impatient with a correspondent who had raised the question of Anglicanism, and she summarily dismissed it as 'a slightly diluted Catholicism.'[3] In 1911 she had been sure for five years, and was still sure that the Roman Catholic Church 'was my ultimate home.' So strong was this conviction that 'to join any other communion is simply an impossible thought,' and 'to have any personal dealings with Anglicanism seems for me a kind of treach-

[1] A friend who read this passage in MS commented, 'The discovery of Anglicanism did not come from within so much as from without, i.e. the children taught their mother not to be a fool!'

[2] See e.g. her letter of May 5, 1941: 'I never go to meetings nowadays nor, I fear, have I much belief in their usefulness. All this discussion about a 'Christian Society,' a 'new Christian England' etc., seems so entirely on the surface, doesn't it? . . . The new life, when it comes, I think, will not be the result of discussions, plans and meetings, but will well up from the deepest sources of prayer.' *The Letters of Evelyn Underhill*, edited by Charles Williams (Longmans, Green, 1943), p. 307.

[3] *Ibid.*, p. 63.

ery.'[1] But twenty years later, by 1931, her position had completely changed, and she explained it to a Roman Catholic correspondent thus:

I feel I owe you an explanation of my 'position' which must seem to you a very inconsistent one. I have been for years now a practising Anglo-Catholic, and solidly believe in the Catholic status of the Anglican Church, as to orders and sacraments, little as I appreciate many of the things done among us. It seems to me a respectable suburb of the city of God—but all the same, part of 'greater London.' I appreciate the superior food, etc., to be had nearer the centre of things. But the *whole* point to me is in the fact that our Lord has put me *here*, keeps on giving me more and more jobs to do for souls here, and has never given me orders to move . . . Of course I know I might get other orders at any moment, but so far that is not so. After all He has lots of terribly hungry sheep in Wimbledon, and if it is my job to try and help with them a bit it is no use saying I should rather fancy a flat in Mayfair, is it?[2]

Two years later, in March 1933, she was writing to another friend, and her position was still the same. Rome was attractive 'because it *does* understand and emphasise worship.' But her place was 'in the trenches' with the Church of England and not in the 'barracks' with Rome. 'The life of prayer can be developed in the C. of E. as well as anywhere else if we really mean it.' In forgetting that, Newman had been guilty of ' spiritual selfishness.' But she would obey her orders and stay where she was, though that did not prevent her from realising that 'there is still a great deal to be done and a great deal to put up with, and the diet is often none too good—but we are here to feed His sheep where we find them, not to look for comfy quarters.'[3]

'We are here to feed His sheep, not to look for comfy quarters'—it is a homely phrase but it exactly describes the great tradition of pastoral responsibility which in every generation carries the servants of the Anglican Church through their personal crises, through their moments of irritation with the Church, and keeps them within it as loyal members. Whatever happens, and though the very skies fall, there are still sheep to be tended. It is our office in the Church which gives us our charge to tend them. It is unthinkable that we should desert them, or let them down. But we cannot serve them if we are in opposition to their Church and ours; we cannot serve them fully if we are out of love and loyalty with the Church. For their sakes, therefore, we stay in our quarters, and discipline ourselves to talk less about our discomforts. Such thoughts as these must have rescued from ecclesiastical bitterness hundreds of churchpeople, and steadied them. The same thing is true of those moments of great

---

[1] *Ibid.*, p. 125. [2] *Ibid.*, pp. 195, 196. [3] *Ibid.*, p. 210.

perplexity when the pressure of trends, and tendencies, and events so enlarges opportunity and complicates duty that we can hardly discern between our right and left hands. It was so throughout the twenty years 1919 to 1939, and it is so still. But nothing that can ever happen in the world can absolve the Anglican Christian from fidelity to his pastoral charge, and this thought again steadies him for in the time of the breaking of nations there is always the anchor of clear knowledge of what the next pastoral job is.

III. *Giants and Heroes*

To read many of the documents by which the Church sought to stir and guide its witness during those twenty years, and to stretch memory backwards to recall the events of those years and the persons who shaped them, is to be left with two main impressions. These are that the Church was served by an unusually large number of men and women of the highest quality, a few of whom were giants; and that the events with which they had to deal were more than usually bewildering in their variety and complexity.

Certainly there were giants in the land in those days. A single generation of the Church which saw on the throne of Augustine first Randall Davidson, then Cosmo Gordon Lang, and finally William Temple, could not be said to lack leadership of a very high order. As the years pass by one has less and less desire to quarrel with the judgement that Davidson was one of the two or three greatest of all the Archbishops of Canterbury. If towards the end of his years the firmness of his grasp faltered a little, as it seemed to do over the matter of the Revised Prayer Book, he had nevertheless raised his high office to a pinnacle of eminence and a height of authority which it had never before known. It provided the whole Anglican Communion with a badly needed centre of gravity, and through the influence of Lambeth when he reigned there the Church of England was held together and its unity was intensified. 'Certain it is that in Randall Davidson's tenure of the archiepiscopal see the office of Archbishop of Canterbury acquired a commanding position in the communions of Christendom unprecedented in the previous history of the Church.'[1] The judgement is not a word too strong.

This office he handed to his brother of York, Cosmo Gordon Lang, who might well have quailed as he contemplated the standard set. Probably he did quail for in his heart he was a humble man. To some he gave the impression of prelacy, but it was the impression of something set only skin deep in him, if indeed it was there at all. The true man displayed when he spoke, as he sometimes did, of his

---

[1] Bell, vol. ii, p. 1153.

unworthiness for the office he held, and when, near the end of his life, he said he must retire because he needed a few years to make his soul's peace. His courage was great, and it came out when he publicly rebuked the entourage of The Duke of Windsor just after the Abdication. It made him violently unpopular, as he knew it must, and it is difficult to think of another archbishop who would have dared to speak publicly in such a way and at such a moment. He was perhaps the most polished orator of his generation, and he was characteristically at his best when overseas missions were his subject. On the occasion of the marriage of the Duke and Duchess of Kent, he gave an address which was a classic of its sort, and his lovely voice graced the beauty of the words he chose. He was an archbishop with whom people came first and public affairs second, and he had a wonderful discernment and patience. He was, for instance, Dick Sheppard's constant anchor, offering him a friendship which never wearied and never failed, and an understanding which that tormented soul could find nowhere else. In a very black moment of his life Basil Jellicoe, too, found great comfort and strength from the Archbishop. All who knew him well thanked God they did.

But if any one man can be said to have towered over all his contemporaries and to have dominated the Church of his day, that man was undoubtedly William Temple, successively Bishop of Manchester, Archbishop of York, and Archbishop of Canterbury.[1] He would never admit that it was due primarily to himself that the Enabling Act was passed, and likely enough it would have been passed without him, but certainly not so quickly. He always used to say that the creating of the Life and Liberty Movement, and therefore the passing of the Enabling Act was due more to Dick Sheppard than to any other man. Indirectly, the Church Assembly, on this view, owes its existence to Sheppard, which is an ironical thought, seeing how constantly the Assembly infuriated him. But the two great conferences at Birmingham and Malvern, which did so much to gather together, to intensify, and to guide the Church's thinking on the relationship between religion and sociology, might never have been held without Temple's initiative or succeeded without his chairmanship. Without them, the witness of the Church would have been sadly impoverished. But that is true of every single thing which Temple ever did, and the list of his undertakings is staggering in its variety and its range. Other men besides him have done much (but

[1] It is true that Temple became Archbishop of Canterbury in 1942, whereas the penultimate date of this book is 1939. But the terminus of 1939 is approximate only, and will not be adhered to with academic and Chinese exactness. It simply serves to indicate that this book makes no attempt to describe the Church in the war of 1939 to 1945.

few, if any, did so much as he) to establish the inevitability of the connection between Christian Theology and Social Order, to widen the recognition of this connection, and to give to this conviction a policy to pursue. He was not the only evangelistic apostle to the student world of his day; and there were others besides himself who could give retreat addresses and write devotional books of the highest spiritual order. The Church had other philosophers, though not many. There were even one or two who could make shift to explore the borderland where literature and theology join hands, though it is hard to think of any who wrote more effectively of that exploration than he did in *Mens Creatrix*. He was by no means the only great diocesan bishop of his day, not the only one whose slightest look was law and his whisper gospel to all his ordination candidates, though no other has ever given presidential addresses to his diocesan conferences of Temple's quality. But if he was not absolutely unique in each and all of these fields, he was a master of them all, and he was absolutely the only man who was. Nor was there anyone else who was loved, trusted, and admired as he was throughout almost the whole range of society. No one but he, moreover, could have been quite so fully the architect of the Oecumenical Movement. In his time he was the real leader of the whole of Christendom lying outside the Roman obedience. He spoke with authority, and everyone conceded that authority, in every one of these spheres of Christian witness, and in others as well. It was in his first big book, *Mens Creatrix*, that in a sense he wrote his own epitaph, 'We need very urgently someone who will do for our day the work that St. Thomas Aquinas did for his.'[1] Aquinas constructed the *Summa*, and Temple also dedicated himself to justify and to serve exactly the same wholeness of all twentieth-century life when God is its centre. Whether he succeeded as Aquinas did is doubtful, and he himself knew well the dangers of too absolute a success in such a quest.[2] But no other figure in modern history has come so near success, and if it be held that the sum total of Temple's teaching, leadership, writings, and episcopates is not quite a modern *Summa*, there is no doubt that he was authentically in the Aquinas succession. We still stand too near to him to attempt to decide the exact differences made to the witness of the Church because Temple towered over it. But they are evi-

[1] William Temple, *Mens Creatrix* (Macmillan, 1917), p. viii.
[2] In 1925 Temple spoke thus of the achievement of Aquinas and the Schoolmen: 'Magnificent as it was, its very magnificence constituted a danger. Indeed, one desires to say that while we should aim, as they aimed, at trying to preach, if we can, or in the measure that we can, a view of the world inspired by Christ which really puts every feature of human activity into its own place, we shall immediately be on our guard if we feel we have done it with completeness . . . We ought not to have a complete system.' *Essays in Christian Politics* (Longmans, Green, 1927), p. 196.

dently considerable, and in some ways they are probably decisive for the course of its history. The presence of William Temple was the greatest of all the assets the Church possessed as she marched through a profoundly difficult era.

Nor was the Church without priests who by their preaching and living had the power to quicken the hearts of vast masses of ordinary people—men who were indeed popular preachers but who never became glib or cheap. Such were Dick Sheppard of St. Martin-in-the-Fields and Geoffrey Studdert-Kennedy of the Industrial Christian Fellowship. These two were not alone in this power—there was also Gough McCormick, Dean of Manchester—but no one else had quite the same pre-eminence. Of each it was true to say that the crowd would throng to suffocation any church or hall in which they were billed to speak. Each of them was on fire and burned up with the love of Jesus Christ, and each had a love for all His children, most of all of the erring and luckless ones, that would never let them rest. Yet they were very different men. Sheppard's genius was for friendship. He could make a man or woman his friend for life after only five minutes conversation, and it would be no surface friendship. It would touch the depths of life. Kennedy, on the other hand, was not immediately at ease with those who met him casually, and he could sit withdrawn and silent for hours together. But his preaching of the Gospel was possibly the finest, the most memorable and moving, of any heard in English pulpits in this century. It was sometimes slangy, but it also often contained passages of such beauty that one could hardly tell whether they were poetry or prose. It was not always in 'language understanded of the people' and yet they always understood it and listened with breathless eagerness. Behind all he said there was a profound and coherent system of philosophy. His sermons went well into a book, as Sheppard's could not have done. To Sheppard on the other hand the Church owes much of the grand chance it has always had to proclaim the Gospel by broadcasting. His services were the first to be broadcast and he himself had a great flair for broadcasting, a medium which Kennedy could probably not have used successfully. Both were men who carried about with them the visible stigmata of suffering, their own, but far, far more of other people's. Each had developed to a remarkable degree the power of inspiring trust in others, and wherever they went there were those who took one look at them and murmured, 'That man I know would understand my trouble.' Thus each carried on his shoulders an unimaginable, crushing burden of the woes of others. They both died what were, to human seeming, untimely deaths; and yet both had reached the point where they simply could not have gone on any more, dragging their weary bodies round the country. The wealth they gave in the Church to the cause of Christ cannot be estimated, but it was very great.

Besides its leaders and its prophets a Church must have its theologians, and of these the Church was not starved. Perhaps the most influential of them all was Clement Hoskyns—a judgement presently to be defended. Besides him there was Oliver Quick, a master of analytical theology, whose forte it was to disentangle the different threads of truth in a dogma and then weave them together in a new synthesis. His two great books, *The Christian Sacraments* and *Doctrines of the Creed*, quickly became classics of the art of theological integration. Fr. Lionel Thornton, of the Community of the Resurrection, reached far fewer people than did Quick, for he wrote for the pure scholar. But his book *The Incarnate Lord* was one of which other theologians speak reverentially, and most competent judges regard it as one of the two or three outstanding theological works of the period. It went far towards cutting a new road through a jungle down which scientists and theologians could walk hand in hand. In a far more popular way the same task was assayed by B. H. Streeter, both in his lectures at Oxford, and in his best known book, *Reality*. It had a very wide circulation, and did much to commend the Faith effectively to educated agnostics.

The theologians were matched by men and women upon whom another vocation was laid. It might be called the vocation of keeping alive the social conscience of Christians. There was a long roll of those who worthily bore that charge to the Church's good. Fr. Basil Jellicoe and Conrad Noel, James Adderley, Robbins of Leeds, and, above all, William Temple were but a few of them; and among those who are alive still there are Maurice Reckitt, Charles Jenkinson, and Canon V. A. Demant. The same period saw the veritable prince of all principals of theological colleges, B. K. Cunningham of Westcott House, Cambridge, at the very height of his power. It would not be extravagant to suggest that, William Temple alone excepted, no single man did quite so much to shape the Church as B. K. Cunningham. Among the many other vocations of which the modern Church stands in need that of the professed religious life of monastery and convent is conspicuous. In this field too there was uncommon distinction. A generation which saw Frere and Talbot at Mirfield, Kelly at Kelham, and Mother Maribel at Wantage could not regard itself as starved of monastic and conventual superiors of a high order.

But perhaps the outstanding feature of the leadership given to and within the Church during those twenty years was the rising prominence of laymen. No clerical author taught the Church half so much about mysticism as Evelyn Underhill: few taught us so much about worship. It is quite possible, too, that in her work as a director of souls and a retreat conductor she brought fully as many souls to God as any clergyman; and she spoke with an authority to which the whole Church, clergymen and lay people alike, listened with profound respect. In her most difficult art she trained successors who are with us still.

An uncountable number of lay people, and indeed clergy too, learned much of their theology at lay hands, and the Church was tremendously blessed by a host of lay theologians who had the art of effectively using new mediums for the popularising of theology. How many people have had their theology at the hands of Mr. C. S. Lewis, and how many have been forced to think again and yet again about our Lord by Miss Dorothy Sayers, through her broadcast plays, *The Man Born to be King*, and her admirable newspaper articles on the Creed? Side by side with them stood Mr. T. S. Eliot, perhaps the most considerable poet of our time. As a poet no one could ignore him, and the fact that he was content to be a loyal member of the Church of England must have made many an intellectual agnostic wonder if the Church was as dead and as despicable as he had assumed. The power of Charles Williams, a 'romantic theologian, i.e. one who is theological about romance,' was very great upon those who understood him. He was a towering figure as a poet, a critic, and a writer of celestial romances; and as a person his quality was such that when he died C. S. Lewis said of him, 'No event has so corroborated my faith in the next world as Williams did simply by dying. When the idea of death and the idea of Williams thus met in my mind, it was the idea of death that was changed.' For Williams was 'a masculine angel, a spirit burning with intelligence and charity.'[1] To all these may be added those laymen who taught the Faith through their art, Ralph Vaughan Williams, Sybil Thorndike, and, no doubt just as effectively as they, Lord Hugh Cecil and Sir Stafford Cripps from their opposed political points of view.

A Church which, in a single generation, could number among its members such a host of men and women of the highest talent, and so many of them laymen, cannot reasonably complain that it lacked the lustre of great names. The list is astonishing in its length, its eminence, and its range; and it is far from being complete. Has there been any other period of twenty years in the history of the Church of England quite so distinguished by men and women of the first rank of achievement?

The events, problems, and issues with which these people and the

[1] *Essays Presented to Charles Williams*, with a Preface by C. S. Lewis (Oxford University Press, 1947), pp. xiv and ix.

whole Church had to deal were both numerous and varied. These twenty years were very crowded. The Church Assembly had been born, and with it there had been set up an army of subordinate councils and conferences for every diocese, rural deanery, and parish, the total effect of which was to influence and to modify the life of the Church at a thousand points. Because the Assembly existed a mass of legislation was made possible—measures changing, inaugurating, or controlling such matters as Clergy Pensions, Dilapidations, Patronage and a score of others. A further consequence was the new method of governing the Church through central boards or committees. Throughout the period the sufficient supply of ordination candidates and their training remained a problem. There were many controversies. The Revised Prayer Book provided the most celebrated of them, and to that must be added the controversies caused by the Modernist Conference of 1919, by the public challenges of the Bishop of Birmingham to the Archbishop of Canterbury over evolution, and by the invitation of a Unitarian to preach in Liverpool Cathedral. The place of the Church in the educational world was always being debated, and so was the duty of the Church in matters social, political, and economic. The problem of reunion occupied at least as much time as any of these; and the problems of the Churches overseas in such matters as their relationship to government, to native marriage customs, and their maintenance, never ceased to be pressing. More and more attention was paid to the growing Oecumenical Movement; while at home the grave facts of the moral situation of the people of England, and the lamentable statistics of divorce, were always before the mind of the Church. Pressing upon it day and night were the secularist challenge, and the constant efforts the Church made in theology, in devotion, in renewal to meet it.

It would have been easy to continue with this list almost indefinitely, and to fill several pages with a catalogue of the matters to which the Church had to pay attention, for these twenty years were exceptionally crowded. Such a chronicle as this must perforce pick and choose between them, selecting the few and leaving the many entirely untouched. Selectiveness of this sort, though essential, is apt to become very arbitrary, and it must be exercised by the light of some intelligible criterion of choice. But what criterion can there possibly be which is more and other than the personal preferences, even prejudices of the author? Must he be reduced to heeding only the events and problems which happen to interest him most? It would be an irresponsible way of procedure. But there is a criterion of selection more valid than this, though it is still personal. It is to say, That matters most which illustrates best what, in the author's belief, twentieth-century Anglicanism as practised in the Church of England is meant to be and is trying to do. That may be personal but it is also intelligible. It is personal because it depends on a personal view of Anglicanism. It is intelligible because the only possible justification for there being many Churches and not one is if the members of each Church believe that their Church has something to give to the total wealth of Christendom which other Churches have not. If that is so, the history of any Church becomes the record of its success or failure in making its own characteristic contribution. If it is not so, there is really no reason for continuing in the membership of any Church of which this is not believed. Therefore it is necessary to explain what this personal view of Anglicanism is if the principle of selection which it governs is to be made clear. To this, then, the last section of this opening chapter is devoted.

IV. *Anglicanism—a Personal Statement*

Anglicanism is a way of corporately following Christ. It is a way which bears the marks both of catholicism and of protestantism, for Anglican Churches are catholic and they are also reformed. The biggest achievement of Anglicanism is the worldwide Anglican Communion of Churches. Starting from the Church of England Anglicanism spread slowly over the globe. For the most part it followed the flag, and where British colonists or governments went the English Church went with them, to the Americas, to India, to Africa, to the Arctic, to West Indian plantations. Where in process of time the colonised or annexed lands won their independence the British governments came home but the Anglican Church remained, as in the U.S.A. yesterday and in India and Burma to-day. Anglicanism has spread also to many lands, such as China and Japan, where the British flag has never flown. Wherever this way of following Christ has spread, there it has taken root, and it has been proved to be a way which can be followed by peoples of every race, every colour, every level of culture and civilisation. Always its essential spirit has been missionary, and every Anglican Church founded has looked to see what others it could found. Anglicanism may have been begun and long sustained by the Church of England, and its beating heart is still in the two provinces of Canterbury and York, but it is as wide as humanity because there is in it that which all humanity can adopt and make its own.

This is a stirring achievement indeed, unique in the long history of Christendom. Not even the Church of Rome has spread further geographically; and that Church remains the Church of Rome, whereas the various Churches comprising the Anglican Communion are bound together by wholly different ties and are in no sense the Church of Canterbury. If this is the biggest achievement of the Anglican Communion, the heart of Anglicanism ought to be found in whatever it is that successfully holds all the Anglican Churches in the world, from Japan westwards to California, in living communion with each other, and makes possible the decennial gathering of all their bishops in the Lambeth Conference. What is this tie? It is not our loyalty to the Scriptures, for they are not the exclusive possession of any Church. Neither establishment, nor any other particular relationship to the state has anything to do with it: the Church of England is the only Anglican Church which is established, and a Church may be in a nonconformist position, as is the Episcopal Church of Scotland, and still be Anglican. It is not that Anglican Churches are pervaded by the spirit of England. Tell that to the members of the Episcopal Church of the U.S.A. and see what they would say. The Anglican Church in Japan grows steadily more Japanese and eastern, that in Uganda steadily more African. Wherever the Anglican Church is planted it becomes all the time more native to its new soil and less native to the soil of the land whence it came. Yet all these Churches, African, Australian, Indian, and Chinese remain in formal and living communion with each other, cherish their Anglicanism, and regard Canterbury as their focal point and its archbishop as the natural chairman of their assemblies.

The tie that binds them is the Book of Common Prayer as the norm of their worship, and with its implications as the criterion of their corporate living of Christianity. The revisers of 1662 dimly foresaw something like this when they wrote that the new service for the baptism of those of riper years 'may always be useful for the baptizing of natives in our plantations.' The revisers of 1928 had the same thought in mind when they prefixed to their revision a preface which brought together the thought of a whole world to be won for Christ, and the thought of the Book of Common Prayer. 'We are living in a new world; it is ours, if we are true to the faith that is in us, to seek to make it a better world.' The book of Common Prayer has been retained, with slight modifications, by all the Anglican Churches as their official service book. In all of them, from Westminster Abbey to the tiny mission station on stilts in a Malayan jungle or the igloo church in a snowfield in the Arctic, the liturgical worship follows the same familiar Anglican pattern, with the same epistles, collects and gospels. It is not only Rome which can boast that in every Roman Catholic church in the world the service is in essentials the same as in St. Peter's in Rome. It is as true of the Anglican Communion with this difference that in all Roman churches the service is in Latin, but in all Anglican ones it is in the vernacular native tongue which the people understand; and this surely is far better.

The common use of the Prayer Book Ordinal registers for the whole Church the continuance of the visible notes of catholicity, and the threefold ministry, given within the apostolic succession, ensures that the shape of the Church shall be the same in all its provinces in every land. Everywhere there is the ministry of bishops, priests, and deacons; and in every Anglican Church the Communion is celebrated and given by ministers who have been episcopally ordained. The admission to Communion is always by Confirmation by a bishop. This has the result of securing uniformity in outward shape between the different Anglican Churches, and without this it is hard to see how the whole Communion of Churches could be held together. But the Ordinal, the apostolic succession in the ministry, and the rite of confirmation, are not jealously preserved chiefly as a piece of mechanism which secures unity, but because all Anglicans believe that this Church order is a part of the will of God for all Churches which prize their catholic status. This status is embodied still further in the ineradicably sacramental tone and emphasis of the Book of Common Prayer.

All this the Anglican Communion shares with the Roman Catholic and the Orthodox Churches. But where our system, as exemplified in the Book of Common Prayer and enshrined in centuries of history, differs most strongly from theirs is in the tremendous emphasis it places on the spiritual freedom of the individual. Throughout the whole range of our worship and our life the permissive 'You may' or 'You should' predominates over the dominical 'You must.' The Prayer Book says 'You must' to the clergy in the ordering of public worship, and in the recitation of the daily Offices of Morning and Evening Prayer. It says 'You must' to the laity only in the matter of communicating three times in the year, including Easter Day. This emphasis has coloured the whole expression of Anglicanism, and there is no Church in the world which so passionately believes in freedom and which so positively demands it from clergy and laity alike. Anglicanism is an assertion of spiritual freedom, and there is nothing of which the Anglican Communion is more completely convinced. As a result no priest in all Christendom is as free as an Anglican priest, and his freedom is more nearly absolute, safeguarded as it is at every turn and point, than that of any other stipendiary in any other profession in the modern world.

So strongly does Anglicanism believe that the best work is done and the best lives are lived when clergy and laity are trusted with freedom as nearly absolute as makes no matter that it faces squarely the fact that many will abuse that freedom, and that in consequence, some scandals, many inconsistencies, and much wastage must mar its picture. Anglicanism knows very well that it carries a higher proportion of spiritual passengers to weaken its witness than any other Church does. It knows too that the wastage under a system which so exalts freedom must be heavy. But its belief in freedom is so fundamental that it deliberately rates these considerable dangers as less than the gain which freedom brings. It is a sign of the maturity of Anglicanism. But the dangers of freedom are real, and though we cease to be Anglicans in heart and mind if we say they are more real than the benefits of freedom, we must never forget them. There are some words of Archbishop William Temple which puts this gravely and clearly:

> The whole desire of the Church has been to offer the fullness of God's help to every soul but never to dictate to any soul precisely how that soul may best receive the benefit. It sets a high standard for the individual member. No doubt it involves comparative failure for very many who might, by a more strict and more military discipline, have been led to a fuller use of all the means of grace than in fact they practise under the Anglican system. None the less I believe the Church of England did deliberately adopt that attitude and I believe it did so rightly. For with all the dangers—in fact, humanly speaking with all the certain loss involved— there is made possible in this way for all the members of the Church a fullness of individual apprehension and appropriation which is almost impossible and is certainly discouraged under a system which so marks out for men quite clearly their religious duties so that when they have performed these they feel that their duty is done.[1]

From this basic principle of freedom an important corollary follows. It is that in the Anglican system, or scale of values, the average counts for more than the exceptional. Anglican Churches have produced great men and women in abundance, and the Church of England in our generation has been served by a long list of people of high eminence and uncommon ability, as we have already seen on an earlier page. No one underestimates the value of heroism or disputes the immensity of our debt to their leadership. Nevertheless there is no Church in Christendom in which the leadership principle counts for less. In the Anglican way of life what really counts is the cumulative pressure upon society of the anonymous host of the average; and certainly the Anglican Communion believes that its own particular part of the Kingdom of God will best be occupied and won for Christ by the rank and file membership of the Church. Our real heroes are those whose names can never be known, the ordinary parish priest, the Sunday School teacher, the member

---

[1] *Essays in Christian Politics* (Longmans, Green), pp. 201, 202.

of the Mothers' Union, the sidesman, and most of all the small band of the faithful who make the congregation at the Eucharist on weekdays. On their continued and utterly obscure fidelity the entire worldwide Anglican Communion of Churches ultimately rests. If that were everywhere withdrawn for only one generation the Church would collapse and no amount of specially gifted leadership by those in places of eminence and authority could save it. It is perhaps not the least of the high distinctions of Anglicanism that within it is solved the dilemma which torments the rest of the world. The dilemma is this: since most people must in any case be obscure how can they be saved from believing that obscurity is the same as insignificance? In the secular world of the twentieth century it *is* the same. But in the Anglican Church it is not, because instinctively Anglicanism organises itself as though the aphorism, Look after the Community and the Leadership will then look after itself, were really true, as of course it is.

In the forefront of the Anglican array of battle, then, we place the average, the rank and file member of the Church. Our leaders are like the generals in a modern army—absolutely necessary for victory, but they do their leading from behind. Side by side with this tradition of Anglicanism, therefore, there has grown up another distinctively Anglican characteristic, the emphasis on the office of a pastor, and the primacy of this office over that of the prophet, the scholar, or the administrator. One could argue for ever whether this scale of comparative values is just or unjust. The point is that this is how Anglicans instinctively think or feel—how they *must* think or feel if they are to lay all the responsibilitues of heroism upon the anonymous and obscure average of churchpeople of all races and languages. For this emphasis on the pastoral is the only thing which could save the Anglican spiritual economy from the heresy of rating the collective above the individual, of preferring to deal with crowds and herds, of laboriously estimating power in terms of mass trends and tendencies, rather than the dealing with individual people, individual families, and small groups one at a time. That is why the parochial system is the characteristic Anglican device for seeing that for every soul there shall be his own pastor. The Anglican Church is essentially and fundamentally pastoral. It cannot be said too often for nobody will ever understand Anglicanism who ignores this basic fact. It is always the great pastors who remain beloved heroes for one generation after another. It is possible that Archbishop Laud did more for the Church than George Herbert, but through the centuries it is Herbert who is loved while Laud is at best admired. Those bishops are loved best who know their sheep and are known by them, like Chavasse the universally beloved 'Little Bishop' of

Liverpool. Frank Weston, Bishop of Zanzibar, was known to have a passionate and sacrificial love for each one of his dear native spiritual children. His tiresomenesses, which were many, will all be forgotten but he will live on in Anglican memories because he was a wonderful pastor. Tell any Anglican priest in any part of the world that he is no prophet and he will cheerfully agree that this is indeed so. Tell him that he has no gifts of leadership and while he may not like it he will not greatly resent it. But tell him that he has no pastoral sense and he will be really hurt, and feel deeply wounded and insulted in the house of his friends. For he will feel, and rightly, that if it is really true he is without excuse. Few can be leaders, and fewer still prophets, but everybody can be a faithful pastor. The gift is utterly commonplace; anybody can have it who pays the price, and the price is heavy. For nine-tenths of the prosecution of its worldwide mission Anglicanism relies on the most commonplace of all spiritual gifts, the gift of the pastoral sense. Failure elsewhere can be redeemed, but failure there is for Anglicans absolute, and the dominical injunction which the Anglican Church has taken more deeply than any other is, 'Her sins which are many are forgiven because she loved much.'

No Church in the world is so completely Anglican in mind, temper and spirit as the Church of England for, after all, she is the mother of all Anglican Churches. This passion for freedom, this vision that real heroism lies in the average and the unknown, this belief that effectiveness lies in the slow cumulative pressure of a community upon a society, this exaltation of the unspectacularly pastoral office, and, with it all, this supra-national and unprovincial view—all these mark the Church of England. No one who does not know this will ever understand her. No one who does not share this scheme of values will ever succeed in adequately explaining her to others. But undeniably it makes the process of explanation difficult. It is so much easier to write about the famous men and the resounding events. They are indeed part of the scene and cannot be ignored if the portrait is to be true. But if they occupy the stage all the time, as in so many ecclesiastical histories they do, the result is not a portrait but a cartoon.

This book is a portrait of a great Church in its daily life and work in a profoundly difficult epoch of its long history. It is not a history. Many years must pass before anything like a history of the Church in our own times can reasonably be attempted. It is a portrait, an impression of corporate spiritual vitality in action. Its material must therefore be highly selective. But it is not a purely arbitrary selection for it rests on the clear principles of Anglicanism as the author happens to see them.

So it is that a portrait of the Church is of necessity a book about ministering. The ordinary parish priest occupies much space in it. The great heroes occupy but little. Some of the events which made most stir at the time they happened, such as the rejection of the Revised Prayer Book, occupy no space at all. But because the history of the Church is after all the story of what priests and people do with its theology, an account of the broad development of theology and its immediate consequences take precedence of other themes. The broad interaction of the Church upon the people is seen most easily in terms of how the social conscience of church-people slowly grew, and some of its effects in the sphere of housing are described since this was indeed one of the notable features of the Church in action. There follow chapters on the position of the clergy and the many ways in which the Church sought to fulfil its pastoral office. The effects of this ministry of Church to people are summarised by taking typical spheres of the Church's action and trying to show what the Church did and how it fared in each one of them during the inter-war epoch. But all the time and in every sphere the Church was vehemently opposed by the characteristically modern instrument which the devil uses to undo her, the secular view of life. Every priest and every congregation had to struggle with this, and a description of some of the forms it took is therefore part of the portrait to be drawn. Finally the Church of our own time has always been sensitive about its relationships with other Churches, and mindful of the opportunities given to it by its central position to promote the unity of Christendom. Nor could a Church which had spread within five hundred years from two tiny provinces to become the mother of the whole Anglican Communion ever forget her mission-ary obligations, and the whole supra-national aspect of her witness. The last two chapters, therefore, give a portrait of the Church in action in some of the many spheres of reunion and of its consciousness of its international relations.

No one is more conscious than the author of how much is ex-cluded and how little is included. But this is quite inevitable. It is his hope that what remains after the sieve of selection has been so drastically wielded constitutes a consistent and recognisable portrait of the mother of all the Anglican Churches passing through twenty years of travail with dignity and with hope.

CHAPTER ONE

IN THE SPHERE OF DOCTRINE

I. The 'Liberal' Heresy

In the early nineteen-thirties Sir Arthur Quiller-Couch devoted one of his Cambridge lectures to the answering of Mr. T. S. Eliot's abuse of Liberalism in his book, *After Strange Gods*. On one page of it Mr. Eliot had allowed himself to use the phrase, 'In a society like ours, worm-eaten with Liberalism,' and when Q's eyes fell upon these words they flashed with fire. He gathered his armour and advanced to give battle in the Arts School in Cambridge. What, he asked, is this Liberalism which so many Christian thinkers seemed to dislike so much? What does Mr. Eliot himself understand by it? Q himself found it difficult to discover.

What he means by 'Liberalism,' except that it is something he dislikes, one must use patience to discern, so dexterously he shuffles religion into politics, politics into literature, tradition into dogma, to and fro, until the reader—let alone a listener—can scarcely tell out of what category the card (so to speak) is being dealt.[1]

Since then the denunciation of Liberalism has been the most constant theme of Anglican theology, and the theologians have regarded their condemnation and repudiation of it almost as though it were a Crusade laid upon them by the most urgent needs of their times. They have thought of it as not less than man's second disobedience, which, like the first, has brought death into our world and increased our woe. By 1945 the theologians had succeeded in so discrediting it that to-day very few religious thinkers would venture publicly to approve of Liberalism. But what is this Liberalism which Gore distrusted, Karl Barth loathed, T. S. Eliot abused, Niebuhr denounced, and Hoskyns did so much to destroy? No one can hope to describe and gauge the temper and the effect of Anglican theology in the years after the first world war without first trying to find the answer to this question. The most superficial examination is enough to show that Q was justified in his bewilderment; for Liberalism is a spirit, a climate, an ethos, and it has to do with politics as well as with religion, and with literature as well as with politics, for its terms of reference are the ultimates of life and death.

The Liberalism with which the twentieth-century Anglican theo-

---

[1] Sir Arthur Quiller-Couch. Lecture on *Tradition and Orthodoxy* in *The Poet as Citizen* (Cambridge University Press, 1934), p. 61.

logian had to do was in all essentials the same spirit which Cardinal Newman so detested a hundred years ago. He denounced it, and its practitioners, almost as personal enemies. 'The men who had driven me from Oxford were distinctly the Liberals,' he wrote many years after the event; and the Liberalism with which they indoctrinated the eternal truth of religion was, he said, 'the half way house to Atheism,' potentially damnable because it preferrred 'intellectual excellence to moral.'[1] But it was in Note A of his *Apologia* that he gave the most careful definition of what he meant by Liberalism.

Now by Liberalism I mean false liberty of thought, or the exercise of thought upon matters, in which, from the constitution of the human mind, thought cannot be brought to any successful issue, and therefore is out of place. Among such matters are first principles of whatever kind; and of these the most sacred and momentous are especially to be reckoned the truths of Revelation. Liberalism, then, is the mistake of subjecting to human judgment those revealed doctrines which are in their nature beyond and independent of it, and of claiming to determine on intrinsic grounds the truth and value of propositions which rest for their reception simply on the external authority of the Divine Word.

Thus Newman in 1865. It is virtually the same pronouncement which St. Bernard of Clairvaux had made centuries before in his quarrel with Abelard, only Newman was more polite than Bernard. But the intellectual climate of Europe has changed very greatly since Newman's day, and the liberal attitude which he described has added to itself the prestige of science and its technique, and the assumptions of democracy. Yet change the wording of Newman's definition but slightly, and we seem to be listening to the voice of the commissar. It is to the rule of the commissar that what the theologians call Theological Liberalism leads. Schweitzer saw that when he declared that German criticism of the Gospels was inspired by German nationalism. Nevertheless the theologians have acquiesced too tamely in the name Liberalism. A darkening of counsel always attends the transfer to theology of a title valid in politics; and whereever in Europe Liberalism (in the political and cultural sense of the word) has been destroyed it has given place to a state of affairs which overthrows every Christian principle.

There is no beginning of the history of Liberalism on this side of the classics, and anybody who wants to dig down to its roots must go back at least as far as Plato, for ancient Greece is the true home of both the scientific spirit and of the highest ideals of man as great in his own right and perfectible by his own power, and it is the amalgam of these which makes theological Liberalism. In the

---

[1] John Henry Cardinal Newman, *Apologia Pro Vita Sua* (Longmans, Green, 1865), from edition of 1904, p. 225.

history of the Jews in biblical times there is nothing of this, and from *Genesis* to *Revelation* the Bible continually asserts the exact opposite: the virtue of the world lies in its divine creation, history is the story of divine action in the world, and progress for humanity and perfectibility for man is a function of divine grace. Tension between views so diverse is inevitable and endemic, especially as both are noble, and in some senses both are true. The discovery of truth about man depends upon the discovery of the synthesis which holds this tension at the creative level of tautness. The Middle Ages at their best, in the twelfth and thirteenth centuries, were in a fair way not only to discover this synthesis but to apply it to the whole social body of Christendom. But the attempt faltered, and by the fifteenth century it had failed. Then the two extremes of revolutionary Protestant theology and Renaissance classicism parted company and the synthesis was broken with a finality which lasted for at least four hundred years. Geneva drew from the Bible its ideas of the total depravity of man and of history as being no more than the record of human sin in the city of destruction. Florence looked to the ancient Greeks and asserted the dignity and freedom of man, the high status of the artist, history as ordered progress, and scientific verification as the only test of theory. The one idea produced John Knox as its apotheosis, and the other produced Benvenuto Cellini. Both are considerable creations of the human spirit, but neither is really satisfactory. The failure of both Knox and Cellini as types of humanity is due to the fact that neither Geneva nor Florence looked to the Bible as a whole, nor yet to the Catholic Church as a whole, in whose joint keeping the only possible synthesis was held.

There is no need in such a work as this to attempt the task of tracing down the centuries the action and interaction of these contrasted ideas about the revelation of God, the nature of man, and the purpose of history. But the history of this process in England entered a new phase in 1859, the year of the publication of Charles Darwin's *Origin of Species*. Few people who speak of it as an intellectual landmark have ever actually read it. But its most important findings and conclusions were immediately popularised, and everybody knew that through Darwin science had given judgement that the method of progress was by evolution, that the mainspring of evolution was natural selection, that nature was a closed, coherent, and uniform system, and that evolutionary thinking had come to stay. The acceptable picture of man as harmless and innocent, as destined by the sheer power of automatic progress to create at last the civilisation of his dreams, as perfectible by his own efforts, above all, as the centre of his own world, had been so powerfully reinforced as to become the only possible view of life to be entertained by anyone who cared to be thought intelligent. To believe oneself modern was to accept the evolutionary thinking about life together with its basis of the theory of the impregnable uniformity of nature. A God who created such a world might be acceptable, provided that one steered clear of the *Genesis* account of the process. But a God who disrupted the iron theory of the uniformity of nature by revelation, by miracle, or, worse, by acting within it at His own will and in ways utterly unpredictable could not be squared with the theory. The biblical picture of man as standing every day of his life in need of a grace and salvation other than what he could draw from nature if he were to accomplish any good thing was no less at variance with the accepted evolutionary thinking. It was all miles away from the broad faith of the Bible whether interpreted by the catholic or protestant traditions. The Bible believed that salvation came by faith; the Liberal often doubted whether salvation was necessary, and if it was, he believed it came by man's own effort in righteousness. The Bible forbad trust in princes or any children of men, and held that our trust must be in God alone; the Liberal placed his trust in the systems and codified techniques of knowledge in science, education, and politics to bring society to perfection and man to sanctity, or to complete him and make him every whit whole. Catholic and Protestant alike held with the Bible that the natural man is in opposition to God; the liberal believed that man is by his own nature made in the image of God and that Christ was divine through the perfection of His humanity.[1] Once accept the religion of the Bible as true, and there is no escaping from the conclusion that Liberalism is justly described in the great anathema of the Commination Service in the Book of Common Prayer:[2] 'Cursed be he that putteth his trust in man, and taketh man for his defence, and in his heart goeth from the Lord.'

'Cursed' may seem to be an extravagant, an uncharitable, even a vicious epithet to apply to Liberalism, even though the rest of the anathema precisely describes its ethos, for it was a great tradition and it attracted and convinced the characteristically high-minded. The attitude towards life of men like Thomas Huxley and Lowes Dickinson, Professor Bury and Hastings Rashdall, Bishop Percival of Hereford and T. R. Glover was not likely to be ignoble. It might indeed be mistaken through excess of optimism, as the passage of time has proved it to be. But Liberalism's prestige was enormous, and in its heyday, the period of Asquith's administration, its optim-

---

[1] There is an excellent tabular list of these contrasts, of which the above is a very condensed form, in *Catholicity* (Dacre Press, 1947), p. 42.
[2] Incredibly, the form of Commination in the Revised Prayer Book of 1928 totally omits this anathema.

ism did not seem unreasonable. As a philosophy of life it had nevertheless parted company with the faith of the Bible, and had taken away from those whose thinking it influenced (probably the greater part of the nation) the armour which the Bible had given earlier generations. A faith over-optimistic about man, and deficient in every statement about man's need of God, could not guide humanity through the dreadful fires which were to come. As a consequence every noble cause in which Liberalism so passionately believed, the perfectibility of man by human resources, man's necessary freedom as a glorious being, the free expression of knowledge, and the idea that natural man will normally choose the righteous course, lies to-day in ruins, and has to be re-built all over again. The disaster of Liberalism is the most tremendous tragedy of this century, and theologians who do their duty by renouncing it in order that they may free the ground to build again should first salute it for the elements of greatness that were in it. As a philosophy of life, as a political need, as a climate of culture, Liberalism has certainly failed. As a school of theology it is already dead. But there is no cause for rejoicing in this. Its failure has not proved to be the prelude to a revival of religion, and modern disillusion with the liberal view of automatic progress—and indeed with progress of any kind— is no help whatever to evangelism. The loss of belief in progress is perhaps the gravest danger of our time, because a vacuum in human imagination has been created, and this vacuum is certainly being possessed at present by demoniac suggestions. The Church can only cast out these devils if it succeeds in filling the vacuum by an acceptable and realistic doctrine of progress of its own, and this has still to be done. Violent denunciations after the manner of the *odium theologicum* serve nothing that is good, and to indulge in them is to invite the judgement that an illiberal theology is savage and barbarous.

II. *The Decline and Fall of Modernism*

Both as a political creed and as a dominant cultural influence Liberalism rose to the height of its prestige in the period from 1906 to 1914. In those glittering years it carried all before it. Its spokesmen supposed that even if they had not yet achieved all their purposes, at least they had at their command every instrument by which they were automatically bound one day to achieve them to the full. Yet even then, in the very heyday of their success, their prophets betrayed a certain uneasiness. They were not happy to be without a religion, and they desired the religion they knew they needed to be no new form of worship of the goddess of Reason of the French

Revolution of 1789, but one which should retain' every element of Christianity which evolutionary thinking could leave unimpaired. They had no desire—very far from it—to turn their backs on our Lord, whom even the most 'humanist' and 'rational' among them regarded as their Lord too. The ethics of the Gospel were vital to Liberalism, and Jesus was captain of the liberal's salvation. But the corner stones of their creed were the rigid uniformity of Nature and the perfectibility of humanity by human power and resource. It was therefore required of the self-conscious and high-minded liberal of the type of Lowes Dickinson and Oliver Lodge that he should be a crusader under the banner of Jesus Christ and yet at the same time reject the whole element of the miraculous in the Gospel story, shy away from the category of the supernatural, discount every statement there found that man cannot save himself because 'the heart of man is evil continually.'[1] This was a dilemma which tormented him. He showed it by the way in which he found it simply impossible in his books to leave religion alone. Was there any way out of it? Would the application of the new knowledge and the scientific study of ancient documents show him that way—how he could keep the Jesus he genuinely loved and reverenced as his Lord without treason to his liberal presuppositions? The Modernist movement in Christendom, and particularly in the Anglican Church, was convinced that he could, and that it could show him how. 'I believe,' wrote Professor Sanday to Dr. Randall Davidson, Archbishop of Canterbury, 'that the cultivated modern man may enter the Church of Christ with his head erect.'[2] This endeavour, promoted by the immense prestige of Liberalism, set the pace of theology in the Church for a generation.

In 1925 Dr. H. D. A. Major, Principal of Ripon Hall, Oxford, and Editor of *The Modern Churchman*, sailed for the United States of America to deliver the William Belden Noble Lectures in the University of Harvard. He had chosen as his subject the character, aims, and method of Modernism in England; and certainly if this phenomenon was to be explained, there could be nobody better equipped than Dr. Major to explain it. For a cool, informed, and ample statement of what English Modernism stood for it would still be difficult to find anything more suitable than these lectures, where the modernist speaks for himself through the mouth of the acknowledged leader of his movement.

He was quite sure that it was proper to speak of English Modernism, and that there was in fact a Modernism of England which was

[1] See vol. i, pp. 48–52 of the present work for an ample documentation of this judgement.
[2] Bell, vol. i, p. 678.

both different and distinguishable from the Modernism of America or Rome. Their very enemies were different. The Roman modernist opposed mediævalism, the American modernist opposed fundamentalism, while the English modernist had to take up arms against traditionalism. But what was it that English Modernism positively believed? His vital principle which underlay all he did, and from which everything that he believed hung suspended, Dr. Major defined as fidelity to the 'operation in human history of the Spirit that was in Jesus Christ'; and immediately he added to those unexceptionable words the following expression of hostility which, by a curious association of images, the word Spirit always provokes in the modernist mind, 'and the aim of the English Modernist is to set free that Spirit from those archaic dogmatic shackles and ecclesiastical burdens, great and grievous to be born, which are hindering it from exerting its full and proper influence in the modern world.'[1] The English modernist, he was sure, was a separately recognisable identity; and he bore four positive marks of recognition. His Modernism is 'the outcome of an education which makes people acquainted with New Truth';[2] and this New Truth he must of necessity be resolved to use, thereby showing his faith in it. Yet because a man 'may know the New Truth and have faith in it, and be sure that it has a good use, he may not be a Modernist, he may be, and most often is, an Agnostic.'[3] To be a Modernist, he must believe that the New Truth serves religion, and that religion is absolutely necessary for all humanity. But not even this is enough, for in addition to it the modernist must ' love and value a Beloved Community —a community which enshrines our moral and spiritual ideals for humanity.' This community is the Church of Christ, and the modernist is bound to be a churchman, and has no claim to the title if he is not.

To be a Christian Modernist one must be convinced that our civilisation needs not only the Christian Religion, but also the Christian Church. Probably the historic Christian Church seems to the Modernist to enshrine Christ's ideals very imperfectly. If so it will be his duty as a Modernist to strive to make it embody them more perfectly, but he may not sever himself from its membership, or believe that the Christian Religion can dispense with the Christian Church.[4]

On modernist terms, loyal churchmanship is not only compatible with Modernism but essential to it, which no doubt is one reason why modernists in England have always opposed the disestablishment of the Church.

---

[1] H. D. A. Major, *English Modernism: its Origin, Methods, Aims* (U.S.A. Harvard University Press, 1927), pp. 6, 7.
[2] *Ibid.*, p. 55.   [3] *Ibid.*, pp. 55, 56.   [4] *Ibid.*, pp. 56, 57.

Dr. Major then proceeded to furnish a list of the things which the Anglican modernist has cast away on coming over from Traditionalism to Modernism, and in which therefore he does not believe, and which he seeks to end. This list comprises seven doctrines. It is significantly longer than the list of what he does believe, for one of the ineradicable marks of the modernist is that he is always so much more conscious of what he does not than of what he does believe. The modernist, then, refuses assent to the following propositions:

1. The conception of God the changeless despot who 'from a throne in the heavens governed the earth in accordance with certain inflexible principles.' In His stead the modernist asserts 'the God of emergent evolution, who is ever bringing new things to pass.'[1]

2. The doctrine of everlasting punishment, 'grotesque, absurd, incredible.'[2]

3. The doctrine of the propitiatory sacrifice of Christ. Here the words in the Prayer of Consecration in the Liturgy, 'who made there by his one oblation . . .' are called 'terrible'; and objection is made to the formulæ 'for Jesus Christ's sake' and 'through the merits of Jesus Christ' at the end of prayers.[3]

4. The doctrine of original sin when interpreted as involving original guilt; and as a consequence he refuses assent to any doctrine of baptism which goes further than a statement of baptism as necessary to assert the protection of God and to admit to the Church.[4]

5. The eschatological doctrines of judgement and the second coming of Christ, but it is more the imagery under which these are traditionally asserted than the truths which these images assert which is repudiated.[5]

6. The belief in the infallibility of the Bible. It is not an infallible but an inspired Bible. 'The statement that the Bible is the Word of God is being replaced by the statement that it contains the Word of God,'[6] and we must now accept 'the assured results of criticism as to the origin, dates, composition, integrity, historicity, and scientific value of the various books.[7]

7. The traditional view of divine revelation, which 'presented the knowledge of God as a unique system of truth miraculously communicated from heaven to earth.' In its place the modernist would claim that 'revelation is implied in the very structure of the human mind, so that the process of thought, conscience,

[1] *Ibid.*, p. 102.
[2] *Ibid.*, p. 106.
[3] *Ibid.*, pp. 107, 108.
[4] *Ibid.*, pp. 110–12.
[5] *Ibid.*, pp. 112–16.
[6] *Ibid.*, p. 117.
[7] *Ibid.*, p. 118.

affection, truly understood, involve the recognition of the Infinite and Eternal. It is because we are what we are, and are becoming what we are becoming that God can and does unveil Himself to us, that is, *in* us. Hence the Modernist teaches that the divine method of revelation is internal—God speaking, not as Traditionalism teaches, in tones of thunder from the sky, but with a still, small voice in the human consciousness.'[1]

From that it is clear that there are many things of high spiritual importance which the modernist believes, and which he has done much to safeguard. He believes in man, his greatness, his heroism, his high calling and destiny: he believes it is a most splendid thing to be human, and he believes it passionately. Over and over again Dr. Major says that the modernist continues to assert this or that Christian dogma because it supplies something which is necessary to human life. Thus the modernist generally argued from the perfection of Christ's earthly life to His Godhead, not vice versa. Thus again Dr. Major writes about the dogma of the Incarnation that modernists think it precious because it 'conserves the highest values in life' and promises 'an augmentation of those values.' Its use to human beings is the criterion of its credibility.

The historic evidence upon which the Church believed the Incarnation was, much of it, false; its significance in many respects was misrepresented and misinterpreted: the Church held fast to the dogma, incredible and indefensible as it seemed in some respects. Why? Because it promised an augmentation of values in human life.[2]

Everything that the political liberal meant by his fine slogan, Trust the People, the modernist meant also, and he supplied the liberal with theological grounds for his political and social faith.

He believed too in a God of energy who is eternally revealing Himself in history through the Holy Spirit and in the human consciousness. The modernist's God was emphatically a deity who was awake, alive, alert; and there has been no historic school of theology which has held a richer version of the doctrine of divine inspiration. And because this realm of spiritual realities was to him the richest, the nearest, the most verifiable fact of life, he believed that in his very iconoclasm he served a truly religious purpose, and he saw no presumption in his claim that in him a sage had at last arrived who had the right and the knowledge to judge between what was true and what was false in the whole body of traditional catholic theology. This rich scheme of the faith delivered to the saints, the 'modernist

---

[1] Major, *English Modernism*, p. 119.
[2] *Ibid.*, p. 93.

claims freedom to investigate as a Christian right, and also freedom
to reject what is false.'[1] So far as the doctrines of the Creed are
concerned he was prepared to separate them into the categories of
truth and error:

> As editor of the *Modern Churchman* for thirty years I have no know-
> ledge of Modern Churchmen who do not believe in 'the incarnation, the
> atonement, everlasting life, divine judgement,' but I do know a great
> number of Modern Churchmen who do not believe in the virgin birth, in
> the resurrection of the physical body of Jesus Christ, in the descent of
> Jesus Christ into Hades between his death and resurrection, in his return
> at the end of the world to judge the quick and the dead at a great assize ...
> These beliefs are all affirmed in the Apostles' Creed and have been held by
> orthodox Christians until recent times ... If asked why Modern Church-
> men do not believe these things, the reply is that modern biblical, historical,
> and scientific studies have made them incredible.[2]

Nor did this claim seem to him presumptuous. His right, even his
duty to sit in judgement followed upon his doctrine of divine inspiration, and upon his belief that he had in his hands what his predecessors had lacked, the two instruments of biblical criticism and
scientific method of investigation to guide him. Such was his faith
in them that he never questioned their competence, and when their
use seemed to bring out of the very Gospels themselves a divine
authority for liberal humanism and even made of their Hero the
Liberal Christ, he rejoiced the more. He was supplying the modern
cultivated man with a Christianity credible to his initial presuppositions, but he was also sincerely seeking for truth. The amalgam
was a spiritual basis within a purged Christianity on which liberal
humanism could stand erect. A Christianity so treated was at once
Liberalism's source and goal.

The modernist believed he served a truly religious purpose. There
are, for example, few more iconoclastic examinations of St. Mark's
Gospel than Professor R. H. Lightfoot's Bampton Lectures of 1934,
with their notorious conclusion, 'For all the inestimable value of the
Gospels, they yield us little more than a whisper of His voice: we
trace in them but the outskirts of His ways.'[3] Nevertheless he is sure
that the second gospel is a deeply religious, doctrinal, and spiritual
document, and he values it precisely because he believes that this
rather than the composition of a biography of our Lord was its
author's purpose. Thus he may well say 'I hope that critics will pause
not once or twice but many times before they decide to level the

---

[1] *Ibid.*, p. 94.
[2] Dr. H. D. A. Major in a letter to *The Times* of September 4, 1945.
[3] R. H. Lightfoot, *History and Interpretation in the Gospels* (Hodder &
Stoughton, 1934), p. 225.

charge against me that I destroy and do not build.'[1] That is sincerity, and the modernist is sure he was safeguarding *spiritual* truth, which is what matters to him.

But he was always apt to make man, and particularly modern man, the criterion by which spiritual truth is to be discerned and judged, thus magnifying modern man above all other man. He came latest in a movement of automatic progress and so ought to be more wise and intelligent than all his ancestors; and he had what they had not, the blessings of scientific discovery, technique, and method. Thus the modernist claimed for him an irrelevance of original sin, and claimed for himself the recognition of an infallibility for the instruments of enquiry he used, in short for the 'modern knowledge' to which he was always appealing. It seemed to others that his estimate of the virtue and intelligence of modern cultivated man was optimistic, that his treatment of Bible and Creeds was cavalier, that his worship of liberal humanism contradicted the Gospel, and that his version of the Christian religion was all very well for fine and fair weather but useless to provide the shelter of a rock in storm and tempest. There were many who knew they must oppose the modernist because for all his virtues, which were very many, he seemed to them to be flattering man in such a way as to ruin him, and to be taking his doctrine of God's energetic inspiration to the point where it was no longer reasonable to believe that God had spoken in Christ once and for all.

Many of the theologians and leaders of opinion in the Church, laymen like Lord Halifax and bishops like Gore, would if they could have had such modernists as were clergymen indicted for heresy, and have taken away from them their licences as accredited teachers of the Church. This they could never do, partly because they could not take the whole body of the Church with them, and also because the whole process of trial for heresy and withdrawal of licence is made far more difficult in the Church of England than in any other Church in the world. The modernist priest, like any other who was intensely irritating to ecclesiastical authority, could take refuge behind the three barriers which Hensley Henson once approvingly described as the Church of England's 'inability to legislate secured by its subordination to the State, the relative moderation of its denominational confession, and the tradition of clerical independence distinctive of its legal system,'[2] given legal form in the parson's freehold. So they were saved from any persecution and were able to say exactly what

---

[1] Lightfoot, *History and Interpretation in the Gospels* (Hodder & Stoughton, 1934), p. xiv.
[2] Herbert Hensley Henson, *The Church of England* (Cambridge University Press, 1939), p. 112.

they liked with almost complete impunity. Modernism was a campaign, a guerilla war, without casualties.

On the other hand, if the main body of the clergy and laity were markedly unenthusiastic about any attempt to coerce the modernists, they remained intensely suspicious, and they were never convinced by them. Very few churchpeople were equipped to argue with modernists, but they got the impression that the modernists wanted to lead them into a theological land of haze and quicksand, where they would never know where they were, and from which every landmark and every patch of solid, firm ground had been carefully removed. Perhaps the teachers among them got hold of the Cambridge Biblical Commentaries, and read there, as Hensley Henson did on Good Friday 1934, their handling of the Passion narrative in St. Luke's Gospel. The bishop read it, seized his diary, and wrote:

From the standpoint of the Humanitarians what special and perpetual significance can the Crucifixion of Jesus be said to possess? The critics have passed their rough desecrating hands over the evangelical narratives, and left little in them of all that has most touched the hearts of men. I read through the Cambridge Commentary on the Passion chapters in St. Luke's Gospel and realised how spiritually desolating is the method of Bible study which it represents . . . *'A sublime touch, but probably not historic'* is the note on the words, 'the Lord turned and looked upon Peter.' The dramatic episode in which Barabbas is preferred to Jesus is *'somewhat unlikely.'* The whole account of Pilate's contact with the people is contained in a narrative which *'it is impossible to accept as history.'* The wailing of the women 'is probably unhistorical,' being made up of a number of Old Testament reminiscences. The words, 'Father, forgive them, for they know not what they do,' are marked as doubtful. 'But *whether the words are part of Luke or not, they are entirely characteristic of the spirit of Christianity, and of Jesus Himself; even if not historical, they are a supreme tribute to His memory,'* The mockery by the soldiers *'is unlikely.'* The touching record of the two robbers *'seems to move rather in the realm of legend than of history.'* It is difficult to make devotional use of a sacred scripture which is thus to be regarded.[1]

What conclusion could the teacher draw, except that either scripture was completely untrustworthy, or that modernist criticism of it led him straight into Cloud Cuckoo Land?

Further, the ordinary Christian could see no justification for the modernist's reiterated statements about the finality of modern thought, modern scientific knowledge, or modern methods of historical research. All of these criteria-not-to-be-questioned, these twentieth-century taboos, led to the enthroning of the men who used

[1] Herbert Hensley Henson, *Retrospect of an Unimportant Life* (Oxford University Press, 1943), vol. ii, pp. 317–18.

them in a position of infallible eminence, so that all the ages of the
world must abide the question of modern cultivated man, who alone
was free and uninhibited. People read their papers, looked at the
world where they lived, inspected such modern cultivated men as
they knew, lived and died and agonised in the wars they made, and
knew that modern man was no angel to sit in judgement upon every
century. The modernists might be very learned, but they seemed to
be talking very great nonsense. It is for these reasons that in writing
or talking about modernism to-day one instinctively uses the past
tense.

III. *The Modern Churchmen's Conference at Cambridge*, 1921[1]

All these traits of Anglican modernism were given the most public
airing they ever enjoyed at the conference of Modern Churchmen,
held in Girton College, Cambridge, in 1921. There has perhaps been
no conference of churchpeople in modern times which created quite
so much sound and fury. When it had ended and its proceedings
were published, the secular no less than the ecclesiastical newspapers
were filled for days with denunciations and defences of it. So far
did one newspaper go in attacking Hastings Rashdall, that he accused
it of libel and obtained damages out of court.[2] He probably gave
them all away, for few men have been more generous than Rashdall.
Protests poured into Lambeth Palace. There were angry debates in
Convocation. The issue of *The Modern Churchman* which contained
the conference papers sold more than 6,000 copies. It was a celebrated occasion, amply trumpeted by all the resources of publicity;
yet out of it but little came. It did not wear well. The modern student
who obtains a copy of the relevant number of *The Modern Churchman* and reads the papers in it will not find himself much stirred.
He is unlikely to be greatly moved even by the editor's introduction,
which, at the time, caused particular anger. It all reminds him a
little of the vigorous argument of Fluellen, Macmorris, and Captain
Jamy in *Henry V* as they were standing in safety debating the academic art of war at the siege of Harfleur:

> Captain Macmorris, I beseech you now, will you vouchsafe me, look
> you, a few disputations with you, as partly touching or concerning the
> disciplines of the war, the Roman wars, in the way of argument, look you,
> and friendly communication; partly to satisfy my opinion, and partly for

---

[1] All quotations from the proceedings of the conference are identified by the
numbers of the pages in which they occur, and these are given in brackets in the
text. All these references are to *The Modern Churchman*, edited by Dr. H. D. A.
Major, vol. xi, No. 6, September 1921.
[2] *Theology*, March 1940, p. 153.

the satisfaction, look you, of my mind, as touching the direction of military discipline, that is the point.

Nevertheless, this conference had a real significance for the twentieth-century church, though it was other than its members or their opponents seem to have supposed.

The conference had been called to consider the question or 'Christ and the Creeds'; and on that question it had nothing of lasting significance to say. But again and again, as it were in a parenthesis or a bracket, the speakers showed themselves to be most concerned about another question, the glory of man. They were conscious of the need to find a new and a surer theological foundation for the Christian doctrine of man, though they did not discern that for the twentieth century this was to be the problem of problems, and they showed no awareness that even then it was specially under attack. But in 1921 they were not peculiar in this.

When the organisers of the conference announced what its theme was to be, even their friends were apprehensive. Hensley Henson, then Bishop of Durham, caused a cautionary note to be sent to them through a third party. He wanted them to take heed what they were about lest they might 'create another crisis in the matter of belief before we have well made good such liberty as we have.'[1] It was not the advertised list of speakers which made him utter the caution. It was obvious what nearly all of them would be certain to say on such a subject, for most of them had been saying it steadily for years. But Dr. Kirsopp Lake, who had carried his own variety of modernism to such lengths of negation that he had scandalised his own friends, had just published his theories on the subject in his *Landmarks of Early Christianity*, and they were very alarming. If the members of the conference should be carried away by the excitement of the occasion and give Kirsopp Lake their support, they would be compromising the whole movement and carrying it into a quicksand. But the organisers would not listen to the bishop's advice. Far from that, they added a paper by Dr. Foakes Jackson to the published programme, and it was known that this paper was intended to represent the joint views of Lake and himself. This paper was duly read by its author at an early stage in the conference. The conference, he said, had

deliberately chosen to discuss the very fundamentals of the Christian faith, and to face and not to shirk that most pointed of all questions: 'What think ye of Christ?' The reason for this choice is, I have the vanity to suppose, republication of the first volume of *The Beginnings of Christianity*, which Professor Lake and I have edited. (229)

---

[1] *Theology, loc. cit.*, p. 152.

The conference did not dissent from this attribution of motive, but made it clear that it intended not to commend but to repudiate the book. Of Dr. Lake's own book, the editor of the *Modern Churchman*, writing in the name of the whole conference, observed that it was to be condemned as giving a portrait of Christ

historically unjustifiable and psychologically inadequate. The Liberalism which Prof. Lake jettisons may be alleged to have stripped our Lord of His miraculous characteristics, but it left Him His moral and spiritual supremacy. But Prof. Lake's conclusions seem to deprive Him of the latter as well as of the former. (194).

It was certainly no wonder that the modernists were much more alarmed than the traditionalists by Lake and Foakes Jackson, for the 'Liberal Christ' which the modernists had been at such pains to create was the very Christ whom these two scholars supposed they had dethroned. Foakes Jackson, speaking with grim relish to the conference, made precisely this claim.

We have been most severely rebuked by the Liberals of our own Church, who have my sincere sympathy. They are fighting a hard fight. On the one hand they see they are losing the support of the public because there is little demand for a reasonable presentation of Christianity. There is a growing conviction not the less dangerous because it now rarely finds a voice that Christianity can be ignored.

Then he turned to rend the modernist liberals of the type gathered in the lecture room at Girton:

They have lost the historical Christ and have not regained Him by converting Him into a social reformer, a moral legislator, a revealer of a new conception of God. They are preaching an entirely new religion and concealing the fact even from themselves. (229-231).

By Lake and Foakes-Jackson, as by Schweitzer before them, the modernists were being mortally wounded in the house of their friends.

The conference, then, had been called to discuss the relationship of Christ to the creeds. But what Christ? The 'uninteresting' Christ of Lake and Foakes-Jackson was offered to the conference, and flatly rejected. The rigidly eschatological and partially deluded Christ of Schweitzer's *The Quest of the Historical Jesus* had always been repudiated by English modernists. To accept his arguments would be to undermine the infallibility of scientific New Testament criticism, and this was the cardinal dogma of the modernist creed. Their own predilection was for the 'Liberal' Christ; but the papers read at the conference demonstrated that for them such a title was misleading and inaccurate, even though they liked to think of themselves as theological liberals—an excellent illustration of the darkening of counsel which always attends the transfer of political terminology to theological speculation. The Christ of this conference was really the 'humanist' Christ; and the broad effect of most of the papers was to justify and to explain this title. That Christ was perfect man they all passionately believed. That He was God they believed no less; but they derived His divinity from the perfection of His manhood.

Although the papers did not betray it, and indeed the fact was hardly even mentioned, the delegates were always under the compulsion of the fact that they met within three years of the end of the first world war. Universal human disasters on such a scale as that always cause imperative questions about the nature of man. Until they are satisfactorily answered, no further human progress seems possible. What is man as he seems to be at the end of a world war? He is unquestionably heroic and therefore more than animal. But he is also unquestionably devilish, revelling in a brutal cruelty to which few animals ever descend. He is powerful to defend the right but powerless to promote it, when once defended. Man is never so puzzling as when some great and protracted catastrophe pitilessly reveals what is really in him. The Christian doctrine of man is never in so great danger, and his freedom as a social personality hangs on a hair. Anglican modernists, like other Christians, were thoughtful and sensitive men and women. They hated cruelty and every form of evil not a whit less than the traditionalists. Deep in their minds and on their consciences lay the contemporary failure to agree upon any doctrine of what humanity was and is. They knew that in this very failure lay the most potent threat of the tyranny they loathed. Having chosen to discuss the problem of our Lord's relationship to the creeds they could not help but struggle to find in it an answer to the vital questions about the nature of man. They were sure that within the mystery of Christ's nature the only satisfactory answer was to be found. But they thought they could find it there only if they began with the humanity of Christ and then fitted His divinity into what they believed to be true about His humanity. 'I would urge (the orthodox religious teachers) to make sure of the Humanity of Christ and the Divinity will make sure of itself' (307). In saying this Dr. R. G. Parsons spoke for them all.

In that there is nothing to which the traditionalist could object. But most other speakers said the same thing so much more extremely. Canon M. G. Glazebrook approvingly quoted Professor Henry Jones:

The error (of Dr. Denny) does not spring from maintaining the divinity of Jesus but from denying the divinity of man. Nor can it be corrected by maintaining that Jesus was a 'mere man': the implications of that phrase are themselves profoundly erroneous and unjust to man (211).

C*

Dr. Major declared:

> Jesus Himself did not claim to be the Son of God in a *physical* sense such as the narratives of the Virgin Birth affirm, nor did He claim to be the Son of God in a *metaphysical* sense, such as is required by the Nicene Theology. He claimed to be God's Son in a *moral* sense, in the sense in which all human beings are sons of God . . . I think historically to-day we must be strong to declare that the consciousness of Jesus was a full human consciousness, and that it was not supernatural and miraculous in any sense that cannot be attributed to a human personality (276, 277).

Dr. Hastings Rashdall perhaps caused more wrath than the reader of any other paper when he said:

> Jesus did not claim divinity for Himself . . . Never in any critically well-attested sayings is there anything which suggests that His conscious relation to God was other than that of a man towards God—the attitude which He wished that all men should adopt towards God. (278).

And again, from the same author:

> There is no more reason for supposing that Jesus of Nazareth knew more than His contemporaries about the scientific explanation of the mental disease which current belief attributed to diabolic possession than that He knew more about the authorship of the Pentateuch or the Psalms. (281)

Now all that may well appear in equal degrees optimistic, credulous, and shocking to anyone who reads it a quarter of a century later. But the courage of its faith in the perfectibility of man may well strike him as more remarkable still. This faith he based on the perfection of the humanity of Christ, not on the subsequent experience of the moral capacity of man in history. These men thus held a high standard of value of humanity, and they refused to be over-impressed by the depressing picture of man which had emerged from the war just ended. But when this was put as they put it, they involved themselves in heresy so deadly that all other more formal heresies paled beside it. This was the heresy of taking man and deducting God from him: it was to make God in the image of man. 'Orthodoxy, in beginning with God, began at the wrong end,' said Dr. Bethune Baker (287). This was really shocking, for it was only another way of saying what Swinburne had said in his famous lines:

> Glory to Man in the highest! For Man is the master of things.
> But God, if God there be, is the substance of men, which is man.

This faith was at variance with the main delivery of biblical witness about the relationship between God and man, and it was therefore bound to be inconsistent with much of the orthodox creed. The credal doctrine immediately affected was that of the Incarnation, and on that the view taken by most of the readers of the papers was

certainly dejective. But it was not deliberately dejective. Indeed, the
Christology of the conference was often strikingly positive. C. W.
Emmett spoke for many when he declared, 'I really want to show
that the ordinary man may trust the general impression of the personality of Jesus which he gets from the Gospels' (214). Professor R. H.
Lightfoot was passionately devotional and richly orthodox in his
answer to the question, What do we know about Jesus? Professor
Bethune Baker followed the invariable modernist dogma in refusing
the miraculous element in the gospels:

> I can only regard this idea of the miraculous birth (of Jesus) as ætiolo-
> gical and honorific—in those days a natural and reasonable way of account-
> ing for a great personality and the experience of which Jesus was the cause
> and centre, as it would be unnatural and irrational to-day (288, 289).

But apart from this he was not unorthodox, and did not think of
himself so. Indeed he claimed that in many respects his thought
about Jesus marched in step with that of Baron von Hügel (295). But
it is not recorded that this great sage agreed.

The modernist yielded to members of no other party in the Church
in the absoluteness of his devotion and loyalty to our Lord, but the
members of this conference answered the question of the relationship
of Christ and the creeds by separating them at more than one crucial
point, and this brought them into conflict with the whole body of the
catholic minded, who at no time have believed that a personal devotion to our Lord, however absolute, is enough to make a man free
of the whole Christian tradition. That they did make this separation
between Christ and the creeds was recognised and admitted by their
spokesmen. On the last night of the conference Dr. E. W. Barnes,
now Bishop of Birmingham, preached them a sermon in which he
gently chided them for allowing their modernist enthusiasms to take
them too far, and for attempting to shuffle from under some of the
vital doctrines of the Faith. He was, he said, an evangelical. As
such, he was really disturbed that

> one or two, in discussing subjects where language cannot adequately
> describe feeling, have seemed to doubt whether the Jesus of history was the
> unique Person in Whom St. Paul and St. John saw the Only-begotten Son.
> I weigh, without prejudice, I trust, all that they have said. In the end I feel
> no hesitation in affirming that Jesus rose from the dead to become the
> living Christ, one with the Holy Spirit (345).

And again, in the same sermon:

> I imagine that our ignorance in this realm (the interaction of the human
> and the divine) has caused us to avoid questions concerning reconciliation,
> redemption, salvation. I regret the omission because such matters are
> central in Christian experience (347).

When the conference was over, Dr. Major printed in a special number of *The Modern Churchman* all the papers of the conference. To them he added a long and considered preface, in which he frankly admitted:

> It would be idle to pretend that all the views expressed at Girton are in harmony with popular orthodoxy, or even with traditional orthodoxy. All that those who expressed them could hope is that they may be in harmony with progressive orthodoxy . . . The Girton Conference speakers were more concerned to adjust their orthodoxy to the orthodoxy of the future than to harmonise it with the orthodoxy of the past (193).

The whole idea of the 'Faith once for all delivered' was cast away by such an argument. Small wonder that this preface caused more trouble than all the conference papers put together. At the end of it he asked two questions of 'our traditionalist fellow-Churchmen and the whole Anglican Communion':

> 1. Will they accept the affirmation, 'God was in Christ,' with the practical recognition in daily life that 'Jesus is Lord' as constituting the irreducible minimum for modernist membership in the Church and in the teaching and ministerial offices? If they will, then a Truce of God can be attained. But the question needs to be answered frankly and without delay.
>
> 2. Will they concede to modern Churchmen the right to modify the use of the Creeds, and to produce, if they will, alternative Creeds for use in parishes where they are desired by the parishioners, provided always that this be done in a wise, loving, and orderly fashion and with the authority of the Bishop? (200).

There was of course no hope of an affirmative answer to either question, and this Dr. Major must have known very well. But in the mere asking of such questions there was nothing specially shocking or even novel. For years modernists—and not only they—had been struggling to find words and phrases for an acceptable, alternative Creed. The whole of the preface suggests to the reader of to-day that neither its author, nor the members of the conference, were really prepared for the volume of the storm of wrath which followed.

The storm raged and its winds blew from many quarters. But there was a note of furious irritation in it for which the actual accusations made hardly accounted. It was partly due to the infuriating sense of superiority which modernists blandly assumed ; and this was expressed, for example, in a remark of Bethune-Baker's:

> We ought perhaps to be content if most of our friends get on to the bridge (from the past to the future) and stay there safely, refusing to follow the more active among us who are exploring the country beyond (292).

But their friends did not at all appreciate the suggestion. They did not like being regarded as timid sheep, bleating 'Safety First,' and refusing to set foot on dangerous ground: and in any case they avoided the ground chiefly because it looked so very like Cloud Cuckoo Land. But even more the storm was due to an instinct that to make modern man the criterion of all values, and even of the truth of the Incarnation, must in the end result in the overturning of the whole Christian Faith by reducing it to the level of the ordinary and the tame. Yet that was exactly what the conference had succeeded in doing for those who believed what they said. It had inexorably been led into the position where that was what they must of necessity do. Just this was involved in the primary assumptions of most of the papers read that the element of the miraculous proves nothing in the realm of faith, that the divinity of Christ lies in the perfection of His manhood, and that 'Orthodoxy, in beginning with God, began at the wrong end.' It is in effect a deadly heresy in that it leads to death, but the death not of God but of man. It delivers us all tied and bound into the hands of those who would have us to be human animals, meet and fit for enslavement. The conference did an even more direct and immediate damage. Dozens, perhaps hundreds of lonely parish priests were deeply disquieted and even daunted by the weight of intellectual authority apparently arrayed against the orthodox presentation of the Faith which had sustained their fathers and ancestors. Many became hesitant in delivering their message, and pastoral-hearted and truth-loving men began to find they could no longer say confidently, 'This is the way: walk ye in it.'

As soon as the conference papers had been published, Hensley Henson publicly protested his repudiation of 'the extreme modernist opinions' expressed in some of them.[1] Dr. Headlam, then Regius Professor of Divinity at Oxford, reviewed the papers in the *Church Quarterly Review* of January 1922, and administered a very judicious castigation which fell upon authors and critics alike.[2] It was, however, in the Convocation of Canterbury that it was decided whether the occasion was to be regarded as a great crisis, or as an awkwardness which time would smooth if only people would refrain from exacerbating it. The question was raised first in the Bishops' House on May 22, 1922, in a very long debate, remarkable for the way in which each bishop who spoke showed depth of conviction matched by charity of judgement and real knowledge of the subject. The bishops were dealing with a petition (or a 'gravamen,' to use the technical term for it) from some sixty Anglo-Catholic members of the Lower House, and with a counter-petition asking them to refuse

---

[1] *Retrospect*, vol. ii, pp. 143, 144.
[2] *Theology*, March 1940, pp. 193, 197.

assent to the petition. The one asked them to declare that the doctrines asserted at the conference were 'contrary to the teaching of the
Bible and the Church'; the other stated that 'questions of essential
truth can only be decided by the slow process of research,' and
demanded freedom of enquiry.[1] The bishops accepted neither.
Instead they produced a resolution of their own:

> This House declares its conviction that adhesion to the teaching of the
> Catholic Church, as set forth in the Nicene Creed—and in particular con-
> cerning the eternal pre-existence of the Son of God, His true Godhead and
> His Incarnation—is essential to the life of the Church, and calls attention
> to the fact that the Church commissions as its ministers those only who
> have solemnly expressed such adhesion.[2]

This resolution was the work of the Bishop of Gloucester (Dr.
Gibson); for he had joined with the Archbishop to persuade the
bishops that to deal with the matter as the petition of the Lower
House had suggested would be useful only if announcements of
episcopal authority had power, and they had none. The Archbishop was careful to pour cooling streams of water on the idea that
the conference had amounted to

> a great phalanx of heresiarchs set in battle array against the doctrine of the
> Church Catholic, and that we were called on to rally the Church in defence
> of the Christian Faith.[3]

He also said plainly that it had been the preface to the conference
papers in *The Modern Churchman* which had caused most of the
trouble:

> The papers were edited with a preface which attempts to speak in the
> name of everybody concerned. I realise that the word WE may be merely
> editorial, but it has all the appearance of meaning, 'We, the writers of the
> papers,' and that seems to me gravely misleading and mischievous.[4]

On the same subject the Bishop of Gloucester had been still more
crushing:

> It would be interesting to know whether any one of the members of the
> conference was consulted as to the Preface, or would be willing to take any
> responsibility whatever for the singularly ill-judged utterances of the
> writer of the Preface.[5]

It was, however, made very plain both in the Convocation debate
and in the Archbishop of Canterbury's letter to Bishop Gore[6] that
the Archbishop had no intention at all of exercising discipline upon
the members of the conference, and without him nobody else would

---

[1] *Chronicles of Canterbury Convocation*, 1922, pp. 263, 314. (Cited hereafter as
C.C.C.)
[2] *Ibid.*, pp. 325, 326.   [3] Bell, vol. ii, p. 1140.   [4] *C.C.C.*, 1922, p. 354.
[5] *C.C.C.*, 1922, p. 322.   [6] Bell, vol. ii, pp. 1141–2.

be likely to move in the matter. So the storm blew itself out, and no modernist was called upon to suffer even the mildest martyrdom. Perhaps it was the wisest course because as by instinct or inspiration the course of theology followed thereafter very different and much more suggestive paths, which, in time, were seen to be leading to a position of vital importance. Thereafter modernism in the Anglican Church might remain as an organised party, and might also give birth to occasional aberrations, as in the Open Letters of the Bishop of Birmingham in 1927 to the Archbishop, but its contentions were seen to be side-issues and its characteristic language to be archaic jargon. The Girton Conference of 1921 was the last breathing of a one-time giant soon destined to become a living corpse. The breath of life was not in it because as the years passed, and the iron in them steadily dissipated the liberal idea, it was seen that the characteristic modernist attitude towards Christianity was able to lead only to a place where nobody could possibly wish to go.

Nevertheless the Girton conference had one positive influence upon the development of doctrinal thought in the Church of England during this period. The storm it caused helped to change the Archbishop of Canterbury's mind; and whereas he had previously refused to appoint a Commission upon doctrine in the Church of England, he now acceded to the many requests that he should do so.

It was in 1920 that a group of young theologians, headed by Dr. Burge, Bishop of Oxford, propounded to the Archbishop a scheme for a new report on doctrine, to be drawn up by an authoritatively appointed commission consisting of theologians from each of the recognised parties in the Church. Their purpose would be twofold: first to declare what the teaching of the Church of England is, and secondly to end doctrinal strife by the sheer weight of the fact that the declaration would be made by theologians of all parties. Over this work they were sure they ought to take many years. The Archbishop was very critical of this, and pointed out that only a commission with some kind of conciliar authority behind it could achieve what they desired, and this kind of authority he had no intention of giving. Would it not be far better to hold some kind of unofficial enquiry of the kind which had produced *Lux Mundi* in an earlier generation. To this Dr. Burge replied that *Lux Mundi* was the work of men of one school, whereas he had proposed a commission of men of all schools. There was deadlock, but the Girton conference broke it; and in 1922 the same proposal was made to the Archbishop by nine bishops, seventeen priests, and one layman. Dr. Davidson was again cautious. He harped on their youth in his reply, and feared lest they should try to produce a new criterion of orthodoxy. Dr. Burge sent an immediate disclaimer:

In reply to your Grace, we would wish to make clear that we do not con-
template, and have never contemplated, authority being given to a commission to frame either a statement of doctrine which would be binding on
the Church or the clergy, or even a statement of doctrine which would *ipso
facto* be held to be the official teaching of the Church.[1]

The Archbishop hesitated for six more months, but on December 28,
1922, he agreed to do what was asked, and, together with his brother
of York, appointed the commission, with these terms of reference:

To consider the nature and grounds of Christian Doctrine with a view
to demonstrating the extent of existing agreement within the Church of
England, and with a view to investigating how far it is possible to remove
or diminish differences.[2]

It seems likely that the commission on doctrine would not have had
even this mild amount of authority behind it had not the Girton
conference forced the pace. It did not make its report until 1938.

IV. *Sir Edwyn Hoskyns and the Eclipse of Liberalism*

To attempt to trace the movement of theological study and conviction through a period of a quarter of a century is to enter a maze,
for no other field of knowledge attracts a greater volume of literature
and eloquence. It is the common fate of the explorers of a maze to
begin by following an attractive-looking path and then to find, after
a few turns and twists, that it leads only to a dead end. Such had
been the experience of those who had trusted the modernists to guide
them through the maze. After 1921 increasing numbers of these
camp followers realised that they must go back to the beginning
and start again; and this chronicle must follow them. But there is no
hope of reaching the centre of the maze, no hope of our believing
that theology during the last twenty-five years has moved in any
identifiable direction, unless we can be provided with some thread
of Ariadne to guide our steps. This thread, it has been suggested,
is the steady growth of our consciousness of the Church as the Divine
Society:

Indeed, one may say, (declared the Regius Professor of Divinity at
Oxford, Canon Leonard Hodgson) that the outstanding feature of the
theological development of the last thirty years has been the recovery of
the conviction that Christianity is essentially the religion of the Church,
that is, of a society called into being by God to be the instrument of His
work on earth. And bound up with this conviction, that the Head of the
Church, the risen and ascended Lord Jesus Christ, is Himself God.[3]

Other threads might perhaps be chosen, but this one has a definite
and identifiable starting-point, and it leads us clearly all the way

---

[1] Bell, vol. ii, p. 1148.   [2] *Ibid.*, p. 1150.
[3] In *The Guardian* of August 18, 1944, p. 284.

until at last it leads us home to the centre of the maze. When we get there we shall find it is exactly the same place that we shall also reach when we follow the ramifications of the Christian social movement in the Anglican Church. Anglican theology to-day has come to the point where its strongest conviction is that the Eucharist, as the characteristic rite of the Divine Society, is the heart of the practice of Christianity and points symbolically to the only cure of a sick world. The Christian social movement is to-day convinced that in the Eucharist is dramatically enacted the moving picture of the healthy social order. The two movements of thought and effort started from different ends of the world of Christian experience, and they have travelled by very different roads. But they come at last to one and the same centre of the maze, and thenceforward can travel onwards hand in hand through a future journey of limitless possibilities of blessing for the world. But to choose this particular thread to guide us through the maze inevitably involves the neglect of all the others. It means that we must spend all our time with the theologians who taught the theologians, rather than with the theologians who taught the non-specialist educated Christians. Of these perhaps Oliver Quick achieved more in his two great books *The Christian Sacraments* and *Doctrines of the Creed* than anyone else. But the period was exceptionally rich in writers who could teach theology to ordinary people, and Quick was one of a considerable company, which included men like Streeter, A. E. Taylor, William Temple, and, more recently, Dean Matthews, Canon Michael Ramsay, and Fr. A. G. Hebert. These are but a few of the many names which might be listed. In a history of theology between the wars all would find their place. But in a work like this it is necessary to choose the one thread and follow it, resolutely ignoring all others.

With this thread to guide us we come quickly to the first landmark and have no difficulty in identifying it. In 1927 *Essays Catholic and Critical* was published. It was an important volume of essays by various Anglican theologians, all of broadly catholic convictions, and edited by Dr. E. G. Selwyn, now Dean of Winchester. In his preface he claimed that the volume was in the succession as well as in the tradition of the *Lux Mundi* essays of 1888, and in fact it was the first volume of comparable importance in that field which had appeared since then. The purpose of Dr. Selwyn and his authors was to reckon fully with the great changes which had come over the theological scene since then, and to restate the catholic Faith in their light. They had been convinced of the need and the possibility of a synthesis between critical scholarship and catholic tradition ever since before the war of 1914; and the possibility of writing a book of essays to prove it was discussed between Dr. Selwyn and some of his contributors at a meeting they had at that time. The years had brought into play the high prestige of the critical movement in New Testament studies, which had triumphantly uncovered the origins and foundations of the Gospel. But they had also brought 'a keener discernment of the supernatural element in religion, and a renewed interest in the expressions of it which are seen in Catholic unity and authority, in whatever form these come.'[1] Their purpose was to weave these two new forces into a synthesis, and to use this synthesis for the reinterpretation of the historical basis of the Christian religion. This purpose and scope of the book was brilliantly expressed in its title. No one has seriously doubted that the authors did succeed in what they attempted, and their book at once became seminal, in the sense that it laid upon all subsequent theological study the necessity of reckoning with it.

Many fine things were in it. Perhaps there has never been a better short apologia for the necessity of religion as a whole than Professor A. E. Taylor's *The Vindication of Religion*, a beautifully clear and wonderfully even-tempered essay of such quality that a single reading is a memory which time does not efface. *The Spirit and the Church in History*, by the present Dean of York, is a lyrical piece of writing from which one finds oneself quoting again and again. The editor's own contribution, *The Resurrection*, is still a classic example of the art of assembling complicated evidence, clarifying and interpreting it in the briefest possible compass. There were other jewels as well, but the passage of time has left no serious doubt about which of these essays turned out in the end to be the most influential. It was Sir Edwyn Hoskyns' *The Christ of the Synoptic Gospels*, which has ever since exercised a profound effect upon Anglican theology. If there was ever to be a public competition in which one was asked to quote the most influential sentence in the field of theology written during the last thirty years, there would be many who would at once enter the first sentence of this essay, and they might well win the prize:

For the Catholic Christian 'Quid vobis videtur de Ecclesia? What think ye of the Church? is not merely as pertinent a question as Quid vobis videtur de Christo? What think ye of Christ? it is but the same question differently formulated.[2]

The man who thus challengingly opened his essay, and in a single vivid sentence made plain its theme, was the Dean of Corpus Christi College, Cambridge. In 1926 he was known only to three very different circles of men; to the students of the Cambridge theological faculty, and to them he was a beloved master; to the men of the

---

[1] *Essays Catholic and Critical*, edited by E. G. Selwyn (S.P.C.K., 1926), p. v.
[2] *Ibid.*, p. 153.

Lancashire territorial division he had served as chaplain during the war; and to the little company of academic New Testament scholars. To-day people speak reverentially when they use the name of Hoskyns, just as they do when they use the names of Temple, Chavasse or Gore. Hoskyns mattered to fewer than did these others, but he exercised upon them, and on the students they taught in their turn, an influence profound, decisive, and lifelong. He had no remarkable gifts of leadership. His writing was not particularly attractive; it was indeed wrought out of a constant struggle, and so was often rough and obscure. His mind was essentially academic, though it was also catholic in the exact sense of that word. The catholicity of mind which made the *Farmer and Stockbreeder* a weekly treat led the devotee of exact, dispassionate scholarship to write on one occasion a splendid description of the academic mind as the layman sees it—'the innate tendency of the academic mind first to complicate what is obvious, and then to perform mental gymnastics as prodigious as they are unnecessary.'[1] This was never true of him, but it must often have seemed to be true to those who heard him for the first time; and even old students of his have said that in his later books he was apt to write after the manner of one who was always saying to himself, 'No, it can't be as simple as that: I must have overlooked some difficulty.' Yet there was certainly magnetism in Hoskyns, and to-day he rules much of the theology of the Church of England, ruling from the grave through his pupils, and their pupils after them.

The centre of his influence (wrote one of his pupils) lay in Cambridge; and for the past fifteen years it was true of him . . . that young ordinands gravitated to this University for the express purpose of studying theology under his direction. It is no dishonour to the Divinity Professor to record how men, and women, came to Cambridge for the sake of Hoskyns . . . In his hands theology became dynamic and creative. His lectures on the Theology and Ethics of the New Testament were exceptionally vivid, forceful, trenchant, and unexpected, and were delivered with a sustained enthusiasm and excitement which it is impossible for anyone who heard them ever to forget: by contrast, his sermons, though equally emphatic seemed curiously restrained. It was through these lectures, and through his college teaching and his supervisions, that he left his abiding mark upon the Church of England: for through them he exerted an unrivalled influence upon the younger clergy, who remain to carry on the work from which God in His inscrutable wisdom has now recalled him.[2]

There are no overtones of personal loyalty in this testimony. Any enquiry among those whom Hoskyns taught at once draws similar expressions of gratitude. Another pupil writes as it were anony-

[1] *Ibid.*, p. 160.
[2] Charles Smyth. Introduction to *Cambridge Sermons of Edwyn Clement Hoskyns* (S.P.C.K. 1938), p. xix.

mously in a private letter, 'He was indeed the bright and morning
star of the Theological Faculty at Cambridge in my day, when the
alternatives were the mistiness of X., the stodginess of Y., and the
scepticism of Z.' To make a list of the men whom Hoskyns taught
and then to place against each one the office he now holds would be
to see at once that what he taught at Corpus now dominates half the
theological colleges, and is well represented in university, cathedral,
and parish church. Thus a bias of theological teaching which twenty
years ago seemed bewildering, foreign, and harsh to all who knew it
by hearsay or from books has now become so customary among us
that its characteristic approaches and idioms are now perfectly familiar, and it is their absence not their presence which excites remark.

The secret is in the fact that those whom he taught knew that they
owed to him a great deliverance. Others before him had set themselves to remedy the mischief wrought by the application of the
assumptions of liberalism to theology. Others, too, had realised as
Hoskyns did just what this mischief was—a paralysing uncertainty
about the Christian message, a haunting suspicion of the supposed
intellectual inferiority of Christian theology when set over against
current evolutionary thinking, a temptation to despair when all the
promises of progress for humanity were one after another broken
like straws. Both G. K. Chesterton and Charles Gore (to mention
no other names) had in their different ways set themselves to perform
just such a task. But Hoskyns was more radical than they; he went
down to the roots of the mischief. These roots were embedded in
the long reign of the negative criticism of the New Testament, which
had ended by leaving the reader with only 'a tattered copy of St.
Mark's Gospel' in his hand, as Schweitzer had said, which had
shrouded with mistiness the Christ of the Gospels, and had clothed
with dubiety all the presuppositions which Jesus took for granted
and the evangelists used as foundations. That was where so much
of the contemporary despair among sensitive people had begun,
where the refusal of freedom by so many of the young and ardent
had started. That too was the point where the cure must begin. The
same critical process which had been used to drive a wedge between
Jesus and St. Paul and to separate Christ from His Church must
again be used—the same techniques, the identical methods—to
destroy the conclusions to which it had seemed to lead. The theologian of the New Testament had compromised the present and only
the theologian of the New Testament could restore the future.
Remedies as well as judgements must begin with the scriptures read
in the Church. It was with this conviction that Hoskyns began his
essay in *Essays Catholic and Critical*, and when he had finished it
he has so hoisted the modernist critics with their own petards that

they have never again been able to hypnotise the Church. 'The Liberal Christ' still had His canvassers; of whom Dr. Cadoux was the most famous. But fewer and fewer Christians hearkened to their charming. Hoskyns wrote much else besides this essay, but perhaps it had a wider range of effectiveness on the theological sphere than anything else he wrote.

The essay is really its own summary, and any précis of it is bound to be arbitrary in its selection and relatively unjust. The problem was to discover the 'relation between the life and teaching of Jesus of Nazareth and the Christ of St. Paul, of St. John, and of Catholic piety,' and further the relation 'between the little group of disciples called by Jesus from among the Galilean fishermen and the *Corpus Christi* of St. Paul of the *Civitas Dei* of St. Augustine.'[1] The modernists, or liberal protestants, thought their studies had brought them to the point where they could say what these relations were. Hoskyns used five pages to state in summary form but with scrupulous fairness what their solution was. The spirit of it can be most conveniently shown by a quotation from Professor E. F. Scott's book, *The New Testament Today*, which Hoskyns himself copied for his essay, and put into a footnote.

Above all, the figure of Jesus stands out all the more grandly as the mists of theological speculation are blown away from him, and we come to discern him as he really sojourned on earth. It is not too much to say that by recovering for us the historical life of Jesus criticism has brought Christianity back to the true source of its power. The creeds, whatever may have been their value formerly, have broken down, but Jesus as we know him in his life, and all the more as his life is freed from the accretions of legend, still commands the world's reverence and devotion. The theology of the future, it is not rash to prophesy, will start from the interpretation of Jesus as a man in history.[2]

Now in that passage there are two main assumptions—that it is possible to blow the mists of theological speculation away from Jesus and that this has in fact been done, and that the historical life of Jesus which criticism uncovers shows Him as standing aloof from the credal statements about Himself, and separated from the content of super-nature of which the creeds are full. Such was the spirit of what Hoskyns called the 'Liberalism Protestant solution.' Its results had been to separate our Lord from the Church, from St. Paul, to minimise the element of the supernatural in the Gospel, and not merely the element of miracle. Jesus, concluded the Liberal Protestant solution, 'did not claim to possess a divine nature,'[3] did not found the Church, did not foresee a worldwide mission to

---

[1] Smyth, *op. cit.*, p. 153.   [2] *Ibid.*, p. 159.

[3] *Ibid.*, p. 156.

preach His Name, and meant by the title 'Son of Man' 'his consciousness of the dignity of his essential humanity.'[1] What had been
achieved by the use of the weapon of critical scholarship was a new
sanction for 'modern idealistic humanitarianism,' and, still more
important,

> A basis is now provided for a new reformation of the Christian religion,
> capable of ensuring its survival in the modern world. In the Gospel of
> Jesus is to be found the pure religion of civilised and united humanity.
> Thus the assured results of liberal historical criticism form as necessary a
> prelude to the Christianity of the future as the preaching of John the
> Baptist did to the original proclamation.[3]

To the Scriptures they had appealed, and to the Scriptures Hoskyns
determined to take them; and in the Scriptures he took them more
particularly to the Synoptic Gospels from which they themselves had
chiefly drawn their own Christological 'solution.' No one was more
competent to do this than he, a New Testament scholar of European
reputation, whom nobody would have dared for a moment to accuse
of selecting evidence to prove a case. These gospels were in fact the
sacred writings of a living community, the primitive Church. The
epistles were the records connected with the processes of building
the community. The only genuinely historical way of reading the
gospels was to read them in the light which the epistles shed upon
them. Nor could they be read at all in a patterned literary form
unless the way of the Cross and the triumph of the Resurrection was
the vital principle which bestowed shape upon the narratives. No
one could possibly make sense of Good Friday and Easter Day who
began by emptying that event, a single event, of its supernatural
content. Furthermore, it was a first principle of objective historical
criticism that gospel stories in which the normal and the supernatural
are inextricably mingled must not be read with the pre-conceived
and fixed idea that 'what is supernatural has been superimposed by
the irrational credulity of later enthusiastic believers.'[3] This is to
reduce the gospels to tales told, if not by idiots, at least by men who
had no glimmerings whatever of literary craftsmanship, and the
synoptic writers evidently had far more than glimmerings of it,
whether it came to them by the inspiration of God, the light of nature,
or (as possibly with St. Luke) by literary training. Hoskyns went on
to a long exposure of the fallacies in the 'Liberal Protestant Reconstruction.' It led to the demonstration that the only possible way of
reading the basic documents, the synoptic Gospels, was to regard
the supernatural element as being at least as primitive as the moral
element; and that the 'exclusiveness, which is so obviously a char-

---

[1] Smyth, *op. cit.*, p. 155.   [2] *Ibid.*, p. 156.
[3] *Ibid.*, p. 165.

acteristic of Catholic Christianity, may have its origin in the teaching of Jesus rather than in the theology of St. Paul.'[1] Furthermore, he showed that the belief about modern life to which the 'Liberal Protestant' handling of the gospels pointed was in fact completely at variance with the belief about life held by the synoptic writers, and derived by them from the teaching and practice of Jesus. 'The conception that the human order can be transformed into the kingdom of Heaven by a process of gradual evolution is completely foreign to the New Testament.'[2] He had in fact no doubt that the Gospel is ineradicably supernatural, and that the four written gospels which contain it (the first three not less than the fourth) maintained at every stage of their growth the balance between natural and supernatural in Christ. Thus the radical criticism of the Gospels had results quite other than had sometimes been supposed. It inseparably joined Christ to St. Paul, and Christ to His Church, and formed a new and sure foundation for the catholic traditions of faith, life, and worship. Perhaps the heart of Hoskyn's work can best be summarised by a single quotation from the last section, the conclusion of his essay:

> From this reconstruction it will be seen at once that a whole series of contrasts underlies the Synoptic Tradition . . . The contrast is not between the Jesus of history and the Christ of faith, but between the Christ humiliated and the Christ returning in glory . . . The contrast is not between a reformed and an unreformed Judaism, but between Judaism and the new supernatural order by which it is at once destroyed and fulfilled: not between the disciples of a Jewish prophet and the members of an ecclesiastically ordered sacramental cultus, but between the disciples of Jesus, who, though translated into the sovereignty of God, are as yet ignorant both of His claims and of the significance of their own conversion, and the same disciples, initiated into the mystery of His person and of His life and death, leading the mission to the world, the patriarchs of the new Israel of God. The contrast is not between an ethical teaching and a dreamy eschatology, or between a generous humanitarianism and an emotional religious experience stimulated by mythological beliefs, but between a supernatural order characterised by a radical moral purification involving persistent moral conflict and the endurance of persecution, and a supernatural order in which there is no place either for moral conflict or for persecution.[3]

The high importance of what Hoskyns had done in this essay did not immediately disclose itself to all eyes. But little by little it came to be seen that theological Liberalism, having been attacked by a master-hand wielding its own weapons, had been smitten in a mortal place. Since he wrote less and less has been heard of the 'Liberal Christ' and to-day that mythical figure appears no longer in works of theology. But that is not to say that theological liberalism has disappeared from the land. The idea of the 'Liberal Christ' may be

---

[1] *Ibid.*, p. 169.   [2] *Ibid.*, p. 171.
[3] *Ibid.*, pp. 177, 178.

dead in the world of scholarship, but it still permeates the educational system of England, where millions of children are given Christian ethics but deprived of the Christian dogma which makes them intelligible and of the denominational teaching which offers membership in a worshipping community within which alone they can be practised. But if Hoskyns had not delivered the schools, he had done much to deliver the parochial clergy from their mesmerised state. Much of the authority previously conceded to the modernists by the average parish priest had been due to their learning. Though they might seem to him to be all the time blowing pieces out of the rock of the Scriptures, and so destroying the basis of the Gospel he believed and was commissioned to proclaim, he had the discomforting feeling that they knew far more about the science of biblical criticism than did their opponents, and that they had been abused rather than discredited. But here, at last, was a new portent—a university professor, who knew at least as much and possibly far more about New Testament scholarship than any don who had spoken at the Girton Conference of Modern Churchmen, and whose standards of disinterested academic research could not be questioned. Hoskyns was an acknowledged oracle, and the oracle, having accepted the challenge to appeal to the work of the critics on the primitive evangelical writings, had done so and had given his judgement.

Hoskyns had destroyed an idol. He had shown that a particular treatment of the New Testament made nonsense of history. He had next to show that an application of the new knowledge to the Bible revealed the real faith of the Bible, and that this faith was worth the holding, because it was true, because it made history intelligible and consistent with ordinary human experience, because it was demonstrably the faith of the forlorn hope which conquers in the Spirit. He had to begin by exploding the Liberal Protestant fallacy, but his really basic and seminal work was to reanchor Anglican theology to the Scriptures, and to show that out of the Scriptures came the Church. Thus both Scriptures and the Church were equally given by God as parts of His very Word to man, and endorsed by Christ as such. The Scriptures as he expounded them became, so to say, more of a rock than ever, and became it precisely because of what the new methods of historical criticism had brought to their interpretation. They had brought into bolder relief than ever before the 'Scandal of Uniqueness' which is the distinguishing mark of the Faith of the Bible; and, as Hoskyns spoke or wrote of this 'scandal,' he had the power to show clearly that as the God of the Scriptures was clothed with a rigid exclusiveness from all other imagined deities of man, so the demand of the Scriptures upon all who took them seriously was that because the mere holding of such a faith would be an offence, they too must accept the reproaches of exclusiveness. It was dangerous doctrine (the truth is nearly always dangerous) and liable to be misunderstood. But it was not tame and dull. It is small wonder that many students went to Cambridge simply to be taught by a man who spoke to them in accents like these. Hoskyns was no Barthian, though he understood Barth and greatly admired him. None the less, he became to Anglican theology the same kind of moving and disturbing force that Karl Barth was to European Protestantism.

The Scriptures are the Word of God, who has spoken; and the Church is inseparable from the Scriptures. The Church is therefore the Divine Society. This, in briefest possible form is what Hoskyns lived to teach. One illustration of his own peculiar and infectious manner of teaching it is in his delight in etymology. 'Can we rescue a word and discover a universe? Can we study a language and awake to a truth? Can we bury ourselves in a lexicon, and arise in the presence of God?' He asked the question in a sermon in the chapel of Corpus, and undoubtedly he thought we could, for he went on to preach a course of sermons on Sin and the Remission of Sin, which he characteristically began with an examination of the word Church. The next term he began another course of sermons on *The Language of the Church*, and prefaced it with the words, ' The Church has a language: it possesses words and phrases: for example, Faith, Righteousness, Sin, Judgement, Flesh and Blood, Spirit, Death, Life, Darkness—Light, Wrath,—Love, Evil—God, the Devil— God.'[1] But the use of them is hard and difficult, he pointed out, to those who had forsaken biblical and adopted evolutionary patterns of thought. Similarly, he opened his book *The Riddle of the New Testament*, published in 1931, and written in collaboration with the Rev. Noel Davey, with a chapter on *The Language*; and it is fascinating to see how this sets the pace of the entire argument, which comes at last to the conclusion:

It must be quite definitely affirmed that neither the Jesus of history nor the primitive church fits into the characteristic nexus of modern popular humanitarian or humanistic ideas. This is not merely because they belong to another age, of which the thought moved in an entirely unmodern idiom, but because their idiom was entirely foreign to that of any age, including their own. The gospel was as much a scandal to the first century as it is to the twentieth.[2]

Thus to the ancient terms Bible and Church Hoskyns had given a new content and a new emotional force. If to-day we think of the Church as having an ineradicably scriptural basis, and of the Bible as the living Word of the living God, it is largely due to him.

[1] Smyth, *op. cit.*, p. 93.   [2] Hoskyns, *op. cit.* (Faber and Faber), p. 180.

CHAPTER TWO

THE RESULTS OF THEOLOGICAL PRINCIPLE IN THE DAILY LIFE OF THE CHURCH

I. *The Decline of Partisanship*

Many people are apt to think that theology is the splitting of hairs of academic theory and of the work of theologians as having no relevance to the practical problems of life. They are of course wrong, and the truth is the exact opposite of what they suppose. Nothing is so powerful in practice as a theological idea. As a matter of mere historical demonstration, notions about God and His purpose for the world do change history and alter continents, and they affect for good and ill the whole manner of man's life in the world and his relationship to his environment. Because Luther once insisted that justification before God is by faith alone all Europe was changed, and the getting and the spending of every peasant and every aristocrat altered its pattern and its rhythm. The power of theology is not less in a mechanical than in a pastoral age, and the work of Hoskyns and those who echoed and followed him, and developed still further the principles he had established, began to show itself in the daily life and worship of the parish churches within a very few years, and therefore to affect many thousands of people who had never heard his name or theirs.

He spoke the words for which so many were waiting and in accents which made them hear. His deepest conviction could be put in a phrase, or a motto: the Faith of the Bible as the Word of God to be Practised in the Church of the Bible as the Body of Christ. That is exactly what Fr. A. G. Hebert, of the Society of the Sacred Mission at Kelham, has been steadily teaching for years. The mere recitation of the titles of his books shows it—*Liturgy and Society, The Throne of David, The Form of the Church, The Authority of the Old Testament.* The two great books of Fr. Lionel Thornton, of the Community of the Resurrection at Mirfield, exhibit exactly the same theological movement, for he followed *The Incarnate Lord* by *Common Life in the Body of Christ,* and the latter study is radically biblical throughout in a sense in which the former is not. The same assumptions also underlie the whole work of Fr. A. G. Hebert and many others on the Parish Communion, and the great liturgical study of Fr. Gregory Dix of Nashdom Abbey, *The Shape of the Liturgy*; and they give form and shape also to a work

so different from these as Dorothy Sayers' *The Man Born to be King*.
Archbishop William Temple himself was moving fast towards it and
away from the old emphases of liberal catholicism when he died.
Soon after he was appointed to the Primacy he declared in the
Christian News Letter that the Christian thought of all the world
was steadily converging on some half-dozen affirmations, and the
first of these he phrased as 'a Decision for God who has spoken.'
In his introduction to the Report of the Archbishops' Commission
on Doctrine, which he wrote in October 1937, he described how
theology was changing direction, and moving at last away from the
tradition of *Lux Mundi*:

> As I review in thought the result of our fourteen years of labour, I am
> conscious of a certain transition of interest in our minds, as in the minds of
> theologians all over the world . . . In our country the influence of Westcott
> reinforced by that of the *Lux Mundi* School had led to the development of
> a theology of the Incarnation rather than a theology of Redemption . . .
> A theology of the Incarnation tends to be a Christocentric metaphysic . . .
> A theology of Redemption tends rather to sound the prophetic note . . .
> If the security of the nineteenth century, already shattered in Europe,
> finally crumbles away in our country, we shall be pressed more and more
> towards a theology of Redemption. In this we shall be coming closer to the
> New Testament . . . If we began our work again to-day its perspectives
> would be different.[1]

Now, twelve years later, we can see it more clearly than even he
could in 1937. The classical schools of theology had all broken down.
Liberal Protestantism led nowhere: if Hoskyns had not broken it,
some other must have done so. Liberal Catholicism was admirably
meeting a need which was no longer widely felt. In their places the
new interpretations of Calvinism on the one hand and Thomism on
the other were addressing themselves to the real needs of the day
and saying the things which needed to be heard. The revival of
biblical theology and the consciousness of membership in the Divine
Society was the characteristically Anglican *via media*, and it is in
this tradition that nine-tenths of the younger clergy of to-day have
been and are being trained.

The immediate 'practical' result of this movement of theological
emphasis is that the strife of the historic parties in the Church has
almost completely ceased, for once it was accepted the parties themselves were seen to be quite irrelevant to the situation created in the
Church by this theology, and outside the Church by the strife of
nations and the predicament of man. Partisanship on the century
old lines rapidly became out of date. For what was being taught was
essentially a rediscovery and reassertion of the authority both of the
Church and of the Bible—not the one by itself or the other, but both.

---

[1] *Doctrine in the Church of England* (S.P.C.K., 1938), pp. 16, 17.

Protestants and Catholics in the Church thus found much common ground. Protestants saw that many indubitably catholic theologians were laying more and more stress in their teaching on the Bible, while their own theologians were enthusiastically exploring the authority of churchmanship.[1] In these changed circumstances High Church and Low Church rapidly became technical terms without meaning. It is very largely to this that we owe the blessed relief from the strife of tongues and pens between them. If to-day we tend less and less to affix the labels Protestant or Catholic to parsons or parishes, and if in nearly every diocese there is between them a happy co-operation and a brotherly love which is instinctive and makes no draughts on the wells of Christian charity, it is to this theological movement that we owe it. The last really discreditable outbreak of sectarian strife between them was on the occasion of the debating of the Revised Prayer Book of 1928. It was most violent while it lasted, but it subsided with remarkable speed, and it is doubtful if in our time we shall see any revival of it. When parties find that they have so much more in common than they once suspected, partisanship ceases to be.

II. *Baptism and Confirmation*

The new teaching about the Church is at once exciting and disturbing to those who hear it for the first time. The Church of our baptism is the Divine Society and the Body of Christ. It is likened to a garrisoned fortress standing a siege; or, alternately, to a series of sallies against the entrenched, worldwide armies of secularism, carried out by forlorn hopes of brothers. It is the divinely given social mould within which alone it is possible to practise the Beatitudes of the Sermon on the Mount. Set, as it is, in the twentieth-century world, our own Church of England is again a missionary body, offering redemption to a country needing reconversion and in a society which has now become sub-Christian. We are again the Church of the New Testament, living in biblical times re-born, and having a closer kinship with the Church of the first three centuries than could have been claimed by any generation of the Church between the first and the twentieth centuries. Since this is so, we are constantly told by those who have made the new teaching of Church consciousness their own, that the Church of the first three centuries must be our model to-day.

All these implications of the new teaching are commonly accepted by those who hear and accept it. We claim membership in the Church

---

[1] See, e.g., a first-rate study from the Protestant side, F. J. Taylor, *The Church of God* (Canterbury Press, 1946).

of our Baptism, and the mere utterance of the word Baptism in this context at once brings one face to face with the first barrier which prevents the Church from becoming in practice what the theologians and the prophets have been declaring that it is in the mind of God. It is now generally acknowledged that the way in which infants are commonly presented for Baptism comes near to being a denial of the true nature of the Church, and a mockery of the actual situation in which it finds itself. 'Indiscriminate Baptism' has been the practice of the Church for at least fifteen centuries, but it is only in the last twenty or thirty years that the clear knowledge has come that something is very wrong. To-day there is no single problem which more deeply disturbs the clergy, and there is no rural deanery in England where this disturbance is not constantly voiced. Infant baptism, as we have been practising it for so many years, has now become a chronically sore place in the ecclesiastical conscience of the Church of England, and of other English Communions besides. The real trouble is that the spirit of baptism in the Early Church no longer applies, where, after the initiation, it followed the 'Easter Mass in the dawn, and first communion as the beginning of Christian life in the midst of the exultant Church.'[1] 'Exultant' is the ringing word in that sentence. We have made it almost impossible for members of the Church to 'exult' because a new member has been admitted. It is not nowadays a rare thing to hear priests who undoubtedly hold the full catholicity of the Church both in faith and in practice declare that the Church has 'gone wrong' over infant baptism, and that baptism of an infant should be a rare privilege reserved for the infants of parents whose Christian profession cannot be doubted because it has been steadily asserted in the practising membership of the Church for years. They believe that the normal practice should be baptism only after full preparation, and therefore administered at the age of confirmation.

The whole theological problem has been carefully analysed by reference to the baptismal practice of the Early Church in the pamphlet from which quotation has just been made. Fr. Gregory Dix finds the root of our trouble in our separation of baptism from confirmation and both from the first communion, whereas in the early days these three were all parts of one and the same rite. Diagnosis is not the same thing as remedy, and to suggest remedies was not Fr. Dix's purpose. But our practice of baptising every baby presented to us regardless of whether there is the least likelihood or even possibility of its being trained to be a Christian not only makes nonsense of the whole doctrine of the Church as we have received it,

---

[1] Dom Gregory Dix, *The Theology of Confirmation in Relation to Baptism* (Dacre Press, 1946), p. 12.

but also (and precisely because it does so) it seriously hampers and embarrasses the whole witness and proclamation of the Church.

The most pressing aspect of the pastoral problem to-day lies precisely in those millions of English people of goodwill who sincerely regard themselves as practising Christians, who are Baptised and insist on the Baptism of their children in infancy, but who regard the Christian life as something a man does for himself, individually and privately . . . Of the Church as organic, as the Body of Christ, of the Divine life within it, of their own responsibility to it and for it, these people know and acknowledge little or nothing . . . The existence of this vast amorphous mass of Pelagian goodwill, at least three or four times as large as the living Body of the Church which seeks to live by grace, is what muffles the whole impact of the Gospel, and the whole witness of the Church in England to-day. Deal with this problem, incorporate these people effectively into the life of the Church and you will have some prospect of making an impression on the equally large mass of sheer paganism behind . . . The foundations of any long term policy lie in the field of right *teaching* about Baptism and Confirmation. A right change in this must in the end do something to dissipate this immense and disastrous misunderstanding.[1]

Thus when, in 1941, the editor of *Theology* wrote an article about Baptism and called it *Baptismal Disgrace*, he was only echoing with dramatic abruptness what many had long been thinking, and what their acceptance of the new exalted teaching about the Church necessarily led them to think.

Anxiety had been expressed and agitation had been carried on in a desultory and sporadic way ever since 1898 when two Yorkshire rural deaneries, Dewsbury and Birstall, had delivered the burden of their consciences about it. But it was in 1920 that a strong joint committee of the Convocations of Canterbury and York made its report.[2] Dr. Chase, Bishop of Ely, had been its chairman, and six bishops had been among its members. The report was a very cautious document, and it betrayed itself, among other ways, by the weakness of its language about the sponsors which the Church requires in infant baptism. The primary difficulty first of finding suitable sponsors, and then of training them, was certainly mentioned; but the committee shied away from the suggestion that there might be certain babies whose baptism the Church ought to defer until there is a reasonable likelihood of its requirements being met. 'One caution is necessary. The command to make disciples of all nations . . . ought not to be restricted in such a way as to 'forbid little children' to be brought to Christ because those who present them do not understand the blessings which Christ bestows in baptism, or the responsibilities which corporate fellowship with God involves.'[3]

---

[1] Dix, *op. cit.*, p. 34.　　[2] *Administration of Infant Baptism* (S.P.C.K., 1920).
[3] *Ibid.*, p. 5.

The report used much of its space to chase the red herring of a revised form of the Service of Baptism, but it said nothing which betrayed any consciousness of what was really at stake.

That this committee of 1920 had solved nothing and satisfied nobody is shown by the fact that since then others have had continuously to put their hands to the work it had been charged to do. In 1937 the Social and Industrial Commission of the Church Assembly had produced a report on The Church and Youth, in which a great deal was said on the problems of baptism. The relevant part of this report was considered by the House of Bishops in the Convocation of Canterbury in a long debate. It brought out the useful fact that the remarks about baptism in the report had been the work not of clergy but of a body of young people. They had asserted that 'the present confusion seems to us to jeopardise the spiritual purpose of Holy Baptism'; and they had gone so far as to make certain practical suggestions. They were that parents should be asked to attend preliminary instruction concerning the nature of baptism, that times of baptism should be much less frequent and much more should be made of the sacrament when these times came round, that sponsors should always be prepared, and that the parents of a child should be asked to sign a solemn promise: 'We do solemnly promise, with God's help, that our child shall be brought up in the Christian Faith according to the teaching of the Church of England.'[1] These suggestions were sympathetically received by the bishops, who, one after another, testified to the universality of uneasiness, They were not, however, officially endorsed by them. But there is to-day at least one big industrial parish (and probably there are more than one) where all the above recommendations have become conditions of the giving of baptism. It means that baptisms ordinarily happen only once in three months, and that the baptism of a normal and healthy baby is deferred until it is twelve weeks old. In those twelve weeks both parents and sponsors are given a thorough preparation for the responsibilities they undertake; and the service of baptism, when it comes, is a big and important occasion and the whole body of the congregation is always present.

In January 1939 the Upper House of the Convocation of Canterbury turned again to the same problem. They produced most alarming statistics. In the last twenty-four years sixty-seven per cent. of all the babies born in England had been baptised by the Church of England—that is, eleven and a half million babies had been baptised in our churches in that period. Yet the Easter communicants in 1937 had numbered only two and a quarter million.[2] There was agreement both among the bishops and the mass of the clergy that

[1] *C.C.C.*, 1937, pp. 294–5. [2] *C.C.C.*, 1939, p. 229.

while there might be many remedies for that most disturbing fact, the reform of baptismal procedure was certainly one of them. The bishops agreed that the priest of one parish ought not to baptise babies from another parish except by the consent of the other priest. But Dr. C. S. Woodward (Bishop of Bristol) in urging a resolution to this effect, regretted that it was advisory only, and said frankly: 'The difficulty is one which I confess I do not know how to deal with.'[1]

A further resolution that 'the clergy are justified in delaying the baptism of an infant on the ground that the parents are not ready to fulfil the Church's requirements concerning sponsors' was not carried. The Archbishop at the end made the blameless comment that we 'must make a sustained effort to see that the ideal, so far as possible, is realised.'[2] This was the report which caused the editor of *Theology* to write an article entitled *Baptismal Disgrace*.

There, to-day, the matter still rests. Mention the administration of baptism in any clerical gathering and a storm will certainly be caused, for everybody agrees that indiscriminate baptism as it has been practised for many centuries is quite inconsistent with a vivid belief in the Church as it is in the New Testament and with the actual facts of the Church's situation in the twentieth-century world. The discussion has gone far enough by now to isolate the vital problems which have first to be faced and solved. These are the whole question of infant baptism, the relationship of baptism in water to baptism of the Spirit, the relationship of baptism to confirmation considered as two parts of the one rite of Christian initiation. Most immediately 'practical' of all is the question of how we can secure the same universal acceptance of the need of the preparation of all concerned in a baptism as we have secured in the case of confirmation in the last hundred and fifty years.

III. *The Bible and the Bible Reading Fellowship*

'If the Church is the Household of grace, it is the Bible which anchors the Church to the true Word of God and which equips Christians for their warfare.' The words are those of the present Archbishops of Canterbury and York in their message to the Bible Reading Fellowship on the occasion of its twenty-fifth birthday.[3] It would be difficult to put more neatly the vital kernel of the theology which Hoskyns taught and his pupils and disciples are spreading so widely. There is health and vitality in such an affirmation, but it

---

[1] *C.C.C.*, 1939, pp. 241–3.   [2] *C.C.C.*, 1939, p. 245.
[3] *Twenty-Five Years; 1922–1947* (The Bible Reading Fellowship), p. 1.

is obviously inconsistent with the wide ignorance of the Bible even among many who go regularly to church. If churchpeople generally are to discover and make their own the knowledge that the Church is the Divine Society and they are in it, they must first be persuaded to read and to know the Bible just because it is the Word of God who has spoken. If churchpeople neither know nor use their Bibles the power of God has not free course in them and the Church's witness is weakened. Where people who are living without God know nothing of the Bible the first step towards their conversion is to persuade them of its relevance to them and their needs. Redemption cannot be dissociated from the Bible, in which its scheme is to be found; nor can anyone know Jesus who knows nothing of the historic records of His teaching and His life. No one, once converted, can be trained in the Faith without the Bible. Christian life depends on Christian theology; and Christian theology, above all in the Anglican Communion, is scriptural theology.

Long ago, in that other world of 1911, the tercentenary of the Authorised Version of the Bible was celebrated. A flood of eulogistic literature poured from the presses. But it marked not the beginning but the end of an epoch in the history of the Bible. For three hundred years English Christianity had been Bible Christianity, and English literature had been moulded, nursed, and fed by the language of the Authorised Version. But for the next thirty-five years the influence of the Bible on the life of the nation, and even on the life of the Church, was to become steadily less, as the legend spread among the people that the Bible was no longer trustworthy. As Bible religion was the only religion the man-in-the-street knew, he ceased to practise any religion at all when he ceased to read the Bible, and to bother whether his children ever opened it or not. This is, perhaps, the greatest religious change of this century, and it has been devastating. The testimony of parish priests of long and wide experience is virtually unanimous. Thirty years ago a priest might begin a sermon with a reference to Nicodemus—'You all remember what Jesus said to Nicodemus, except a man be born again'; or he might preach about Joseph as a foreshadowing of Jesus. To-day he would have to begin by telling the whole story of Nicodemus or of Joseph, for he cannot count on his hearers knowing who either was or what either did. Thirty years ago, when one visited the sick, one might begin by reminding them of Jesus' care for the sick, and what He did and said to them. It would only be to revivify knowledge they already had. Nearly all people, even those who had claimed no effective membership of the Church for years, knew that much of the gospel. They knew, too, at least some of the Old Testament stories and characters; likely enough, they had one or two texts by heart, and

D

even knew that at the point of death it was good to read the twenty-third psalm and the seventeenth chapter of St. John's Gospel. It is but rarely to-day that the ministration to the sick can take for granted even this modicum of biblical knowledge.

Of all the agencies which have set themselves to remedy this disturbing and potentially disastrous state of affairs, the Bible Reading Fellowship has probably been the most successful and effective. The story of the Fellowship is one of the great romances of Anglican history in the twentieth century, and it constitutes an example of the true spiritual adventure, for it is throughout the story of God's action in power upon an enterprise begun and continued in fellowship, at every stage deliberately offered to God for His pleasure, and every plan made prefaced by a conscious act of waiting upon God, and therefore made in the belief that such was in fact His will and His plan. It is the first condition of creativeness in every spiritual venture. Beginning in a single parish in Brixton in 1922, the Fellowship's leaflets of Bible readings and notes go to-day to 351,000 readers every month in many parts of the world. They find queens and prisoners to read them, and every kind of person between these extremes; and when any priest of the Anglican Communion has a confirmation candidate who wants to read the Bible regularly but does not know how, it has become virtually an instinct to suggest first of all the use of the appropriate monthly leaflet of the Bible Reading Fellowship.

A chance conversation began it all. Or 'was it just chance?'[1] asked Canon L. G. Mannering twenty-five years later. Probably it was not. He was at the time vicar of St. Matthew's, Brixton; and he was talking of the needs of the parish with his staff. What was needed in this typical and ordinary South London parish of 13,000 souls? They did not answer at once and off-hand; 'we talked and prayed about it.'[2] Then they knew. The need was not for more machinery, but for something basic and seminal, something to promote and spread and deepen the revolutionary simplicities of Christian living, prayer, the reading of the Bible, communion at the Eucharist, and all practised in conscious fellowship with others. The circumstances of the parish seemed to make necessary the monthly publication of a paper giving subjects for intercession and Bible passages for reading, with brief and simple notes. But it was not to be a purely private thing; those who took the papers must be in a conscious fellowship, with a weekly service for intercession and an exposition of the readings for that week, and a corporate communion each month. The papers were to be the badges of membership of a definite parochial society, the Fellowship of St. Matthew. 'We will make the venture,' wrote

---

[1] *Twenty-Five Years*, p. 15.   [2] *Ibid.*, p. 15.

the vicar to his people, 'believing that God calls us to this.' This leaflet of a parochial fellowship in Brixton was the first publication of what was presently to be the Bible Reading Fellowship; and it soon begot a mighty progeny.

At first it grew slowly. When the first year ended 175 people were taking and using the leaflets in the fellowship, which was still parochial. Then three other parishes joined in the scheme; St. Jude's, Brixton, St. John's, Eastbourne, and St. Andrew's, Aysgarth, in Yorkshire. Between them they had brought the number to 500 at the end of the second year. Then Canon Tom Pym, at that time Canon Missioner in Southwark Diocese, took a hand, and gathered a number of South London clergy to tell them of what St. Matthew's, Brixton, had been doing. Other parishes came in, and by the end of 1926 the circulation of the papers had risen to 1500. There were now too many parishes to make it possible for a single leaflet of subjects for intercession to suit all their needs. Thus each one was bidden to make its own list of intercessions, and the Fellowship's leaflet was confined to Bible readings and notes. It also changed its name to the Bible Reading Fellowship. Plainly it had outgrown the capacity of a single parish to deal with it, and that further and much wider growth was before it seemed clear. These things constituted not a crisis but one of those moments in the history of any movement which grows naturally from small beginnings when fresh decisions have to be made. Those in charge of the Fellowship's fortunes recognised this, but characteristically they would decide nothing until they had together sought to discover the decision of God:

> The Fellowship entered upon a new phase. There were indications that it might grow rapidly—all the more need therefore for prayer and guidance. What might be the purpose of God for this Fellowship? What line ought we to take? In May 1927, again under the leadership of Canon Pym, a group of us met for prayer and conference at the Diocesan Retreat House in Carshalton. It was unanimously agreed that the movement should be left to grow naturally and without publicity.[1]

A lame and impotent conclusion? At that moment it might perhaps have seemed so, for the only light they had was to carry on and not to force the pace. The decisive moment produced no new decision.

Yet in the next three years the circulation jumped from 600 to 20,000; and the papers were being read and used in many parts of the world. The original series of monthly leaflets had gradually to be multiplied into four or five different series. The leaflets were regularly published in a dozen different languages, and soon a special Braille edition was added. The work grew so fast that its direction had to be moved from Brixton in 1930 to an office in Westminster;

[1] *Ibid.*, p. 28.

and a full time secretary, Miss Margery Sykes, was engaged in 1930, and a full office staff to support her. Miss Sykes is still doing this vital work for the Church. Since then the office has had to be moved three times, as the work outgrew the accommodation. Through the horrible years before the war the work went on; and during the war itself, though many of the Fellowship's members were cut off from their source of supply, there was still an increase of 98,000 new members. But what of those who had grown to rely on the Fellowship's leaflets for their Bible reading, and could no longer receive them? There were many, and one of them, in Haarlem, later told the story in words which constitute the best of all tributes to what the Fellowship had achieved.

When in May 1940 the Germans took possession of this country, a small group of members of the Church of England at Haarlem—mostly British wives of Dutch husbands—were left here without a padre, a church, or anything and by the end of the month those of us who were of the B.R.F., some six or seven, realized that no more leaflets would be coming either. We set to work and had a meeting every fortnight in turns at our houses, and put together all the old B.R.F. Notes we had (one of us even had them from 1933), and made a sort of 'circulating library' using the months of bygone years for our meetings and at home, e.g. my family always read them at family prayers. So we kept going, and thank God the Germans never discovered our meetings. By 1945 we were very much at the end of this circulating library, and when at the liberation the first Canadian Army Chaplain gave us a handful of the green 'For those on Service' B.R.F. leaflets we were very pleased, and now we can join again since January. Last year we still depended on friends getting them for us because we couldn't pay for them. So when you are together presently to give thanks for the many blessings of the B.R.F. our thanksgivings will be with you in the spirit, for a fellowship which meant so much in the hard time we had.

Facts and figures can etch no more than the dry bones of such a story. They cannot by themselves give any indication of what the story means in terms of the immensity of achievement, nor what the achievement means in terms of the lives it helps to mould, nor yet how it has come about that there is so remarkable a story to be told. There is no doubt about its grand scale. From 100 members to 351,000 in twenty-five years, and all done without publicity, without over-organisation, without any use of the techniques of high-pressure salesmanship—it is probably the biggest thing done in the Anglican Church since 1919.

Those who were privileged to be present at the great twenty-fifth anniversary gathering in London on June 5, 1947, did perhaps realise something of the numerical greatness of what had been achieved, for they saw it with their own eyes. When, for example, they arrived at the Central Hall in Westminster for the Bible exhibition they saw, perhaps with consternation, that it was not going to be easy to get into the hall at all, large though it is. Had they not been there in very good time, they might perforce have been among the hundreds who were forced to wait outside, while to be among those standing in the long queue down the corridor would have been good fortune. Only those who arrived early got into the hall for the speeches, and they crammed it. Then, in the afternoon, came the anniversary service in Westminster Abbey. It did not start until 4 o'clock, but already by 2 o'clock the members of the Fellowship were streaming in to make certain of a place, and very soon every seat was filled, every corner and cranny where one might at least stand was taken. Children from schools which had groups of the Fellowship were placed in the choir, overflowed it, and were found seats on the sacrarium steps. In the evening came the big meeting at the Central Hall, for which 14,000 applications for the 2,700 seats had been made. Two other halls near by were taken, and they too were packed, though those in them had not thought to see the speakers, but only to be together to hear the speeches through loud-speakers. This was the great occasion, for they were to hear a fellow member of the Fellowship speak to them. This member was H.M. the Queen. When she arrived she was told of the two overflow meetings and insisted on going first to them before she went to the big hall to speak to the members.

I am very glad indeed to be present at this meeting, which celebrates the twenty-fifth anniversary of the Bible Reading Fellowship. Twenty-five years is not, from an historical point of view, very long, but the spiritual significance of things cannot be estimated in terms of time, and who would imagine in 1922 that in a quarter of a century the membership of this Movement would have grown from a small parochial group into a world-wide fellowship? The daily readings and notes chosen and written by scholars have been the means of helping tens of thousands of grown-ups and children to understand not only the riches incorporated in the Scriptures, but the implications of their spiritual truths in ordinary everyday life. I myself am a member of the Bible Reading Fellowship, and so I can say from my own experience how valuable it is to have the help of these notes in one's daily Bible reading. As during the past years of war, so throughout the present days of reconstruction we all have great responsibilities to shoulder. If we rely upon our own strength, either as an empire or as individuals, we shall indeed find the burden too great, but if, through prayer and Bible reading we learn to live each day in the strength and power of God, we may well go forward with confidence and hope.

At the Bible Exhibition which was opened this morning, I believe a scene is depicted of Queen Victoria presenting a Bible to an African emissary. Her words as she presents it are: 'This is the secret of Britain's greatness.' It is my prayer and hope that these words may become true again in our generation. These are challenging days in the history of the world: a new era is struggling to be born, and what sort is it to be? We, in our nation and empire, are called upon to give a moral lead to the world. We can only do this if we are true to our great Christian traditions. To what greater inspiration and counsel can we turn than to the imperishable truth to be found in this treasure house, the Bible? To read it regularly, to read it intelligently and devotionally, this will deepen our discipleship and enable us to take our share in creating and extending the fellowship which may be used by God to build the kind of world He meant and wants it to be.

It was the great moment, but presently, when others too had spoken, came another moment, only a little less memorable. The Bishop of Gloucester, as chairman of the Fellowship, beckoned its founder, Canon L. G. Mannering, to the front of the stage and handed to him a leather bound volume signed by the Queen and many another member of the Fellowship, and inscribed with fitting words of tribute.

We, the Council and members of the Bible Reading Fellowship, on this the twenty-fifth anniversary of its foundation, wish to express to you its founder, our deep appreciation of the work you have done in creating the Fellowship, and in helping by your vision and faith to make it what is is to-day. Beginning in a small way in your own parish twenty-five years ago, the Fellowship has now extended its circulation of monthly notes for Bible-reading, both at home and overseas, to some 350,000. Since its inception your counsel and leadership have been of inestimable value to its growing work. We assure you of our affectionate gratitude and we also thank God for the vision He granted you twenty-five years ago.

To few men is it given to plant a seed and then to see in their own lifetime so great a weight of fruit.

To most people the society is known by the monthly Bible reading leaflets it publishes, and a very substantial proportion of them must be used in solitariness for private reading. But both its earlier and its present title contain the word Fellowship, and from the beginning it was a fellowship of readers of the Bible which the founders intended to create. In part this fellowship was spiritual, the fellowship created between one reader in Aberdeen and another in Penzance by the fact that each read the Bible according to the same plan, and this fellowship is real and precious. But the ideal of the society is that its members should study the Scriptures together in small groups with the aid of the leaflets, which are composed with an eye to corporate study, and thus fulfil the petition in the Fellowship prayer, 'that we, with all who devoutly read the Holy Scriptures, may realise our fellowship with one another in Thee.' During the years a large number of these groups have been formed in every kind of sphere of life. They are inspired by a careful fostering of this spirit in the London office of the Fellowship (it must be one of the busiest as well as the happiest offices in London) where 'each day begins with morning prayers and a reading from one of the series of Notes,' and where, as a natural consequence, 'the office is undoubtedly a happy one and even at the busiest times the work is done so cheerfully and with such interest that there is no sense of strain, and one is inspired with the sense of fellowship that exists and the pride and satisfaction that each member takes in her work.'[1] Thus the Bible Reading Fellowship takes its place in the whole movement of the Spirit towards the cellular expansion of Christianity which has been so marked a feature of the history of the Church in our time.

The Bible Reading Fellowship is so evidently one of the most successful movements in Anglican history during the last thirty years that it is worth while to ask how this success has come to pass. There are two answers. It fills a need which is basic and simple. Christian practices and doctrines which are generally neglected for a period always reassert themselves and take their own revenges. The denigration of the Bible at the hands of many critics, and the neglect of the evident duty laid upon all Christians to read it regularly, have had dire consequences for English Christianity. In due course, and inevitably, the Bible reasserted its own authority in a new form, through processes and instruments described in the previous chapter. The inspiration and the scholarship of these theologians, could only have free course in the Church through a great army of unscholarly and ordinary Christians who were reading the Bible intelligently and devoutly. This army the Bible Reading Fellowship has done more than anyone else to provide. The theologians created the need and the Fellowship supplied it, and in doing so greatly strengthened the platform on which the theologians were standing. Throughout they have played into each other's hands. The second reason for the phenomenal witness of the Fellowship is that its founders began and developed their task in a manner exactly suited to the genius of the Anglican Church. The vision has always been pursued with a decent modesty. They were content to let it begin in a small way, experimentally and naturally; and the organisation and the publicity followed in the wake of the demand, and were at no point allowed to exploit the vision. The extent of the response determined the amount and the complexity of the organisation, which was gradually provided to fulfil a proven need and not to create it. Throughout its course the principles of those in charge of it might have been thus expressed, Pray first and act afterwards, and, Let the organisation be completely simple, and never more than the bare minimum necessary to supply the need. It is the way of doing things which the Church understands, and at every point it is consistent with biblical principles. Thus it is that the Bible Reading Fellowship has done more than any organisation whatsoever to get the Bible actually read by members of the Church, and there seems hardly any limit to its promise.

[1] *Twenty-Five Years*, p. 32.

IV. *The Eucharist and the Parish Communion*

It is impossible to think of the Church without also thinking of the Eucharist, for it is the sacrament ordained by the Founder of the Church and the rite given to be used in the Church by which the Church's people are united to their Lord and to each other. The rediscovery of the phrase in the Creed, 'I believe in the Holy Catholic Church' by the Oxford Movement more than a hundred years ago led at once to a revaluation of the Holy Communion; and it is common knowledge that the great increase in every parish church of opportunities for people to receive their communion, and the steady growth in decency and solemnity when it is celebrated is due to the Oxford Movement. In other words, say something vital about the nature of the Church and get it widely accepted, and the immediate results will show themselves in the field of the Eucharist. In our own time, as we have seen, theologians have been saying things about the Church, and what they have said has found eager ears to hear it; in consequence, we are witnessing the growth of a new kind of emphasis on the Eucharist. What the theologians of the Oxford Movement said about the Church and what our own theologians of yesterday and to-day have been saying is not quite the same thing. Although neither would dream of contradicting the other, their emphases have been different.

The term 'The Church' could not mean to Newman and his peers quite what it means to us to-day. It was not then a beleaguered garrison set in a largely pagan society. They knew nothing of the modern knowledge of the Scriptures, and the connection between the Word of God and the Divine Society was then neither as real nor as rich as it has now become. It would not have occurred to them to adopt as the chief evangelistic motto, 'Let the Church be the Church.' As a consequence, their teaching about the Eucharist was broadly personal and individual: it was primarily an act of personal devotion. To-day one is much more likely to be told that it is a social rite, that it contains and asserts a whole philosophy of social health, that it is the gathering of the faithful in the Church to offer corporately the sacrifice of our redemption.

The outward and visible sign of this prevailing view has come to be the Parish Communion, and the meaning of it was first set out at full length, in 1937, in a composite book of essays by various writers, called *The Parish Communion*, and edited by Fr. A. G. Hebert. The broad insight of all the writers is this: if you express your philosophy of the Church and the World by the phrase 'Let the Church be the Church,' then you are led straight to the Parish Communion as the rite which most naturally expresses what you believe. The Parish Communion is the Eucharist at which all, or nearly all, the confirmed members of the parish make their communion all together as the one family of God in that place. It is a joining of whole human families to offer the Great Sacrifice in order that they may be made into one supernatural family in the Church. The hours of Communion which the Oxford Movement have made customary, 8 o'clock and 11 o'clock, are neither of them suitable for such a purpose as this, and the Parish Communion is generally celebrated between 9 and 10 o'clock: it is often followed by a common breakfast at which all the worshippers join. This is now the normal Sunday practice of hundreds of churches up and down the land.

This conception of the place of the Eucharist in the life of the parish is a clear implementing of the conception of the Church rooted in the Bible and set over against the World. Those who believe in the Parish Communion do so because they believe these things about the Church.

> The real aim (of the book, *The Parish Communion*, writes its editor) is to set forth a conception of the nature of the Church, which appears to compel the adoption of the Parish Communion as its necessary expression in liturgy. It is the idea of the Church that is primary.[1]

And what a theology 'compels,' the facts of the modern situation of the Church encourages. The Church is so plainly face to face with a secularised world; all the more reason, then, that the chief service in the parish church on a Sunday morning 'should fully set forth the nature of the Church and that the members of the Church should fully know what the Church is.'[2] It is one with the Church of the Scriptures, and one with the primitive Church of the first three centuries, and as such should be conscious of its separation from the World and its position of privilege in the divine scheme of things.

> Deep in the mind of the primitive Church, and colouring every strand of her belief, is the strong consciousness of the unique privilege with God of the 'Holy Church.' She is the new 'Israel of the Spirit' which has replaced the old 'Israel according to the flesh' in the Divine love and in the Divine plan for the universe.[3]

The Parish Communion, the authors believed, would help to inculcate this sense of privileged separation. The aggression of the modern world, moreover, makes this sense of separated privilege empirically necessary, and especially in the case of a national Church, like the Church of England, since the pressure of the state will always seek to persuade or compel the Church to accommodate her Gospel to 'the religion which the nation holds,' and as a speaker demanded

---

[1] *The Parish Communion*, edited by A. G. Hebert (S.P.C.K., 1937), p. vii.
[2] *Ibid.*, p. 13.   [3] *Ibid.*, pp. 127, 128.

in the debate on the Revised Prayer Book in 1928 'to bring the doctrines of the Church of England into accord with the doctrines of the people.'[1] Against this danger, too, the authors see the Parish Communion as a shield.

Whether the Parish Communion fulfils all these purposes or not, it is now the normal eucharistic practice in many parishes, and it is slowly changing and enriching the common understanding of churchmanship, its relevance and its value. One picture of it may stand for many. In the country parish of Temple Balsall in Warwickshire it has been celebrated at 8.45 for thirty years or more. The service which lasts an hour is congregational throughout, and well interspersed with hymns, and the people come to it from all corners of the parish. For various reasons it is held 'in a room in the Almshouse court, known as the Parish Room, but originally the parish Boys' School, where many of the older men received their education, and with the schoolmaster's rostrum still *in situ*.'[2] There, in that room made holy, the Eucharist was offered in, for, and by the whole family of the faithful in the Household of Faith Sunday by Sunday. The people were their own choir. They sang Merbecke, and did not tire of him, and 'a very little musical talent went, by the blessing of God, a long way.' Everything was done to emphasise that this was the characteristic act of worship of a family. The notices and biddings were of simple homely things, causes, and persons—known to all and the concern of all. The people came in large numbers, and in families—the little children, parents, and grandparents all in church together: and the actual communion lasted long enough for three hymns to be sung during its course. All felt the Service as their very own. A farmer milked his cows, delivered the milk, and then came two miles with his family on a motor bicycle and side-car. A cowman rose at 5 A.M. to get his work done, another came with his wife who 'received the Blessed Sacrament with her baby in her arms and a little one of two years old by her side.' They all worshipped together in this way every Sunday. It taught them that they really were the Church, all alike in it and of it, an island of sanity and love in a frantic world; and that in the Church they walked with God for just so long as they walked together. When the service was over, they all had breakfast together, and

it was interesting to note how the congregation sorted themselves out at the breakfast. There were five tables in the room, one being appropriated to the children, who, for economical reasons were supplied with treacle instead of marmalade, and besmeared themselves accordingly: the boys and growing lads took possession of a smaller table . . . On the other side of it were to be found the maidens of the congregation seated at a table specially

---

[1] Quoted in *ibid.*, p. 297 (note).   [2] *Ibid.*, p. 262.

claimed as their own—though they always welcomed the intrusion of guests of either sex. The middle-aged had a trestle table for themselves, while the clergy, church-wardens, and other leading members of the congregation, and visitors, occupied a central table in close proximity to the fire. Such is the courtesy of youth, and such the happy instinct for the fitness of things which prevailed in the little family which gathered there Sunday by Sunday after Holy Communion in church. Sometimes visitors would be present both in church and at breakfast. The unselfconscious and simple humility with which they would share the family meal, and the sensitive courtesy with which the village people welcomed them, were good to see.[1]

Such is the outline of Sunday morning family worship, which though still exceptional, is becoming the normal practice of an increasing number of parishes every year. In the city of Newcastle-on-Tyne, for instance, nineteen parish churches have the Parish Communion every Sunday.[2] It is a movement which seems bound to grow, and before very long it is likely that the exceptional parish churches will be those who still observe Sunday mornings as the Oxford Movement taught them, with an 8 o'clock Celebration for communion and either Matins or Choral Eucharist (or High Mass) at 11 for worship. It is idle to speculate just what effect this movement will have when it is the normal practice, but it is bound to work towards the integration of the members of the Church, and to do much to fulfil in worship and in life at least some of the promise lying hidden in the gradual unfolding of the dominant theological insight of Anglican history in the last thirty years. Its emphasis has been on Bible and Church, and it is already leading us to a new focus on pulpit and altar.

[1] *Ibid.*, p. 263.
[2] See pp. 207, 208 of this book for a description of the Parish Communion in Newcastle.

CHAPTER THREE

THE CHURCH OF ENGLAND AND THE SOCIAL ORDER

I. *Prologue: John Locke*

The story of the responses of the Church in the twentieth century to the challenge of evil social conditions must be taken back over many generations before its beginning can be found. There is no satisfactory starting-point less distant from us in historical time than the life and thought of the philosopher John Locke, prophet-in-ordinary to the whig revolution of 1688 which set in motion the train of events leading to the establishment of the Hanoverian dynasty, and a new England. In this England was founded the idea of man as a rightly acquisitive animal. Locke was the profoundly influential justifier of this picture of man, of social order as an organisation framed to promote the getting of wealth, of government as a machine to encourage the citizens to amass property and to protect and to guarantee their enjoyment of it. All this he derived from interior Christian convictions so real, so sincere, so deep that it occurred to no one to doubt the loftiness of the sources of his thought. He maintained for many years a power of concentrated industry which was of heroic stature, and he was equipped with a prose style which made philosophy easily intelligible and clearly demonstrated that abstractions of thought might be immensely influential in the sphere of verifiable, concrete results. The principles he maintained and made popular about the purpose of a man's life in society dominated the course and shaped the pattern of the social thinking of both Church and State in Britain until the middle of the nineteenth century; and all the early social rebels like Cobbett and Morris were really rebelling against the immemorial intellectual tyranny of Locke. He made the Acquisitive Society seem to be more moral, more in accordance with God's will than the Theocratic Society of the Middle Ages; and what he urged was accepted with but little question by men of goodwill for centuries. The social movement of the Church from Ludlow and Maurice onwards has been and still is fundamentally an attempt to repudiate Locke, to get this repudiation positively accepted by the mass of Christians, and to find the more excellent way.

John Locke was one of the most eminent thinkers England has ever produced, and perhaps no other English philosopher has enjoyed an authority so unrivalled and so long-lived. His political function was to justify the revolution of 1688, and to ground the Hanoverian political and social order on the rock of a sufficient philosophy. But the authority of his writings lasted long after the immediate political occasion of them had passed out of living memory. George III had come to the throne and the rule of the House of Hanover had long been accepted as the normal order of things, and Locke himself was no more remembered, but still he ruled the society he had done so much to shape. He ruled it from his grave.[1] In his own person one of the most attractive of Englishmen, the reality and sincerity of his attachment to Christianity is not open to question. He was absolutely loyal to what he conceived Christianity to be, but it was a religion of his own finding, not the religion of the Catholic Church nor even of the New Testament. But because this defective religion was the spring of his life and the arbiter of his thought, it involved his social pronouncements in error, and out of his work a picture of what he supposed to be a genuinely Christian Social order emerged, but it was at almost every point opposed to the social theory of Catholic Christendom.

In religion Locke was a synthesist. He used his private judgement to select what seemed to him good from this religious system and that. Of these gatherings he made his own highly individual amalgam, which he submitted to no man's scrutiny. If to believe firmly in the doctrines of the Incarnation and the Atonement of Christ makes a man a dogmatist, Locke held a dogmatic faith. But he was a very limited dogmatist. His belief in Jesus as Lord and Saviour did not wean him from his uneasiness with the idea of mystery; nor did it deliver him from being as rootedly anti-ecclesiastical as he was anti-mystical. He had strong objections to the granting of any temporal power to any ecclesiastical body. Every form of theocracy was an abomination to him. Even in the sphere of a spiritual direction of souls he would not admit any priestly competence. He would have each man his own interpreter of the Bible, of the things of God. His ideas of churchmanship could be almost completely drawn out of this single significant passage from his *Essay Concerning Toleration*:

Religious worship—being that homage which I pay to that God I adore in a way I judge acceptable to him, and so being an action or commerce passing only between God and myself—hath in its own nature no reference at all to my governor or my neighbour, and so necessarily produces no action which disturbs the community . . . If I observe the Friday with the Mahometan, or the Saturday with the Jew, or the Sunday with the Christian; whether I pray with or without a form; whether I worship God in the

---

[1] The phrase is that of G. M. Trevelyan, *English Social History* (Longmans, Green, 1944), p. 306.

various and pompous ceremonies of the papists, or in the plainer way of the Calvinists; I see nothing in any of these, if they be done simply and out of conscience, that can make me either the worse subject of my prince or worse neighbour to my fellow-subject.[1]

This liberal latitudinarianism had its own fine flowering in the great service he gave to the cause of religious toleration, but religious individualism could hardly be taken farther than he took it, and this too had its consequences.

A religion of any kind must be based upon a theory about life and its purpose. Locke was a religious man as well as a philosopher. In both capacities he had to answer the vital questions about life. His answer, which was very simple, he stated again and again in his books and his letters. Happiness is the purpose of a man's life; to pursue happiness is the function of man in the world. But because human reason can so plainly demonstrate the existence of God, the relevance of the world to God, and the revelation of God in Jesus Christ, happiness cannot be achieved in isolation from God, nor in defiance of His laws. Nor can it be achieved in isolation from other men; and because social contract must involve social contact, the happiness of man involves the defining and seeking of a just relationship between man and man and between human government and creative social order. To fail to achieve this is to deliver man into a state of insecure misery which it is precisely the purpose of both God and man to avoid. For happiness is the end and misery is the bane of man.

It is a very modern doctrine. Half the novelists and most of the newspapers preach this sort of thing every day. But it is an anti-catholic doctrine, taking no account of man's vision of God at one end of the scale and the continuous evil in the heart of man at the other. A doctrine of man's nature which does not put these at the strategic centre of its scheme leaves but little for God to do in the present, and sooner or later undervalues what He has done in the past. To be with God and enjoy Him for ever is only possible if God continually and actively reveals Himself. To have the blessed experience of sin forgiven is only possible for those who believe that He actively forgives. To suggest that man lives primarily to avoid misery and win happiness is ultimately to drive out of man the spiritual hunger by virtue of which he is man and not merely a human animal. Man is then valued at less than the Gospel's estimate and far less than the Redeemer's price. He is no longer but little lower than the angels. He soon becomes much lower than the beasts of the field.

The social consequences of this attempt to hold a Christianity

---

[1] H. R. Fox Bourne, *The Life of John Locke* (Kegan Paul, 1896), vol. i, p. 177.

shorn of the element of mystery and deprived of the doctrine of original sin are seen in Locke's exalted view of the majestic rights of property. 'The great end of Men's entering into Society is the Preservation of Property.' This teaching of Locke's was even used by him to justify certain kinds of slavery. It caused him to abuse the poor, saying that their troubles were due to a 'relaxation of discipline and corruption of manners.' He advised that all hale and workless men under fifty should be pressed for the navy, that those over fifty should be sent to work in penal establishments, and that those who were willing to work should have no choice of work, but be sent to labour in whatever trades paid their masters best. These are terrible doctrines for a Christian to hold, when the sort of world they helped to found and remained potent to justify contained Hogarth's Gin Alley, the Newgate stews where Macheath's gang roistered and betrayed each other, and workhouses for pauper children in which more than half were annually starved to death.[1]

But such were the social findings and pronouncements of the foremost thinker of his time, and they found their way into the minds of later prophets in many spheres and into the statute book.

The reigns of George I and George II have perhaps the scantiest crop of important legislation in our parliamentary records ... This was only to be expected in an age when the chief function of government was held to be the 'Preservation of Property,' and when absolute freedom of contract, however oppressive such a system might be to the weaker members of society, was regarded as essential in a free community.[2]

In the sphere of law Blackstone reached back to Locke; so did Adam Smith in economics, and Hume in philosophy. Each derived from him the views he held in matters of the function of government, sociology and economics. The sum of it might be expressed in the phrase, Property Justifies Itself, even though a social order is thus built in which it not only happens that the poor and the weak are defenceless but it is regarded as right that they should be so. Locke lived and died, he thought, spoke, and wrote as a Christian. That he held a form of Christianity very much *sui generis*, very far from what is taught in the Scriptures and defined by the Church seems to have escaped the notice of other Christians for many years. But perhaps it is not so remarkable that Christians for the most part swallowed all Locke taught them and remained for so many years blind to the social implications of the Gospel. We who have now overthrown every single doctrine which Locke ever held—the splendour of toleration, the necessity of freedom, and the primacy of reason

---

[1] See Basil Williams, *The Whig Supremacy* (Oxford University Press, 1939), pp. 5 ff, 126.
[2] *Ibid.*, p. 8.

among them, all of which our civilisation has repudiated no less completely than his views on property—forget the long compulsion of his unquestioned authority.

II. *The Slow Awakening*

It is very hard to make headway against the force of incessant and ubiquitous suggestion; and when suggestion and exhortation are in conflict suggestion has by far the greater power. Particularly this is so when the suggestion is implicit in the structure of a whole social order or pattern of life. Locke had left behind him an agreed doctrine of getting and living and spending which became the universal tradition of Britain, accepted without much examination and with hardly any challenge long before the real social dislocation came with the strains of the war with Napoleon and the Industrial Revolution. Thus the poverty and misery which these caused, and which were terribly accentuated by the inadequacy of an eighteenth-century governmental machine to deal with them, passed far too often without any protest by the Church and were but seldom perceived as a grotesque, horrible denial of every human sanctity and right which all Christians have been divinely ordered to maintain. Bodies of protesting victims, like the Luddites on the one hand and the Tolpuddle Martyrs on the other, were savagely handled by the law, but the force of social suggestion and the very natural fear of revolutionary Jacobinism were such that few good men even among the clergy thought it right to protest and too many even approved when half-crazy loom-breakers were hanged, and pioneers of peaceful workers' organisation were transported to Botany Bay.

The idea that Christian theology was one thing and social ethics quite another and a very foreign thing had taken deep root. Many years had to pass before this unnatural separation could be buried in the darkness where it belonged. We marvel now that Christians could have been so long blind to the fact that the gospel they were presenting was lop-sided and incomplete. The Church as a whole heeded the missionary challenge nearly a hundred years before it woke to the social challenge. Yet the social evils of slums and sweated labour and pauperdom were all at home, very near to them, held before Christian eyes day after day, while the missionary stories of the woes of black men and yellow and brown far away were sympathetically heard and caused resolute action. But though we now may marvel, so it was; and no doubt our descendants will one day wring their hands too over the terrible embarrassments which our present crass but unperceived blindness will be causing them.

The fact that the Church has a mission to society as well as to the

individuals who compose it, that these are not two missions but one
and the same, and that this missionary responsibility is part and parcel
of the Gospel, is to-day accepted by most Christians as commonplace and obvious, and no responsible Christian spokesmen would
dream of denying it. The whole doctrine of John Locke is very
thoroughly dead. But it has taken nearly a hundred years to kill it,
and the story of how this has been done is long and complicated.
It has been told many times,[1] and there is no need here to repeat it
in more than the barest outline.

Locke's views on property and the purpose of government were
not the only influential doctrines which hindered the Church's
recovery of its social mission. There was also the publication of
Darwin's *Origin of Species* in 1859 and the whole welter of evolutionary thinking which spread over the world in the wake of that
epoch-making work. The theories of natural selection and biological
predestination when applied to the government and the social life
of human beings were devastating indeed on any Christian view of
the ordering and the purpose of man's life in society, or of the relations between the individual and the collective. How necessarily
hostile ideas of natural selection by automatic processes are to
Christian ideas of the nature and purpose of a man's life can be
estimated from a reading of Benjamin Kidd's *The Science of Power*,
which was published in 1918, and ran through eight editions in a
year. It is a sustained denunciation of the consequences for humanity
of Darwin. The line of thought he set in progress is accused among
other things, of giving to the doctrine of biological necessity a new
and deadly lease of life in the Prussian military text-books,[2] of denouncing acts of charity for interfering with the process of natural
selection,[3] of exalting the individual at the expense of society,[4] and
of sanctifying the individual's natural aggressiveness.[5] In particular
Kidd had no doubt that Darwin had made the task of Maurice and
the Christian social reformers many times as difficult as it must
otherwise have been:

Almost every argument of the *Origin of Species* appeared to represent a
generalised conception of the effectiveness of the war of competition. The
conditions of the social war which Maurice, Ruskin, and a crowd of
writers had condemned . . . seemed to have been justified at a stroke. The
central thesis of Darwin appeared as nothing less than a culminating
scientific condemnation of all the labour programmes of the west conceived
in a spirit of socialism.[6]

---

[1] Notably in Maurice B. Reckitt, *Faith and Society* (Longmans, Green, 1932),
and in the same author's *Maurice to Temple* (Faber and Faber, 1947).
[2] Benjamin Kidd, *The Science of Power* (Methuen, 1918), p. 32.
[3] *Ibid.*, p. 70.   [4] *Ibid.*, p. 258.
[5] *Ibid.*, p. 153.   [6] *Ibid.*, pp. 45, 46.

Certainly Darwin had placed the acquisitive fighting male on a new pedestal, and Darwin's prestige was not far short of Locke's before him. It hindered and side-tracked the slowly awakening social conscience.

The idea that because the Church is entrusted with the Gospel it has the positive duty of sitting in judgement upon the social and political institutions of the world, and the belief that the Gospel itself is maimed if it does not take society as well as individuals into its offer of redemption were the commonplaces of the Middle Ages. In 1850 they were strange archaic notions, and hardly anyone in England believed them. The few who did knew well that years of propaganda and teaching must pass before they could again be accepted by the Church as a whole and in retrospect there is far more success than failure. This story is punctuated and annotated by the work, almost incredible in the sheer volume of output, of the great men whose names are still alive, Ludlow, Kingsley, Maurice, Barnett and their peers. But they did not dominate the movement. They hardly even charted its course. They inspired it and they taught it. Most of the 'field' work was done by the little societies to which it gave birth. They had an influence out of all proportion to the smallness of the number of their membership, and though they were sadly given to splitting into fragments and going off at wild tangents, which was their characteristic disease, their persistent devotion was profoundly influential. These little societies between them did most to bring us to where we now stand.

In 1877 was born the first of these societies. The Rector of Bethnal Green, Stewart Headlam, whose portrait Bernard Shaw is held to have painted in his *Candida*, founded the Guild of St. Matthew. He was very much of a freak and an oddity—the sort of socialist who is no democrat, but who is at heart more deeply tinged with individualism than any believer in free competition and enterprise. But he had a superb courage, and an instinct for the telling dramatic gesture. When, for example, a young workman was killed in a socialist demonstration in London through being ridden down by the police horses, Headlam marched in front of his funeral procession from Bow Street, up the Strand to St. Paul's and thence to Whitechapel cemetery. He forced the Guild into his own mould and painted it all over with his own colours. Its tone was catholic, its approach to social problems eucharistic. It held as its ideal the vision of a genuinely corporate Church within an omnicompetent State, at work in a society the citizens of which had undergone all the processes of economic levelling by means of socialist political action. Headlam and the Guild had so great an affection for the secularists they hoped to convert that they allowed the political affiliations of secularism too large a share in determining the policy of what was after all an avowedly Christian body. But though the Guild remained quite uninfluential in any political sense, for it never could boast more than 400 members, it has a niche in history, for it was the first corporate attempt to do something which had been badly needed since the Reformation and yet left undone.

In 1889 *Lux Mundi* was published. Those who have heard about but not actually read these essays are apt to suppose that they were all devoted to theology, and that their importance is due to their inclusion of Gore's first public avowal of the kenotic theory of the consciousness of Christ. *Lux Mundi* was indeed a landmark in the history of Anglican theology, but its editors had a sociological purpose as well, and two of the essays were purely social. There had been nothing of that sort in *Essays and Reviews*: between 1863 and 1889 theology had widened its borders. This greater width of interest testified to the catholicity of the book, and in the year of its publication its leading contributors, headed by Gore, founded the Christian Social Union. They had hoped that the Guild of St. Matthew would serve the purpose they had in mind. But its colours were too bizarre and its politics too premature to suit their sagacious minds. Their purpose was to find out by the method of group research just what a Christian social order in the twentieth-century world ought to be. Until they had done this preliminary work they did not feel able to commit themselves to political socialism. As a group the Christian Social Union hardly succeeded in this main purpose of research, partly because it never succeeded in attaching to itself enough of the economists and scholars without which it could hardly be done, though it did have R. H. Tawney. But it 'taught its senators wisdom.' Idealists like Westcott and Gore became realists in matters of reform, It also did a fine work in a secondary sphere by pressing continually and effectively upon the conscience of the Church the evil of social conditions and it performed a great deal of the early education of Christian opinion, which was indispensable if Christians were ever to believe again that their very religion meant that they could not ignore the worlds of politics and industry. Here the fact that it had Scott Holland to write for it made a world of difference. But the Union was by no means content with its academic work. It struggled with the casualties as well as with the diagnosis of industrial disease. Gore, for instance, began his Oxford episcopate by publicly espousing the cause of the strikers in a Reading strike, subscribed to their funds, and

caused a thorough investigation to be made by social experts into the conditions of the working classes in Reading . . . showing that at least three thousand families in the borough had an income insufficient to maintain their members in efficiency.[1]

The Union was a larger and a less neurotic affair than the Guild of St. Matthew. In 1910, its peak year, it had 6,000 members.

In 1906 the Parliamentary Labour Party was formed. Socialism had begun to state its claim to a legitimate place in the constitution of Britain, and to make its bid for political power. Spurred by this significant event, another group of Anglican sociologists came together and decided that neither of the two societies already in the field met the needs they saw, and so founded another, the Christian Socialist League. This new Society was intended to be the infant Labour Party's soul. In politics therefore it was committed to socialism. In religion, however, it was much less uncompromising. It set out to be as 'comprehensive' as it supposed the Anglican Church was, and it refused to become partisan in its ecclesiastical sympathies. The particular contribution it sought to make to sociology was to be found in the emphasis it ceaselessly laid on guild socialism, and, negatively, in its steady denunciation of the whole idea of the omnicompetent state. It argued for the *Communitas Communitatum* as the ideal form of polity, and thus it approached catholicity by another road. To picture the body social as consisting of an endless series of various small and vocational communities, bound up in and held together by a single large community to which all alike owe loyalty, and which in turn has the duty of guaranteeing the freedom and autonomy of each is the federal approach to the ancient catholic idea of the State. The League had Father Neville Figgis as its fugleman who expounded its ideas tirelessly and brilliantly in lectures and books; and time has showed that it had a clearer idea of what were to be the really important social issues of the twentieth century than either of the senior societies in this field. But in 1910 it had only 1,200 members as opposed to the 6,000 of the Christian Social Union at the same date.

The mere fact that there were three separate societies all trying to do the same work had weakened the social witness of the Church as a whole. They were working in competition. Two of them had been founded to repudiate some of the ideas of the first, but they soon began to emphasise most of them afresh. Presently there was a fourth, for in 1918 the catholics in the Church Socialist League became uneasy about the lack of a definite catholicity in its basis. Conrad Noel broke away, taking a number of its members with him, to found the Catholic Crusade. The alarmed remnant of the Church Socialist League promptly revised its constitution, now making it so rigidly catholic as to have the unhappy result of driving out the whole of its protestant

[1] G. L. Prestige, *Life of Charles Gore* (Heinemann, 1935), p. 335.

wing. The Catholic Crusade, like most movements which start as a protest against a parent body, quickly became and remained more eccentric than creative. The results of forty years of work by these societies in the field of social witness and awakening had not been outwardly impressive. Taken together, their membership did not total more than 8,000. But figures rarely tell the whole tale, and events showed that in many ways these societies had done more to awaken the Church than they could possibly have known; just as other events showed that they had done less than they supposed.

In 1908 came the first indication that these fifty years of propaganda had left a good many churchpeople with the impression that the socialist pattern of society was not incompatible with the Gospel. In the summer of that year the Pan-Anglican Congress was held in London, and was attended by delegates from every Church in the Anglican Communion. The second day of the Congress was devoted to the subject, 'The Church and Human Society.' This vast theme covered far more than socialism. Marriage and rural housing were among the many other matters debated on this day. But it was the meeting on 'Christianity and Socialism' which saw the greatest enthusiasm. The previously prepared papers agreed in affirming that nothing in Christian doctrine was incompatible with socialism, though Gore sounded a note of caution when he wrote in his paper, 'We have no socialistic State in existence, or near to coming into existence.'[1] But when he went on to say:

> This, then, is the first great claim we make upon the Church to-day: that it should make a tremendous act of penitence for having failed so long and on so wide a scale to behave as the champion of the oppressed and the weak: for having tolerated what it ought not to have tolerated: for having so often been on the wrong side. And the penitence must lead to reparation while there is yet time, ere the well-merited judgements of God take all the weapons of social influence out of our hands . . . we must identify ourselves with the great impeachment of our present industrial system. We must refuse to acquiesce in it. But more than this, we must identify ourselves, because we are Christians, with the positive ethical ideal of socialistic thought.[2]

he found words for the frame of mind which most of his audience had made their own. The subsequent discussion clearly showed it. Speaker after speaker identified himself with Gore's judgement, and then went further than Gore had done and identified Christianity with socialism considered as a way of governing the State as well as with its ethical ideal. Two young priests, perhaps more far-sighted than some others, ventured to warn the congress that socialism, too, might become a tyranny. But they were heard heedlessly, and the

---

[1] *Report of the Pan-Anglican Congress* (S.P.C.K., 1908), vol. ii, Paper S.A. 6a, p. 3.
[2] *Ibid.*, p. 5.

gathering's true character was registered by the *Nunc Dimittis* of the veteran J. M. Ludlow, then 87 years of age, a friend of Maurice and Kingsley and one of the last surviving Christian socialists of 1848, the breathless year of socialism. 'In those early days,' he said, 'we could never have hoped to see such an audience gathered for such a purpose, and I believe that a true Christian socialism is the faith of all present.'[1]

The enthusiasm of a Church meeting may perhaps not amount to much in terms of practical action; nor are the sort of people who can come from many parts of the world to attend a week's congress in London genuinely representative of the rank and file membership of the Church. It cannot be argued that the atmosphere of the Congress on that day reflected a corresponding atmosphere in all the dioceses and parish churches from which its members came. In 1908 there was still far to go before the Church as a whole could arrive at the position of accepting the social implications of the Gospel and of regarding the social order as well as the individual soul as a field of grace. But it was indeed much that by 1908 a congress geographically representative of the whole Anglican Communion had gone so far. It was also perhaps a little surprising. All this had come from what looked like such feeble instruments—a handful of small societies, one bizarre, one academic, and one politically socialist. They had the invigorating teaching of Maurice to hand down but they always looked like very earthen vessels to hold it. Nevertheless they had offered themselves, and unquestionably they had been used.

It would be a mistake, moreover, to give the impression that the only use which had been made of them was the prophetic one of judging and inspiring. Much other work had grown out of the movement, some of it practical and some academic. A fair sample of the former is the intervention of Bishop Westcott in the coal dispute in Durham in 1892. In 1891 the price of coal fell, and as a result in 1892 the coal owners of Durham resolved to reduce the miners' wages. The result was a famous strike. What gave it its fame was that it was settled by the personal efforts of the Bishop of Durham. From Auckland Castle Westcott anxiously watched events. He saw distress spread fast as the consequences of the strike were felt by every ancillary industry. Most households in the county were soon in debt. He decided that as a Christian bishop it was his proper business to act, and try to play the part of a mediator. He began by writing to the strikers' leaders, but 'had no encouragement whatsoever to attempt any service.'[2] Then he published an open letter

---

[1] *Ibid.*, p. 103.
[2] Arthur Westcott, *Life and Letters of Brooke Foss Westcott* (Macmillan, 1903), vol. ii, p. 116.

to the Vicar of Bishop Auckland to suggest a conference between three coal-owners, three miners, and three business men from other trades. 'Would that I could do anything to further the meeting of such a conference as I have sketched. It would be truly a bishop's work.'[1] This also had no result. But the bishop refused to be rebuffed into silence and impotence. Three weeks later he wrote to both owners and miners to ask them to meet him together in his house at Bishop Auckland, and added that he would propose to both sides that, first, there should be an immediate reduction in wages of ten per cent. (the owners were claiming 13½ per cent.) and that the pits should at once be opened; and, secondly, that the question of any further reduction in wages should be referred to a wages board with power to decide on the claim. After some correspondence both sides accepted, and the bishop skilfully began the negotiations by providing a meal which he forced both sides to eat at the same table. Having thus prepared the ground, and created the only conditions which might make success possible, he sent them off into separate rooms, and himself went to and fro between them. This went on for five hours and all the time a huge crowd was gathered in the park outside, slowly waiting for news, and trying to guess how things were going by noting the movements of the heads of the different delegates in the windows. Eventually he had to make a very strong appeal in the name of humanity to the owners to persuade them to accept a ten per cent. reduction in wages. But at last they did so, and the strike, or more properly the lock-out, was settled. It had been a great strain for Westcott. 'The last half-hour of waiting was terrible. I dare not think what failure would have meant.'[2] Afterwards he had to go out into the streets, and the crowds cheered him there.

It had been a very long time since an Anglican bishop was cheered in the streets. Less than a hundred years before an Archbishop of Canterbury had dead cats thrown at him through the windows of his carriage and a Bishop of Bristol had his house burned about his ears. But in only a few years to come another Archbishop of Canterbury, Randall Davidson, was to be cheered in the streets on the occasion of the general strike because he had intervened in such a way as to show sympathy for the claims of a proletariat in revolt, and his own independence of judgement in the face of the Very Important Persons. This tradition of episcopal peacemaking in industrial quarrels persisted. In the great coal strike of 1926 several bishops co-operated to seek ground of intervention, and were content to draw upon themselves the wrath of the government of the day.

[1] *Ibid.*, vol. ii, p. 119.
[2] *Ibid.*, vol. ii, p. 132.

Mr. Baldwin, then Prime Minister, asked how the Bishops would like it if he referred to the Iron and Steel Federation the revision of the Athanasian Creed, and this was acclaimed a legitimate score.[1]

It is significant that on each occasion the bishops carried the general body of the Church with them and spoke in the name of Christian conscience; and this they could hardly have done had the work of the various ramifications of the Christian Social Movement in its early days been wholly uninfluential. To it we really owe the fact that in England to-day we are not hampered as the Church in Europe is hampered by the terrible tradition that to be a socialist is automatically and necessarily to be an atheist.

Most of the credit was due to Methodism, but some part of it can justly be awarded to the early years of propaganda by the societies dedicated to the service of the Christian Social Movement. But there were large blocks of practising Christians upon whom their work had had little or no effect, and as an illustration of how hard it is to persuade the whole Church to hearken to the pleading of a self-evidently righteous cause when it involves the overturning of a tradition of long standing, it may be worth while to tell the story of the awakening of the Student Christian Movement to the challenge uttered to the Gospel by evil social conditions.

There never was a more alert, more imaginatively sympathetic, or a better directed movement than the S.C.M., nor one in which a higher proportion of the members genuinely meant business by their religion. Yet it was not until 1909, when it had been in existence for 17 years, that it dawned on its members that the Gospel had to do with society not less than with individual persons, and that a strong sense of responsibility for the Chinese coolie could not compensate for a failure to realise any corresponding responsibility for the English wage-slave. 'In the Student Movement the evils and disorders of society and their cause were never mentioned during the first seven or eight years of its history,'[2] wrote Canon Tissington Tatlow, its director; and he added, 'I knew nothing about social questions.' Nor had he so much as heard of the Fabian Society.[3] The record of the Movement in the fields of evangelism in the universities and in the sending out of men to work in the mission field was one of the glories of the Church in that generation, but Maurice and Kingsley might never have written a line and the various societies might not have existed for all the effect they had had on the leadership or the rank and file membership of the Student Movement.

[1] William Temple, *Christianity and Social Order* (Penguin Books, 1942), p. 7.
[2] Tissington Tatlow, *The Story of the Student Christian Movement* (S.C.M. Press, 1933), p. 338.
[3] *Ibid.*, p. 340.

Early in the century a few lone spirits in the S.C.M. had tried to remedy this neglect. As a result of their agitation the social problem was given a little space on the agenda of one or two S.C.M. conferences, and a few study groups came into being. But these tentative fumblings were dismissed by the annual report of the central committee in a single sentence.[1] Before the S.C.M. could awake out of its social sleep the wind had to blow upon it from without; and perhaps one of the most ultimately influential things the Movement's directorate ever did was to open the pages of its magazine to Dr. Adriani of Holland in 1903. He used this invitation to deliver himself of many firm words on the subject of the social blindness of the Movement. He began his indictment by accusing it of not daring to face the real world of everyday secular experience:

Dare we know the world fully, and dare we feel how the world opposes itself to our faith? Our relations in life are based on commerce and industry. Ask the merchant. He will tell you that he approves of your going to Church and reading the Bible; he will offer you a gift for missions, but at the same time he will tell you that it would be ridiculous to apply the teachings of Christianity to commerce. Ask the manufacturer. His answer will be, 'I know many influences in my department, but those of Christianity are out of place there.' Ask the lawyer, 'Can you apply the laws of the Gospel in your profession?' He will look at you in amazement.[2]

Dr. Adriani continued his catalogue, and then drew an acid conclusion:

When we study the literature of the World Student Federation and of the different national Movements we generally receive the impression that for us social and political life does not exist. No one acquainted with the life of the Movement would think that its members did anything but attend Bible circles and conferences, read books on missions and live in an entirely spiritual world.[3]

It was a bitter judgement, and it took some courage for the Movement to publish it in its own magazine. But it did what was needed. From that time onward the Movement slowly awoke. But in this matter also its directorate remained faithful to the S.C.M. tradition of gathering information first and acting afterwards, and Dr. Adriani's article was followed by six years of social study circles, and occasional references to them in conferences.

In 1908 the Movement judged that the right moment had come for the whole of its work, in every department, to be tried and sifted by an impartial tribunal. Problems of great moment had arisen in every sphere of its life and they clamoured for solution. It seemed right therefore to submit the whole organisation and life of the Movement to the independent scrutiny of fresh minds. A general Commission 'to wait upon God to know His will regarding the

---

[1] *Ibid.*, p. 341.   [2] *Ibid.*, p. 342.   [3] *Ibid.*, p. 341.

Movement'[1] was thus appointed. One of the features of the Movement's work which this commission found reason to criticise was the poorness of the response of the Christian student world to the social challenge, and it suggested this remedy:

> The executive should arrange a meeting of four days' duration, and they should summon those who feel upon their hearts the burden of the problem of modern society to come apart and intercede with God for guidance. While we recommend that addresses should be given to guide prayer, names of speakers should not be published, nor should any details of the programme be given which would tend to obscure the central issue—that of intercession for the guidance of the Movement in face of human suffering and alienation from God.[2]

The phrasing was significant and characteristic. It suggested the spirit of humble reliance upon the energy not less than the love of God which had always been characteristic of S.C.M. and made it in so many ways one of the most fully seminal of all modern Christian movements. It was proved to be true on that occasion, as indeed on all others, that an assembly which meets in that spirit, and implements it by a programme expressing that the first and deepest of all its concerns is to learn God's will and to draw on His strength together will quite infallibly be used by Him. Thus this Conference, which met at Matlock in the spring of 1909, became one of the memorable occasions in the history of the Christian Social Movement in England.

It was seminal, for its importance lay more in the stimulation and impetus it bestowed on the minds of the students present than in anything it said or did. Before the Matlock Conference it had been possible and even usual for Christian students to match their ardour for foreign missions by a curious lack of sensitive response to the godless social order at home. But after this conference the Christian student was generally socially conscious, and the missionary work of the Movement did not suffer. About a hundred people were at the conference, and it was the sort of conference at which the members really conferred, not the sort at which they provided an audience for speakers with famous names. There were, it is true, some who had been asked to introduce the subjects for discussion. Among them were William Temple, Kenneth Maclennan, and H. G. Wood, all of whom were later to become famous. But it was a gathering of equals, and not an audience for experts to dominate and lead. Thus the great occasion was a meeting which had no chairman and no set speeches, in which those hundred men and women simply waited on God in spontaneous and mostly silent prayer to see where the Holy Spirit would lead them.

---

[1] *Ibid.*, p. 324.　　　　　　　　　　[2] *Ibid.*, pp. 345, 346.

There was no confusion. Some spoke to us, some led us in prayer, but it was felt that what everybody did was a real contribution to the gathering, and that in literal fact we realised what it was to be led as a body by the Spirit.[1]

After the conference ended a pamphlet was prepared and published called *Discipleship and the Social Problem.* Its purpose was to embody and express what it was believed that the Holy Spirit had impressed upon the conscience of the students who had thus waited upon Him. This is a document of no slight importance in the history of the social movement in English Christendom. Its publication did not of course cause slums to fall down, unemployment to cease, and social security to be won. But it did register a new conviction of corporate sin and a new determination on the part of what is after all the most ultimately influential section of a civilised national community to pray and work and, if need be, fight for social righteousness as a vital part of the whole Christian Faith which these students had always held with vigorous conviction. The decisive things in it were two. First, it frankly recognised that the student world owed its whole privilege of higher education to the system which allowed so much social wretchedness for so many. 'The money which unlocks to him the glorious opportunities of a modern student would not come to him but for the labours of working men.'[2] It was much to have it publicly recognised in such quarters that all universities and colleges were ultimately carried on the backs of men and women in the series of mean and grimy streets in Manchester and Liverpool and elsewhere. That this was—and is so, showed, as Bernard Shaw wrote *Major Barbara* to declare, that there was no such thing as clean money in an unclean social system, not even though 'we gain it cleanly ourselves.'[3] This conviction that the corporate, anonymous but most real sin running through the whole social body was also personal sin was the second point of high importance in the pamphlet. It is we who are the social problem, admitted the students—we the privileged, not only the slum-dweller or the unemployed docker, we not less than the employer of sweated labour himself. Therefore 'from our hearts too must rise the generative force of good.'[4] The pamphlet ended with a noble definition of the vocation of the student who was called to be a moral person in an immoral social order:

This discipleship must be a very costly thing, and day after day the price will be paid. It will mean a slow and painful surrender of self-will and a daily attempt to walk in humility before God and men. Expenditure, pleasure, the choice of our life's work, and, above all, speech and thought

[1] *Ibid.*, p. 352.   [2] *Ibid.*, p. 349.
[3] *Ibid.*, p. 349.   [4] *Ibid.*, p. 350.

as they touch those round us, must be modified. We are called to be meek.
Since no quality is further from the practice and respect of our country, we
shall do well to count the cost.[1]

Such words were not platitudes. They reflected a real determination.

III. *From Propaganda to Research*

Any movement which has as its purpose the bringing of the
Church to realise both in theory and in practice the fact that the
Gospel is the good news of redemption of society no less than of its
individual members must always pass through two stages. First it
must awaken the consciences of churchpeople to the social evils
surrounding them, and try to bring them to the point where they are
ready to say and to mean, *Mea Culpa Mea Maxima Culpa.* Then it
must turn to showing to the awakened Church the practical steps
which must be taken if the promised redemption is to be applied to
the actual concrete situation of society so that it may be transformed into the likeness of the vision of God for it. The first stage
is therefore one of persuasion or of propaganda. The instruments
which the Christian Social Movement must use while in this first
stage are such as will best stir up the sleeping consciences of Christians to the facts. The evils of an immoral social order are described
as vividly as possible, and such descriptions are disseminated as
widely as possible. Such is the function of a Kingsley, a Stewart
Headlam, a Ludlow. At the same time desultory skirmishing takes
place which pricks the hide of the immoral social order here and
there, and serves the purpose of a double demonstration that at least
some Christians are alert and on the march, and that secular reforming bodies, like the Parliamentary Labour Party and the Fabian
Society, are not wholly without allies within the Church.

The blacklisting of shops which paid sweated wages and the refusal
to trade with them was always a favourite form of this preliminary
skirmishing. In this field one of the heroes had been J. E. Watts-
Ditchfield, Vicar of St. James-the-Less, Bethnal Green. In 1902 and
1904 he organised public exhibitions of sweated home work, such as
matchboxes and pieces of tailoring. This led to the *Daily News*
exhibition in Queen's Hall in 1906, and paved the way for the
Trades Boards Act. Another was voluntary ambulance work of every
kind, and such ventures as the work of socially minded undergraduates in setting up and running boys' clubs in the grimmer districts of
university cities. But this first stage has a beginning, a middle, and
an end, for unless it wholly fails the day eventually comes when the
Church as a whole begins to realise that precisely because it is a

[1] *Ibid.*, p. 351.

Christian body it has a social charge, and that corporate indifference
to social evil is both corporate and individual sin. When the bench
of bishops pronounces the principle that adequate wages are the
first charge on industrial profits; when those who in the name of
Christ attack slum landlords know that in this they have the mass of
churchpeople behind them; and when the general body of the clergy
and very many of the laity are no longer shocked by the statement
that the Church has much to do with politics and economics, but
rather take it as axiomatic—then the day has come when the Christian Social Movement has completed the first stage of its purpose
and must be ready to pass over into the second and in many ways the
more exacting stage. In so far as it is ever possible to do more than
give the vaguest date, it may be said that by 1918 the first part of the
journey was virtually completed.

The second stage is that of research. The awakened Church must
be told what is wrong with society and how it may be put right, and
in this the thinkers and academicians of the Movement came into
their own. These two stages naturally cannot be too neatly separated.
Much of the work of the second stage was done in the early days of
the first by F. D. Maurice, and the time will never come when ambulance work ceases to be an obligation upon Christians. Moreover,
the office of persuasion has to be continued afresh in every generation, for Christians may at any time become inert and drowsy with
original sin. Thus important work in Christian Social Research was
being done long before 1918, and one of the charges made against
the Christian Social Union by the more ardent spirits of the Movement was that it was too academic, and not militant enough.

Charles Gore, for example, though no one felt more keenly than
he the injustices of the social order, was always more active in the
sphere of research. He was sure that the whole lamentable state of
society was due to the Church's failure to find a satisfactory doctrine
of the relationship of Property to Personality; and this conviction
caused one vital piece of social research to be undertaken under his
leadership in 1913, when he edited a composite book of high importance on the problem of property in a Christian society.[1] In 1912
Dr. Vernon Bartlett, of Mansfield College, Oxford, addressed to
the *British Weekly* a letter about Property and Christian Steward-
ship. He then asked Gore to join him in issuing some popular
literature to set out plainly what the biblical doctrine of property
was. Gore replied that he could not do so. 'Before engaging in
popular propaganda I needed to clear up the principle of property.'[2]
He therefore edited a composite volume of essays, in which every
contributor found that he had to go to the Old and New Testaments,

---

[1] *Property*, edited by Charles Gore (Macmillan, 1913).   [2] *Ibid.*, p. ix.

and to the glosses of the early Fathers and the mediæval writers, before he could find what he wanted. They all found that the Christian social pronouncements of the Reformation and after had nothing useful to say, and much that was so harmful that this alone did much to account for the fact that the social order had become the Acquisitive Society. The contributors examined the problem from various points of view, and eventually they agreed upon five main principles which should govern the view that a Christian ought to take of his own property and of the function of property in a social order organised on Christian principles.

First of all they draw a distinction between the purposes for which the institution of private property exists. There is property which is used for power and property which is held for use. The former generally attacks freedom but the latter is necessary for freedom to exist. But if property exists for the sake of freedom and not for the sake of power, one needs to hold but little of it—'a very limited quantity on the whole.'[1]

But personality can only develop when man practises the art of living socially. No one can live a full social life unless he is a free being in a free society, and therefore it is the function of the state to foster and to guard the freedom of its citizens. The state therefore has a duty to curb the holding of property for the purposes of power, and this it can do only by levelling the amount of wealth citizens may hold. Those who possess too much property, more than is necessary to guarantee their freedom, must not complain about the levelling process.

It is, however, evident that unless such a process is to defeat its own ends it must be gradual, and in the meantime the need of charity will remain. But charity is justice. It is something to which the poor have a right in any Christian scheme of things. Here the argument makes use of a very striking quotation from Lucian, who was scoffing at Christian social ideas on exactly this ground, that property is for use and for freedom and not for power, and that the poor have a consequent right to charity, which is their due because it is not so much charity as justice:

> Their Leader, whom they adore, had persuaded them that they were all brethren. In compliance with his laws they looked with contempt on all worldly treasures and held everything in common. It is incredible with what alacrity these people defend and support their common interests—the interest of any of their number—and spare nothing to promote it.[2]

From all this it follows that the present laws of property are indefensible in Christian principle because they are so framed that the many are inevitably and legally sacrificed to the few.

---

[1] *Ibid.*, p. xi.   [2] *Ibid.*, p. xiii.

But there will be no change which is a change for the better until people realise that the only authority they have for saying of anything, That is mine, rests on their readiness to say first, I am God's.

It is probable that very few people now read Gore's composite book on property and it is impossible to trace any effect it may have had on the progress of social reform. But nevertheless it was a real portent if a concealed one. It charted the course by which the Christian Social Movement was to go. From 1914 onwards the researchers more and more took charge of it, and the propagandists, while still having a vital work to do, as the post-war career of Studdert-Kennedy showed, became steadily less influential. In future the great names in the Movement were to be of such men as Maurice Reckitt, its historian, Canon V. A. Demant, and W. G. Peck—all of them concerned primarily with social research and criticism.

But from the beginning the Movement had had a deep evangelistic purpose. Its first affirmation had been that our Lord had come to save society as well as individuals, and that the Church's purpose was to offer God's redemption to man in man's contemporary world. There could be no separation between the individual and society because man is a social being. Therefore any movement which was trying to reclaim a social order in the name of Christ was working for the sake of the men and women who composed it; and the members of the Movement always knew what secular reformers are apt to forget, that Christian principles and influence can only enter, say, the Lancashire Cotton Trade or the Stock Exchange by way of the people who are engaged in these spheres. Thus a Christian Social Movement is by necessity evangelistic. That was not overlaid by the new necessity to concentrate more and more on research. These two main preoccupations of the Movement after 1918 were in fact to make it less of a 'Movement' and to integrate it more and more fully both with the Church through its evangelism, and with society as a whole through its increasingly radical criticism of the whole basis of social living in a mechanised civilisation.

The fact that it was to become more and more a movement of the whole Church, rather than of small groups of prophets within the Church who spent their time crying in what looked like a wilderness, did not mean that there was no longer need of a society to contain and express it. But it did mean that the society would have to be one of a new kind—larger, with greater resources of money and organisation, and more fully integrated with the official life of the Church. Thus at the end of the first world war, the old Navvy Mission, which had been the purely evangelistic and 'converting' instrument of the Movement, amalgamated with the Christian Social Union, previously the chief instrument of social research and criticism, and together they gave birth to the Industrial Christian Fellowship. This quickly proved to be the sort of society which the Movement needed to contain it and to guide the next steps of its growth. It was presided over by Prebendary P. T. R. Kirk, who rapidly showed his uncommon skill at holding in creative balance these two very different traditions. He was determined that the I.C.F. should be equally faithful to both of them, as indeed it has always been. More than that, he was determined that the two traditions should not be maintained in separation from each other, but that each should partake of the insights and methods of the other, and in this too, much the harder task, the I.C.F. has been markedly successful, so that it was from the beginning one society, not two relatively independent departments operating under a single name. We are so accustomed to the I.C.F. being a unity in itself that we are apt to forget how difficult it must have been to make it one.

The I.C.F. took the whole of Britain as its territory and divided it into vast districts. Over each of these it appointed a priest to direct the whole of its activities in the area and, if need be, to initiate new ones. Under the priest director worked a number of lay agents, and on these agents the real burden rested. They were the 'front line' of the I.C.F.'s battle to convert industrial Britain. Besides these, the I.C.F. organised a kind of flying squad of men and women of special abilities who were prepared to take its message by sermon and speech to any part of the country. The most celebrated of these was Geoffrey Studdert-Kennedy, whose every speech and sermon was a sustained spiritual effort of the most demanding kind, and who wore himself into an early grave by his incessant travelling and labour. It was not, perhaps, an untimely grave. It was given to him and to one other priest, Dick Sheppard, to move all sorts and conditions of men as no one else could do in those years, and early death was the price demanded from and gladly paid by both. At the headquarters of I.C.F. in Westminster the General Director reigned supreme, with a bishop (at first Dr. Kempthorne of Lichfield) as the chairman of his executive committee, and to him fell the organising of what quickly became the largest and most ambitious of all societies for the preaching of the Gospel to the industrial world of Britain. It was characteristic of a society which had to do this work in the new conditions of post-1918 society that one of the great features of the whole organisation was the bureau of social research and the directorate of social and theological studies in London, which had the double office of compiling and publishing social and industrial surveys of a high quality, and of guiding and ensuring the study of the lay agents up and down the country, all of whom read under the direction of this office and had to submit for its correction regular papers on what they had read.

To be a lay agent of the Industrial Christian Fellowship was no easy task. He it was who week by week sustained the Christian cause in open-air speaking in such forums as Stevenson Square in Manchester or the Bull Ring in Birmingham, where a man had to stand upon his soapbox and gather an audience as best he might, attracting them from his multitudinous competitors by every art he could command. Then he would preach the Gospel to them, and declare its social principles. Sometimes he would have the help of some local priest, and on very great occasions the bishop of the diocese. But usually he must keep his pitch alone, or with the help of another agent if the district was big enough to justify two men working together. He nearly always did attract an audience, and though it was generally not so crowded an audience as those of the communist on one side of him and of the amusing crank or charlatan on the other, the I.C.F. audience once gathered was apt to stay until the end, which was always a prayer. This normally happened on a Sunday evening, and during the week the agent would probably speak at one or two dinner-hour meetings in factory canteens. In the years of heavy unemployment he would have much to do with the organisation of the local occupational centre; and indeed where the local committee was vigorous and enterprising there was hardly an end to the number and the variety of the tasks which the I.C.F. agent would have to perform. Some of them had more specialised work to do. Two, for instance, were always travelling up and down the length of the pipe-line which carried the water from Thirlmere to Manchester, and acting as pastors to the navvies who kept it in repair. Two in Manchester persuaded the local committee to hire, decorate, and furnish a room in a slum street. This they made their headquarters, studying there during the mornings, and holding innumerable little gatherings of shop stewards or trades union officials or labourers of all kinds in the evenings, teaching the Faith by argument, and creating fellowship by cups of tea and patient listening. In a normal working week he might very well address some hundreds of men and minister in one way or another to a score of others. But it was not possible for him to see any results, and he had few if any means of knowing whether he succeeded or failed. His life might well be a Christian saga, but no bards chanted it.

These activities of the I.C.F. through clerical director, lay agent, and the central bureau for research and study went on all the time, day in and day out, summer and winter. Periodically the Fellowship would supplement these and draw them together by two types of

E

venture with which its name became more and more associated as
the years passed. They were the district mission and the great conference.

The district mission they called a Crusade. Periodically—perhaps
every other year—the I.C.F. would gather together everyone on
whom it could lay hands. Its lay agents were torn from their ordinary work. The special messengers, such as Studdert-Kennedy,
were assembled. To them were added many of the local clergy. In
all the crusading team might amount to a hundred people. For many
weeks the ground had been prepared, and when the day came this
evangelistic host would descend on a whole town or district, Birken-
head perhaps, or Barrow, or the Rhondda valley. There would be a
long procession, and a great service in the parish church at which the
crusaders were commissioned for the venture by the bishop of the
diocese. Then for six nights or ten the crusaders would divide into
little teams of three or four and speak on a pitch in the open air, and
all would be brought to an end on the last night with a mass meeting
in the market place or in some large hall. The crusaders met every
morning for the Eucharist, for prayer, and to compare notes. The
course of addresses they took was planned for them by the I.C.F.,
and the outlines were printed as a pamphlet, and all crusaders were
expected not to deviate far from it. It was an exacting and exhausting adventure, and what did it all amount to? Were working men
and women converted and brought into active membership of the
Church? No doubt some were, perhaps many, but there is no knowing how many. The giant district mission, however carefully prepared and well organised, cannot help but be a gallant blundering
in the mist. But lack of the possibility of verifying and analysing
results is no argument against such adventures. There comes one
picture drifting down the years of the atmosphere which an I.C.F.
crusade not seldom created. Let it stand for all the others which
cannot be known. It is a picture of Bishop Hough of Woolwich at
a crusade in the Midlands. He laboured under many physical dis-
advantages, but he made such an impression on rough working men
by the sheer power of his holiness that when he walked through the
crowd after his meeting they were seen to touch the border of his
garment.

IV. *William Temple and his Conferences*

Up to the present this narrative of the course of the Christian
Social Movement in the Church of England has been like a length
of rope. One end of the rope is so tightly woven that it is hard to
distinguish the separate strands. The tightness of its weave is due

to the fact that this end of the rope is held by Frederick Denison Maurice. The other end of the rope is just as tight. It is held by Archbishop William Temple. But between Maurice and Temple there is a distinct loosening of texture, and the different strands which make the rope can be separated and examined one by one. This is because no single hand was capable of grasping all the strands and holding them in synthesis. The various strands of the rope can be roughly sorted into four groups of threads. First, there is the cry, 'Have pity on the poor in the Name of Christ.' Second, there is the endeavour to make Christians admit that it is their vocation to pity the poor because they hold the doctrine of the Incarnation. Third, there is the realisation that such a pity must involve economic and political thinking and proclamation, and that this is the Church's proper sphere because the Church is the Body of Christ. Fourth, there is the knowledge that these insights, which are brought into focus largely by propaganda and research, must lead also to an intensification of evangelism and of the office of the pastor because the socially disinherited are not, on the Christian view, a class or a group but so many individual persons, one at a time. We have seen each one of these strands vigorously plucked by the prophets and by the different guilds, unions, societies, and fellowships. Often more than one of them were taken up in a single hand, as, for example, by Gore or Studdert-Kennedy, or Scott Holland.

William Temple grasped them all, added another to them, and wove them into a new synthesis, so that the rope in his hands became a unity again—just a strong rope and not so many threads. This new thread is the characteristic ethos of Christian social thinking from the economic crisis of 1930 onwards. The heart of this ethos is a new realisation of original sin as a social fact governing all other facts, and the experience of the claims of the totalitarian state upon the essential privacies, individualities, and freedoms of man. The terms of its discussion are the tensions between the ideas of the collective, the good citizen, the good man, and the Christian. The thread is a radical criticism not of a particular economic doctrine, not of any one political party, but of the whole basis of society. The whole corporate life of man in the world, the full range of his getting, spending, and associating, his relationship to the state and collective organisations of every kind, his dependence on nature, his tragic predicament in his world, in his family, and most of all within his own soul—nothing less than all of this became the proper terms of reference for the Christian social thinker, and his analysis became more and more radically critical under the pressure of world disasters of every kind, culminating at last in war.

Now all this was a vast field of learning for any man. But there have been those in our time who mastered it all, Canon V. A. Demant, for instance, on this side of the Atlantic, and Reinhold Niebuhr on the other. These, with Temple, gave the impression of moving at ease in these fields. But Temple had something which no other sociologist of his time possessed—an unrivalled power of clear and intelligible exposition, and also a great position in the Church. In the field of Christian sociology other voices were perhaps more authentically prophetic than his, but no other was the voice of leader and synthesist. And in his own genius for synthesis he was the cause of it in others. He had the power to draw from each member of a conference his own contribution, and then of weaving them all into a synthesis acceptable to everybody. So it was that the characteristic method of the Church's social learning and proclamation in his time came to be the kind of vast conference which was particularly associated with his name, of which the conferences at Birmingham in 1924 (COPEC) and at Malvern in 1941 were the most famous.

When Mr. Maurice Reckitt published his Scott Holland Memorial Lectures on *A Century of the Social Movement in the Church of England* he aptly chose *Maurice to Temple* for the book's title. He could have found none more fitting, and none which more exactly indicated the facts. Already in 1919 William Temple was one of the dominating figures in the Church of England. From then until the day he died he rapidly came to be the most considerable personage in the whole of Christendom, and one of the two men who mattered most to English folk of every kind, of all religions and of none. When he died so suddenly it was as though a light had gone out, and in that light millions of people had walked. A few days after his death a priest whom he had ordained and who loved him as fully as he reverenced him was in an underground 'wash and brush up' establishment in London. Four young labourers, stripped to the waist, were trying to wash with one shaving of soap between them. There was no more, so they offered the priest a share, and, seeing his collar, at once began to talk of Temple. They were deeply concerned with the social problem after the war. They knew nothing, nothing whatever, of the Church's social record in the previous hundred years, nothing of the social work of any other Christian leader. But they did know much of what Temple had said and done, and they knew roughly for what he had stood. But that is a cold way of describing what those four labourers were feeling. They clamoured to make it plain that they had seen in him their hope for better things, and had personified that hope in him. They knew him to be the friend of such as they, and that he had done much to redeem what still seemed to them the shameful social record of the

Church. Not one of them had ever seen him, but their grief at his passing was as full and as sincere as that of the priest to whom they spoke.

The sum of his immense strength does not quite account for this. His knowledge was immense, his charm illimitable, his courage absolute, and his expository power unrivalled. No one was ever more lovable. But there was something more than all this which those labourers in Leicester Square had sensed. It was that he stood, and was known to stand, for the conviction that organised Christianity must count in every part of life, that the Church had a message of salvation not for persons only but also for the furthest corner of the range of activity dominated by principalities and powers, by economic systems and financial policies. Others indeed stood there with him, and had for years been saying all the things he had said. But he was universally known to stand there, and to have said them, as others were not known; and when he spoke his words were pondered and believed in the little streets in Whitechapel and the Gorbals. He was the Christian social movement in his own person, as no one had been before him and no one would be after him—all that, and so much more besides.

It would probably have been impossible to find anyone else but Temple who could have both conceived and carried through the two great conferences at Birmingham, and at Malvern. The conference at Birmingham called COPEC[1] took place in 1924, but it had of course been planned years before that, and was intended to give focus to the characteristically Christian expression of the social idealism which was the mood of the nation for some years after the end of the first world war. There were many social evils which Christians should be fighting: COPEC was intended to provide them with a tactic, a strategy, and a goal. This purpose its secretary, Miss Lucy Gardner, described as the establishing of a 'norm of Christian thought and action for the further working out of a Christian order.'[2] The conference, which was of course inter-denominational, was heralded by a series of commissions which prepared for the conference studies of many aspects of the social problem as Christians saw it. The first of these, and also the ablest, was, however, theological: *The Nature of God and His purpose for the World*. It was symptomatic both of the temper of the conference and of the climate of sociological thinking of that time, that this report was never discussed. Perhaps it is also significant that the circulation of this volume was much larger than that of any of the others. It was presented by some of those who had prepared it, and when that had

[1] That is, Conference on Politics, Economics, and Citizenship.
[2] Maurice B. Reckitt, *Maurice to Temple* (Faber and Faber, 1924), p. 172.

been done the conference passed on to the kind of subjects which in 1924 seemed to be its proper business. There was much vigorous criticism of the 'isms which at such a conference are always disliked—capitalism, imperialism, industrialism—and a good deal of bellicose denunciation of war. More than once Temple had to refuse to put a wildly idealistic or denunciatory resolution to the conference until its members had had time to bethink themselves that they might someday be held to their words. Under any other chairmanship, it was said by not a few of those present, the conference must have got out of hand, so bent were the majority of its members on light-heartedly promising new worlds for old at once and on the spot. All this was due to the fact that the conference was discussing sociological problems out of their theological context, and was therefore continually surrendering to the impulses of a transient mood of idealism. One of its most memorable moments was when Gore appeared on the platform in the city he had loved so well as its Father in God. He was received with tumultuous cheers, but replied to them by uttering forebodings:

This conference will be judged by its practical work, and for that I tremble. We need tremendous courage to ask ourselves frankly whether we are really prepared to accept these fundamental principles and to apply them whatever the effect upon our party politics.[1]

The event was to show that there were many churchpeople who were prepared for precisely that, and chief among them the chairman of the conference. Nor is it just to suppose that because one cannot precisely trace any direct influence of the proceedings of the conference upon the sociological development of the next twenty years that therefore there were no effects. Temple himself thought there had been, and at Malvern in 1941 he remarked:

It is said that gatherings of Christians have said similar things for a very long time, and nothing happens. My answer would be that a great deal happens. Of course much depends on the pace at which anyone expects human history to develop; some people want Utopia tomorrow, and of course they are disappointed. Between the two wars three great changes took place in England: the whole penal system was reformed in a wholly Christian direction; there was a vast extension of secondary education; and the proper housing of the people was at last undertaken on a great scale. I call that a good deal to happen in twenty years. It is true that no one can say just how much the Church or specifically Christian principles had to do with it. But the Church was solidly behind all these reforms.[2]

To this solidity COPEC had plainly contributed.

There was no other conference of this kind until the one held at Malvern in 1941. Temple was its chairman, and it was gener-

---

[1] *Maurice to Temple*, p. 171.
[2] *Malvern 1941: The Proceedings of the Archbishop of York's Conference.* (Longmans, Green, 1941), p. 217.

ally called the Archbishop of York's Conference, but in fact it was very different from its predecessor of seventeen years earlier. The pressure of lamentable national and international events had changed the world. At home, the general strike and the long miners' strike which followed it, the economic crisis with its aftermath of heavy mass unemployment and the challenge of the means test to the worker's standard of living and his sense of personal dignity and family integrity, left no one in England just where he had been in 1924. Experience was deep, bitter, and swift in those years, and many characters were changed. Add to that the steadily mounting horror of news from abroad, the perfidy and wickedness of the totalitarian state, wars in Abyssinia, in Spain, and in China, and finally the coming of a second world war, and all of these dire tidings delivering just the same challenge to the idea of human dignity. It was clear that a conference held in 1941 would have to go far deeper than the one held in 1924.

Nor had the Christian Social Movement in the Anglican Church stood still during those years. It had kept pace with the movement of events, and its prophetic thinking went deeper with every year, continually extending the area of its competence until it was dealing in every utterance with nothing less than the entire range of human social life and the whole nature of the human beings who lived it. Events, as they came, were spontaneously met and challenged by a Christian response from the Movement in the Church. The general strike was met by the famous intervention of Randall Davidson, still Archbishop of Canterbury. The miners' strike was responded to by the initiative of the bishops, headed by Temple and Dr. Cyril Garbett, then Bishop of Southwark, who came within a hair's breadth of finding a basis for settlement, and were scolded by the Government for their pains. The economic crisis and the means test produced the famous letter from Temple to *The Times* asking the Chancellor of the Exchequer to use the budget surplus to restore the cuts in unemployment benefit rather than to lower the rate of income tax. The long years of heavy unemployment found the Church neither quiescent nor silent. In hundreds of parishes clergy and people undertook the heavy labour of providing and maintaining occupational centres, and of course responded fully to the sudden increase of the demands made for 'ambulance services' of every conceivable kind. The prophets and thinkers wrestled continuously to discover the causes of all this mounting woe, and to prescribe remedies which might be both Christian and effective. It was in this sphere and at this time that Canon V. A. Demant showed himself to be a prophet of uncommon power and deep perception; and he, perhaps more completely than anyone, has so married theology to sociology and economics and finance to both, that to-day no reputable Christian thinker seeks to separate them. From the point of view of total culture, Mr. T. S. Eliot entered the field with his very influential book, *The Idea of a Christian Society*, while the influence exerted from across the Atlantic by Reinhold Niebuhr, through his clarifying of the bearing of the original sin of man upon the tragic dilemma of his life in industrial society, was so wide that he influenced Christian thought in England as deeply as (or, it may well be even more deeply than) in America. The Christian Social Movement, had undoubtedly not failed to awaken the social conscience of the Church of England, nor to loose the strings of its tongue.

The Movement, too, did not cease between 1924 and 1941 to dig new channels and weave new patterns for its self-expression, and in this it was true to its own traditions of a hundred years. The further awakening of the Anglo-Catholic wing of the Church to the inevitable connection between Sacramentalism and sociology as a direct consequence of Bishop Weston of Zanzibar's electrifying appeal at the Anglo-Catholic Congress of 1923:

It is folly, it is madness to suppose that you can worship Jesus in the Sacrament and Jesus on the Throne of Glory when you are sweating Him in the bodies and souls of His children—

had led some of the older catholic stalwarts of the social movement to seize their chance to carry the fruits of his appeal onwards from works of mercy to the fields of sociology. Chief among them was Percy Widdington, an old but an increasingly critical member of the Church Socialist League. He had gathered round him a group of thinkers, who had collaborated in 1922 to write *The Return of Christendom*, an influential Christian sociological treatise of the new kind, which insisted on going to the roots of all philosophy and theology in order to find a sociological synthesis. He added to this group men like Fr. Tribe of Kelham, and women like Ruth Kenyon, and they formed the Anglo-Catholic Summer School of Sociology, which met annually in Oxford for many years, and did remarkably able work. It was largely out of this enterprise that the famous Christendom Group sprang. To this men as various as the veteran Percy Widdington, Professor R. H. Tawney, and Canon V. A. Demant brought their insights and treasures, and 'the basis for a Catholic sociology was securely laid. A willing and energetic band of labourers set to work on the superstructure, and their activities, in what is now known as the Christendom Group, are not yet at an end.'[1]

The Christendom Group is the chief link which joins COPEC to

[1] *Maurice to Temple*, p. 178.

Malvern; and it was this body of people which Temple entrusted with the preparation of the programme and the reading of many of the papers at the Malvern Conference. He himself emphasised it:

I have been asked whether it is of deliberate design that most of those who have been asked to read the papers . . . are representatives of one school of thought and one angle of approach. That is quite deliberate. Our time is very limited, and there will be far more coherence in our thought if we enter on the consideration of each part of the subject from the same angle . . . And as far as I know there is no single body of thought which is at once so extensive in its survey and coherent in its interpretation as that which these speakers represent—not without considerable differences, but with substantial unity of method.

Thus the pressure of events, the deepening tragedy of experience, and the widening in the terms of reference in sociological Christian thought as exemplified in the Christendom Group, all combined to make of the Malvern Conference something much less readily intelligible, less idealistic, but far more thorough and penetrating than its predecessor at Birmingham had been.

The conference consisted of about 240 bishops, clergy, and laity. The mere citing of the date when they met—1941—is enough to show that no such elaborate preparation preceeded it as had been used to prepare for COPEC, and indeed the long studies of the sociological Summer School and the Christendom Group had in effect done what preparation was necessary. At the beginning the Archbishop stated clearly what the purpose of the conference was. It was to find the 'Middle Axioms' of Christian Sociology; and his own words are the simplest explanation of this technical term:

Theologians, and Christians who . . . have minds trained by education to appreciate the work of theologians should think out the general implications of fundamental Christian principles in relation to contemporary needs, so supplying what among the ancients were called 'middle axioms' —maxims for conduct which mediate between fundamental principles and the tangle of particular problems. This is the work we attempted at Malvern.[1]

From such a stem grew a bewildering profusion of branches—what is the attitude of the Church to the planned society? Do the formulas of the Church offer any guidance to family life? Is the Church's witness concerned with the possible end of civilised life? What is the relationship between sociology and redemption?—these were but a few of the themes coming out of the main purpose of finding the 'middle axioms,' and any one of them might well have had a full conference to itself. The value of the actual answers returned to them was probably less than the enthusiasts and certainly more than the

---

[1] *Malvern*, p. vii.

E*

denigrators supposed. The former view was represented by the title of a book written in America about the conference, to which its author gave the title *From Pentecost to Malvern*, while the latter was neatly expressed by the editor of *Crockford*, who surveyed the findings, reached for the works of Charles Dickens, hunted through *Martin Chuzzlewit*, and let Sairey Gamp express his mind with the immortal, 'Betsy, who deniges of it?' As the event showed, there were many who definitely 'deniged of it.'

It is, however, probably true that the chief value of the conference lay in the papers read and the discussions which followed them. They were difficult, for everybody was so obviously wrestling with immensities and imponderables, and struggling to move forward through tangles of jungle too tough for anything less than the co-operative efforts of the best minds of all mankind. It was inevitable, therefore, that at least some of the speakers were not really understood. But all this was a registration of actuality, and it showed plainly how great a distance the Church had travelled down the sociological road since the days of COPEC. Before all else the Malvern Conference was realistic, and not in the least optimistic, so that it had hope, and was able to convey it to others.

There were many differences from COPEC. Both in scope and in method Malvern was more theological. Problems were always referred to the Christian pattern of natural order in the doctrines of creation and redemption. It was as much about man as about the systems man makes. More was said about God and Nature than about capitalism and imperialism, more about original sin than about the particular sins of the warmongers and the profiteers. In his opening speech the Archbishop paused to commend the writings of Reinhold Niebuhr, because his 'whole mind is possessed by the sense of that aboriginal sin of man,' and it was this which gave an impression of him as 'a deeply Christian mind grappling with the realities of to-day.'[1] At the end he returned to the same point. The whole world and its systems of relationship were chaotically out of control primarily because 'we have neglected the true end of man.' Thus it was asserted again and again that all ills had sprung from a desertion of natural order, the divinely given balance between God, Nature, and Man. The conference, as a direct consequence, had much to say on a subject on which COPEC had been entirely silent, the creative significance of community in the Church, and the need for radical reform in the Church of England's finance and administration, if the Church in its own fidelity to the natural order was to show the world the things that belonged to its coherence, and thus to its peace.

[1] *Malvern*, p. 224.

What did it all mean, and where lay its merit and its importance? Thinking over it all after it had been ended, the Archbishop found its significance partly in the stimulus it had given to the Church itself by 'gathering recent Christian thought on these matters into a focal expression and so setting it forward once more.'[1] But, more important still, it had put 'the Church on the map again for many who had ceased to regard it as having any relevance for these problems.' This was in the tradition of the Christian Social Movement which made the conference, but not many realised that the Church had any relevance to their problems, and some of them were perhaps 'startled to learn what a body of Churchpeople gathered for such a purpose was ready to say.'[1]

V. *Sociology through Liturgy*

The work of finding the connection between Christian redemption and social disease, and of discovering how to join them, is a charge upon Christian thought and prophecy in every generation. In this chapter we have merely followed, and in briefest outline, the bearing of this charge by only one branch of the Church for not more than fifty years. It is but a tiny part of an immensely long story. But it has been enough to see a definite pattern of conviction emerge. The weight of social conviction in the Anglican Church, as in others, has been ever more steadily settling upon the *persona* of man, as being both the discernible heart of the disease and the corner stone of remedy. It is man himself who is the real problem, and the core of the whole predicament of society. The prophetic thought of the whole Christian Social Movement has converged upon the manifold maladjustments of man's *persona*—maladjusted to Nature and so out of natural order, maladjusted in industrial society by the mass-production methods of a machine age, maladjusted to management, to the planned and the totalitarian state, maladjusted to God and to sin, and so to other men.

Hitherto, Christian sociologists would have been inclined to say, 'That being so, we must now discover the Christian remedies, and then we must persuade people to apply them.' But the diagnosis has now gone so deep and ranged so widely that there is no such thing as one self-evidently Christian remedy to be found. If there were, it would be an impossible task to persuade all peoples and their governments to adopt it; and even if that could be done, the recurrence of original sin in every generation means that this task can never be completed in this world.

Is there no escape from this dilemma? In the last few years

---

[1] *Ibid*, p. 225.

Christian sociologists have been casting about for a new line to follow which may lead them out of the impasse and at last lead them home. The line they have found is new in one sense, a new strand to the rope they have been steadily weaving, but in another sense it is as old as the hills. This line is to trace and apply the connection between liturgy and sociology. If our trouble lies in the maladjustment of our association, as the endemic facts of war and social injustice and inequality of privilege testify, and if as Christians we believe axiomatically that God and worship and 'going to church' are not only relevant but crucial, then liturgy, or the things people do together when they meet to worship God, ought to have something to say to the problem. More than that, what it says must itself be a social proclamation of immense force about the Good Life.

In our generation it was perhaps Fr. A. G. Hebert who first outlined this point of view to the Church in so persuasive a way that many heeded him. In 1935 he published his significantly named book, *Liturgy and Society*. He was thinking more about the evangelistic than about the social problem of the Church (though of course the latter was also present to his mind for they are really inseparable) and the primary thing he wrote is contained in this sentence, 'The church building and the liturgical acts performed there express something about Christianity which the preacher's words can never give.'[1] He was convinced that the key to the evangelistic problem lay in the phrase, 'Let the Church be the Church,' and that the best approach to that desirable consummation was through liturgy, for liturgy alone could resolve the tangle of maladjusted associations within the Church. Liturgy, for good or ill, had social force of a dynamic kind.

The same idea was heard at the Malvern Conference in the paper on *Revelation and Social Justice* read by the Rev. D. M. Mackinnon, which very strongly emphasised the 'immense importance of liturgical practice as a formative influence upon men and women.' The very tensions and qualities which modern man most needs will 'be most surely effected through liturgical revival. For the sacraments . . . are the theology of the common man.'[2]

By diligently searching it would no doubt be possible to find other Christian thinkers who have been saying the same kind of thing in recent years. But incontestably this method of approach to the great sociological problem has been most fully explored by Fr. Gregory Dix, who would probably not call himself a sociologist at all, but a theologian and historian. What he has done, in fact, is to take us on to ground where theology, sociology, and the history of Christian

---

[1] A. G. Hebert, *Liturgy and Society* (Faber and Faber, 1935), p. 41.
[2] *Malvern*, p. 109.

worship blend so completely that they are no longer distinguishable. In his long and great book, *The Shape of the Liturgy*, published in 1945, he more than once gives chapter and verse for the belief that liturgy is effective in sociology as well as in the spread of the Church. He shows for instance that in history a departure on any large scale from the classical shape of the liturgy has detectable social consequences. For example, some individualistic aberrations of Latin eucharistic piety in the late Middle Ages helped to shape the post-renaissance individualism both in religion and in social life, and thus led to the philosophy of John Locke, and through him to 'acquisitive man.'

It may sound exaggerated to link comparatively small ritual changes with great social results. But it is a demonstrable historical fact that they are linked: the ritual change can always be detected before the social one.[1]

Thus the liturgist may be, and indeed is, a prophet of Christian social order. Fr. Dix asserts this, and, semi-humorously groans that this is not how men of his trade are commonly regarded:

What are called liturgiologists are apt to be treated by English churchmen with that vague deference accompanied by complete practical disregard with which the Englishman honours most forms of learned research . . . Liturgists have no particular reason to be pleased with the mandarin-like position thus accorded them. They are in reality only students of what actually goes on and has gone on in every parish or other church in Christendom . . . ever since thirteen men met for supper in an upper room at Jerusalem—the 'common prayer' of Christians.[2]

They study, that is to say, what is elemental and basic in the association of men with other men, and men with God. They are almost as deeply concerned as the sociologists with the fundamental simplicities of the social problem.

The most suggestive of all the statements recently made in this sphere is a passage in Fr. Dix's preface where he says that the liturgy of the Eucharist traces for us the outlines of a new title for man in society:

. . . Over against the dissatisfied 'Acquisitive Man' and his no less avid successor the de-humanised 'Mass-Man' of our economically focused societies insecurely organised for time, christianity sets the type of 'Eucharist Man'—man giving thanks with the product of his labours upon the gifts of God, and daily rejoicing with his fellows in the worshipping society which is grounded in eternity. This is man to whom it was promised on the night before Calvary that he should henceforth eat and drink at the table of God and be a king. That is not only a more joyful and more humane ideal. It is the divine and only authentic conception of the meaning of all human life, and its realization is in the eucharist.[3]

---

[1] Dom Gregory Dix, *The Shape of the Liturgy* (Dacre Press, 1945), p. xii.
[2] *Ibid.*, p. xiii.   [3] *Ibid.*, pp. xviii, xix.

This is a really important statement, which opens up fresh vistas in
a field of study rapidly becoming bare with the treading of so many
feet, and produces in the reader that 'wild surmise' of imagination
of which Keats wrote. It is deeply suggestive, for though it does not
answer all the questions that one would like to ask, it does set one
asking questions of a new kind, creative questions which seem to
point to a road promising to lead at last to the haven of the Christian
sociologist's long journey.

Canon Demant remarked at Malvern that the most 'inclusive and
fundamental form' in which the 'economic deadlock of industrialism' can be stated is to state it 'in terms of types of man.' In the
same passage he himself stated it as 'the lordship of Business Man
over Artist Man.'[1] Fr. Dix's lay figures go deeper: Acquisitive
Man and Mass Man, and the domination of either leads to a desert.
They are lay figures, but they live and have potency; they are not
figures of straw. In the liturgy of the Eucharist we have at last the
real figure of the true man's life in spiritual association, Eucharistic
Man, and in him alone Artist Man and Business Man and Mana-
gerial Man may find their true relationships. He goes on to give the
briefest outline of what is in his mind:

In this period of the disintegration and attempted reconstruction of
thought about our secular society, the individual's relation to society and
his need for and securing of material things are the haunting problems of
the age. There is a christian pattern of a solution which is expressed for us
and by us at the eucharist. There the individual is perfectly integrated in
society, for there the individual christian only exists as a christian individual
inasmuch as he is fully exercising his own function in the christian society.
There his need of and utter dependence upon material things even for 'the
good life' in this world is not denied, or even ascetically repressed, but
emphasised and met. Yet his needs are met from the resources of the
whole society, not by his own self-regarding provision. But there the
resources of the Society are nothing less but the total substance freely
offered by each of its members for all. There, too, is displayed a true
hierarchy of functions within a society organically adapted to a single end,
together with a complete equality of recompense.[2]

The freshness and importance of such a statement does not need
emphasis for it is plain. Every time the Holy Communion is celebrated it is a demonstration of Christian social order, and a proclamation of it in terms of liturgically acted drama. Such a proclamation, endlessly repeated, is potent with suggestion, and the
repetition of potent suggestions is the really irresistible weapon.

What this means and may mean for the future of the Church and
the Christian Social Movement no one now knows or can know.
We have brought the story to the present moment, and all the rest

[1] *Malvern*, p. 109.   [2] Dom Gregory Dix, *op. cit.*, p. xviii.

lies ahead. But here the future is also the past. In the earliest years of Christendom a handful of men and women and their successors imposed their will upon the whole then known world within three centuries, and it is universally agreed by historians that they did it by the quality of their associated life in the Spirit. More than anything else it was what they made of the Eucharist which gave that quality to their common life, and we still have the same Eucharist. It was their evangelistic and social proclamation. It had power then to claim and to change the kingdoms of this world, and it has still.

The last three chapters have traced the outlines of very different journeys. This has told the story of the development of the Christian Social Movement, whilst the others traced the unfolding of theological stresses and convictions in the Church of England in the last thirty years. But all have irresistibly led us to one and the same place, the Altar of God.

CHAPTER FOUR

THE CHURCH AND HOUSING

I. *Accepting the Charge*

Both Churches and Governments suffer from the same characteristic temptation. It is to spin an endless web of theory, and to surround themselves with clouds of words; but to be coy and chary when theory should have come to the point of begetting action. The Christian Social Movement for a hundred years had been chiefly occupied in propaganda, analysis and diagnosis. It had come to the point where it had done much to make good the Christian right to claim the whole social order as a proper field of redemptive grace. By the end of the 1914–1918 war it was time to do something tangible about it, to demonstrate that Christian social theory could by Christian social action take hold of enemy occupied territory and transform it.

Where there is social wretchedness the Church is, and has always been, actively at work, sweetening life at a thousand million points of strain. The only book which could record all this is the Book of Judgement. The revolutionary, and even the ardent reformer, is too apt to speak of this ceaseless, ubiquitous, anonymous work as 'playing about with palliatives,' or 'mere ambulance work.' Over and over again, that is all that can be done to meet the need at its most clamant moment. It is futile, and heartless too, to say that because to act through the parish coal and clothing club or the sick and needy fund is not all one would wish to do, one should not do this sort of thing at all. Nevertheless they remain palliatives in that they do nothing to change the system which causes the need of them, and sometimes they even serve to give it a longer lease of life by salving the consciences of those who could change the system if they would. On a larger scale just the same thing was true of the movement to provide occupational centres for unemployed workers which became such a feature of life in the distressed areas in the thirties, and in which the Church took so great a weight of responsibility and work upon its shoulders. It was all that could be done at the time and it was the obvious thing to do. A Church which refused all traffic with the occupational centres because their existence did nothing to cure unemployment would have stood under every condemnation of the Parable of Judgement.

There was one sphere of social action between the wars which was

basic and seminal, not palliative, in which churchpeople and the
accredited leaders of the Church played a leading and a conspicuously successful part. This was the sphere of slum clearance and new
housing. This work more than any other was the Christian Social
Movement on its practical side, crowning it with tangible things like
human family life, bricks and mortar, investments and dividends,
and the eloquence and thought of many generations of the prophets
of the social movement. What churchpeople, acting under the
inspiration of their faith, did to build flats and houses for the
unfortunates condemned to dwell in slums is at once a thrilling, a
copious, and a most diffused story. Merely to list the titles of the
many public utility societies which Christians all over the country
from Penzance to Tyneside set up, managed and financed in order
to take people out of slums and give them decent dwellings at rents
they could pay would occupy several pages of this book. Memory
goes back, for example, to Canon Thomas Shimwell of Manchester,
passing all his days hand in hand with physical pain got from a backbone injured in swimming at a camp for his Ancoats boys, and living
contentedly year after year in his fantastically comfortless rectory
with slums all round him, and having for company the railway horses
in the stables across the road, with odours of dung all summer, and
troops of rats all the year round. By devoted work for years he
became the corner stone of an enterprise which took many families
away from the Manchester slums, and built for them an entire
housing estate in the suburbs. Or there was the persistent and gallant
work of the Church in Penzance, starting with petitions from the
Parochial Church Council of St. Mary's church to the Town Council,
and when the city fathers would take no action, the formation of a
Rate Payers Association to sweep them from office in the annual
election. In all this Canon Carr was the rector and moving spirit.
He and Basil Jellicoe stood in the market place all day long to collect
money to begin the scheme, and before all was done many families
had been rehoused in Penzance. To take one more sample from a
varied store, there was the action in the same sphere of the priest
and people of St. Nicholas, Guildford. When Guildford was certi-
fied as free from slums they looked round to see what they could do
elsewhere to help the Church's housing ventures. Their gaze lighted
upon the Bethnal Green Housing Association, and the parish raised
the money to adopt and equip some of the flats they were building.
They went further and formed a committee to establish friendly
relations between themselves and the tenants. To this day these
friendly relationships are steadily cultivated. Others of these Bethnal
Green flats were adopted by enthusiasts of the Christian Social
Movement and named after its heroes, Gore, Maurice, Chesterton,

Adderley, and others. The tenants are all told something of their own heroic patron, and like to know it.

There is indeed a grand story to tell of the Church's adventure in building houses and clearing slums, of how it blazed the trail which others, governments, and local authorities who could vote money and need not laboriously collect it, followed later. But only by rigid selection can it be made a manageable story, and one sample must represent a hundred. Let the story of Basil Jellicoe and the achievement of the St. Pancras House Improvement Society Ltd. in Somers Town, perhaps the most conspicuously successful and certainly the most romantic and picturesque of all these stories stand for all the others, and let the gaps which still remain be filled by token in the stories of what was done under Christian inspiration in Leeds, and in London by the Ecclesiastical Commissioners.

II. *Basil Jellicoe and the St. Pancras House Improvement Society*

Out of all the thousands of people who come into Euston Station from the north every day, how many are there who realise that as they get out of their train at one of the arrival platforms they are within one or two hundred yards of the famous Church of St. Mary's, Somers Town; out of which grew certainly the most famous and probably the most conspicuously successful of all the Church's feats in the field of housing? How many, indeed, realise that lying just behind that black wall on their left lies what was until recently one of the most desperate slums in London, but now a slum no longer? Yet so it is. Leave the station by the overhead way which empty taxis use to enter it, and pass through the parcels office entrance, and opposite, across the dreary length of Eversholt Street, is a plain, ordinary, not very beautiful, and unadorned church. There is absolutely nothing externally to distinguish it from a hundred others in just such districts as this. But it is a very famous church. From its altar came the vehement compassion, the drive, the resource which conceived a forlorn hope and thrust it onwards and onwards until that hope became accomplished fact, and the slums at that end of the Borough of St. Pancras were only an evil memory. At this altar worshipped Fr. Basil Jellicoe, and from it he drew the strength and power to become the most famous missioner for decent housing which the Church has produced. Many others were in this venture beside him, and indeed it still goes on though he has long been dead, but no one doubts that but for him it would never have been a movement but only a dream.

Spontaneity is the word which comes at once to mind as one

thinks of Basil Jellicoe. There was in him the basic element of freedom, the power to meet all experience with immediate response,
ungrudging, spontaneous, unselfconscious. He could always make
the experience of other people vividly his own, for he lived so fully
in and for others that their hurts were his hurts, and their joys his
own. He went to a place where almost everybody was deeply hurt
by scandalous housing, and thus the very existence of slums anywhere was to him an affront and offence, a nagging pain in his mind.
It gave him no rest by day or night, and so he was able to give no
rest to himself. He was a flame of mingled suffering and joy.
But the flame blazed so fiercely that it swiftly burnt itself out in
death, and the quicksilver was stilled.

He was the most picturesque and, perhaps for that very reason,
one of the most effective of all the priests who became notable
warriors in the battle of the slums in town and country. Archbishop
William Temple said of him, 'There are some with whom it seems
to be a necessary quality that they should die young—Mozart
among musicians; Keats and Shelley among poets; and among
saints, with many another, Basil Jellicoe.'[1] The Archbishop had
weighed his words. He deliberately placed Jellicoe in the company
of the very greatest, and, judged by the standard of the immensity
of personal achievement, he was worthy of that place. It is to compare the like with the unlike, but the fine blocks of flats hard by
Euston Station and Keats' *Ode to a Nightingale* or Shelley's *Pro-
metheus* are, considered as testimonies to the greatness of the human
spirit, comparable. A saint is not a word to be lightly used, but
Temple used it of him; and if to be a great poet in the sphere of
living is to be a saint there is no doubt about the rightness of claiming that title for Jellicoe. If we canonised nowadays, he would be
an obvious candidate for beatitude. The Anglo-Catholic movement
was his inspiration and a wonderful home was his background.
Between them, they made him what he was. His field of competence
was persuasion and action: in the sphere of intellectualism he was
always at a loss. He was the type whose utter unselfconsciousness
creates a deposit of story and legend wherever life took him. Many
pictures of Jellicoe come drifting down the years. He would wander
about Somers Town clad always in an elderly cassock, and surrounded by hordes of clamorous children over whose heads on wet
days he would spread his cloak like a giant umbrella. He preached
on one occasion in Westminster Abbey on housing, rather startling
the congregation by his choice of a text, which was a Somers Town
obiter dictum of any wife with a recalcitrant husband, 'What! Me

---

[1] In his preface to *Basil Jellicoe*, Kenneth Ingram (The Centenary Press,
1936), p. viii. I am heavily indebted to this biography throughout this section.

send for the copper! He's my old man.' On that day he had picketed
every door into the Abbey with his Somers Town friends, who thrust
leaflets about the housing scheme into the hands of everybody who
entered. He liked to go to Chichester Theological College from time
to time, and the students and principal loved his every visit, even the
visit when he brought a monkey with him, a new pet he had im-
pulsively bought on the way. His capacity for sheer enjoyment was
immense. Every year he made a point of going to the annual fair
at Bude, and would stroll round it, still in his cassock, and go on all
the roundabouts—alone if nobody offered to go with him—and
somehow gathering all the fair's workers round him in a cheerful
talk, with flashes of spiritual fire in it.

If any priest ever led a 'busy' life, he did; and yet seemed never
pressed for time, and always gave to everyone who sought him all the
time that might be necessary. He gave the impression always that
the one to whom he was talking was the one in all the world who
mattered most to him. His strength lay in his scale of values, and
he knew that his real mission was a pastoralia to individuals. His
work for housing was always conceived of as a direct consequence
of his mission to individual persons. With him it was human beings
first and 'humanity' a long way afterwards—a scale of values as
creative as its opposite is deadly.

Somers Town is the district of the mission of Magdalen College,
Oxford, and it was as the college missioner that Jellicoe went there
in 1921. He was still a layman; his age was 22. In the next year
he was ordained deacon, and priest in 1923; and in that year Percy
Maryon-Wilson joined him as assistant missioner. He was thus only
attached to the parish church of St. Mary, not its vicar; and the
serious trouble was that the attachment between the mission and
the parish church had become unhealthily loose. The mission's
clubs had thus become undisciplined and unruly. It is an indication
of the courage of this young man that his first action was publicly
to speak his mind to the offenders. 'I'm a very young man,' he told
them, 'but I'm the new missioner. And you won't like me at all.
You won't like the things I'm going to do. I'm going to close down
all this for a time. We've got to start again and start quite differently.'[1] How differently this was to be neither he nor his audience
dreamed. The first difference was a re-tying of the knots which held
the mission close to the parish church and its altar, for it was to be
the literal truth that the power house of the housing scheme was the
altar of the parish church.

Somers Town, when he went to it, was not a creditable locality.
For some obscure reason great railway stations are often surrounded

[1] Ingram, *op. cit.*, pp. 20, 21.

by slums, and in this Euston was worse than most others. Slums are only superficially alike. Each one has its own distinctive marks. The slum houses of Somers Town have gone to their own place, but photographs and pictures of them remain. From these it seems that bugs and the rotting, peeling plaster of bad stucco were their particular sign manual. There is one photograph of a large flat piece of wood. It is covered so thickly with dead bugs that hardly any wood can be seen. All those bugs came out of a single wardrobe. The houses were mostly tall and tenement-like. Each house found room for many families, and for all of them there was just one outside lavatory-cum-washhouse. The yards were haunted by rats, choked with debris, and covered with bricks fallen from the walls, which no one bothered to repair. Gruesome photographs exist of damp narrow death-trap staircases, with cracked walls and peeling paper; of a court's back entry at night, with pools of liquid, looking as though it might be made of blood and tears; of bent, broken and rusted railings guarding the approach to a portal of peeling stucco and a closed, paintless door, hiding horrors. There is overcrowding in every slum, but in this more than in most. The first seven houses the society bought had twenty-one families in them. One room, measuring ten feet by eight, housed a man and his wife and five children. There was a bed (the family kept all their clothes under that) three chairs, a table, some shelves and a kettle, but no oven. A final photographic record exists of a family group posed outside the door of their hovel—six adults, five children, the baby, and the cat. The cat was fat and well-liking. The baby and its white clothes were clean—and by what prodigies of sacrificial effort had that been achieved. The rest were clothed in what looks like sackcloth and tatters, and on the faces of the children is a terrible expression of puzzled desperation, and no hint or trace of gaiety.

The L.M.S. Railway had built some blocks of decent flats for its employees, but otherwise, said Jellicoe, Somers Town homes were

the Devil's holiday, a kind of perpetual festival of All Sinners. It has been produced by selfishness, stupidity, and sin, and only Love Incarnate can put it right. The slums produce something much more terrible than mere discomfort and discontent. They produce a kind of horrible excommunication; a fiendish plan on the part of the Powers of Evil to keep people from the happiness for which God made them, and from seeing the beauties of His world . . . It is not more policemen who are wanted in places like Battersea and Somers Town: it is God Incarnate in the hearts of loving human beings.[1]

In his daily visiting these were the scenes before Jellicoe's eyes; their human wreckage his hourly business. He saw them all, the child

[1] Quoted Ingram, *op. cit.*, p. 36.

consumptive who might have lived, but not in Somers Town, the mother of children struggling to keep the family decent in conditions militating against the bare possibility of every decency, the husband and wife who got drunk most nights to drug despair, and the thief and criminal who found the railway station and its parcels office a good hunting-ground. But he saw them under the symbolic imagery of the Incarnate Lord of the Parable of Judgement and the Holy Sacrifice of the altar—Christ in people, Christ in his people, and so Christ in homes like these. The horror of this thought was the flame that burnt him, a flame rekindled every time he celebrated at the altar of St. Mary's.

It was in 1924 that the four enthusiasts, Basil Jellicoe and Percy Maryon-Wilson, Miss Edith Neville and Miss I. N. Hill of the Charity Organisation Society were joined by two old Magdalen men, Francis Hubbard and Kenneth Fraser, and became an unofficial committee sworn to do battle for decent houses for Somers Town. They had their determined enthusiasm. They even had an office. But that was all. The office was the dining-room table of the missioners with a battered tin box on it to hold the money and securities they hadn't got. The next thing they appear to have collected was an architect, Ian Hamilton, another Magdalen man, who had for some time been specialising in the sort of work they wanted done. They were all clear that they must form a public utility society and canvass for shareholders. It was not until July 1925 that they were ready to announce that the St. Pancras House Improvement Society existed and was duly registered, and, still more important, that it had bought the freehold of eight slum houses, and now wanted £7,000 to buy them outright for reconditioning. This money was raised by subscription and in share capital in six months, but this might not have happened had not the appeal been noticed by Lord Cecil of Chelwood who used his name to give it public backing in the correspondence columns of *The Times*.

Lord Cecil's action was a portent, an evidence of things to come. For what distinguished the Somers Town scheme from so many others was the extraordinary skill of its promoters in gaining the support of public men of all kinds and their flair for the right sort of publicity. Priests of the Anglican Church generally have an instinctive dislike of publicity, and there is no reason to suppose that Jellicoe and Maryon-Wilson liked it any better than their brother clergy. But they had undertaken the kind of venture for which publicity was necessary. Very well then, publicity there should be, and plenty of it. But it was publicity always for the great plan to rehouse their poor, never for themselves. They had visits from the Queen and the Prince of Wales, from archbishops and bishops of more

Churches than their own, from admirals and famous authors. They gathered round them a great mass of sacrificial goodwill, and the spontaneous and timely help of Lord Cecil in the earliest days was repeated again and again by others as well placed as he to help in a crisis. They themselves refused no invitation to speak to meetings large and small about the scheme. When they spoke of it, whatever the audience, they did so in Christ's Name. They appealed always and to any and every kind of audience in the Name of the Lord, as the Old Testament prophets had done. There was nothing merely humanitarian about what they were determined to do, for they knew they did it as a vocation from the most High God to assert the sacredness of personality which Jesus had so constantly asserted, and against which the conditions of life in the slum were a blasphemy. Speaking in that Name, they were able to appeal far beyond the circle of Anglo-Catholic parishes (though it was to them they went first) to all who called themselves Christian.

Of these four founders of the society only Miss Neville is still in Somers Town, and she is now the chairman. She has recently written down her recollections of the beginnings of the adventure and of its first chairman:

It is difficult quite to recapture the atmosphere of those early days—our boiling indignation and sense of frustration as we realised how little most people knew or cared that a family of 15 lived in two smoky little attics with the rain pouring in on them, that babies born healthy died after a few months of life in damp cellar rooms, that young men and women were starting new families in conditions which should have shamed our great-grandparents, the heart-breaking misery of it all, and yet at the same time all the excitement and joy of comradeship in a cause in which we passion-ately believed. We were hopeful, and could give hope to others. And then, it was frankly fun to confront absentee landlords with an exposure of the source of their incomes: to interview Cabinet Ministers and municipal officials and say to them 'We are going to rehouse slum dwellers whatever you have to say about it'; to shock complacent people with a faithful account of the habits and ravages of the bed bug. Fr. Jellicoe sometimes talked about our work as a 'sanctified lark,' and those who remember him will understand that original way of describing a hard and serious task. He moved others by his infectious gaiety and his deep sincerity—by his power of loving. He loved all sorts of people—outwardly very unattractive people as well as the people anyone could like—sour, cantankerous people, ugly and dirty people, as well as the gay and the brave, the quick-witted responsive people who made Somers Town so delightful. Fr. Jellicoe was continually conscious that the Devil had made the slums. He never fell into the trap of thinking that 'these people' didn't suffer from such living conditions because 'they' were different: he knew that God did not mean people to live so and that it was no use just to be shocked—only to be shocked into action.[1]

---

[1] *Housing Happenings*, edited by Irene T. Barclay (St. Pancras House Improve-ment Society), No. 31, October 1946, p. 4.

In 1926 the society issued its first annual report. It showed a capital of £6,500; and announced that the first eight houses had been reconditioned, and families who had had to eat, sleep, be born, and die in a single verminous room, or even a cellar, now had self-contained flats, each one with its own bathroom. This had all been done not so much for the tenants as with them, for they had been consulted at every stage as to how the reconditioning could be done most conveniently to themselves. At the end of the first quarter of their occupation the total debt for rent was 12s. 9d.

Then came the first real crisis and challenge. One day early in 1926 to the committee of management was administered a great shock. Three members burst into the room and told their colleagues that a chance opportunity of buying 69 houses and an open space of 10,000 square feet had come their way. They had seized it, agreed to purchase, committed the society, and please could they have a substantial sum for the immediate deposit and a further £25,000 in five months' time! The funds did not even run to the deposit, and as for £25,000 . . .! The committee could of course have repudiated them, and certainly nobody could have blamed it if it had. And yet, on the other hand, this property was geographically the key position of the parish: if they could get it they would have the chance to do far more than recondition old houses; they could build a whole block of flats. 'If we had funked it,' wrote Maryon-Wilson, 'there would soon have been a factory in Drummond Crescent, and St. Mary's Flats—never.'[1] The Committee decided to accept the challenge.

The vital thing to do was to pray, and a day of continuous prayer before the Blessed Sacrament was arranged at Pusey House, Oxford. Then an old friend and a new one came to the rescue. Lord Cecil came to see for himself what was being done, and appealed again in *The Times*. This letter of his was publicly backed by Neville Chamberlain, then Minister of Health. A little later John Galsworthy spent a day being conducted round about the streets and homes of Somers Town. A year or two afterwards he was to make this visit the basis of the charmingly sympathetic chapters in his novel *Swan Song*, which describe the Church at work in a London slum. But his immediate reaction was to write for *The Observer* a full-length article on the slum problem in London, as exemplified in Somers Town, which extolled all that the society was doing, and pleaded for help. The paper sent him a cheque for his article, but he promptly wrote to Maryon-Wilson:

This cheque has been sent to me by *The Observer* for the appeal I wrote for you. I didn't expect it, and I send it on to you for the

---

[1] *Challenge*, a Brochure issued by the St. Pancras House Improvement Society, Ltd., 1933, pp. 47–8.

St. Pancras House Improvement Fund. I hope you are getting the money.[1]

Thanks very largely to him and Lord Cecil, they were; and within the time limit the whole sum they needed had flowed in, and the 69 houses and 10,000 square feet of open space they needed was theirs. In 1928 the foundation stone of the new block of flats was laid by Admiral Lord Jellicoe and blessed by the Bishop of London; and the building of St. Mary's Flats was begun. They were finished in fifteen months, and 52 more families had been provided with decent housing in the Name of the Lord.

This event marked the end of the most difficult part of the journey the society had set itself to travel. Its members had not yet realised all their ambitions. Compared with what had still to be done, they had only just begun. But with the finishing and occupation of St. Mary's Flats they had at last something tangible to show, and a feat actually accomplished, visible to any who care to come to look at it, always eases the path of those who must raise money or solicit investments. St. Mary's Flats had been born out of a serious crisis, but those which were to follow had less painful births, though the purchase of the two and a half acre Sidney Street site was one which required faith and gave anxiety.

The rest of the 'bricks and mortar' part of the story can therefore be quickly summarised, and the dates flash past like milestones seen from a motor-car. 1930 was the year of the Solemn Dynamiting of the first of the old Sidney Street houses; in two months the first brick of the flats was laid by Admiral Jellicoe, and hardly had he done so when Queen Mary came to see what was being done. Next year came the turn of the other side of Sidney Street when General Sir Ian Hamilton came and did a Solemn Burning.

We had previously built a large bonfire, ten feet high, and on the top of this pyre had placed large models of a bug, a flea, a rat, and a louse, all stuffed with fireworks, and these were solemnly burnt.[2]

The year 1932 they called the Year of the Crossing of the Rubicon, but the space to be spanned was 'not a romantic stream of water but a drab and filthy street.' It was in fact Sidney Street, already partly laid low, but now to be for ever closed to allow another great block of flats to be built right across it. In the same year the society was offered another acre and a half fronting on Seymour Street, and had to find £38,000 in four months. Of this they had £12,000 in hand: the balance of £22,000 was subscribed within a month of the appeal for it being made. On that site lived 700 more people for whom new homes would be built. Thus, by 1933, the society

---

[1] *Ibid*, p. 48   [2] *Ibid*, p. 52.

which had started from nothing in 1925, owned six acres of land in Somers Town, had built 170 new flats and made eight others in houses they had reconstructed, had provided a nursery school, and decent homes for 3,000 people. Truly, they found a desert and they made it a garden.

This narrative has now run far ahead of the personal story of Basil Jellicoe. Although it was his vision which created the whole adventure, and although it came to be tied more to his name than to any other, that was not of his choosing. From the beginning he had foreseen that if any part of the dream should come true it must be a permanent structure, the life of which would be reckoned in decades rather than in single years. Therefore others must be drawn in to share the responsibility from the beginning, and as the flats were built a permanent organisation of management must be built alongside them. The original sextet was quickly multiplied, and an estate management committee set up. Even so, it was clear as early as 1927 that Jellicoe was doing far too much work, and he then took the first step of withdrawal in resigning his position as missioner while retaining the chairmanship of the society.

Henceforth his energy was to be given to the work of housing— but not in Somers Town alone. As public-spirited citizens in other places read what was gradually being achieved in Somers Town they cast eyes on their own slums, and said to themselves, 'If in St. Pancras, then why not here?' But many, indeed most of them, realising that the vital thing was to get a start, and that the right start was the kindling of faith and enthusiasm, believed that Jellicoe was the very man to do this for them. They rightly judged. To an altogether unusual degree he had the gift of communicating to others the creative pity and enthusiastic faith which flooded his own soul. In those years everybody who cared about housing said, Send for Jellicoe, and Jellicoe went to almost everybody. From Tyneside to Penzance, and from Cornwall to the Isle of Dogs and the Sussex Downs, and as far away as Canada he went to talk of slums and persuade people to combine to end them. It meant that he was less and less seen in Somers Town, and in 1932 the committee of the society believed it right to ask him to resign his chairmanship—a bitter parting for him, and a discipline most nobly borne, and saluted by the Archbishop of Canterbury when, at the last Somers Town function at which Jellicoe was present, he whispered to him, 'Well done.'

Jellicoe was a most successful persuader, but he was not made to be tied down in any one place, not even Somers Town, and in the end these perpetual journeys killed him. Outwardly he was all gaiety and friendliness. Every quality of an open, sunny nature seemed to

be his, and by the infection of it he caused many others to share his
own courage and faith. All these qualities and powers were really
there; everyone he met felt them. He walked with God, and all
knew it. But it may be perilous to walk with God, for one has then
an intensified sense of the presence and the power of evil, and to
Jellicoe evil was an omnipresent, malignant, personal force, always
seeking a point of entry into his soul. The nearness of the devil, with
all its horror, was hardly less real to him than the nearness of God.
His intense sense of atmosphere, the very power which made him
one of the most effective orators of his day, made him also terribly
aware of anything hostile in it, and persuaded him that his own soul
and body was a battleground in which spiritual powers of good and
evil fought. It is so for all, but not all know it as vividly as he. But
if his working life in the world was a strain—and few men have
driven their bodies as ruthlessly—he could find peace in his spiritual
life. Triumphantly he kept his soul, but it was too much for his body,
which soon paid the inevitable price.

There is one picture of Jellicoe on tour which explains a good deal
about him. He had come to a girls' school, and the headmistress
wrote of his visit after he had gone.

I was a little apprehensive about the meeting because there was a small
group of senior girls who were critical of and hostile to all religion and
were certain to be scornful of what he was going to say . . . He started off by
talking about slum clearance, but he didn't seem to be able to talk at all
easily. It was as if some hostile force were holding him up, deliberately
working against him, thwarting him. He paced up and down the room,
paused and hesitated, went to the stage curtains and tried to pull them
apart, then sat down on the stage and got up again. At one moment I
thought he was going to the back of the room to tell us he couldn't go on.
However after a real struggle he got going and talked for an hour with
magnificent fire and enthusiasm. He told the girls of the origin of the
House Improvement Society, but he talked very little about slums or
housing. He talked most of the time about the implications of our
Catholic Faith: of the heart of man as a slum until it had been touched and
cleansed by the risen Christ . . . At the end of the talk he seemed completely
exhausted and very tired. Immediately when we had left the hall and were
alone, he said with a challenging note in his voice: 'There is the devil in
this place: there was a group of hostile people in the hall who were doing
their best to make it impossible for me to talk.' He said he had almost
decided to give up the effort and tell them that he couldn't talk that evening . . . He then told me how he had felt the same hostile forces in
Somers Town working to destroy all the Housing Society was attempting
to do, and how only prayer and sacrifice could defeat the forces of the
devil. As he talked there was unutterable suffering in his eyes and a strange
radiance about his face: I have never seen such depths of spiritual suffering
or such an ardent love of souls on the face of any man.[1]

---

[1] Quoted by Ingram, *op. cit.*, pp. 56–8.

It is on record that he knew both the mystical vision and the dia-
bolical apparition. One day in 1930 he was expected home in Little-
hampton, coming by road from London. But he did not arrive for
some hours after his time, and then stumbled home, limp, excited,
exhausted. A strange and terrifying thing had happened to him alone
on the downs. 'He had seen a vision of goodness, he had seen
into himself, he had been blinded.'[1] Six weeks' illness in a nursing
home was the price to be paid. The next occasion, two years later,
was also in Sussex; and again he had driven from Somers Town,
this time in a lorry laden with mothers on an outing. His exhaustion
was such that his friends with great difficulty persuaded him to cancel
a preaching engagement and at last he obeyed and he lay for five
days, sleeping little and eating hardly anything. The doctors tried
to drug him, but

he wanted to be left alone on the threshold of a strange unseen world. All
through this collapse there was interwoven a mystical strain. He spoke of
a vision of the Holy Child which was almost about to be unveiled. He was
disappointed, snatched back into the arms of sleep before that promise
could take effect.[2]

The perennial frustration of the mystic! At once comes to mind
that other description of the same experience, written by Emily
Brontë, a very different mystic, in lines which make one of the great
moments of English verse:

> Then dawns the Invisible; the Unseen its truth reveals;
> My outward sense is gone, my inward essence feels;
> Its wings are almost free—its home, its harbour found,
> Measuring the gulf, it stoops, and dares the final bound.
>
> O dreadful is the check—intense the agony—
> When the ear begins to hear, and the eye begins to see;
> When the pulse begins to throb—the brain to think again—
> The soul to feel the flesh, and the flesh to feel the chain.

This time the price demanded was five months in a nursing home.
The third, three years later, in 1935, was the last. Once more he was
in Sussex, nervous, restless, unhappy, struggling to work; and once
more a nursing home was the only answer. It was his last resting
place in this world, and for three weeks he lay there slowly dying.
He talked little, but in the small hours of the last night of his life,
he was heard to cry, 'Oh Lord, haven't I suffered enough! Oh Lord,
let it be soon.' Soon it was: within a few hours the life ebbed away,

---

[1] Ingram, *op. cit.*, p. 107.   [2] *Ibid.*, p. 168.

and the soul of a great Christian was set free, carrying his sheaves to God who made him.

His monument is the great blocks of flats in Somers Town, the outward and visible sign of the service he gave to England. Many others share the glory of having given Somers Town health for disease, cleanness for filth, sunlight for fœtid smelling darkness, of having put in the way of thousands denied it a new chance to live the creative life. But, humanly speaking, it could not have been done without the courage and the faith of Basil Jellicoe. His memorial is more than bricks and mortar; it is also a sacrament of families redeemed and saved.

Let us see for ourselves what has been achieved. It is easy enough. Take the underground to Euston, and leave the station by the side entrance into Eversholt Street—a long, grimy, uninspiring street; there are thousands like it for every town in England has several. There, across the road, wedged among the shops and tenements, is a plain church, built in the worst of all architectural periods. The proportions inside it are as gaunt and unpromising as they are outside, but by loving care, by a skilled use of pictures and flowers, by a statue of the Virgin with a few candles burning before her, and by simple but beautiful altar hangings, someone has charmed away the ugliness and made the church a home. Its altar is the holy common table of a family, who gather there every Sunday for the parish Eucharist, and then adjourn in a body to the mission room and have their breakfast together. From that altar came the vital force which changed a district and created the most famous of all the Christian Public Utility Housing Associations.

Only the tops of the blocks of flats we are looking for can be seen from the station entrance. But go round behind the church and there they are, three or four great blocks, built, it is true, of that regrettable yellow brick which all London seems to love so dearly, but, as dwellings, by how much changed from what stood there before, desecrating the earth! The blocks are five stories high, and each one has its own drying ground, playground, and gardens. One drying ground has twenty-four posts in a circle for washing lines, and perched on each post a blackbird, which, however is much more like a rook! Another has jenny wrens for its decoration. Outside stairs lead from landing to landing. Once inside we are proudly shown specimen flats. They range from the two-room flat for old couples, the rent of which is nine shillings a week, to flats of six or seven rooms for large families. Every flat has its bath and electric light and power. The windows are wide and deep and the sun floods it. On the top floor of one of the blocks is a most charming nursery school with a well-planted roof garden for the babies in the flats.

These blocks are much like each other, yet they give no impression of monotony, no sense of gazing at a barracks. They are not replicas of each other. Scaffolding envelops one wing, which suffered in air raids. It was knocked down, but nobody was hurt, and it now stands erect again. So far some 660 families have been rehoused by the society. Eight housing managers look after the tenants and the properties, working on the Octavia Hill principles; and they direct their own craftsmen who keep all the flats in proper repair. So long as these flats stand, Basil Jellicoe will be remembered, and in the way he would most have wished.

III. *The Bishops Take Stock of the Housing Problem*

The cause Jellicoe and his friends had been serving so well in the limited sphere of Somers Town had all this time been steadily championed by the bishops of the Church of England, both individually in their dioceses and collectively in the Upper House of Convocation. Anyone who reads the debates of the bishops in the *Chronicles of the Convocation of Canterbury* during the period 1919 to 1939 would be cured of the popular delusion that bishops as a class took no interest in social welfare. Among the many social subjects raised in these debates housing stood easily first. It was a subject on which almost every bishop wished to speak and on which those who did speak quickly showed that they had gained an exact and deeply sympathetic knowledge of the facts, which only a personal knowledge of the lives of the underprivileged and a long, persistent study of the technicalities of the housing problem could have given them. It is a complete but a hardy delusion that bishops care little and know nothing of the way the poor live.

Of these debates, that which took place on February 13, 1930, was perhaps the most illuminating, concluding as it did by the bishops passing unanimously the strong resolution:

This House regards the overcrowded and insanitary conditions under which so many are compelled to live as a menace to the moral and physical welfare of the nation: it therefore calls upon all churchmen to do their utmost to remedy these evils in their own parishes and elsewhere, and it urges the Government to introduce as soon as possible legislation which will facilitate the abolition of the slums.[1]

The legislation urged by the bishops was soon forthcoming in the Housing Act of 1930. The debate was opened by Dr. Cyril Garbett, then Bishop of Southwark, who had made the subject of housing

---

[1] *C.C.C.*, 1930, p. 70.

peculiarly his own. He had made careful enquiries, and they showed that by 1930 various schemes had been sanctioned which between them would clear away some 13,000 slum houses. Not all of them had then been carried out. In the meantime the position was still very bad, and the bishop produced many statistics to show how serious it was. In his own diocese the borough of Bermondsey was a typical example. Within it there were still 10,000 houses not really fit for human habitation, and 2,763 families were living in over-crowded conditions. Among London boroughs Bermondsey, Deptford, and Paddington tied for first place in the table of infant mortality figures. In each of them 85 infants died out of every 1,000 born; and this was to be compared with Chelsea and Lewisham, with 48 and 52 deaths per thousand.

Other bishops eagerly joined in the debate, each giving examples of the state of housing in his own diocese, until, by the time the debate was ended a knowledgeable survey of the housing problem in the southern half of England, as it stood in the winter of 1930, had been built up piece by piece. It showed, for example, that in Bristol there were still 25,000 people living under insanitary conditions, and that Leeds still had 72,000 back-to-back houses, while Birmingham had 40,000 and Bradford 33,000. But the chief value of this debate lay not so much in the statistical evidence produced as in the realistic evidence provided of the ratio between the achievements of the Public Utility Societies and the extent of the slum problem as a whole, seen all over the country.

The Public Utility Societies were already numerous. Many of them were Church societies in the sense that from the Church had come the impetus which started them and the lion's share of the work which maintained them. Of these the St. Pancras House Improvement Society was the prototype. Practically all of them were Christian societies, in the sense that Christian people, acting directly under the inspiration of their Christianity, were the prime movers in them. To these every bishop gave high praise, and the work of many of them was mentioned by name, as for example, the Church Tenant Association in Bristol, which had been set up by the Bristol Council of Christian Churches, and had reconditioned many derelict houses in the slums of that city, turned them into flats, and let them at a cheap rent. There was the Fulham Society, which had bought vermin-ridden houses in districts where there was only one water tap for a whole street, and turned these houses into flats let at 8s. 6d. a week. In Birmingham, too, the COPEC Housing Scheme was at work in the same field of the reconditioning of slum property.[1] All these, and many more like them there were, and highly to be praised.

[1] *C.C.C.*, 1930, pp. 71–84.

But remember, said Dr. Garbett, that 'if there were thirty or forty times as many Public Utility Societies at work they would only touch the fringe of the slum problem.' He then summoned his wide and detailed knowledge to strike a just balance between the achievement and the need.

In two test districts, one near Manchester and the other near London, private surveys have been carried out with a certain interval between them to see how far those slum districts had been affected by large building schemes carried out in or near the neighbourhood. Those surveys showed that the result had been practically negligible. Here and there undoubtedly there was an improvement, but taking the country as a whole slums and overcrowding were almost, if not quite as bad as they were some years ago. But whether things were as bad or worse there was agreement on every side that the conditions were extremely bad.[1]

In another episcopal debate in Convocation, in 1933, Dr. Garbett again took up the same point, and declared that out of 1,900,000 houses built since 1918, the Public Utility Societies had built only 30,000.[2] These societies had blazed the trail, and done much to find an outlet in immediate and practical service for the convictions of the Christian Social Movement. But it was evident that the slums as a whole could not be ended by this kind of voluntary effort, and it was useful to have this authoritatively said by bishops who were not in the least likely to be unappreciative of what Basil Jellicoe and his peers had done.

IV. *Slum Clearance and Rehousing in Leeds*

There are more ways than one of creating and harnessing the Christian compassion through which slums are pulled down and their inhabitants less blasphemously housed. We have seen one way of doing it in the St. Pancras House Improvement Society which formed a pattern for many other enterprises of the same kind in different parts of the country. This was the normal form of action for socially conscious churchpeople to take. But it was not the only possible form and it had certain necessary limitations. Where, as in Penzance, the slums were grievous in their condition but not enormous in their extent the method of the public utility society was feasible. But in places where the problem was so huge that the cost of dealing with it had to be reckoned not in thousands or tens of thousands but in millions of pounds no public utility society could be adequate to the need, for none had the financial resources and legal powers of a local authority, all of which would be needed to

---

[1] *C.C.C.*, 1930, p. 71.   [2] *C.C.C.*, 1933, p. 349.

grapple with a problem on that scale. This was the position in Leeds, as indeed it was in other cities as well, but very specially so in Leeds. The slums there were so vast and the conditions of the people immured in them so dreadful that nothing less than the whole-sale clearance of great areas with rehousing undertaken by the municipality could tackle the job as it needed to be tackled. The slums of Leeds had to be dealt with not piecemeal but all together and in bulk, and this was far beyond the power of any private enter-prise of churchpeople, however devoted. There were, as a matter of fact, at least two public utility societies at work in Leeds, one of them working under the ægis of the Church Army, which had to their credit a token achievement.

Leeds provides social history with an outstanding example of municipal housing activity, and a living illustration of the practical consequences which followed in a great municipal housing enterprise when the policy pursued was derived principally from the mind of a Christian determined to apply the implication of the doctrine of the Incarnation in the sphere of housing.

The position that Leeds was in was summarised in 1921 in the Final Report of the Unhealthy Areas Committee, signed by its chair-man Neville Chamberlain, and containing this paragraph:

> The City of Leeds is perhaps confronted with the most difficult problem to be found in any of the provincial towns, owing to the enormous number of back-to-back houses, the building of which was continued to a compara-tively recent date. There were altogether 72,000 of these houses in the city, not all, however, of the same type, but all characterised by the feature that they are arranged in close parallel rows. About 12,000 are of a fairly sub-stantial character, with fifteen feet open space between the front of the house and the road, and with a separate W.C. entered from this space. Another 27,000 houses are built in blocks of eight, which open directly on to the streets and have their sanitary conveniences provided in an open space between each pair of blocks. These conveniences, therefore, can only be reached by passing along the street, and no garden or court of any kind is attached to the houses. The remaining 33,000 of these back-to-back houses are the oldest and worst, built in long continuous blocks opening directly on to the street; they are crammed together at the rate of 70 or 80 per acre, and it is difficult to suggest any method of dealing with them satisfactorily.

The problem was indeed a great one and one can only conclude that Leeds regarded itself as beaten by it. The 33,000 of the worst type of back-to-back houses, in which a quarter of the population lived, had all been built before 1872, and many before 1844. The 27,000 somewhat superior back-to-back houses, were built between 1872 and 1892. Only the remaining 12,000 back-to-backs were of later date and even these were built at the rate of 40 houses to the acre. But in spite of the social consequences of the continuing existence

F

of such dwellings, little had been done in Leeds even to alleviate the situation. Between 1870 and 1930 only 4,500 demolitions took place. The largest demolition scheme which covered 2,790 houses, begun in 1895, was actually suspended before being completed, leaving 732 of the condemned houses still standing inhabited in 1930, with the Leeds Corporation as their owners and landlords. In relation to the size and gravity of the problem Leeds was markedly apathetic.

It was a grievous apathy. Buried in the files of the housing reports are many descriptions of what whole streets of such houses were like and what it meant to live in them. Structurally they were gaunt frames of decay held up by rotting black bricks. The walls bulged. Damp stained them and fungus decorated them. No damp courses had been provided and dry rot had spread like a flame. Workmen were always in and out for only by incessant patching could these houses be persuaded to stand up for just a little longer. The oldest type, of which there were 33,000 or more in 1930, had just the two rooms, a living-room and bedroom. Under the living-room was a small coal-hole. Food had to be kept in a cupboard in the living-room, or on shelves on the stairway to the coal-hole. There was nowhere else to keep it. In the living-room the family sat and fed, cooked and washed, were born, ailed, died, and waited for burial. No hot water was laid on. There was just an earthenware sink with one cold tap. There was, to be sure, a fire—if one had any coal— and a kettle. In that one heated water to wash in, and one did what one could to keep clean. But it all had to be done in the one living-room. Baths took a deal of contriving. Many parents saw to it that their children were tubbed on Saturday nights. But even one bath meant much discomfort for the whole family, and the preparing of it was an exhausting business, so that often enough the parents themselves had no baths at all. The lavatory arrangements were particularly horrifying. No house boasted a lavatory of its own. Outside in the street there might be two built together to serve a whole block, and things were contrived so that there was a bedroom over them. But their only entrance was in the street so that every soul who wanted to go there must go out of doors first, and then, likely enough, found it occupied. Small children, and not they only, generally used the street. Pictures survive of one of the worst courts of such houses —dank, dark, sinister, a scene of decay and filth caused by greed. A little ragged girl poses before the camera and holds protectively a tiny sister, as though trying to shield her from the consequences of life in a place like that. That child has now been rescued. If she is living in Leeds to-day it is not in such a court as that nor in such a house. They have all been swept away, and in their place, on the very same ground, stand the Quarry Hill Flats, one of the finest communities of tenement flats anywhere in this country.

In the rescue of that child the Church, through one of its priests, played a very big part. That the old apathy has disappeared, and that by 1935 Leeds had become, in the words of Mr. Lewis Silkin, the present Minister of Town and Country Planning, 'the Mecca of all housing reformers' is largely due to the work of an Anglican priest, the Rev. Charles Jenkinson.[1] At first sight Jenkinson presents something of a contrast to Jellicoe, except that he, too, clearly has the power to communicate his own enthusiasm to others. Jellicoe was closely associated with the Anglo-Catholic wing of the Church. Jenkinson has had no association with it, having been all his ordained life a member of the Modern Churchmen's Union. But had the two men met, which they never did—though Jenkinson is well acquainted with and has the highest admiration for Jellicoe's work—they would probably not have regarded their apparently divergent theological and ecclesiastical views as in fact fundamentally different. One has only to glance at the church at Belle Isle, Leeds, designed as Jenkinson wished it, with its noble 'English use' altar, its traditional vestments and ornaments, to appreciate that for him as for Jellicoe everything for which he tries to live is summed up in the Eucharist. His speeches at housing meetings were generally expositions of the two Gospel sacraments. 'How can we,' he would ask, 'declare that in Baptism children are made members of Christ, children of God, and inheritors of the Kingdom of Heaven; or how protest at the Eucharist that we are in love, and in that disinterested and universal love which is charity, with our neighbours, and then tolerate such conditions for children and neighbours as exist in Leeds?' Then he would go on to relate the doctrine of both sacraments not merely to the general need for better housing but also to the practical details of housing policy. Jellicoe could have made that speech. What is more, he often did.

It is indeed the details of what became known as 'The Leeds Housing Policy' which made that policy of worldwide interest. Slum clearance, and on a large scale, was being carried out in the middle 1930s in many places; but nowhere previously in any

---

[1] Now Alderman the Rev. C. Jenkinson, Leader of the Leeds City Council, and member of the Central Housing Advisory Committee. Mr. Jenkinson was Vicar of St. John's and St. Barnabas', Holbeck, Leeds, from 1927 to 1938, and on the demolition of practically the whole of that parish became the first vicar of the new estate parish of St. John and St. Barnabas, Belle Isle, Leeds, which he resigned at the end of 1947. He is now an honorary assistant curate at St. Mary's, Hunslet, Leeds, Leader of the Leeds City Council, Chairman of the Stevenage (New Town) Development Corporation, and a member of the Minister of Health's Advisory Committee.

municipal scheme were the human aspects of the housing problem so fully appreciated or more practically met.

Jenkinson's activities in the housing field began in November 1930, when an opportunity occurred for him to become a member of the Leeds City Council. Already, and for over 20 years previously, a member of the Labour Party, party political action, when necessary, had no terrors for him: he had become increasingly convinced that nothing less than a strong political campaign could lead to Leeds housing being revolutionised in the ways he believed to be necessary. The weapon to be employed was to hand in the Slum Clearance Act, 1930, for which the then Minister of Health, Mr. Arthur Greenwood, M.P., had been responsible. But in Leeds, as elsewhere, the Act looked like becoming a dead letter: and Jenkinson was convinced that it ought to be, and determined it should be, operated to the fullest extent. Compelled under the terms of the Act to forward to Whitehall a five years programme of slum clearance, the Leeds City Council forwarded one for the demolition of 2,000 houses in the five years, but accompanied it by a public statement that no guarantee was given that the programme would be carried out in the time. In fact, in the first two years, 1931 and 1932, a total of only 25 houses were 'represented' for demolition. This meagre programme was made by Jenkinson the commencement of his public agitation. In April 1931, he proposed, in the City Council, that a Housing survey of the City should be made by the Medical Officer of Health. His resolution was defeated. At once Jenkinson published his speech, with additional matter as a pamphlet: and nearly 20,000 copies soon found their way all over the city. A press correspondence was opened up, and meetings were arranged; and within a month or two all responsible people in Leeds were aware that someone with considerable determination and no little knowledge of the subject was not going to let the matter of Leeds Housing rest where it lay.

Jenkinson had sent his pamphlet to every clergyman and minister in the city: and in June 1931 the Leeds Chapter, the largest ruri-decanal Chapter in the country, passed and published the following resolution:

In the opinion of this Chapter, housing conditions in considerable areas of this city call for urgent attention on moral as on other grounds. The Chapter therefore represents to the City Council that with a view to arousing the public conscience on this matter, it is highly desirable that a precise statement of the situation and possibilities under the Slum Clearance Act of 1930 should be prepared, and at least a summary of the facts published. The Chapter expresses the further opinion that the housing problem in Leeds should be removed from the sphere of party political controversy.

The last sentence Jenkinson heartily endorsed: and it is one of the greatest satisfactions of his life that now for some years past, by unanimous resolution of the City Council, it is the agreed policy of the Council that not only the still remaining houses of the worst type of back-to-backs, but also the whole of the 27,000 somewhat superior ones, shall be entirely demolished at the earliest moment when circumstances make clearance again possible.

Sufficient had now been accomplished to make Jenkinson's next and decisive move practicable. He tabled a special resolution that the City Council appoint a Committee 'to enquire into, and report upon, the present position and future policy of Housing' in the City. Shaken by the results of the publicity already given to the subject, this time the majority of the City Council gave way, and the Committee was appointed. Working on Royal Commission lines, it took evidence, heard and cross-examined witnesses, and preserved a verbatim record of the proceedings. The medical officer of health, the Churches—Anglican, Free Church, Roman Catholics and Society of Friends—day school teachers, architects, property owners, estate agents, etc., gave evidence: and after over twelve months' work the committee reported. The Majority Report was a typed document of some thirty pages, the nature of it being sufficiently indicated by the central statement that 'no persons, however optimistic, can anticipate that we shall be able to cope with the problem' (of the 33,000 oldest type of back-to-back houses) 'satisfactorily inside the next twenty-five years.' The Minority Report, drafted by Jenkinson, was a printed document of ninety pages, including twenty-two appendices: and by its weight, arrangement and detailed statement of policy, at once occupied the field of public attention. Over twenty thousand copies of it were sold and the local Labour Party, after discussing and finally accepting the policy laid down in it, made it their principal plank in the ensuing municipal elections of 1933.

Jenkinson was lucky in the year 1933 in which elections were held. That year was noteworthy in housing history, for it was in March 1933 that Sir E. Hilton Young, Minister of Health (now Lord Kennet) declared in the House of Commons that the Government would stand no more trifling with the slum problem, and that he meant at once to call upon all local authorities to prepare a fresh survey of their areas and to follow it with programmes for the abolition of the slums, giving a definite date for the completion of their clearance, and with no governmental limit to the number of houses that might be dealt with. On the receipt of the ministry's circular all local authorities had to comply with its demands. The Leeds City Council, with the minority report in its hands, scrapped its earlier five year programme and rejected the advice of the majority of its committee by forwarding a programme for dealing with the Leeds slums at the rate of 3,000 houses a year, but without defining any total to be dealt with. It was when matters had advanced thus far that the municipal election was held, in November 1933, by which the Labour Party, by a small majority, obtained control of the Leeds City Council, and appointed Jenkinson to be the chairman of the housing committee.

Immediately after the election the policy was put into operation. Its principal features were: first, a Housing Committee of the City Council was set up—there had not hitherto been one—and Jenkinson was appointed its first chairman. Secondly, a Housing Department was established and staffed and a leading municipal housing architect brought in as Housing Director.[1] Thirdly, the existing slum clearance programme was scrapped. The Minister of Health was informed that Leeds intended to 'represent' the whole of the worst type of back-to-back houses by the end of 1939—which would have meant the demolition of the last of them by 1942—with the first 8,000 'represented' in batches, before the end of 1935. Fourthly, the Housing Director was instructed to prepare estate layouts and housing plans on entirely new lines to provide for the placing of contracts for 8,000 new dwellings within the same period, to include a block of flats designed according to general instructions given; and also a hostel for homeless persons. Fifthly, an entirely new rent, and differential rent relief, policy was at once put into operation. It was the particular combination of ideas in this policy, even more than the magnitude of the programme, which at once put Leeds in the forefront of advanced housing authorities and brought to it housing pilgrimages from all over the world. The rate at which Jenkinson drove his committee and officials was deliberate and he has, since, often explained his reasons. He knew perfectly well that the ideas, which he and his committee were realising, were far ahead of general Leeds opinion, but he believed they were right and necessary ideas. The difficulty was that what he and a few others could see clearly in their minds most other people would never see at all until the slum houses were going down in thousands, the new dwellings on the new estates going up in thousands and the rent policy actually operating over a wide field. He and his friends were therefore prepared for terrific opposition, much criticism and probable political defeat— and they received all: but he was convinced that in the two years for which his chairmanship was politically secure so much could be started and made certain that thereafter it would be impossible for anyone to depart seriously from the main lines laid down, that pub-

[1] Mr. R. A. H. Livett, O.B.E., A.R.I.B.A., then Deputy Housing Director of Manchester, now City Architect of Leeds.

lic opinion would inevitably endorse his views in the end, and that the political opposition itself, in face of the facts, would be forced to accept his general policy.

The demolition of practically all the slums of a great city and the rehousing of their inhabitants is naturally an intensely complicated business, and it is only possible to give here the barest description of some of the features of the Leeds policy in which the specifically Christian approach to the problem found expression.

First of all came the insistence that houses were to be built for people, and that to provide a mould for the proper development of family life the criterion of measurement of fitness must be in terms both of living and sleeping accommodation—not one and not the other but both. Under Jenkinson's chairmanship the floor area of all new municipal houses was at once raised to the absolute maximum then permitted by the Minister of Health, that is about 775 super feet. To-day the present Minister of Health will not allow a three-bedroomed house of less than 900 super feet, and the Leeds three-bedroomed house to-day is of 1030 super feet. People, he argued, need room to live as well as rooms. But a sufficient number of bedrooms should be the basis of all housing accommodation, the policy of building nothing smaller than the two-bedroomed and nothing larger than the three-bedroomed house was plainly inadequate. Nowhere more than in Leeds was the question of bedrooms urgent. In the worst areas of the old back-to-back houses, there were 14,000 with one living- and one bed-room, and 18,000 with the one bedroom divided into two. The overcrowding in many such dwellings was of course fearful. Clearly, no mass provision of two- or three-bedroomed houses and nothing else could possibly meet the situation. It was therefore decided that on all new housing estates five different sizes of houses must be built, and planned on the basis that there must be enough bedrooms to separate boys and girls from the age of ten, and a limitation upon the number of persons in a bedroom, according to its size. For all ageing people special old people's flats were built, mixed in with the other houses, but having exactly the same amenities as the large family dwellings. Wherever a family had a member suffering from tuberculosis special provision was also made.

The second distinctive feature was the establishment of the principle that for every house demolished one new house must be built. Surprising as it may seem the law does not require this. It only requires the local authority to provide equivalent accommodation for the number of persons displaced, if the accommodation is not otherwise available. Under Jenkinson the Leeds Housing Committee went further than the law demanded. When 100 families were displaced 100 new dwellings of the sizes that the particular 100 families needed were provided. The result was that Leeds rehoused and has kept on its estates 84·5 per cent. of the total number of families of the cleared slum areas. This was an important achievement. It is comparatively easy to make a fair show in the flesh by wholesale demolition. The real test is what then happens to the people who are displaced. Only too often they gradually drift into nearby districts of poor but not yet officially condemned houses. It is not enough to take them to fine new corporation housing estates. The trouble is to keep them there. To have kept 84·5 per cent. of them on the new estates is a much bigger achievement than at first sight it looks.

The Leeds scheme of rent relief, instituted by Jenkinson, and a matter of special satisfaction to him, is probably more responsible than anything else for this achievement. It was invented to implement the profoundly Christian principle that no housing or slum clearance policy can be regarded as humane or successful unless it actually enables families to live without hardship in the size of dwelling they need. It is common knowledge that nearly all municipal houses are subsidised out of the national exchequer and the local rates. The easiest way to distribute these subsidies is to divide the money equally over all the houses. But the larger the house the greater the cost, and therefore the higher the rent. Even if the rent of every house is reduced by an equal amount it is still true that the largest houses are the dearest to live in. But often enough the families which need the largest houses are by no means those who are capable of paying the highest rents. If therefore this rule-of-thumb policy is pursued, many families either cannot afford the accommodation they need, or will only be able to occupy it at the cost of much hardship. Jenkinson's remedy was simple. All municipal rents were fixed at roughly the amount needed to make ends meet, and calculated as though there were no subsidies at all. Those who could pay that rent did so. The subsidies were placed in a separate pool and every family not in a position to pay the stated rent could apply for rent relief wherever the relief was needed, for the amount needed from time to time, for so long as it was needed, but for no longer. The rent relief scheme operates over all municipal tenancies in Leeds, and relief is given down to a minimum rent of sixpence a week for any size of dwelling. It was this rent scheme which more than anything else enabled Jenkinson to see his dream come true—that the families most in need should be properly housed and then be able to live permanently in the new houses.

The majority of the people rehoused preferred to live on the estates in separate cottage dwellings. But there were some, as there were bound to be, whose circumstances forced them to go on living in the centre of the city, and for them it was necessary to provide flats. Therefore 26 acres of slum cleared land in the heart of the city, almost opposite Leeds Parish Church, were selected as the site on which to build what is to-day, with the possible exception of the Karl Marx Hof in Vienna, the most famous block of 'working class' flats in the world. In their planning Jenkinson's distinctive views are evident. There are 938 of them, varying from ageing persons' one-bedroomed flats up to five-bedroomed dwellings. Only 15 per cent. of the area is covered by buildings, and thus there is ample space, light, and air. Every flat has a private recessed balcony, but the commonest form of access to flats of this type by communal balconies was absolutely barred. Jenkinson would have no front doors on a common thoroughfare with consequent lack of privacy. Every flat opens on a landing serving only two flats, and is reached by one of the 88 automatic passenger lifts. There is a communal laundry, a community centre, spaces and equipment for games, and stores for prams and bicycles. All household refuse is poured down a receptacle and then automatically carried by water to a disposal incinerator.

Finally, the needs of the perennially homeless were not forgotten. In the slum areas there were some common lodging-houses which had to be demolished along with the back-to-backs. For their inhabitants Shaftesbury House was built, and it is probably the finest hostel for the homeless in this country. It takes 516 lodgers in self-contained sections for men and women. Each section has its large day-rooms, writing-room, canteen, locker-room and many other amenities. For every lodger there is a separate bedroom, not a cubicle in a bedroom; and thus every lodger has the chance to maintain or to find again the self-respect which is the proper due of personality.

All this work set a problem to the Diocese of Ripon, which rose to it by creating six new parishes and building six new churches for the Leeds estates between 1930 and 1939.

Thus within six years Leeds had been transformed. In 1933 it was still notoriously one of the most slum-ridden cities in England. In 1939 there were hardly any slum houses left. Instead the city had won for itself a tremendous reputation for having provided the best workers' flats in the country, one of the best hostels for the homeless, vast new housing estates, and a system of differential rent relief which is unique and which time has shown to be the instrument which can permanently give the chance of happiness and family decency to those who need it most. And for it all a priest of the Church of England was primarily responsible.

F*

V. *The Ecclesiastical Commission*

There are still too many to whom the appearance of the Ecclesiastical Commissioners in a chapter devoted to the work of the Church for good housing would seem incongruous and even astonishing. Old legends die hard; and the legend that the Church, through the Commissioners, owns slum property and refuses to improve it, is one which has been exploded again and again; and yet people continue to repeat it and even to believe it. The even more wicked lie that the Commissioners own brothels and draw their profits has been nailed down many times—and is still told. When Dr. Lang was Archbishop of Canterbury he once said publicly (and, no doubt, many times privately) that to assert that the Commissioners owned slum property was to utter falsehood, and 'I do not think I need qualify the word.'[1]

The facts about the estate in Paddington have been many times explained. The property, when the Commissioners were forced to take it over, was leased on a perpetually renewable lease, and the estate is held from the Commissioners by their head-lessees for 2,000 years. These had let again to sub-lessees, also on perpetually renewable leases; and thus neither the Commissioners, nor their head-lessees, have legal power to act. The power by which they might have acted they applied for in 1840. But when they asked Parliament for the power to end leases in order to secure control, there was a great outcry, and they were refused. Thus to-day no ground landlord, whether the Commissioners, or a municipality, or a private person can do anything to prevent a house, built on his ground but let on perpetually renewable lease, from being used as a brothel, as some of the houses in the Paddington estate have been.

It goes without saying that the Commissioners derive no profit whatever from the misuse of the houses. They receive merely the ground rent and they have in fact spent on preventive and remedial measures far more than any negligible sum of ground rent (less than a tithe of one per cent. of the income of the estate) which could be related in any way to the property so misused.[2]

The only measure which would really be remedial is the disappearance of prostitution. The power to exercise any control over the use of property built by others on ground they have come to own by very ancient bequest is denied to the Commissioners by law. And yet they must suffer in repute for what is done in some of these houses. It seems hardly fair.

[1] *C.C.C.*, 1933, p. 361.
[2] *Number One Millbank: The Story of the Ecclesiastical Commissioners*, James Raitt Brown (S.P.C.K.), p. 44.

The other charge, constantly made and as constantly denied, that the Commissioners are slum landlords is even more unfair, and has even less substance than the libel of financial complicity in Paddington brothels. This charge is frankly a lie, though the secretary of the Commissioners puts it more politely:

The implication is entirely mistaken. The expert knows its untruth. The instructed Churchman can discredit it, because archbishops and bishops and leading laymen direct the Commissioners' policy. The student of politics rejects it, because he knows the Commissioners to be a public body under statute, with a representative in the House of Commons who can be questioned at any time by any M.P. about any single house in any constituency. But there are others—and they are many—who are content to repeat what they have heard until it is controverted.[1]

The record of the Commissioners in the sphere of housing, both as landlords and builders, is a fine one. In 1884 they became the owners of a working-class housing estate at Walworth in South London. Hearing of the pioneer work that Miss Octavia Hill had already been doing in housing management, they invited her to manage their Walworth estate. She gave much of the rest of her life to managing the Commissioners' estates, and was employed by them until she retired in 1912. The work of the Commissioners was therefore the base from which the famous Octavia Hill system of management went out to bless the country; and to-day the Commissioners are employing twenty housing managers, trained by her.

It was under her persuasion that the Commissioners became builders as well as landlords. This happened in 1893 when the leases of some worn-out property in Southwark and Westminster fell in, and the Commissioners thus gained control. They decided that the houses were too old to stand repair, and must be pulled down. Until then their custom had been to give a building lease to a housing society, but Octavia Hill persuaded them that only if they built themselves could unity of planning over the whole area be gained, since it was too large for any single housing society to undertake by itself. They agreed, and thus created the tradition that the Commissioners are builders of houses as well as the 'exceptionally good landlords' which an independent housing enquiry in 1936 declared them to be.[2] The tradition set up in 1893 was extended ten years later to Walworth where they built a model estate of cottages in accordance with Octavia Hill's ideas. Since then, their building operations have extended to Lambeth, Southwark, Stoke Newington, and Paddington.

[1] *Number One Millbank*, p. 49.
[2] Report of a Survey of the Commissioners' London property made by Miss Marion Fitzgerald in 1936. Quoted in *Number One Millbank*, p. 52.

The Commissioners are in fact a very big concern, but as land-lords they successfully avoid the trap of the great corporation in that they are never impersonal, soulless, and machine-like in dealing with their tenants. The perfect colophon of their long story of social beneficence is a little incident which happened during the last war. Their housing estate in Walworth was badly damaged in an air raid one night, and very early next morning, when it was only just light, their housing manager was there to see what had happened and what could be done for the tenants whose houses had been destroyed or damaged. She found the agent and the builder there already, dis-cussing repair. There was a little group of tenants gazing ruefully at what had a few hours ago been their homes. One of them im-mediately sympathised—with her. 'Isn't it awful, Miss, for you?' Another, thinking of the future, asked the question which evidently mattered most to them. 'It doesn't mean we shall be sent off the Commissioners, does it?'

All through the ages the Church has been a most notable worker in stone and brick and mortar, and in every century this work of hers has been poured into dwellings almost as fully as into cathedrals and churches. The tradition has remained alive and alert down to our own time, and in the years between the wars the Church has been by no means the least of the instruments of the rehousing of the people. These three instances of what the Church did for housing in St. Pancras, in Leeds, and in many parts of London by the Ecclesi-astical Commissioners, are only samples of a socially beneficent story, too vast and various to be written.

CHAPTER FIVE

THE PAROCHIAL CLERGY

I. *Ordination Candidates and Curates*

The 'abundant shower' of curates, which Charlotte Brontë noted in the famous first sentence of *Shirley*, fell in 'affluent rain' upon the hills of Yorkshire in the later forties of the nineteenth century. Every parish had 'one or more of them,' and Charlotte remarked sardonically, 'They are young enough to be very active and ought to be doing a great deal of good.' This must be one of the very few occasions in the history of the Church when the word Curate is not coupled with the word Scarcity. Since that time almost everybody who has had anything to say about curates has begun by complaining how hard they were to procure, and few discussions of candidates for ordination have admitted that there were enough of them. Charlotte Brontë herself went on to say that this prodigality was a new thing. It had not always been so, and particularly it was not so in the days of the Luddite riots, the period of her novel. 'Curates were scarce then . . . Yet even in those days of scarcity there were curates: the precious plant was rare, but it might be found. A certain favoured district in the West Riding of Yorkshire could boast three rods of Aaron blossoming within a circuit of twenty miles.'

At hardly any time, it would seem, has the supply of candidates for ordination kept pace with the demands of the Church and the growth of the population. But during the years between 1919 and 1930 the complaints of a serious shortage of ordination candidates were more widespread than ever before. There were reasons enough, for the situation was very alarming. During the years of the war the flow of ordinations had naturally dried to a thin trickle. By the end of 1918 the Church was very short-staffed, and the situation was steadily getting worse, and must do so for at least two years more, until the candidates for ordination from the army could complete their training. But even after 1920 the position did not seem to be much easier, and for some years, until 1930 at the least, this vital problem caused much anxiety, and almost incessant stocktaking.

A shortage of clergy is the fact which more than any other immediately touches and affects the whole life of the Church. Thus of all the many post-war problems of the Church this was the most widely discussed. But no one did more than the anonymous editor of *Crockford's Clerical Directory* to keep it in the forefront of the

Church's notice. His annual preface to the fat black volume in which he surveyed with astringent wit and sardonic humour the events of the Church's life in the previous year became famous in this period. Whenever *Crockford* came out there was a rush to read what barbs the editor had hurled and to note with appreciation the wonderful neatness of their phrasing. But his prefaces were by no means wholly destructive, not even in the case of his pet subjects for satire, the Church Assembly, the latest conference, or the multiplication of dioceses. In particular he deserved well of the Church for the pertinacity with which he kept attention focused upon awkward problems, and chief among these in his judgement was undoubtedly the shortage of ordination candidates and the consequent scarcity of curates. Almost every year he returned to it, and nearly always he contrived to record the alarm he felt in words which successfully communicated it to his readers. As it was exactly the same alarm every time it was no slight literary feat to be always finding new words and phrases to record it. In 1924, for instance, he wrote, 'In most parishes the Assistant Curate is already one of the rarer migrants, and he promises to become before long as scarce as the bittern or the bustard.'[1] In 1927 things were no better so he used stronger language:

> It is not too much to say that if the history of the last ten years is continued for another ten the effective maintenance of the parochial system will have become impossible in all but a few favoured localities. Anything which can fairly be called *The Church of England* will have ceased to exist, and its place will have been taken by the sporadic activities of a denomination.[2]

In 1931, 'the situation is still going from bad to worse, and a crisis of the first magnitude draws nearer every year.'[3] Furthermore, when the editor commented in 1932 upon the 1930 report of the Church Assembly's Commission on the Staffing of Parishes he was sure that the figures given in that document, though certainly alarming, were not alarming enough. The Report said that 1,168 additional clergy were needed to supply the deficiency, and that an annual average of 588 deacons would suffice. A few weeks after the report was issued its authors raised those two figures to 1,583 and 630. The editor was sure that even this correction was not drastic enough, and that no fewer than 1,830 new clergy were required at once.[4]

How far were the annual cries of alarm in *Crockford* justified? The gloomy predictions have not been fulfilled. The curate is not yet as rare as the bittern. The parochial system is still with us. The

---

[1] *Crockford Prefaces: 1921–1944* (Oxford University Press, 1947), p. 33.
[2] *Ibid.*, p. 62.   [3] *Ibid.*, p. 105.   [4] *Ibid*, p. 118.

work of the Church is not yet reduced to the 'sporadic activities of a denomination.' In spite of the fact that the stream of new ordinations was dried up a second time by the last war, it cannot be said that the 'crisis of the first magnitude' which in 1931 'draws nearer every year' has even yet arrived. There are of course far too few clergy, but there are just enough to keep the machine running, and even enough, as we shall see in another chapter, to set some new dynamos turning.

When a great war begins it does not need exceptional prophetic abilities to see that very soon the Church is bound to be short of clergy, that every year the war lasts the position will get worse, and that no remedy can begin to be effective until several years after the war has ended. It was early in 1916 that the two archbishops began seriously to provide for the difficult situation which would occur when the war had ended. Already there were men serving in the armed forces of the Crown who had said they hoped to be ordained when they were demobilised. Every year their numbers grew. In the spring of 1916, therefore, the Archbishops of Canterbury and York gave a public pledge in the name of the Church that no soldier fit for ordination should be denied it merely because he could not pay for his training. This promise eventually involved the raising of £378,000, and it paid for the training of 1,039 service candidates. But for the training of most of them the ordinary theological colleges were not numerous enough, nor was their curriculum what was necessary for a man coming straight out of the army. To meet this special and temporary need the old prison at Knutsford was taken over and became the place where ex-servicemen intending to take Orders might receive their pre-university training. Altogether 675 such men were sent there, and of these 435 were eventually ordained. It must be the only theological college on record which was housed in a gaol, and perhaps it is the only gaol which its inmates have ever learned to love. Knutsford was a venture of faith and a magnificent one. There is no doubt that it saved the Church from serious disaster, especially in the years 1921 to 1924. Of the men ordained during that period more than 40 per cent. were ex-servicemen, the vast majority of whom had had much of their training at Knutsford. In a debate in the Convocation of Canterbury in February 1920 interesting figures were given which reveal the magnitude of the problem set to the Church by ex-service ordination candidates. At that date there were 3,300 names on the list of the Service Candidates Committee. Of these 95 had already been ordained, 455 were already at the universities, 392 were in theological colleges, 300 were or had been at Knutsford, and 45 were provided for in other and various ways. This accounts for 1,287 out of the 3,300. Of the other

2,013, 92 had died, 500 were still serving, and 1,421 had withdrawn their names.[1]

The Church had thus done its duty by the ex-service ordination candidate. But there were not enough such candidates to fill up the ever-increasing gaps in the ordained ministry of the Church. The average annual wastage from death and retirement was estimated at 550. Thus the same number of fresh deacons were needed every year merely to keep the number of working clergy constant, but it was not until 1932 that this number was reached. In 1921 and 1922 the numbers were 346 and 392. The next year it rose to 463; and this, though considerably better was 70 less than the lowest figure in the ten years before the war, and half of what was deplored as inadequate in pre-war years. In 1924 and the two following years the figures fell again to 436, 370, and 363. It was not until 1932 that the annual wastage figure of 550 was passed, and after that it rose steadily until in 1939 590 men were ordained. This recovery looks better than it really was for all the time the population was increasing. Had it not been for the successful Sponsor Scheme by which generous individuals made themselves responsible, each for the financial needs of one candidate, the situation must have been worse still. By this scheme some 680 men were helped forward to ordination, which was a noble achievement.

This meant that up to 1932 curates were desperately short, and after that very short. In 1930, for example, the number of incumbents was 13,000, the same as for many years past. But the number of curates was 4,080. In 1905 it had been 6,095 so that in twenty-five years there had been a loss of 2,000. In 1930 the number of parishes which normally employed curates was 4,287. Thus over two hundred incumbents who should have had help were forced to do without it. When provision was made in the Patronage Measure for one representative in Convocation from the curates of a diocese if they numbered one-third of its total clergy only the dioceses of London, Southwark, and Liverpool qualified.[2] What all this meant for the pastoral work of the Church can be suggested in another way. In 1905 there had been 19,053 clergy in active work. In 1914 the figure had dropped to 18,180. In 1922 it was 17,162. In 1930 it was 16,745. Thus in the twenty-five years from 1905 to 1930 the number of clergy at work had dropped by 2,308; and in the same period the population had increased by 3,000,000.[3] No wonder that from all over the country complaints were coming in of parishes

---

[1] *C.C.C.*, February 1920, p. 187.
[2] *Ibid.*, 1930, p. 571.
[3] These figures are those given by the Archbishop of York in *The Claims of the Church of England* (Hodder & Stoughton, 1947), p. 130.

with populations of 20,000 and more which were being worked by one priest alone.

The young men who thus approached by devious routes to the calling of the sacred ministry of the Church were markedly unlike Charlotte Brontë's curates in *Shirley*. They had indeed no affinities with any fictional prototype of the *genus* curate that one can remember. To judge by the extreme rarity with which he is successfully portrayed in imaginative literature, the typical curate must be the scarcest of creatures, so hard to find that our novelists in every age can never have seen one. If the men who were ordained after 1918 were quite unlike Mr. Donne, Mr. Malone, and Mr. Sweeting, they were hardly less different from the average run of their own predecessors in the pre-war era. The new men were so much more experienced in life, and they tended more and more to come from a class of society different from what had been normal in the past. Many of them had seen an abundance of horror and violent death and had walked with danger for years on end, and they could not suddenly be as though these experiences had never come their way. Less and less of them came to a theological college by the old traditional journey of a sheltered background of economic security, a good public school, and one of the two senior universities. Their background tended to be one of much economic insecurity, and their personal and family financial resources to be few or none. The candidate who did not need help from some fund during his training became the exception. The young man who has never known economic security and an assured and unquestioned place in society cannot help but be different from one who has enjoyed these blessings from the day of his birth. The man who has learned at a preparatory school, a public school, and a university the art of living in community must be in an advantageous position as against another who has enjoyed no such privileges. It became therefore the business of the post-war theological colleges to make desperate efforts in heroic equalisation, to take both types and make them members one of another, and to train all alike to be good priests and pastors. This was very difficult but it was often successfully done.

Not the least of the great blessings of the Church in the years between the wars was the unusual profusion of principals of theological colleges who could admirably do that very thing. Particularly was this true of the decade of peculiar difficulty 1920 to 1930. During those years B. K. Cunningham reigned at Westcott House, Cambridge. J. B. Seaton, later to become one of the most loved diocesan bishops the Church has known, was at Cuddesdon. Leslie Owen, who eventually died as Bishop of Lincoln, ruled gently but firmly over the Bishop's Hostel at Lincoln. F. R. Barry, to-day Bishop of Southwell, was first at Knutsford and then at King's College, London. There were others besides these, but if none had been of their quality, it would still be true that the Church was unusually blessed in this vital department of its life. Has there ever been another generation in the life of the Church when so many theological colleges were simultaneously under the care of men of like quality? Where such as they were in charge it was certain that the men would be taught to pray, taught the practice of the presence of God, and taught to live in community. That the pastoral work of the Church has gained rather than lost by the opening of the doors of ordination to young men of every social class is largely due to the standards set by B. K. Cunningham and his peers, and sustained by their successors. Of such as they the young men whom they trained spoke with gratitude and love for ever after, and this was the best tribute of all.

The situation of the post-war ordination candidate was often more difficult after he had left his theological college than while he was still a student there. Before he could be ordained he had to find, or be found, a vicar to employ him and a parish to serve. Without this title he could not be ordained. One would naturally suppose that in days when there were more curacies to fill than curates to fill them this would cause no difficulty to the curates since they would be able to pick and choose. For a few years after the end of the war this was indeed so, but not for long. The increasing economic strain of the nation which culminated in the economic crisis and the long years of mass unemployment seriously altered the curate's position. While there continued to be more curacies than there were curates the number of parishes, especially in the industrial districts, which could afford to find the £100 to £150 a year—the average amount that had to be locally raised to make up the sum received from grants to a bare living wage—steadily decreased. The time came, in the middle thirties, when the bishops had to be very cautious in accepting even very suitable men who offered themselves for ordination, because they knew well that it might happen that no parish could be found which could afford to employ them. In those years most of the dioceses which were worst hit by unemployment had three or four men who were in the cruel position of having exhausted their resources on their training, and who could not be ordained because no parish could be found which could afford to take them. The period during which they were unable to earn their living was thus unexpectedly extended for three months or more, and this was a very serious matter for them.

The financial stringency in parishes in industrial areas operated

to the harm of curates in another way. It is of incalculable importance to the whole future of a clergyman that he should serve the first
years of his ministry under the right vicar. If he goes to the wrong
one his lot is wretched and lasting damage may be done to him.
But with the best will in the world the scarcity of money made it very
difficult to pick and choose the parishes to which a bishop would
allow deacons to go. Only too often they had to go to the vicars of
those parishes which could find them salaries, irrespective of whether
they were the right vicars for them. Sometimes the misfits had
results which were hardly short of tragic. If this was bad for the
curate, it was also bad for the Church, which was unable to see to
it that parishes and districts which most needed help got the help
they needed. As individual curates had often to go to those parishes
which could pay their stipends, so areas wealthier than others had
advantages disproportionate to their real needs. The dioceses on
which the real brunt of unemployment fell were those in which the
numbers of curates at work also fell. At the ordinations at Michael-
mas 1933, for example, all the three Lancashire dioceses put together
had 67 men ordained. The dioceses of London and Southwark had
91. Yet at that time the poverty, strain, and distress of Lancashire
was greater by far than anything London knew; and both the population and the extent of Lancashire was also far larger than that of
the dioceses in London. This of course was precisely the reason
why so many fewer men went to the dioceses of Manchester, Blackburn, and Liverpool than to the dioceses of London and Southwark.
It was not the men's fault, nor the bishops'. It was simply that the
Church had not seriously faced, much less solved the problem of the
sensible management of its finances.

One other matter specially affecting the life of the curate in those
years remains to be mentioned. In certain dioceses, chiefly the
heavily industrialised dioceses of the north, he could count on
quicker promotion than was the lot of his predecessors in any age.
In dioceses like Manchester or Liverpool curates were sadly few in
relation to the population to be served, and the parishes to be filled
by incumbents were many. As a natural consequence it was the
normal procedure that a curate was given a parish of his own about
five or six years after his ordination as deacon. But his brother in
Devonshire or Kent could not reasonably expect to wait for less
than nine or ten years, and often longer still. Many industrial parishes in the north were therefore filled by men between 27 and 30
years old. These youthful incumbencies had their dangers as well
as their advantages. There was vigour and enthusiasm in them, and
it was but seldom that such a vicar failed to resist the obvious temptation of becoming puffed up. But he might, and sometimes he did

mistake impulse for inspiration and act without judgement; and his training was necessarily very meagre in view of the heavy pastoral responsibilities which an Anglican incumbency always involves. Moreover, it meant that the older members of the congregation suffered some deprivation, for men and women of 50 and over simply will not go to a man young enough to be their son if their trouble is at all intimate. But it is probable that the Church gained more than it lost by placing many uncommonly young men in sole charge of its parishes.

II. *The Trials of the Incumbent*

The 'povre persoun of a toun' in Chaucer's *Canterbury Tales* was a 'shepherde and noght a mercenarie.' A shepherd his successor of the twentieth century certainly was, and no less than his immortal prototype 'riche he was of hooly thoght and werk.' But he was more of a mercenary if 'mercenary' means one who must give an undue proportion of his attention to matters of pounds, shillings, and pence. This he could hardly help being. Even if his own income was, exceptionally, not a doleful anxiety to him and his wife, he could not hope to escape from giving nearly half his time and about two-thirds of the space in every number of his parish magazine to the soliciting and collection of money for the diocesan quota or the parish funds. It was singularly little use his protesting that he was not ordained to be even this sort of mercenary. He certainly did protest, but it made no difference. If he knew his Housman perhaps he gained some comfort from remembering the epitaph on that other army of mercenaries, 'whose shoulders held the sky suspended'; and indeed it was true—as it always is—that on the shoulders of the incumbents of England the whole Church hung suspended.

Exceedingly little of the wealth of nations ever came the way of the Anglican incumbent, who after 1919 became even poorer than he had been before, and that is saying something. His plight did not go unremarked. Nor had it been unremarked by Chaucer and his successors all down the ages. But though clerical poverty has been one of the constant themes of English literature for 600 years, singularly little had been done to tend the parson's financial need. It is true, and can be placed to the credit of our own generation, that since 1919 more has been done to staunch the financial wound of the parochial clergy than was done in 600 years before that; and though it is little enough, very far from being radical enough, and though the remedy has always lagged behind the breathless inflation of the cost of living, it is something.

The war was barely over before the Archbishop of Canterbury

opened fire on the age-long scandal. He chose the occasion of the presidential address to the Convocation of Canterbury to declare his indignation over

the present intolerable pressure upon the incomes of the clergy. It is a fact that at present in our country's life by far the severest pressure lies upon those who have small fixed incomes, and there are none upon whom the pressure falls more heavily than it does upon the clergy. I am often ashamed at seeing letters from rich men and women saying, 'We wish that you would help us in regard to getting an incumbent for this parish. We want a man of the highest possible qualifications' (that is the usual request) 'but the income is only £180 a year and we find it difficult to get the right man.' [1]

The Bishop of Salisbury suggested in the debate that 'the bishops might well for a time cancel some of their routine engagements and leave their innumerable committees to others in order to gather their people and put before them strongly and authoritatively the spiritual aspect of this pressing problem of clerical poverty.'[2] This some of them did, and there was a campaign in 1920 to bring the facts before the people. Some new money was raised and some benefices augmented. But something much more radical was needed.

The facts were disturbing and apparently intractable. There was not enough money in the assured annual income of the Church to give all its clergy a proper salary, and what there was was so inequitably distributed as to be a scandal and a rather bitter farce. Between 1919 and 1939 various efforts were made to raise the value of the poorest livings, and to make the distribution of income slightly less absurdly inequitable. But in 1939, out of 12,719 incumbencies 3,631 had an endowment income of less than £300, and 5,000 had less than £400. As for the inequalities, the average stipend of incumbents in 1921 was £426, of cathedral dignitaries £850–£900, and of bishops over £4,000. In 1927 a commission appointed to examine the financial postion of the clergy found that the augmentation of benefices had by no means kept pace with the rise in the cost of living, and that the average benefice was worth 16 per cent. less in actual purchasing power than it had been in 1914. Further, during this period the Church relinquished all income from coal-mining royalties and tithe, and the loss on tithe alone was £50,000 a year.

It would be quite untrue to suggest that the Church as a whole remained unmoved by this state of things, and more was done to remedy it between 1919 and 1939 than in any twenty previous years. The long-term financial position of the clergy was undoubtedly improved by the Clergy Pensions Measure and the Dilapidations

[1] *C.C.C.*, 1920, p. 44.   [2] *Ibid.*, p. 50.

Measure, but the gains from these helped the benefice more than the particular incumbent of it, while in the short run it embarrassed still further the incumbent during his working years for he had to pay his pensions premium and, more often than not, the dilapidations premium on his vicarage. A start, however, was made on one difficult aspect of the whole problem, the unwieldy parsonage house and garden. In all dioceses a number of new vicarages of sensible size and construction were built. In the diocese of Winchester, for instance, some fifteen incumbents were provided with new houses by 1939, and their old vicarages sold or let. Had it not been for the war of 1939 and its aftermath, this particular aspect of the problem of clerical poverty might have been well on the way to solution.

But although very much has been done since 1919 towards the improvement of clerical stipends it is plainly not enough. If it were, we should not be having large appeals for this in practically every diocese to-day. The fact is that what has been done, though in aggregate considerable, has not kept pace with the general inflationary process. But it was nevertheless probably as much as could have been done short of a revolutionary change in the whole system. To interfere with the incomes of benefices is to make inroads on the laws of inheritance and property, the rights of patronage, and ultimately the rights of the parson's freehold. To pay to every parson a living wage, and to remove the grosser anomalies and inequalities in the distribution of the Church's money involves all these invasions, and the Church has not yet been willing to pay this price.

But there were some clergy in the Church who were willing to pay it, and to advocate what was nothing short of a financial revolution. In 1935 a group of clergy and laity came into existence under the leadership of Dr. Leslie Hunter, Archdeacon of Northumberland, and now Bishop of Sheffield. It came to be known as the Men, Money, and the Ministry Group from the title of the first pamphlet it put out in 1937. This was a plea for economic reform in the Church, and it started from the two agreed points of conviction that a Church which was really the Household of Faith must order its finances more equitably, and that nothing short of a really drastic remedy could do it. The remedy they proposed was that the whole of the parochial, cathedral, and diocesan endowments of the Church should be swept into a central pool, and then redistributed according to need and to the job to be done. Two years later the same group greatly elaborated this proposal in its second publication, *Putting our House in Order*, and enumerated at the end ten propositions for reform, which received wide support. By these propositions the whole of the Church's endowment income would be pooled. Then the same basic salary, rising to an agreed maximum by automatic

annual increments, would be paid to the whole body of the clergy
from the Archbishop of Canterbury to the youngest deacon. To this
basic salary would be added family and educational allowances
according to need, and an allowance designed to cover the necessary
expenses of the jobs to be done. The parson's freehold would of
necessity be modified, but there would be respect for life interests,
and the need to raise considerable sums of new money was also
recognised.

It was certainly a revolutionary scheme, and it is academically
interesting to speculate whether there would have been any real
chance to carry it into effect had not the war intervened. The pro-
posers knew very well, and always acknowledged, that it could be
done only by free consent of the Church; and up to the present the
Church has steadily refused its consent to any serious modification
of the parson's freehold. The scheme would moreover have involved
a serious strengthening of the hands of the bureaucrats by its dependence on the creation of a single central office for the handling of
all endowments. But though the Men, Money, and the Ministry
Group never were able to go beyond the putting forward of their
scheme for discussion, no one else has suggested anything sufficiently
drastic really to make an orderly justice out of the chaotic inequity
of ecclesiastical finance in the Church of England. This group did,
however, achieve one other thing, and that was not unimportant.
Once and for all it disproved Anthony Trollope's cynicism. In
Framley Parsonage he had discoursed on the tangled web of tithe
and the 'remuneration of our parish clergymen,' and had remarked

One cannot conceive that any approximation could have been made
even in those old mediæval days, towards a fair proportioning of the pay to
the work. At any rate it is clear that there is no such approximation now.
And what a screech would there not be among the clergy of the Church,
even in these reforming days, if any over-bold reformer were to suggest
that such an approximation should be attempted.

In *Putting our House in Order* just such a suggestion was made.
There was no screech: quite the contrary. These suggestions were
signed by twenty-five diocesan bishops, by many deans and archdeacons, by some forty residentiary canons and senior parochial
clergy, all of whom were the very people who stood to lose most if
they were adopted.

So the clergy went on through those years, as still they do, un-
complainingly and faithfully, with poverty for their daily companion
and anxiety as they looked ahead to their future and their children's.
They continued to raise money incessantly for their diocesan quota,
for missions, for every conceivable parochial and diocesan purpose,
but very seldom for their own urgent needs. More often than not

they came low down in the scale of values fixed by authority. And all the time their wives toiled ceaselessly in the house and in the parish, bereft of practically all domestic help, and they did it cheerfully and never complained. It was the wives who bore the brunt of the very heavy burden the Church's financial chaos lays upon its parsonages, and they who at least as much as their husbands carried the mission of the Church to the realm on their shoulders. In no generation has the Church been so splendidly served, in circumstances of incessant strain, by the wives of its clergy; and the financial provision made for the widows of the clergy has been the most terrible scandal of all, which is being put right only with painful slowness.

III. *The Church Assembly and the Clergy*

The Church Assembly was bound to affect the life and work of the clergy for it was after all brought into being with that very end in view. Between 1888 and 1913, 217 bills dealing with ecclesiastical affairs were introduced into the House of Commons: of these only 33, that is 15 per cent., ever became law; the rest were dropped owing to lack of parliamentary time. This was the sort of situation which the Church Assembly was created to remedy, and which it certainly did remedy. The clergy were, moreover, amply represented upon it. It may be true, as is often asserted, that too many senior clergy—as for example practically the whole body of the archdeacons—were automatically members without having to submit to the processes of election. But even granting that, it remains true that the representatives of the general body of the parochial clergy outnumbered the ex-officio members, and therefore to every act of the Assembly which affected the lives of the parochial clergy the consent of their own representatives was necessary.

The first work of the Assembly was the clearing up of the long arrears of administrative reform, which the old system could not compass. Some of the measures which were introduced and passed to do this did undoubtedly bear hard on the clergy, from whom compulsory premiums for pensions and dilapidations were extracted. But very few clergy would really wish to go back to the old days when alone among Christian Churches the Church of England had no scheme for pensioning retired clergy other than the taking of a third part of the benefice income from their successors, and when heavy claims had constantly to be made against the estates of deceased incumbents for the dilapidations of their parsonages. The Assembly also made heavy inroads into the more blatant of the old scandals of patronage, and little by little it has done something to give the lay people a whisper of a voice in the choice of their vicars, and to protect them against the few really unsatisfactory incumbents, and this with astonishingly little modification of the rights of the parsons' freehold. In all these spheres the Church Assembly's actions have on balance been beneficent. There can be hardly anyone who can seriously wish the Assembly had never been created, or who could view with equanimity the prospect of its sudden disappearance now. It has done much that it was essential to do, and which could not have been done without it.

It is not only or even chiefly in matters of financial reform or of discipline that it has most affected the life and work of the clergy. It is not even the facilitating of the passage into law of measures affecting the organisation of the Church, as, for instance, the division of large dioceses and the creation of new ones, which has made the real difference. The really significant change which the Assembly made was the creation of machinery which forced the clergy to consult the laity throughout the whole range of the Church's life, and established the principle that the witness of the Church was not the affair of the clergy alone. In most dioceses and parishes this had, of course, been done before, but it had been a matter of grace and courtesy and prudence. After 1918 it became a matter of obligation. The Enabling Act provided for statutory councils on which the laity were to be fully represented at every level of the Church's life. Through Church Assembly, Diocesan Conferences, Ruridecanal Conferences, and Parochial Church Councils, all of which were forced by law to meet at regular intervals, every geographical area and district of spiritual competence was provided with its representative, responsible body which must be consulted, and on which lay people were fully represented by democratic election. They were given wide powers and responsibilities. Only the actual ordering of public worship was withheld from their competence. This was much more than an act of justice bestowing on the laity a voice by right instead of a voice by grace. The vital thing was the establishment of a principle that the lay members of the Church were equally responsible with the clergy for all the Church did. So far from weakening, it greatly strengthened the hands of the clergy by putting them in a far stronger position to request and even require the help of their lay people. Co-operation made legally inevitable was practically inescapable, and became so settled a habit that to-day it is everywhere regarded as the normal state of affairs. But in the long perspectives of the life of the Church it is an unremarked novelty, and it has worked almost wholly for good.

Thus a vast reservoir of power has been tapped, and new sources of help are now open to the clergy to use. It is true that these sources were there before, and true that they were often used. But it has made a wealth of difference that the groundwork of statutory co-operation has been created. Any clergyman may test it by asking where he would be if all the help given to the Church, and to him personally, by and through the Parochial Church Council were suddenly to be removed. The over-occupied parson is still with us, and still perhaps in the majority. The report of an Assembly Commission may a little exaggerate his submersion in business, but it exaggerates a truth:

> The life of a parish priest in a large town has become a rushing struggle to get through the innumerable tasks which crowd upon him day after day, and to meet incessant unforeseen demands. Besides the exacting round of parochial duty, there is the burden of administrative and clerical work which falls upon him as a trusted public servant, but not as a spiritual pastor. If he does manage to secure an apparently clear hour for reading or study in the morning, the front door bell or the telephone may be relied upon to break into it. This is no exaggeration, and the strain goes on week after week and month after month. Unlike the majority of men, his weekends bring no slackening of pressure, though Sunday is not necessarily his busiest day. Moreover, the possibility of taking a day off each week is frequently denied him; and, with the increasing shortage of priests, even the annual holiday is becoming increasingly difficult to arrange.[1]

Not all town clergymen would recognise themselves in this description, and most would want to add to it some words about what is involved for themselves and their wives by the fact that very, very few of them have any domestic servants. But it is still true that the key to unlock this problem is the help which can be given by the laity, and it was the Enabling Act which did much to manufacture this key.

In another way, too, the Church Assembly has been of positive benefit to the Church and its clergy. It established in every diocese the system by which both the diocese and the Assembly itself are financed by a regular, systematic, and graduated toll on every parish, through the quota payments. The collection of this quota has certainly added to the burden of work the clergy must do, for in many parishes it is still left to the vicar to see that the necessary money is collected, whereas it should be—and by now in most parishes it probably is—the responsibility of the Parochial Church Council. But the system is itself a great boon for it allows the diocese to budget properly, and through it the parishes are helped in a score of ways. There are grants for curates, and for candidates for ordination; and through this quota payment the diocese is provided with much paid and expert help in such spheres of work as moral welfare and voluntary religious education. All of this directly quickens and

---

[1] *Towards the Conversion of England* (Press and Publications Board, 1945), p. 48.

alleviates the work of the clergy, and for most of it the series of reforms made possible by the Enabling Act is responsible.

But in spite of all this, the Church Assembly has never been a popular institution of the Church. From the beginning its choice of the custodians of its powers has always been in marked contrast with the scriptural precepts of 1 Corinthians i. 26–28. This could not perhaps be completely avoided, but the efforts to avoid it, and even the recognition that such a contrast existed, have not been conspicuous. There is also much justification for the common criticisms that its membership is not truly representative either of the clerical or the lay arms of the Church, and that its place of meeting might with advantage be sometimes elsewhere than in London, since it is certainly a delusion to suppose that London is the only depository of the wisdom of the nation or of the strength of the Church. But were these all the criticisms to be offered, the voice of criticism would not have been heard so consistently over the whole period of its life. For indeed this voice has never been still, and when it has been raised it has always found echoes. Undoubtedly one of the reasons why so many delighted so greatly in the annual prefaces to *Crockford* was the apparently inexhaustible wells of acid handy for the editorial pen when it came to chronicle the doings of the Assembly. Criticism has seldom been neater, or more various. In 1921 the Assembly has already 'shown a disposition to vote away more money than it can reasonably expect to command.'[1] In 1924 the barbs of *Crockford* had stuck fast in the thin skins of some of its members, who had protested. They had been wiser to be silent, for the last word was with the editor:

We are sorry if we have hurt their feelings, but the poignancy of our remorse has been mitigated by the tenor of other comments on the same remarks which reached us from other sources.[2]

In 1934 an incautious lay member had said in a speech that he ought to be 'able to change an unsatisfactory incumbent as easily as he can change an unsatisfactory doctor, solicitor, or cook.' The editor rent him, and then remarked:

We may be held to have made too much of a mere piece of impertinence. But as long as such speeches are made and allowed to escape rebuke, Dean's Yard cannot affect surprise if the conviction that 'The Assembly is the Enemy' continues to gain ground amongst the rank and file of the parochial clergy.[3]

In 1936 the Assembly had somewhat airily suggested that the raising of the diocesan quota would be more satisfactorily accomplished

---

[1] *Crockford Prefaces*, p. 7.   [2] *Ibid.*, p. 25.   [3] *Ibid.*, p. 146.

and its own budget more completely provided if 'regular instruction on the principles of Christian giving should form part of the *curricula* of all theological colleges' and if the clergy preached about it oftener. It was certainly incautious to give such an editor such an opening.

> We have pointed out more than once in the Prefaces to former issues that the function of the Christian pulpit is to proclaim the Gospel of Salvation; not to lubricate the wheels of the ecclesiastical machine . . . The clergy are not angels (as St. Thomas of Aquinum justly remarked), and can, therefore, hardly be expected to show very much enthusiasm for an Assembly which as far as it has affected them at all has weakened their authority, threatened their security, added to the work they were not ordained to do, and made it more difficult for them to keep themselves and their parishes out of debt. We believe that the majority of them are doing their best to believe that these things are the indispensable preliminaries of the millenium (like the woes which in Jewish belief were to usher in the Messianic Age), but it is impossible to deny that their loyalty has been highly tried.[1]

And so on and so forth, year after year, *passim!* culminating in the considered summary of judgement in the introduction to the collected prefaces:

> So far (the Assembly) has not come up to the expectation of its originators; which does not mean that it has been of no value. A large number of the clergy distrust and dislike it, for reasons which are not far to seek.[2]

As the editorial critic rent the incautious speaker so it would be perfectly possible to rend the incautious critic in many matters of detail. But that he did voice what a very large number of clergy were thinking, and still think, is certain.

It is likely enough that the editor of *Crockford* was one who before 1918 had shown a marked lack of enthusiasm for the Enabling Act. But volumes of criticism came also from those who had taken off their coats and sweated to bring the Assembly into being. None had worked harder to do this than Dick Sheppard, and no man's criticism was afterwards more persistent or more violent. In 1932 he addressed a letter to the *Church Times* which began:

> Sir—The parochialism of the Church Assembly is becoming almost unbearable. It bids fair to destroy the vitality that remains in the Established religion. Many who did what they could to assist the Church in winning a measure of self-government . . . are now in despair at its proceedings . . . Their main hope was that, at long last, the Church, through a new and alert representative body, which they were told would not be of a purely legislative character, would be enabled to speak with no uncertain voice, and to declare what it believes to be the Mind and Will of God on the

---

[1] *Crockford Prefaces*, p. 173.   [2] *Ibid.*, p. x.

really grave problems that threaten righteousness and civilisation. Here the Church Assembly has completely and ignominiously failed. It has never spoken above a whisper on the things that matter.[1]

This miniature anthology of rude remarks made about the Assembly in those years could be extended almost indefinitely if it were profitable to do so. But in this as in other things enough is enough, and these quotations sufficiently indicate the widespread suspicion with which the Assembly was watched by many of the working clergy. The impression one has as one reads through these criticisms is that they are much more impulsive than analytical, that they reflect a mood and do not draw up an indictment which would be likely to stand up against dispassionate cross-examination.

Nevertheless they were uttered and applauded, and the applause would not have greeted indictments so manifestly thin had there been any other way of expressing a general feeling about the Assembly which gained ground among the rank and file of the clergy as the years passed by. The parochial clergy looked at the Church Assembly, and they saw many good and necessary things it had done, all of which could have been done in no other way and by no other body. They were things for which a centralised body was essential. But they saw also many tendencies towards the centralising of the work of the Church in all sorts of other fields, and the growth of what they were wont to call the Civil Service Mind. They believed that this was to attempt to do the Church's work in the World's way. Almost every branch of the Church's work was gradually provided with a supervisory board which sat in London, and though some of these central boards were excellent (that devoted to Moral Welfare work was a conspicuous example of what a central board should be), many others gave the impression of being merely bureaucratic. All alike were very expensive, for they had to be provided with fully furnished and equipped offices and secretariats. The assumption seemed to be that the work of Christ could not be done properly until it was directed by large central committees, and the result was that more and more power and initiative was taken out of the hands of the dioceses and parishes and seized by these committees which the Church Assembly had created. No doubt a strong case could be argued for the existence and the powers of this committee or that, but the sum total of the impression given was that the Church Assembly thought that England could be won for Christ by good planning and organisation. It may be that this impression was unfair, but, fair or not, it was certainly the impression which the Assembly made upon the working clergy; and they knew very well

[1] R. Ellis Roberts, *H. R. L. Sheppard: Life and Letters* (John Murray, 1942), p. 224.

that it was not in this way that the coming of the Kingdom could be hastened. When one remembers that as early as the summer of 1926 the Church Assembly had created two permanent and fourteen special committees, five boards and councils, and seven commissions, it is hard to see how the Assembly could possibly have hoped to escape a charge of bureaucracy.

This general impression, which the Church Assembly undoubtedly did much to create even if it was not exclusively responsible for it, had two unfortunate consequences. First of all it fostered the legend that it was first of all required of both bishops and parish priests that they should be good administrators, for the whole process of centralisation greatly multiplied the actual administration they had to do. The clergy as a whole became much too 'busy' and their 'business' did nothing whatever to increase their congregations. That there was a real connection between the ever-increasing stress laid upon administration and central planning and control and the smallness of congregations was the definite opinion of an acute, a sympathetic, and a detached observer like Charles Morgan, who wrote in a famous essay on 'The Empty Pews':

> To this layman's plea that the Church boldly resume her splendours of the mind and spirit many objections may be raised. Some will say that it is mistaken policy to talk 'above the people's heads.' To this there is a plain answer: if your doctrine is too difficult for us, speak then in parables, but do not water down the doctrine. Others will say that not enough men of quality as philosophers and scholars are nowadays available to the Church; others that modern vicars are so beset by parish business that they have no time to prepare sermons. Both of these objections are just, but they could be overcome if the Church were determined to overcome them. Is it determined? Is this the direction of its present endeavour? Is not the tendency of many priests and of many laymen active in the Church to pursue an opposite policy, to attach less and less value to saintliness, philosophy, scholarship, eloquence, and an ever-increasing value to a priest's capacity as an organizer and administrator? This is consistent with the whole idea of popularising churches by making them places of entertainment, by regarding them primarily as centres of social endeavour, by performing the tasks of Martha and abstaining from Mary's privilege and authority—in brief, by playing down. The error is the error, which is the curse of modern civilization, of judging men and institutions not by what they are inwardly but by what they do apparently. Priests are promoted because they are active in good works and have the attributes of an efficient civil servant; they are sometimes scorned and passed over as being ineffectually aloof if they devote their lives to meditation and the exercises of the spirit.[1]

Such was the opinion of a friendly critic from outside the Church. Place it alongside the complaint of the Evangelistic Commission

---

[1] Charles Morgan, *Reflections in a Mirror* (Macmillan), pp. 148, 149.

already quoted on page 154, which of course was written from within the Church, and there can be no doubt of the judgement that centralisation in the Church does not help but actively hinders its real work. So far from easing the incessant pressure of secularism with which the clergy had daily to contend, this bureaucracy seemed to them to be itself a subtle form of it, a suggestion of the heresy that man's salvation depends upon human powers, and a transformation of values which left them with less and less time to do the work for which they had been ordained.

This multiplication of centralised administrative machinery had moreover another and an even more serious result. It could have been justified in the eyes of the clergy only if it delivered the goods it promised, and this it conspicuously failed to do. During the period between the wars the Church was gradually submerged under a cloudburst of prophecy and planning, of commissions and reports, of boards and committees with their organisations and officials in every diocese. Most of them were created by the Church Assembly, and most of them promised new worlds for old almost at once if only every diocese and parish would pursue their remedies, and laboriously and simultaneously follow in logical order the stages of their planned campaigns. They took more and more clergy for more and more weeks in the year away from their proper work to sit on committees, and they produced snowstorms of paper to flood the dioceses. These paper plans rained in bewildering prodigality upon the heads of the clergy and faithful laity. But it was noticeable that the practical results always turned out to be much sound and fury and very little else. They were meant to renew hope but they drove hope further away. The constant failure of one plan after another to achieve its purpose produced a sense of frustration directly proportionate to the amount of energy put into them. The superabundance of Commissions, Reports, Calls, Challenges, Appeals, Surveys, and Plans together constituted that deadly over-stimulation which in the end only produces a dull resistance on the part of those whom it is intended to stimulate. So it is that an acute historian, himself a priest, could observe the clergy of the twentieth-century Church and remark that their rudimentary failing was despondency.[1] If this was true of the average parish priest much of the guilt of it lies in the incessant nagging, scolding, and general denigration to which he was subjected by both bureaucrats and prophets. The marvel is that this barrage of denigration had so little effect upon his inborn instinct of pastoral faithfulness.

[1] Canon Charles Smyth, in *The Genius of the Church of England* (S.P.C.K., 1947), p. 46.

IV. *The Way of Renewal*

But whenever an appeal was made to the clergy as pastors and priests by their own proper leaders the bishops, rather than by some Church Assembly commission, the appeal was heard and response was made. Of all such appeals the most famous and the most influential was that made in July 1929 by the two new Archbishops of Canterbury (Cosmo Gordon Lang) and York (William Temple). They had just assumed their great offices, and, as they afterwards explained to the House of Bishops in Convocation, they conceived it to be their first duty to discover what at that moment the Church most needed. They had no doubt that it was the spiritual renewal of the clergy, undertaken in fellowship one with another.

Let any of your Lordships, said the Archbishop of Canterbury, put himself in my position, or in the position of the Archbishop of York, at the beginning of the exercise of the responsibilities entrusted to us. We were bound, as any honest leader is bound, to look round and see what it is the Church that we are called upon to rule most needs. It was a most searching question, and I ask you to believe, so far as I am concerned, that the answer was not lightly given. I did think, and I do think, and every experience of the last year increases my conviction that what the Church does need most is fresh study of and prayer around the Faith which we are commissioned to teach.[1]

With that conviction in mind they issued to the Church a joint pastoral letter, which they required to be read aloud in church to the people on the Sunday morning next after it had been received. The letter is here quoted in full:

PASTORAL LETTER TO THE CHURCH OF ENGLAND

From the Archbishops of Canterbury and York

Brethren in the Lord,

In this first year of our office we are moved to speak to the clergy and people about some of those things which are nearest to our hearts. Can we fail to have the hope that at this new stage in the story of the Church there may come some renewal of its life and power? Such a renewal will not come by mere appeals to the emotions, still less by new organisations. We are convinced that under the guidance of the Holy Spirit it may come if the whole Church will set its thought and prayer towards gaining a deeper and fuller appreciation of God, of His self-revelation in Christ, and the wonder and glory of the eternal gospel of His love and grace.

This gospel has been given. It is for the Church to proclaim it. The great body of truth about God and man which lies behind it has been given. It is for the Church to bear witness to it. But what has thus been given must be ever newly grasped—made real in life, interpreted and expressed to meet the needs of each successive age.

---

[1] *C.C.C.*, 1930, p. 29.

Is there not at this present time a manifest need of thus renewing the hold and unfolding the truth of the Gospel? Consider some signs of this need.

We are enclosed by a material civilisation great in its achievements, confident in its self-sufficiency, in which no place is found for God or even for the spiritual life of man. The Church of Christ is called to give witness to the reality and claims of the things unseen and eternal. How can it give witness to these things unless they are manifestly real and powerful in the lives of its members?

Among our own people, not least among the young, there are many who are perplexed by difficulties or haunted by the fear that new knowledge is shaking the foundations of their Faith. To them the Church owes a twofold duty. It must give them in fuller measure chances of learning what the Christian Faith really is. It must show them that through new light thrown upon the Bible and new discoveries of science rightly understood we are reaching a new knowledge of God and of His ways of revealing Himself. The Holy Spirit of God is worshipped and glorified when men are willing to be guided by Him into all truth.

Within the Church there are, we must thankfully acknowledge, many signs of zeal in the cause of our holy religion. Yet sometimes this zeal is narrow in range and in effect. It tends to be given to sections and parties rather than to the whole body of the Church. And aspects of truth and experience, when they are isolated, become onesided and exaggerated. It is only through the study of the whole Gospel of God that each aspect finds its place in the proportion of the one Faith.

Here may we speak a word about the difficulties in the ordering of our Common Prayer which recent events have brought about. It shall be only a word, for our eager hope is that the Church may rise above them to a higher ground and an ampler air. Suffice it then to say that the true way of solving these difficulties is that men of different outlook and traditions should not only tolerate but learn from one another, should come together, study together, so that all may bring whatever truth or experience they severally prize as an offering for the enrichment of the whole Church.

Once again, must it not be confessed that in many of our congregations there is a dulness of spirit, a languor of worship, a reluctance to make fresh adventures for the cause of God's Kingdom at home and overseas, strangely out of accord with the splendour of the Faith which they profess? Is not one reason this—that people so often take that Faith for granted, make or use no opportunities to grow in the knowledge of its length and breadth and height and depth? If by thus learning what the Faith really is and means they could gain some vision of the Love of God ever 'coming down from Heaven' in Christ to their own lives and their own parishes, drawing them into union with Himself and with one another in the fellowship of His body, speaking to them through His Word, giving His Life to them through His Sacraments, calling them to work with Him in the fulfilment of His Kingdom, would there not come to them new joy and zeal and power— 'the garment of praise for the spirit of heaviness'?

It is difficult and indeed impossible for us within the limits of this Letter to say fully and clearly all that is in our minds. But our aim is very definite. It is to ask all members of the Church, clergy and laity alike, to make some continuous study of the Gospel of God's revelation of Himself in Christ, of the Bible and the Creeds wherein that Gospel is set forth, part of the corporate life and work of every parish throughout the land.

G

We make our Appeal first to the clergy. We know well the difficulties which beset them, the incessant demands which are made upon them. Our heart goes out to them in sympathy and understanding. But this call will not add to their burdens; rather will it relieve them. If they are encouraged and helped by authority to join frequently and regularly with their brethren in their deanery or district in a fellowship of study and prayer, they will find a real refreshment in their labours. They will be inspired to fulfil with new hope and zeal their office as the teachers of the people.

We make our Appeal also to the laity. Let them be willing to set their clergy free for more undistracted devotion to the Ministry of Word and of Prayer. Let them be ready themselves to use whatever opportunities for common study may be offered in due course in their own parishes. Let every parish be a school of sacred learning, wherein groups of men and women, old and young, many or few, may together steadily and prayerfully think out the meaning of the Christian Faith.

We write this Letter with the knowledge and goodwill of our brother bishops. We trust that when the Church's working year begins in the Autumn some steps may be taken in each diocese, in accordance with its own special conditions, to enable first the clergy and then the laity to respond to the Appeal which we have now made to the Church.

May the Divine Teacher, the Holy Spirit Himself, further our endeavour with His continual help. May He take of the things of Christ and show them anew to His Church in England now.

Finally, brethren, pray for us on whom so great a responsibility has been laid that God may frustrate all our Plans which are not His and so guide us by His Holy Spirit that we may serve His Church according to His Will.

Commending all who read or hear these words to the Blessing of Almighty God,

We are your servants in Christ Jesus,

COSMO CANTUAR:
WILLIAM EBOR:

July 1929.

It was a remarkable and a heartening message. It faced the facts of the Church's difficulties in modern society, but without scolding, and in such a way as to give real encouragement and to renew hope. The appeal came from those who had an undoubted right and a plain duty to make it, and it was accepted by the whole body of the clergy as a charge involving an inescapable obligation of obedience.

The phrase 'Way of Renewal' does not occur in the letter, but the whole movement it set in motion quickly became known by that title. In every diocese action was at once taken. The bishop of London, for example, chose 120 from the general body of his clergy to accompany him to High Leigh Conference House for a school of prayer. But the unit of response soon became the ruridecanal chapter, and the clergy of these chapters began to meet regularly together for study and prayer. Sometimes it happened that a chapter was content to meet in a schoolroom and listen to a paper read by its most learned member. When this was the pattern of response it did not last long because the proceedings were apt to be dominated by the naturally talkative, and constituted no more than just another meeting. But the pattern of the average Way of Renewal Group was mercifully very different. The clergy would meet once a month, always in the home of one or another of their members. A celebration of Holy Communion would be followed by breakfast, and this by a period of silent corporate prayer. Then the study would begin—perhaps a chapter of the Bible or of some agreed book. Somebody briefly introduced it, and the discussion which followed was so managed as to give every member his full chance to contribute to it. Then there would be a sandwich lunch, and the party would disperse in the early afternoon. A body of clergy who did this sort of thing every month for some years could hardly help but become a gathering of intimate friends before long, and whether these Way of Renewal Groups taught them much in the academic sense or not, they undoubtedly gave them a new sense and experience of what membership one of another really means. Co-operation became a habit, and even a tradition, and mutual trust displaced suspicion. The sense of solidarity among the clergy was greatly enhanced and the sense of ecclesiastical partisanship was steadily diminished by these exercises in fellowship and prayer; and there is no doubt at all that the Way of Renewal gave to the clergy what they urgently needed, and gave it to them not as medicine but as joy. Many of these Way of Renewal Groups continued in regular fellowship until the beginning of the second world war, and a few of them continue still. For not a few clergy these meetings are among the pleasantest of their memories; and not the least of the services which Dr. Lang and Dr. Temple together gave to the Church was their first, the issuing of their pastoral letter.

CHAPTER SIX

THE RELIGIOUS FAMINE

I. *Godlessness Renascent*

One of the governing factors in the Church's prosecution of its mission during the two decades between the wars was the tendency of so many clergy to be despondent about the prospects for Christendom in their time. The larger hope they always held firmly: if God is God, His will must infallibly be done in the end. But the nearer hope for the visible growth of His Kingdom in their own time they found the most difficult of virtues. Christian literature discussing these prospects was apt to be governed by the constant use of the word Frustration. It became so much of a theme song that many came to dread the very sight of it. Yet it expressed a real and ever-present experience of the clergy as they went about their daily work and tried to relate it to the wider issues of the whole Christian mission. An acute observer, himself an Anglican priest, fastened on this despondency when he wanted to find a word to express the rudimentary failing of the twentieth-century parson—the failing so commonplace and widespread that it escapes censure by escaping notice.

Look at the history of the English parson, and of the particular temptations by which he has been particularly assailed in particular centuries; in the 16th century, by ignorance; in the 17th, intolerance; in the 18th, lethargy; in the 19th, social worldliness; in the 20th, despondency.[1]

This despondency, this expectation that whatsoever is tried is bound to fail, has not been the special preserve of the clergy, but the temptation of the whole Church and the experience of all who held the primacy of spiritual values as the basis of their philosophy. As an ever-present temptation it was throughout those twenty years, and it still is, the most prominent characteristic of the general climate in which the whole ministry of the Church has had to be pursued. But an experience which is felt by the whole Church is especially the travail of her clergy.

Several causes combined to put a cutting edge on this temptation to be despondent. But there was no reasonable doubt as to which of them was the chiefest and most malign. It was the general pre-

---

[1] Canon Charles Smyth in *The Church of England in History and Today*, an essay in *The Genius of the Church of England*, The Rt. Rev. A. E. J. Rawlinson and Canon Charles Smyth (S.P.C.K., 1948), p. 46.

valence of the whole disease called secularism spreading fast and
wide over the world, and penetrating in depth as well as horizontally
wherever it travelled. In the idea that God is a hypothesis which
progress does not need there is nothing new. In one form or another
it has been the stock insolence of every revolutionary since the world
began. But in most ages of the world secularism has been a ceremony of aggression, not an atmosphere of acquiescence. The Rab-
shakehs,[1] the Mirabeaus, and the Lenins stridently proclaimed it as
a gospel to peoples most of whom were shocked and revolted by it;
but in the twenty years between the wars there was less need of
fuglemen than ever before (though, as we shall see, they still blew
their trumpets) because secularism had moved into a new phase of
its journey and had become an imperceptible atmosphere of the daily
life of the western world, a ubiquitous suggestion from which no
living person could escape. This ultimate of pride which regarded
the earth as Man's Own Show and put at all its points of entry a new
flaming sword of Eden to keep out the trespassing God was in the
air they breathed, in every current of the wind that blew upon them.
Against this ceaseless psychological conditioning the power of exhortation was a little thing and denunciation a less. Even argument
could not avail much for although it was easy enough to demonstrate
the intellectual deficiencies of the secularists and to convict them of
error piled upon error whenever they presented the anti-Christian
case, secularism had got to the point where it was no longer greatly
disturbed or embarrassed by having its intellectual pretensions torn
to tatters before its eyes. It had at its command the potent weapon
of mass suggestion and no amount of argument could blunt it. Nor,
as the event showed, could even the worldwide experience in the
second war of the agony secularism causes disturb the faith of
governments and peoples in human perfectibility by a planned use
of human resources and no other. Even that calamitous immensity
of suffering did not teach the world a decent humility, and did not
disturb the sway of secularism. Only a suggestion can cast out a
suggestion, and a suggestion powerful enough to catch up its enemy
and prevail against it could not be produced by clergy or people at
a moment's notice. The despondency was inevitable.

The heart of secularism is the belief or the assumption that human
progress, however defined, does not require the action of God.
Whether the progress is to be made towards the perfection of a
person, or the equality of persons in a just social order, or the
bringing of assured peace to the world, the secularist believes that
human beings have at their command by their own right every instrument needed to pursue these ends successfully. When they

[1] II Kings, xviii. 19–36, and especially 33–35.

manifestly fail to do so, it is attributed either to a defective education which is about to be finally rectified, or to a corrupt political or
economic system which is always on the edge of being mended or
ended. It is not attributed to any sin which man has not the power
to redeem, or to any demon over which man has no authority. There
is nothing left for God to do; and it is worth while neither to deny
Him nor to learn to think rightly about Him. If He exists, He is
merely an irrelevant category which may be discarded. It is an
enormity of pride and the essence of human sinfulness; and it has
been the devil's chief stroke in our time to have persuaded multitudes all over the world to accept it heedlessly as a working philosophy, and to prevent them from ever examining it, since if they
once did so, they would recognise its pretentious and blasphemous
absurdities and reject it with horror. Such are the powers of the
ceaseless suggestion and the resources of psychological conditioning
which modern inventions have bestowed upon us. It is not surprising that this demon is not easily cast out, not wonderful that he has
cheated many Christians of all immediate hope.

Although the disease afflicted most those countries which had
gone furthest in industrial development hardly any part of the world
was immune. All the great ecumenical conferences of the period
were full of complaints about it, and whatever the context of the
conference or its agenda the complaints were certain to be made and
were never irrelevant. The conference of the International Missionary Council at Jerusalem in 1928 can be taken as a fair specimen.
It was the direct successor to the Edinburgh Conference of 1910,
but it differed from it in two significant ways. Nine-tenths of the
speeches at Edinburgh could have carried the heading, Now or
Never: Make the world Christian in this generation or the chance
will be gone for a thousand years.[1] At Jerusalem in 1928 they no
longer talked like that. At Edinburgh it was supposed that the chief
enemies of Christianity were rival religions but at Jerusalem the
delegates from every country represented there agreed that the real
enemy was secularism, one and the same from China to Peru. 'I
believe,' said Professor T. C. Chao of Pekin, 'that the battlefield of
Christianity in China is not in the realm of the non-Christian religions, but in the realm of secularism.'[2] Professor Rufus M. Jones
from the United States of America echoed him, 'The greatest rival
of Christianity in the world to-day is the world-wide secular way of
life and interpretation of the nature of things.'[3] From the republic
of Uruguay came the same complaint, but more bitterly phrased:

[1] See vol. i of this work, pp. 213 ff.
[2] *Record of Jerusalem Meeting of the International Missionary Council* (Oxford
University Press, 1928), vol. i, p. 358.   [3] *Ibid.*, vol. i, p. 284.

This progressive little republic has the reputation of being one of the
most fanatically radical and secularistic in the world. Some years ago it
set about eliminating all religious associations from the calendar, changing
Holy Week into Touring Week, and Christmas Day into Family Day. In
no town in South America is it more difficult to get an audience for a
religious message than in Montevideo, the Uruguayan capital.[1]

There was a ferocity about Uruguayan secularism which was extreme, but it only exaggerated a universal feature of South American
life. Paris was its cultural capital, and the cultural penetration of
French thought and literature was 'almost wholly sceptical and
humanistic.' Thus out of 6,000 students in Buenos Aires, only 20
admitted that they believed in a personal God; and when a law
student was asked to represent his faculty in a Y.M.C.A. camp he
' declined in anger that they should consider me willing to attend a
meeting held under religious auspices,' and he went only after the
third time of asking.[2] An official of the International Labour Organisation at Geneva, who had the best of reasons for knowing of
what he spoke, told the conference that secularism was spreading
fast. His work brought him into touch with those parts of the world
'to which secular civilisation was being exported; and what was in
fact being exported to them' in the most efficient, persistent, and
enthusiastic way were precisely those elements of secular civilisation
which in the past had produced social injustice and the most widespread suffering.'[3] From the U.S.A. came just the same lamentation,
and in 1925 the bishops of the Episcopal Church had sent a pastoral
letter to their clergy containing these words:

We see in our land tens of millions of men and women who acknowledge
no connection with religion, and, as a result of this, a large proportion of
our children are growing up without religious influence or religious
teaching of any sort.[4]

All the world over people looked at the Russian experiment, with
its passionate secularity, and Bolshevism had everywhere immense
emotional force and attraction, which it still enjoys. The whole
testimony of the Jerusalem Conference, and of all other Christian
writing and speech about the prospect of Christendom, was of the
rapid, universal, and intensely disquieting spread of the secular habit
of thought and way of life.

In England the landslide had not gone as far as in many other
parts of the world: in France, for example, secularity was far more

---

[1] *Record of Jerusalem Meeting of the International Missionary Council*, (Oxford
University Press, 1928), vol. i, p. 455.
[2] *The Review of the Churches*, July 1929, pp. 387–98.
[3] *Record of Jerusalem Meeting*, vol. i, p. 374.
[4] Quoted in *Bishoprick Papers*, by H. H. Henson (Oxford University Press),
p. 306

deeply entrenched. But here too it was the enemy of enemies. When Arnold Bennett declared in his *Affirmations* in 1929 that in England, 'the intelligentsia is for the time being godless; and as for religion the affair is over and done with,' his pertness described a fact of English social life which stretched much further than the rarified circles in which the intellectuals moved, and which was in fact the normal attitude in many a factory and the condition of whole streets in the great cities. Not only factories were affected by the secularist plague. It was strong in universities and schools. 'Officially the University of Oxford was almost wholly secular in outlook,' commented Lord Elton on the Oxford he knew;[1] and added that the pride of intellect he found there, which is the food on which secularism flourishes, 'was fostered at every turn by the whole character of a University which obviously set so much store by the mind and so little by the Spirit.'[2] It was to be found in the highest places of government. When the Cenotaph was erected in Whitehall to the memory of the fallen in the first world war, no Christian symbol was engraved upon it. Before it was unveiled the Archbishop discovered that some members of the Cabinet ' had wished, or the Prime Minister had wished that the proceedings should be wholly secular, alleging as a reason that Mahommedans and Hindus were among those to whose memory it stood.'[3] He had to bring much pressure to bear to prevent it. Over the schools, too, the same tide was flowing; and one very acute observer, Bishop Henson of Durham, saw little hope that the schools could turn this tide for they were themselves too deeply affected by it.

> The rapid secularisation of English life during the last two generations has created an attitude of mind hostile to the continued association of Religion and Education,[4]

he wrote, and caused the sentence to be printed in italics. He went on with deep foreboding:

> But when I speak of the secularisation of English life I am thinking less of the practical exclusion of religion from the educational system than of the atmosphere and habit of society itself. There has been a strange decline in the prestige of Christianity. The war did not create the avid secularism which now marks English life, but it certainly gave a powerful stimulus to the secularising factors which were already present. It is not easy, perhaps not possible, to indicate the causes of the periodical religious famines which visit the civilised world. But the fact cannot be mistaken. Religion is for the time being at a discount.[5]

---

[1] Lord Elton, *Such is the Kingdom* (Collins, 1947), p. 69.
[2] *Ibid.*, p. 70.　　　　　　　　　[3] Bell, vol. ii, p. 1037.
[4] *Bishoprick Papers*, p. 303.　　　[5] *Ibid.*, p. 303.

Not all, but nevertheless many of the state schools exemplified it; and the attitude of many teachers and even some local education authorities showed plainly that any obligation to teach any sort of scripture in the schools was resented.

The best criterion of the extent to which the secular view of life holds sway in society, as also of the success of the Church in combating it, is what happens on Sundays. The keeping holy of Sunday, and churchgoing on that day, is always the first religious obligation to be disregarded, just as it is also the acid test of the success of any work of evangelism. Anyone who observed the fashion in which English people used their Sundays in those two decades could have little doubt of the extent and ubiquity of the sway of secularism over all classes of society. Every bishop found he had to address himself to that sore subject again and again at his diocesan conference and in pastoral letters to his people. Again Hensley Henson spoke vividly for the whole uneasy Church:

> The secularisation of Sunday is no new thing but it has recently acquired a new urgency. For since the fatal year 1914 three new factors have had to be reckoned with. First, the general disregard of Sunday rendered necessary by the war has weakened the Christian tradition throughout the community. Next the disgust with every kind of authority which marks post-war society has found frank expression, even among Christians, in the lax treatment of Sunday. Thirdly, the notable increase in travelling facilities has greatly stimulated the secularising process . . . It needs not to elaborate the picture. The secularisation of the Lord's Day, which now proceeds throughout the parishes, portends a spiritual catastrophe of the utmost gravity.

And then he goes on, as in a prophecy of which every word has since proved true:

> Other consequences are beginning to disclose themselves, and these carry the secularising process far beyond the parochial boundaries. The motorists and cyclists are beginning to resent the obstacles to their complete enjoyment which Sunday observance creates. They arrive at famous churches only to find them occupied for Christian worship! Why are not the ruins of Glastonbury Abbey open to visitors on Sundays? asks one newspaper correspondent indignantly. Why is Tewkesbury Abbey inaccessible to tourists on Sundays? demands another. Why should the cathedrals be closed between the Sunday services? protests a third. The secularising argument is pushed over the whole area.[1]

The effect of all this upon the congregations in the parish churches was notorious and needs no description, and this in turn had a depressing effect on the parochial clergy who are accustomed to estimate the effect of their ministries by what they observe in church on Sundays. It is perhaps the only test they can apply, and the march of secularism struck them at a point of peculiar sensitiveness.

[1] *Ibid.*, pp. 275, 276.

G*

II. *New Lords and New Morals*

For the many, secularism was just a matter of acquiescing in a prevalent atmosphere. They gave it no more thought than they gave to religion. To all appearances they were content to live without God in the world. They did their work in the production line of the factory, and on Saturday afternoons they went to the football match and sang 'Abide with me' with their fellows, and they came no nearer to religion than that. They were not in the parish church on Sundays, and they could not see any particular use for a parson except perhaps to sign forms for them. They just accepted an atmosphere of secularity and applied it, and in so doing they nearly broke their parson's heart. But of course they did not know that, and would have been astonished and incredulous if they had been told.

But this shambling acceptance of an atmosphere was matched by a ceaseless assertion of its intellectual necessity. This was a ceremony or a ritual of aggressive secularist justification by very many writers, most of them of the front rank and bearing names which commanded attention. Their propaganda was indeed a ceremony and followed a monotonous ritual, for the ceaseless attacks on Christianity of these articulate intellectuals all followed much the same pattern, and their pleading soon became drearily familiar. It did not much matter which of them it was that wrote the anti-Christian book of that month. One knew in advance just what its flavour would be, what it would say, and that all the stock ignorances and misrepresentations of Christianity would be once more displayed with an air of great originality and brilliance. It made little difference which particular author wrote it, for they all said the same things, they all followed the same steps of the ritual ceremony. There are many different kinds of parrot but they all make the same noise.

In their own spheres of competence these writers enjoyed a deserved reputation, and all wrote really well. This gave them the semblance of authority in spheres where they had no competence. To very many it made a difference that it was the author of *Kipps* who was denouncing the Church, a great scientist like J. B. S. Haldane who was insulting the clergy, and the author of *Chrome Yellow* who was pointing out that Christian morality had been history's great mistake. By some queer and innate perversity the English like taking their theology from the amateurs, so the famous scientist and the clever novelist found a credulous audience for their attacks on the Faith, but the counter-attack of the bishop or the Christian moralist was apt to be listened to by only the already convinced. The audience of an H. G. Wells would give no heed to them. They

were professionals and suspect. This partiality was particularly true
of clever young people in universities and colleges. Of many of them
it was true to say that when Aldous Huxley or D. H. Lawrence had
delivered themselves on any subject whatsoever they supposed the
oracle had spoken and the cause was decided. And the literary
oracle delivered judgement a great many times in those years. No
publishing season was complete unless two or three new books
appeared which demolished yet once more all the criteria and moral
standards of Christianity. The barrage made a great noise. It was
outwardly very impressive and it impressed most those who liked to
be thought intelligent, and would rather be dead than be out of the
intellectual fashions of the moment.

Christianity, they assumed, was out of date, and in the scientific
age its pretensions had been exploded. There was therefore no
obligation to treat it, or even its founder, with reverence, and this
was convenient for there was no virtue quite so unfashionable as
reverence, no attitude quite so demeaning as humility. Everything
in earth or heaven was fitly to abide their question. Accordingly no
reverence was paid to Christ—not even the respect was given Him
of discovering what it actually was that He had said and done. It
would be easy to compile a miniature anthology of the crass errors
of fact that these writers made when they spoke of Christ. It would
also be very dreary, and so one example can suffice. It shall be given
anonymously, for the writer cited, a man of the highest intellectual
stature, has, in several subsequent books made virtual recantation.
But in those days, desiring to discredit Christianity by using again
the archaic argument of Celsus that it is a religion for slaves, not
free men, he wrote that its success in the Roman Empire was due to
the fact that numerous slaves naturally embraced a religion which

assured them that they alone were virtuous in this life, and would alone be
happy in the next; the religion which exalted pity as the first of duties and
condemned power as the worst of crimes; the religion which proclaimed the
equality of all men, that preached universal love, and at the same time (for
the love was tempered by envy and hatred) promised the weak a posthu-
mous vengeance on their masters.

It would be difficult to make more errors in one sentence. Even the
slightest acquaintance with the gospels would have saved him from
mistakes so glaring. He seemed not to have that acquaintance. He
had not thought it necessary to discover what the gospels said before sitting down to discourse on the absurdity of the moral teaching
of Jesus. This neglect was in effect treason to the scientific spirit,
but he and other literary secularists were cheerfully neglecting the
obvious, committing that treason, and propagating crass errors of
fact every day. They simply did not suppose that Christianity was

intellectually respectable enough for them to make any attempt to
discover what the case for it might be, or even what it had to say.
The Christ they demolished or patronised never bore much relation
to the Christ of the Gospels or of Christian experience.

It was, however, easier to criticise Christ and the religion He
founded through a ceaseless denunciation of the philosophy and the
system of morals Christianity had established. The heart of the
philosophy was the relevance of spirituality to life as the first and
highest category of value known to human beings, and the heart of
the moral code was self-sacrifice as the condition of all true and
effective living. Both terms were invariably greeted by the new
literary hedonists with streams of abuse. Spirituality they thought
of as the denial of life; self-sacrifice they equated with self-murder.
Here again we may illustrate most fitly from the author quoted
above, since he was the most considerable artist of them all.

Spirituality was his 'King Charles's Head.' To this malign bent
of mind he ascribed all the multitudinous woes of India. He has
but to turn to Spinoza, Socrates, St. Francis, Swift, Baudelaire,
Pascal—very different men, towards each of whom he exhibits the
same attitude of impartial disdain—to be immediately betrayed into
the reflection that what was really wrong with them was their ambition to have their being in heavenly places and to hold sweet communion with the inherently unknowable. They were not content to
be human, he complains again and again; they must try to be superhuman. Naturally men, they must fancy themselves angels. Made
worms, to use Spinoza's image, they aspire to become butterflies,
and actually are 'inferior half-dead versions of their old selves,
bombinating on the wings of imagination in a void.' He would sing
the demons' chorus in *Gerontius* with all the fervour and heartiness
of an evangelical conviction:

> Low-born clods
> Of brute earth,
> They aspire
> To become gods
> By a new birth
> And an extra grace
> And a score of merits!

'How sour, how uncouth a dissonance,' rejoins the Soul in the poem.
But since it is ordained, he says, that we are to be low-born clods of
brute earth, let us aspire only to be the best of possible clods, to
realise our cloddish composition, that we may fully exploit all its
capabilities.

He bids us look at history, at the dire results of this presumptuous
and absurd trafficking with the superhuman. Look at the hermits of

the Egyptian desert; look at the average monk. They sacrificed themselves, performed the Christian acts of mutilation and death worship, that they might see God. Where is the guarantee that they succeeded? And if the reality of the mystic's vision be conceded for the sake of argument, the horrible, the blasphemous self-tortures of eremite asceticism is a price far too high. Look at St. Francis, whose interest was really ended with the passing of his wild and unconverted youth. Look at Swift, the complex-ridden; at Baudelaire, the Christian pervert; at Pascal, the intellectual and diseased worshipper of death. Theirs are dreary stories, and the dreariness, a blasphemy against life, is all due to this extraordinary Christian notion that in order truly to live, truly to achieve that impossible state of being, communion with God, it is necessary to commit a prolonged self-murder. They, like Paul, did not merely protest that they died daily. Stunted by consistency, they did it. Contrast with them those adorable pagans the Greeks. 'Their behaviour, according to our standards, was very frequently outrageous and disgusting,' but they had no nonsense of spirituality or self-sacrifice about them. Their religion sensibly corresponded with the facts of their experience by pointing them to many gods, yet made one in Zeus. Thus they were *men*, true clods of brute earth, 'incomparably completer and more adult than the decayed and fossil children who, at our Universities, profess themselves the guardians of the Greek tradition.' Or take those later saints in the life-worshipper's calendar, the tumultuous Elizabethans, Marlowe, Essex, the Queen herself, Shakespeare, Leicester, and their like, brutally refined, sensually spiritual, cynically religious. 'We watch them enviously.'

These things are perpetually misunderstood and wrongly valued by historians and philosophers. But the priests and not they are his main enemies. Both of them smell, as he himself suggests, but whereas the smell of a don is faintly aromatic like that of withered leaves, the smell of a priest is like something else, not aromatic. For in the priests lies the real danger to life-worship, in that they are the guardians and propagators of the great tradition and admittedly attractive ideal of Christianity.

The end proposed by the Christian ideal is attractive, its power to stimulate inexhaustible. But if the means to the end are bad, then the power to go on stimulating indefinitely will be a power to go on indefinitely doing mischief. And, as we have already seen, the means *are* bad . . . because those who take the ideal seriously . . . do vital damage, not only to themselves, but also by their precept and example to their fellows. Even to those who do not take it with such a suicidal or murderous seriousness, the superhuman ideal is harmful. Their belief is not strong enough to prevent them from living inconsistently, but it *is* strong enough to make them regard their inconsistencies as rather discreditable.

If it is held that spirituality is treason to the human spirit, that self-sacrifice is self-murder, and that our only moral guide is the state of our feelings at any given moment, the whole of the New Testament and the Christian ethical tradition is effectively taken away from him who believes it. Christ Himself becomes no more than a safely dead hero in a book, who has in history exactly as much and as little authority as Socrates or Plato.

Clever special pleading like this did have this effect for many who were deceived by it, and for them the kingdom of Thelema ousted the Kingdom of God. Many dwelt in this new kingdom of the twentieth-century hedonists, where a man's desires were his only criteria and his whims his authority, where adulteries were encouraged and trial marriages and abortions were openly advocated, and where no God was suffered to reign. This ceaseless advocacy of scores of prolific writers both in England and the U.S.A. made of Christianity a dated, archaic thing for multitudes of the callow and unsteady. Over every traditional sanction by which ordinary people had tried to rule their lives and build up a decent social order they cast the mantle of a paralysing agnostic uncertainty. They did much to fasten on their generation and the next the heavy chains of the idea that morality is never final and always contingent, which more than anything else has made our world a hell. They were *les clercs* who committed *trahison*, and they have much to answer for. As the years went by and the best of them saw what they had done, they were appalled. They wrung their hands, crying, 'But this isn't what we meant.' But it was too late then.

The Church, through its clergy and people, had to deal with the situation thus created, and found it astonishingly difficult. It was not indeed difficult to demolish the arguments of the hedonists, since they seemed to be very ignorant of the most elementary facts of the Bible, and, for all their bluff, their philosophy was vulnerable at a thousand points. But so many of the Church's people themselves lacked biblical knowledge, and did not really know the groundwork of their Christianity and its moral code. The Church had to pay for the destructive criticism of many modernists who had too successfully spread abroad the impression that the Bible was untrustworthy. Of those who could argue with the hedonists, not many had a tithe of their literary skill and could not command their audience. They were indeed answered, but the answer was apt not to come the way of those who had been led away captive, and the refutation had to wait for desperate experience to be effected.

III. *The Refined Idolatries*

The pleadings of the literary secularists led straight to a twentieth-century version of Rabelais' ideal Abbey of Thelema, the home of balanced excess, where the legend Do What Thou Wilt decorated the gatepost. In Thelema, moral consistency was the one intolerable vice, and its ethical heart was to follow gladly whatever desires one had. If the desires were inconsistent—for chastity one day and for lust the next, for gluttony one moment and for fasting at another, as in fact most of our desires actually are—so much the better. The one form of excess corrected the other and a decent balance was thus achieved. At least, that is how the theory ran. But even while it was being most enthusiastically canvassed, its propagandists had to warn their readers that these free and untrammelled delights were only for the few, and for the rest, the enormous majority of mankind who were so undisciplined that they would run to excess in one direction only, the restraints of the law and of the moralists would always be necessary. In the heart of even the theory the principle of inequality was erected. It was the first social consequence of the repudiation of our Lord and His Teaching.

Thelema was quickly abandoned even as a dream by those who had espoused it. The vision melted away before the fires of the failure to make the world safe for peace, of the economic crisis, and of the rise of the Nazis to power. Moreover, the best of the secularists realised that their brilliance had not charmed evil away, and that there was a grim truth in the parable about the house which was swept and garnished, which not even the most progressive enlightenment had made irrelevant. Thus in the middle thirties the idea of Thelema abruptly disappeared from their pleading, and they set themselves to find a new secularist purpose and destiny which should fit people to live in the new iron age and at the same time endorse their major premise that Christianity, with its whole range of deity, moral suppositions, and works, was a finally discredited and exploded superstition, of which the kingdom of man still stood in no need. Those who could sing only the songs of Thelema dropped out of the chorus of secularism and faded into an embarrassed silence. The others, pliable enough to change their tune and high-minded enough to recognise a social duty to do so, set themselves at once and with energy to the work of finding that which would not contradict the anti-Christian negations they had established, and which was positive and vast enough to fill the vacuum they had created in the souls of so many dupes.

They found it in the idea of civilisation as the supreme goal of history and of man. They proposed civilisation as the alternative end and inspiration of humanity to that of Christianity. To fill the place which God once had in all human hearts, they suggested whatever kind of incarnate representation the idea of civilisation might be supposed to possess. They put the values of Christianity and civilisation in opposition, and they set about persuading people that civilisation was the word of high repute, while to the word Christianity they assigned a value which was either hostile, or irrelevant, or at the best a lower ideal.

It was necessary, therefore, to define civilisation. What were its basic elements? They were tolerance, good manners, æsthetic awareness, the primacy of reason. These states of mind made civilisation, and religion had nothing to do with it. A good many secularist writers joined in this argument, and most of them were continually glancing at it. But the most thorough examination was a very brilliant (in the exact use of that overworked word) book by Clive Bell. Every secularist assumption was taken for granted, and he drew this portrait of the truly civilised person:

He is made, not born: he is artificial; he is unnatural. Consciously and deliberately he forms himself with a view to possessing and enjoying the best and subtlest; and yet in another sense, all sophisticated though he be, he is the least distorted of human beings. He is the least distorted because his reactions are the least biassed . . . He is a man of taste in all things. His intellectual curiosity is boundless, fearless, disinterested. He is tolerant, liberal, and unshockable; and if not always affable and urbane, at least never truculent, suspicious, and overbearing. He chooses his pleasure deliberately, and his choice is limited neither by prejudice nor fear. Because he can distinguish between ends and means he values things for their practical utility. All cant about 'rights,' 'duties,' and sanctities' blows past him like grit and chaff, annoying without injuring. His sense of values, intelligently handled, is a needle to prick the frothy bubbles of moral indignation. He is critical, self-conscious, and, to some extent at any rate, analytical. Inevitably, he will be egregious. Conscious of himself as an individual, he will have little sympathy with the unanimity of the flock.[1]

The godless civilised person was in fact something of a selfish lout, and the godless civilisation as propounded by the secularists took colour from his loutishness. For though it was held to be a state of society in which æsthetics and intelligence stood for everything and God and goodness stood for nothing, every secularist cheerfully accepted the division of mankind into two classes, those who were worthy to practise the arts of a civilised community and the many who were unworthy, whose only function was to work and sweat in order to provide a secure leisure for the civilised few. The literary secularist was perfectly ready to propose that the ideal kingdom of civilisation should be economically supported by herds of wage

[1] *Civilisation* (Chatto and Windus), pp. 185, 190.

slaves who could never themselves enter it. Clive Bell, following Buckle and all secular writers on civilisation, was prepared to write:

How are the civilising few to be supplied with the necessary security and leisure save at the expense of the many? The answer is that nohow else can they be supplied: their fellows must support them, as they have always done. Civilisation requires the existence of a leisured class, and a leisured class requires the existence of slaves—of people, I mean, who give some part of their surplus time and energy to the support of others. If you feel that such inequality is intolerable, have the courage to admit that you can dispense with civilisation, and that equality, not good, is what you want.

This is deadly reasoning. It is true that the glory of the Periclean age was carried on the backs of the Athenian slaves: it is also significantly true that that glory was a very brief candle. But here were writers with no little following who were prepared to say they saw nothing particularly wrong about that, for to them civilisation was a goal of intelligence, and equality only of goodness. The new secularist goal was in fact even more of a blasphemy against the Christian doctrine of man than the old had been against God and the moral code raised in His name.

The attitude of mind which preferred civilisation to the Kingdom of God was apt to create its own standards of moral value. The new absolute was intelligence, and to say of someone that he was intelligent became the highest possible commendation. The adjective became overworked and was often applied with considerable inappropriateness, but by its endless use it did often come to be accepted as the one valid distinction between the sheep and the goats. The Gospel virtues unite and integrate people; the secularist virtues divide and disintegrate them. Intelligence, though indeed a good, is not praised in the Gospel, no doubt because it is a term of distinction and not of unity. By their perpetual use of it as the crown of irreligious virtue, the secularists did much to separate men who might have been united, and to implant the evil spirit of pride in themselves, for those who talk most about intelligence never doubt that they themselves possess it.

IV. *The Little Man and the Very Elect*

The secularist intellectuals had proposed a set of surrogate virtues to take the place of the repudiated Christian dogma and the moral code erected round it. But these new surrogates, self-expression without let or hindrance, and intelligence as more important than goodness, were such as only a small minority of the human race could be expected to value and to practise. This they realised perfectly well. They cheerfully accepted, they did not shrink from advocating the division of society between the elect and the herd, the managers and the managed. They made it evident that secularism is not compatible with either equality or freedom: on their terms indeed both ideals become vices. Their work of putting away, ignoring, or even patronising Christ, and of valuing intelligence more highly than love, had in fact done much to undergird totalitarianism. When that desperate heresy once more plunged the world in war these same intellectuals denounced it as fiercely as anyone. In this they were neither consistent nor honest since they themselves had done far more than the millionaire terrified for the safety of his dividends to bring it about. The millionaire was the lay figure of the socialist cartoonists; the secularist intellectual was no one's lay figure, but a flesh and blood creature, the treasonable clerk. Those whom the common phrase, 'Too clever to be Christian,' fitted bore an awful responsibility for the rise of totalitarianism.

For they created or endorsed its basic philosophy in their division of mankind into an *élite* and an average mass, and in their constant attack on any kind of human greatness. With nobility of any kind they were acutely uncomfortable. It did not matter whether the figure proposed for admiration was the ordinary soldier in the trenches or the hero of the history books. Taught by Lytton Strachey, to whom Christianity was as faintly ridiculous as the eminent Victorians who had built their lives upon it, the intellectuals hastened to disavow all belief in greatness.

These men and women, so ran the thesis, were not heroes and heroines; they were not even villains; like everyone else of whom the man in the street has made a hero, they were only mildly ridiculous . . . All achievement, like the fundamental human virtues on which achievement depends, was faintly 'bogus.' It could titter at almost anything and could admire almost nothing.[1]

The indictment is severe, but also just; and the heart of its discernment is the instinct of the intellectual to repudiate instinctively all the gods of the man in the street just because he is the average man, and the thing of which the intellectual is always most conscious is that he is not as other men are. He found rather tame the virtues of love and self-sacrifice, which ordinary folk can compass as well as men of high analytical intelligence. He set out to feed his pride by discrediting them, and would have no qualities called virtuous except those beyond the reach of simple people. For the chance of unity he offered only the certainty of division, and in the process inaugurated the idea of the Little Man, rejoicing in his very ordinariness, fodder to be exploited by the tyrants and the lying propagandists into whose hands he delivered him. And all the misery which came of this

---

[1] Lord Elton, *St. George or the Dragon* (Collins, 1942), p. 28.

fundamental blasphemy against the Christian doctrine of man seems
to have taught him nothing, for he is blaspheming it still.

V. *The Problem Set for the Church*

The Church could not possibly sit still and dumb under this
incessant barrage, but it was exceedingly difficult to know what to
do and to say. There was an argument to be met and an atmosphere
or a suggestion to be countered.

The meeting of an argument was very easy and very difficult—
both at once. It was easy because the secular intellectuals simply
did not know what the Bible contained (except in the most slavishly
literal way) and had very little notion of what Christian teaching in
belief and morals really maintained. They could be convicted of
error almost every time they put pen to paper. But it was difficult
too because all too few churchpeople had the scriptural and doctrinal knowledge which the intellectual lacked. When, for instance,
it was solemnly stated:

> There is no evidence whatever that Jesus regarded His death as part of a
> divine plan . . . On the contrary the Synoptic Gospels make it plain that
> He was hopeful of escaping the Cross, for he went into Gethsemane in the
> very hour before His arrest, and there prayed piteously, 'Let this cup pass
> from me.'[1]

any member of the Mothers' Union, any boy or girl newly confirmed,
ought to have been able to demolish in two minutes a comment of
such clod-hopping ignorance. But only too often they could not do
so because their own ignorance of the Scriptures was only a little less
abysmal than the intellectual's. It was difficult again because the
ordinary man and woman in the pew did not read the books containing the blasphemies; and even if they did, they generally had not
the pens of ready writers. Nor had more than a small proportion
of their clergy. Moreover, even if an indignant rejoinder was forthcoming from these quarters, it was unlikely to be read by the sort
of people whose minds were daily feeding on the current anti-
Christian literature.

Another difficulty in effectively countering the doctrinal and moral
arguments of aggressive secularism was the deep gulf which separated the average mind of the modern student and the mind of the
traditionally trained priest. This was put very clearly by a young
woman who wrote to a bishop in a moment of exasperation:

> You older clergy have no idea of the gulf which separates you from us.
> You were educated before Natural Science entered, as it has entered to-day,

---

[1] The example comes from America, in H. L. Mencken's *Treatise on the Gods.*
Quoted in *Whom Do Men Say that I am?* (Faber and Faber, 1932), p. 361.

into general education. We were nurtured and trained to take the scientific view, and therefore your way of stating your views is impossible to us.[1]

The deepest obstacle which separated the bishop from the young science student was the utter inability of the latter to believe that finality in the field of religion, or an ultimate in the process of divine revelation, could have been reached at a particular moment in history, and that moment occurring two thousand years before. That indeed ran contrary to every assumption of the current evolutionary thinking.

What was wanted was a successor to G. K. Chesterton. He lived through most of the inter-war period, but died before it ended. His last book *The Everlasting Man* was a sustained attack on the evolutionary thinking taken for granted by secularism, but it had not quite the fire and brilliant wit of his essays in *Orthodoxy* and *Heretics*, and though he was still read by the students who had been taken captive by the anti-Christian intellectuals, he no longer possessed the authority over them that he had wielded over their parents in the early years of the century. The new generation felt that they had taken his measure and so they discounted his technique. Moreover he had become a Roman Catholic, and though this naturally made no difference one way or the other to the effectiveness of his apologetics they cannot be placed to the credit of the Anglican account.

But the Church did not permit the challenge to go unanswered even though the answers which counted were seldom framed as such. These answers can be roughly grouped under two headings, those which were part of the worshipping life of the Church, and those given by Christian writers in lectures and books. The first place among the defenders of the Faith must undoubtedly be given to Dr. William Temple. While still a junior fellow of Queen's College, Oxford, he had given a series of lectures, *The Faith and Modern Thought*, and these were an earnest of what was to come. Students were always especially dear to him, and he was at ease and at home in their company. His intellectual distinction was such that even to the most convinced disciple of the secularists it made a difference to the respectability of Christianity that Temple believed it. A clever undergraduate could believe himself intellectually far superior to the senior curate of St. Agatha's, Coketown, or the Vicar of Nether Backwoods, but he could hardly dismiss Temple as a mere ignorant victim of superstition, or as one whose belief was a form of clinging to a vested interest. Both at Manchester and at York he lost no chance of commending the Faith to the student world; and this was not only because he believed that world to be crucially important in

[1] *C.C.C.*, 1930, p. 19.

the Christian economy, but because he definitely liked being in it, and this liking was sensed by the young. Few young secularists, dazzled by the brilliance of the anti-Christian intellectuals, were likely to emerge from an evening spent with Temple without a good many holes in their secular armour. The work he did in this sphere was incalculable, but its crown and summit was in the mission he conducted to the University of Oxford at St. Mary-the-Virgin's church. This church, directed by a succession of skilfully chosen vicars, was not the least among the instruments God used to commend the Christian Faith to such undergraduates as denied it; and its great work had much to do with the phenomenal success of the mission Temple took there in 1931. His addresses were subsequently published under the title *Christian Faith and Life*, and they, both in their spoken and published form, must have been one of the two or three most powerful hammers of the secularists—perhaps all the more so because secularism as a creed was never described or denounced, and in fact not even mentioned. Every night for a week Temple gave two long addresses in which he simply described what Christianity is in creed and behaviour, and the intellectual authority on which it rests. It was said at the time that they were difficult, but that was only true if attention wavered. They demanded unceasing concentration, but given that they were not in the least difficult. The church was crammed night after night—and attention did not waver. No one can ever know or estimate the power of such an event, but during that week there must certainly have been many students who at least wondered if the judgement, 'Religion is finished: the affair is over and done with,' was quite so accurate an estimation of the spiritual situation in England as they had previously taken for granted; and some there certainly were who were lost to secularism and won for Christ from that week onwards. Nor did that happen only in that week. In one way or another Temple was doing that work all his life, and he was still doing it when he died.

The second instrument for the confounding of the secularists was the emergence of a number of eminent Anglican laymen and women who suddenly found through their books and writings a new door into the minds of the intelligent young, and who forced them to take their work seriously and to hearken. Chief among them were C. S. Lewis, Charles Williams, and Dorothy Sayers. It is possible that no finer answer to secularism in miniature form has ever been composed than Dorothy Sayers article in the *Sunday Times*, 'The Greatest Drama Ever Staged'; and there have been few better expositions of Christian morality than her pamphlet, *The Other Six Deadly Sins*. C. S. Lewis made a big impression with his *The Problem of Pain*, for not only was it a fine and penetrating book in itself, but it gained in authority among people who were not Christian by its disclosure that the author had himself been a secular atheist, who had abandoned it because he was convinced that atheism was intellectually untenable and Christianity could be accepted by those to whom the authority of reason was paramount. But whereas one could neglect *The Problem of Pain* and yet remain in the literary fashion, one could not treat *The Screwtape Letters* in so cavalier a way. The book was everywhere discussed and it was necessary to read it if one wanted to be equipped to take part in the discussion. It was one of those books of which it was as nearly true as it ever is to use the common phrase, 'Everybody's reading it.' The fact that its frank avowal of belief in demoniac possession shocked a good many readers merely ensured that it was read the more carefully; and those who were frankly incredulous that a man of C. S. Lewis's intellectual attainments could possibly believe such things read the book all the more eagerly out of sheer curiosity. Its sales were immense and its circulation vast, and by many it was read again and again. Its effect on the discrediting of intellectual secularism cannot be computed, but it cannot have been small.

Charles Williams was less well known than these, but his power on those who knew or heard him was electrifying. Neither as a poet nor as a writer of highly original 'spiritual shockers' could he be ignored by any who cared for letters. But as an opponent of secularism he struck the doughtiest blows in his lectures in Oxford on Milton, for in them he did two things. He helped forward the revival in Milton's popularity—and to care for Milton is automatically to regard secularism with distaste; and he made the Christian virtue of chastity exciting. C. S. Lewis has described the power of this lecture over those who heard it:

We elders heard what we had long despaired of hearing—a lecture on *Comus* which placed its importance where the poet placed it—and watched the 'yonge fresshe folkes, he or she,' who filled the benches listening first with incredulity, then with toleration, and finally with delight, to something so strange and new in their experience as the praise of chastity.[1]

This lecture was afterwards printed as the introduction to the edition of Milton in the World's Classics, published by the Oxford University Press, which Williams served. It is therefore possible to quote the passage about chastity which so impressed that young audience, and did so much to reverse in their eyes the libels upon Christian morality with which the secularist intellectuals had fooled so many of them.

[1] C. S. Lewis, *Preface to Paradise Lost* (Oxford University Press, 1942), p. v of Dedicatory Letter to Charles Williams.

The mystery which Comus desires to profane is the mystery of Chastity. It is no use trying to deal with *Comus* and omitting chastity; *Hamlet* without the Prince of Denmark would be an exciting melodrama compared to the result of that other eviction. Chastity (not only, though perhaps chiefly, that particular form of it which is Virginity) is the means, in *Comus* by which all evils are defeated, the flesh is transmuted, and a very high and particular Joy ensured. It may be true that we ourselves do not believe that to be so, but our disbelief is largely as habitual as our admiration of *Comus*. That is why it has been possible to admire *Comus* without any serious realisation of the mystery of chastity, in spite of John Milton.[1]

'Temperance,' he went on, 'is the means of intense Joy.' The early death of Charles Williams robbed English literature of a fine writer and the Church, of which he was a loyal, practising member, of one of her most powerful defenders against the secularist attack.

Intellectual secularism, therefore, did not find a silent and inert Church, but one which rebutted its arguments by strong counter-attack. But the secularism which was an atmosphere and a suggestion, and which constituted just as deadly a blasphemy against the fundamental Christian doctrines of God and man, was much harder to deal with. It was an all-pervasive demon which could be cast out only by the creation of a contrary atmosphere, and this had to be slowly and laboriously created. It could not be planned, for an atmosphere, or the general flavour of a whole culture, is something which grows very slowly and imperceptibly, just as the secularist atmosphere had been steadily and imperceptibly stealing over all Europe and America since the day of the storming of the Bastille in Paris in 1789. Between 1919 and 1939 it had grown to the height of its power, a veritable Giant Despair who was the cause of depression and even despair in many faithful clergy and laity, who believed, many of them, that the lot had fallen upon them in a stony, dismal heritage, that the most they could hope to do was to keep the wheel of the Church slowly turning. They did not believe they would see it quicken, nor that the light would so shine in their time as to banish the darkness. Yet in truth much was being done in many parishes and cathedrals to create that counter-atmosphere and to banish that darkness. At worst we were learning how it might and how it could not be done; but that tale must be told in subsequent chapters.

[1] Introduction to *The English Poems of John Milton* in World's Classics (Oxford University Press, 1940), p. xii.

CHAPTER SEVEN

MINISTRIES ANCIENT AND MODERN

I. *In the Countryside*

It may be true that far more English people live in the towns than in the country, and that 'if local government divisions are taken as a basis for calculation, 80 per cent. of the population is recorded as urban and 20 per cent. as rural.'[1] But it is also true that no Church has a greater stake in the well-being of the countryside than has our own; nor is there any with an initially better chance of promoting that good. Nevertheless the greater part of the articulate thinking of the Church about its whole ministry to the people has been directed towards the better discharging of its work in the towns. But one of the features of the period between the wars was that a far more persistent and searching diagnosis was offered of the disease and health of the countryside than for many generations before. A considerable library of books and pamphlets was written and many committees and commissions investigated the problem between 1919 and 1939. The total flavour of all this oratory and writing was undeniably gloomy. The general ministration of the Church and the wholeness of its impact upon country life and work shared in this pertinacity of examination. One of the common features of this more ecclesiastical research was the invariable testimony to the truth of two opposites, the basic sameness but also the swift and widespread change of social conditions in rural places; and one of the commonest complaints was that the organisation of the Church had not kept pace with this change. Perhaps the most distinguished of these examinations by the Church of its rural problems was the report of a committee appointed by Dr. Cyril Garbett, then Bishop of Winchester. This committee consisted of country clergy and lay people, and its chairman was the present Bishop of Southampton, at that time Archdeacon of Winchester and also the rector of Old Alresford, a typical Hampshire country parish. They called their report *The Church in the Country Parishes*.[2] It is one of the indispensable documents for any consideration of the health of the Church in the country in this period. In his foreword Dr. Garbett vividly sketched the background against which it was written by his insistence that the 'unchanging, immemorial' countryside was in fact changing very fast indeed:

[1] F. G. Thomas, *The Changing Village* (Nelson, 1939), p. 51.
[2] Published by S.P.C.K., 1940. Cited hereafter as *Report*.

In the last twenty-five years changes have come with a rush and the transformation of the village has been rapid. With the break-up of the large estates, and the occupation of the manor houses by new-comers from the town, many of the old traditions have gone: the motor, the popular press, the wireless and the cinema have destroyed the isolation of the village: and the dispersal of the children for educational purposes is hastening the decay of its corporate life. Many of these changes are for the better, but they mean that the old village of English history is rapidly vanishing.[1]

The history of the Church in the village during these twenty years is therefore the history of how the Church struggled to cope with these changes.

The literature about the Church in the village from 1919 onwards is not on the whole flattering, and the indictments it draws are often severe. Let us take the indictment in its severest form. In 1925 a book was published [2] called *England's Green and Pleasant Land*. It consisted of a series of articles about the sadder side of life in the country, and it attracted much comment. The book was published anonymously, and the author's name has not been attached to any subsequent edition. In this book there is very much about the Church and its clergy, and this is a testimony to the fact that it is still impossible to think of an English village without its parish church and parson. But almost every reference stings, so that the testimony is inverted and backhanded. The sum of the author's complaint is as follows:

In the fireside judgement of the mass of agricultural labouring families, the average parson is witless and lazy, a self-satisfied drone, who, by the advantage of his social position, has secured a soft job, to which he hangs on, although he knows, or ought to know, that much of what he keeps on saying about the gravest matters that can engross the human mind is untrue.[3]

There follows a great deal more to much the same effect; and then a passage in which the author admits that he does not believe the truth of the Christian interpretation of life, and himself goes to church occasionally in order to set an example. 'My complete absence would be an excuse for the non-attendance of others who are probably better at church than lying abed or dragging about the roads.' [4]

This abusive judgement would not be worth quoting were it not for the fact that its author tries to justify it by giving character sketches of a dozen country clergy whom he says he knows. He lists them alphabetically.

A.B.—red-faced and hearty, with 'a loud voice and a big belly.' He reads no books, and preaches 'poor stuff.' But he is most charitable and pastorally faithful, and a 'first-class neighbour.' 'There is

[1] *Report*, p. ix.
[3] *England's Green and Pleasant Land*, pp. 90, 91.
[2] By Jonathan Cape.
[4] *Ibid.*, p. 92.

not a kinder, more generous, or pluckier fellow. When there was an epidemic, he was fearless.'

C.D. reads no book and preaches drivel, but he has a 'high narrow sense of duty.'

E.F. is a theologian, and preaches with conviction, though his congregation does not understand him. He gives much service to his village by immersing himself in local government.

G.H. is an amateur poultry farmer, reads no book, and is given to unseemly quarrels with choir and churchwardens.

I.J. is a sincere priest and a fine classical scholar. He plays football with the village boys. But his sincerity 'does not prevent him from being a blithering idiot.' 'After his death it was discovered that he was the anonymous donor of £300 which set the ball rolling for the cottage hospital, and that this was most of his bachelor priest's savings.'

K.L. is a scholar who assured a stranger that 'nothing whatever is needed in this parish' and so gave it nothing beyond the statutory services.

M.N. is a 'genial and generous old hunting man' who preaches for never longer than seven minutes, but he is charitable and kindly.

O.P. 'has lately been sent to a lunatic asylum.'

R.S. is dear, dutiful, and old, and has done a great deal for the social life of his village. He is an evangelical and an expert on the culture of sweet peas.

T.U. likes to be called Father, and is in fact the father of nine children. He is generally in trouble with his bishop because of his high church practices, but he is faithful—'a most assiduous priest.'

V.W. needs a wash and brush-up, and he reads 'little of anything.' But what he does believe he believes with sincere intensity.

X.Y.Z. has no real vocation for the priesthood but is determined to serve his parish with his full powers. He is a zealous and outspoken champion of the poor and in their interests he defies the powerful. 'He asks the right questions at the wrong meetings.'[1]

Thus, very much after the manner of 'Characters of the First Eleven' in the school magazine, a far from sympathetic writer describes in 1925 the country clergy whom he knew. If so hostile a witness could find so much to praise, it is a reasonable inference that the Church was not ill but well served in the twenties by its country clergy. Of his dozen specimens, only one was utterly unattractive. Some of the others were oddities, and one or two of them were freaks, but that is not to say that they were faithless and incompetent clergy. The broad impression left by the catalogue is that the country parson could be counted on for pastoral faithfulness, for great

[1] *Ibid.*, pp. 82–86.

personal generosity, for the service of the rural community, and for
the championing of the under-privileged. Two out of the twelve were
continuing the tradition that the country parsonage is a home of
scholarship. The one valid and (apart from these two) consistent
charge which the author brought against his regiment of parsons is
that they did not read as they should have done—and this, if true,
was a valid ground of complaint for by his ordination vows every
priest is pledged to a life of study. But there might well be excuses
even for that neglect—loneliness, for instance, and sheer poverty so
that the necessary books could not be bought; and of these continuous goads of the country parson's life the author showed no awareness whatever. The country clergy of the twenties, in fact, emerged
with much credit from the exceedingly rough handling they got in this
bitter book.

Such was the country parson as a very hostile critic of the twenties
saw him. Side by side with that we may set the country parson and
the situation in which he lived, and which he struggled to redeem, as
his peers saw him in the late thirties. The best evidence here is the
Report of the Bishop of Winchester's Commission of 1939, the composite work of eight country clergy and five laymen and women.
The commission was appointed in order to

consider the work of the Church in country parishes under present day
conditions, and to report what changes, if any, should be made in methods
of work and organisation to strengthen the work of the Church in rural
areas.[1]

This report is as authoritative and experienced a picture as we are
likely to get of the mission of the Church to the countryside and the
people who live and work there. The fact that it was written by men
and women who were themselves both country-dwellers and pledged
to forward the mission of the Church in the country makes it all the
more worthy of credence.

On the immemorial association between the Church and the Land
the Report declines to build too much. The mystical exaltation of
Land as such, which has occurred as a leading theme in one popular
farming book after another in the last twenty years, preaches a very
superficial and uncritical nature-mysticism, which takes little or no
account of nature's own need of redemption, and is difficult indeed
to square with the Christian theological doctrine of creation. The
Report is clear that this identification is full of danger theologically,
and that, if persisted in, it puts the country parson in a false position
because the point of unity between the Church and the Land as the
practical farmer has seen it has for centuries been the tax called tithe.

[1] *Report*, p. xi.

We regard the Church's association with the land as out of date. The parson is no longer a landed proprietor or a farmer. Tithe was superseded by Tithe Rent Charge, and the Tithe Act of 1936 has almost completed the process of cutting the Church adrift from the land; and in spite of the financial loss suffered, we are glad that a fruitful source of friction between parson and people has been done away.[1]

Other writers, moreover, have in this same period given their testimony that a romantic devotion to the Land is seldom found in the breasts of those who actually work upon it all the year round. There is, for example, the point of view of the tractor driver whom Mr. C. S. Orwin has reported as thinking aloud thus, as he drives his tractor, 'I looks at the bloody earth, and I says, "Blast it".'[2]

The Commission thus began by establishing clearly its own realism of view. The mission of the twentieth-century country parson could not be identified or refounded by attempts to couple the Church to any kind of nature mysticism, however up to date. The heart of his mission, on the other hand, is still friendship and prayer—and prayer comes first.

A country priesthood bravely shouldering the burden of intercession can be the instrument in God's hand for the revival of the whole body (of country life). Miracles would happen if every country parson used to the full the opportunities for prayer and study which God gives him.[3]

In the country, the Commission believed, the Church's mission was very difficult. The rural character made it so. The village community had a bad name for being inert.

There is a lack of zest in village life which shows itself in a childish ingenuity in making excuses, a knowledge of the right thing to do . . . with too much indolence to get it done, and the defeatism which gives a new venture 'three years.' There is a sad element of truth in the epigram that 'Nothing succeeds like failure in the countryside.'[4]

Besides this, there was the resentment of class distinctions which nevertheless went hand in hand with a dour determination precisely by those who most resented them to perpetuate them in such unlikely fields as attendance at Holy Communion. The superstition that the Blessed Sacrament is for the gentry dies very hard in the country village; and what breaks the parson's heart most often is the spectacle of farmers' and labourers' sons and daughters who were prepared by him for confirmation, were then confirmed, made their first communion, and then never came to their communion again except perhaps on Easter Day. Many of the other diseases of country

---

[1] *Report*, p. 8.
[2] C. S. Orwin, *Problems of the Countryside* (Cambridge University Press, 1945), p. 88.
[3] *Report*, p. 19.   [4] *Report*, p. 3.

life, scandalmongering, and the dislike of seeing a bright boy or girl 'get on,' were to be found just as readily in the life of the town. But in the tiny community of the village they loomed larger and were more socially and spiritually devastating. During the years between the wars agriculture was under a cloud, the countryside was being depopulated, and the improved social conditions of the town, higher wages, better houses, more entertainment, were not to be found in the country. The consequence was still a deeper and less easily eradicable lethargy. It needed a fine priest to work well in the country, and the villages needed the best parsons. The country vicar had in many ways a harder time of it than his brother in the town. A very experienced priest who has known both town and country from within has testified to the truth of this:

Like so many town parsons I was guilty of a slightly patronising attitude towards country work. I thought I was in for a soft job. But my nine years at Winchfield provided the toughest job of my whole ministry, and proved to me that it is ten times easier to be a town parson than a country parson.[1]

Loneliness was the hardest and the commonest cross the country parson had to bear. If one compares the accounts given of the country parson's life given by the clerical diarists of the eighteenth century, by men like Woodford, Skinner, or Cole, with what has been written and what one knows for oneself about the lives of their descendants of the twentieth century, one has the impression that the loneliness has intensified. Improved transport communications seem to have done less to cure it than might have been supposed. When St. Clair Donaldson came from the diocese of Brisbane to be Bishop of Salisbury he was shocked to find how isolated and lonely many of the village clergy of Wiltshire and Dorset were. 'The spiritual isolation of many of our country parishes is as great as that of the most lonely I have known in Queensland.'[2] The Bishop of Winchester's Commission drew a distinction between social and spiritual loneliness. The bus, the car, and the telephone, they thought, should dispose of the complaint of social loneliness. But there were still plenty of country parsons who could afford no car and had no telephone, and one or two in their own diocese were living still in hamlets through which passed only a single bus in a whole week. Nor did the car and the bus cure the malaise of spiritual loneliness, which, with hopelessness, 'remain as besetting temptations.'[3] It did sometimes happen that the country parson caught the disease of 'Nobody Loves Me,'

[1] Arthur Hopkinson, *Parson's Progress* (Joseph, 1942), p. 107.
[2] C. T. Dimont and F. de Witt Batty, *St. Clair Donaldson* (Faber and Faber, 1939), p. 111.
[3] *Report*, p. 13.

and the conditions of his life made it an insidious disease which it was hard to avoid. It was very easy for him to suppose that the diocesan authorities were not very interested in him, and that the village did not really want him and saw no particular purpose in the things his parish church stood for.

All these things conspire to tempt a man to lose faith in the worth-whileness of his job. He can easily become a decent-living and sober-minded office-holder who has lost hope in his own efficacy and faith in God's power to convert his people.[1]

There were however two other circumstances of his life which laid siege to his integrity as a priest. The first was his constant poverty, which was underlined by the size of the house in which he had to live, and the broadness of the acres in which it was placed. From a score of sources, national and diocesan, the incomes of the poorest country livings were constantly augmented during the period, but these increments, welcome though they were, did not keep pace with the rising cost of living. A chronic shortage of money is a spiritual as well as a material affliction. It led in one parish after another to the second malign circumstance of the country parson's life—the ever increasing amount of time he had to give to doing all the manual labour which men like Woodford and Cole seem to have enjoyed a sufficiency of cooks, housemaids, gardeners, and sextons to do for them. The parsonage with any domestic servants became a great rarity. The gardener, if there was one, was usually a man of seventy who came for one day or half-a-day in the week. The sexton, if any, dug the graves, and no more. Everything else the parson and his wife usually did. On her fell the cooking and the cleaning, and on him the washing-up, most of the garden work (for the quickest way for the parson to lose the village's esteem is to have a badly neglected garden), and, not seldom the care of the churchyard, the lighting and stoking of the church boiler, and the daily pumping and carrying of water for the rectory in those villages (still not a few) where all water came from wells or a stream and not through the tap. A man who had to do all these daily chores (and many country parsons did) might remind himself that if he offered them to God they would turn into blessings for his people and himself, but it is not easy to do that with sincerity every day, and the pressure of their sheer and ceaseless inevitability made the life of prayer and study desperately difficult to maintain.

The test of whether or not a country priest is seriously trying to maintain it is whether or not he is scrupulous in discharging his obligation to recite the offices of Matins and Evensong every day, and to do this publicly in his church unless he is 'reasonably let or

[1] *Report*, p. 15.

hindered.' It was twenty times harder for a country than for a town parson to do this. Before breakfast he had the chores to do. Afterwards he was apt to get immersed in a mass of duties. The church was bitterly cold on weekdays in winter, for no country church can afford to keep its boiler burning all the week, and even if it could there would be nobody but the parson to stoke it. There would probably be no congregation—at any rate, not for years—and it is hard indeed for most men to be both alone and 'real' in their daily recitation of the services. Yet where these difficulties were faced and the obligation was faithfully discharged the dangers of spiritual loneliness were met and beaten. So it was, for example, in the tiny village of Winchfield in Hampshire, where the rector, Arthur Hopkinson

day by day, for nine years, each morning walked across the fields from our lovely Queen Anne rectory to the lovely Norman church, unlocked it, rang the bell, and said Matins. In the evening I rang the bell again, and said Evensong. For years it was lonely worship; but gradually others joined me. I knew, too, that the men in the fields and the women in their homes liked to hear the bell and to know that someone was praying for them . . . For me, this routine meant habits of discipline . . . for it had not taken me long to discover how particularly difficult it is to maintain discipline *alone* in the country.[1]

The twenty years between the wars did not pass without any alleviations of these things being attempted. The ruridecanal conferences brought into existence by the Enabling Act did something to break down the isolation between one village church and another, while the diocesan conferences did much to bring the parson, his wife, and some of his lay people into touch with others all over the diocese, and gave him the pleasant illusion of being, in part, the arbiter of its policies. The Way of Renewal Movement of Lang and Temple, when fully used, did more still for the renewing of the springs of his spiritual life in the regularly gathered community of his peers and neighbours. Nor were these alleviations limited to the spiritual or democratic spheres of his life. It was in these twenty years that the Church began seriously to tackle the problem of the vast, unwieldy, and expensive country rectory. Many of them were sold, and new rectories of reasonable size and inexpensive to run were built instead. In the diocese of Winchester alone about twenty of the country parishes received new parsonages for old in the five years before 1939. It is reasonable to suppose that but for the second world war, which stopped all house-building, the problem of the vast country parsonage would by now be solved.

Such were the weaknesses of the country parson's position. But they were matched by strengths; and first among these the Com-

[1] Hopkinson, *Op. cit.*, p. 114.

mission put the fact that he was resident, independent, and leisured at least in the sense that he was the arbiter of his own time-table. He was resident, and so could really be a pastor especially in times of family crisis; and he was available to take the lead in all kinds of village affairs. He was independent, and in a largely feudal atmosphere, such as still makes the background of many villages, he was often the only champion the poor and underprivileged could trust, and whose battles he often fought. He was leisured, and leisure is over and over again the condition of faithful pastoral work because it is an activity which needs time and cannot be hurried.

> The country parson has plenty of time. While others are driven from pillar to post, hurrying about to classes, to committees, to meetings, scarcely able to fit their engagements into the crowded pages of their diaries . . . he has the priceless advantage of leisure. He has time to think and replenish his stores; he need not act without due deliberation . . . He should never be idle but he need never be in a hurry. And that is one of the outward marks of sanctity . . . the saints are never in a hurry.[1]

As a consequence of this time to think, which the pressure of domestic chores does not destroy since they are largely mechanical, he could deliberately choose how best to serve his people and the Church. There was of course the inner life of prayer and study, and the round of services, and these were fixed marks. Being an Anglican priest there was also the demand of personal relationships to be met, and these 'still count for more than anything else in a village.'[2] But on these primary foundations the country priest could choose his own way of ministry. It was often the scholar's life, and oftener still the life of public service on the local government board or the hospital committee. If a census could be made of the many different types of service which the country vicarage rendered to Church and State between the wars, the list would be as impressive as it always has been, and the conditions were probably harder than for many years before.

But the greatest single change that came over the position of the Church in the countryside was certainly the uniting of country benefices. As the value of money sank, and the depredations of the Tithe Act began to operate, it became more and more difficult to provide each country parish with its own parson. Men simply could not be found who could afford to accept the livings. On paper the obvious solution of the dilemma was to add the vacant parish to the charge of the nearest vicar and to add part, if not all of the stipend to his own. Not only was this the best solution on paper: it was often the only solution in sight. It had solid advantages:

---

[1] Charles Bigg, *The Spirit of Christ in Common Life*, p. 79. Quoted in *Report*, p. 10.
[2] *Report*, p. 11.

If through a union of benefices (the vicar) is enabled to receive a stipend which will free him from anxiety and an excessive share of 'chores,' the chances are that he will do better pastoral work . . . But apart from economic considerations, a variety of opinions has been expressed, some clergy saying that it is an advantage to their ministerial life to have the wider scope afforded by union; others saying that it makes no difference either way; others again claiming that an incumbent does his best work in one parish with one church, and that a country parson has a whole time job even with quite a small population.[1]

It was certainly true that very few of the villages affected liked it. When it came to the point each one always wanted the exclusive possession of its own parish priest. But none had a practical alternative to offer. The Winchester Commission made a rough calculation that 63 per cent. of the united benefices had become content, that 28 per cent. had resisted the suggestion but had become resigned to the accomplished fact, and that the rest were discontented. Often the parson sought to allay this discontent by providing each of the parishes with its full quota of services on Sundays, and by keeping going the organisations of each parish separately. Where he did this he had a truly dreadful Sunday, with perhaps three or four Celebrations, two morning and two evening services, and at least four sermons in the day. Sometimes it happened that one luckless vicar had three places of worship to serve; and by 1939 the number of country clergy with only one church was rapidly diminishing.

This account of the ministry of the Church to the village has been wholly concerned with the country clergy. In the country that is how things were; the mission of the Church was mostly a mission of the clergy. But it is possible to write that sentence in the past tense. Since 1929 there has been a considerable extension of the numbers and the influence of the Lay Reader in the village, and the range of society from which he is drawn has also been considerably extended, so that the Lay Reader is to-day a more influential figure than he has ever been before. In other ways, too, there are signs that it is at last being realised in the village that the mission of the parish church is a mission of the whole body of those who habitually attend it, and that it does not consist solely of the work of the parson. The experiment of the country deanery of Whitchurch in the diocese of Winchester, for example, is particularly significant, for its purpose has been to unleash the lay power and enthusiasm of the parishes through the members of the Parochial Church Councils for the work and the leadership of the evangelistic country church. This has been going on for several years and it seems to be markedly successful. But it did not begin until 1945 and so it falls outside the limits of this volume.

[1] *Ibid.*, p. 59.

H

II. *In the Town*

To describe the work of the Church in the cities and towns is an impossible task, so many and so various are they. It seems best, therefore, to proceed by the method of taking samples, and letting them speak for the whole mission of the Church to urban England. Here then are two such samples, the one of Tyneside, and the other of the smaller unit of the country town, Alton in Hampshire.

Newcastle upon Tyne

In a vast modern industrial city which numbers its inhabitants by hundreds of thousands, religion is always at an initial disadvantage. Its people are too far from the sights of nature to be able easily to comprehend the realm of supernature and its relevance to their lives and concerns. Their crowd is too inchoate, too enormous for the sense of community, which is at the heart of the practice of Christianity, to be instinctive and unremarked. There is apt to be an initial estrangement between the great industrial city and the realm of the supernatural. Without awe, wonder, and reverence there can be no spiritual outlook, and without that there can be no religion worth the name, and these qualities are certainly rarer in the town than in the country. Religion can and does constantly overcome this urban handicap, but it remains a handicap.

The work of the Church in a great city is therefore never easy. On balance it is more difficult than its work in the village because it is always more pioneering and more evangelistic, and therefore it needs a strategy and tactic. If it is to be effective, the Church in the city must act in loyalty to a policy, and the policy has to change according to circumstances which in any two towns are never the same, and which in a single town may alter bewilderingly from one period to another. But a village has something more permanent and timeless in its life. The work of the Church in a Westmorland village is much the same as its work in a Sussex village, and it changes little in either from one decade to another. In both it is within the compass of possibility. The village priest has not the same dilemma as his urban brother who is always confronted with a bewildering mass of possible duties many of which he must perforce leave unattempted because there are only twenty-four hours in the day. Therefore he must pick and choose which duty he will discharge and which he will leave alone, and he cannot do this satisfactorily unless he has a criterion of choice, that is, a considered policy or plan, a strategy and a tactic.

The history of the Church in any great city would illustrate this fact, but it is seen more clearly in medium-sized cities like Newcastle or Bristol, with their own cherished traditions and clearly marked

individualities, than in the enormous cities like London or Manchester which are altogether too vast to possess any particular character of their own. A full picture of the life of the Church in urban
England would require the telling of its story in each city in turn,
which is an impossible task. But it may be illustrated in broad outline by trying to describe its witness in the period after 1919 in only
one city, Newcastle upon Tyne.

Everyone who belongs to Newcastle claims that it is a city with a
strongly marked character and individuality of its own. Those who
write about it concede the claim. Geography has made it so, for
throughout its history Newcastle has been more fully separated from
the rest of England than any other city of like size. Scotland, it is
true, is distant from it by only the length of a county, but beyond the
border one is in a very different country. The Pennine cuts it off from
Cumberland and the Lancashire towns. South of it lay miles of
moorland for generations, and though in the last hundred years the
moors have been tamed and cut by macadamised highways and by
railways, it is still true that Newcastle is widely separated from the
West Riding of Yorkshire. For many centuries Newcastle had to
provide for itself all it needed in religion, in culture, in learning, and
in medicine; and it provided all of them with vigour. Its trade, too,
was markedly individual. Only Glasgow shared the particular bounty
of nature which brought coal and a navigable river together in such a
way as to make the building of large ships the specialised domestic
occupation. All these circumstances, operating unchecked over centuries and still potent, have made Newcastle and Tyneside as a whole
perhaps the most independent, most fiercely patriotic, and most isolated industrial area in England. Its special character was described
by an acute and trained social observer, Dr. Henry Mess, in 1928, in
these words:

There is a curious abruptness of manner which is very disconcerting
until one has got used to it. The general temper of the area is individualistic, and hard to move along new lines . . . There is a great love of outdoor
sport; an unusual knowledge of wild life; a great deal of interest in local
history and antiquarianism . . . Tyneside is—we will not say militarist—
exceptionally interested in all that concerns armies and navies. It is easily
understood when one looks at its history. There is first of all the Border
tradition; for centuries there was watchfulness against the Scot, and the
great leaders of Northumberland were, above all, leaders in war. In the
second place, Newcastle and Tynemouth are barracks towns, and the
former is a great recruiting depot. . . . And in the third place, Tyneside grew
and thrived on the race in armaments. Battleships and big guns meant
wealth to the captains of industry, work to the rank and file, and dividends
to thousands of local investors. Men love what they create and the Tynesider followed the fortunes of his craftsmanship all over the world.[1]

---

[1] Dr. Henry A. Mess, *Industrial Tyneside* (Ernest Benn, 1928), pp. 25–26.

Such a city may have many black spots, but at least it is vital, it has a colour of its own, and it has in its bones all that is needed to create a sense of community. It has, in its very situation, that is to say, all the raw materials of the corporate Christian life. It is therefore one of the happiest places for a priest to work, for local history gives him a chance. It is noticeable that a priest who has once worked in Newcastle for a time and then left it to go elsewhere, often likes to get back there if he can.

The quotation given above is from Dr. Henry Mess's social survey called *Industrial Tyneside*, and an account of the genesis and purpose of this authoritative document may well serve as a starting-point of a description of the life of the Church in Newcastle[1] after 1919, since it was the initiative of Christians in Newcastle which caused the survey to be made and the book to be written. The great Conference on Politics, Economics, and Citizenship (COPEC) which was held in Birmingham in 1924 was followed by many local conferences of the same kind, and among them one in Newcastle. The Newcastle COPEC stirred those who came to it to consult together in order to see what they might do to apply Christian principles to the whole life of Tyneside. They decided that the first service they could offer was to discover and set out in intelligible form the actual facts of social life on the banks of the Tyne in the post-war age. Until the facts were known, and so assembled that they could be seen clearly and be easily weighed against each other, Christian social action must remain a form of fumbling in the dark. In 1925 these men and women set up a survey committee. It had Sir Theodore Morison, Principal of Armstrong College, as its chairman, and its membership consisted of industrialists, social workers, trade union officials, professors, and clergy. They decided to set up a social services bureau, and to appoint Dr. Henry Mess to be its director. The survey, *Industrial Tyneside*, was the first consequence of this action. It is a measured, dispassionate, and astonishingly full account of what it was like to live on Tyneside at that time. Crammed with facts and figures, it is nevertheless written so that they are clear; they are left to speak for themselves, and no commentary underlines them. It was this cool and lucid presentation of the facts which gained the admiration of so difficult a critic as Hensley Henson, who came from Durham to meet the clergy of Newcastle and Gateshead to commend it to them in measured terms of praise. It poured on the social life of Tyneside, he said, 'maximum light with minimum heat.' William Temple, then Archbishop of York, also gave it the highest praise when he came to

---

[1] In this account 'Newcastle' means primarily the city, and secondarily Tyneside as a whole. It does not mean the diocese of Newcastle, which takes in the whole of the county of Northumberland, which consists mostly of rural parishes.

Newcastle Cathedral to preach at the service at which this survey was solemnly received at the hands of its author by the Church and offered at the altar. In all this the vigorous co-operation of the Free Churches played a big and perhaps a decisive part, and the salary of Dr. Mess was provided by the munificence of a congregationalist layman.

The facts of social life on Tyneside in 1928, as the survey revealed them, were certainly disturbing; and they pointed to a poverty in the quality of family life of the majority of people which no Christian who believed the creed could tolerate with equanimity, for by it the doctrine of man implicit in the Incarnation was derided. By the building of ships and the hewing of coal Tyneside chiefly lived, and unemployment in both these basic industries was alarming indeed. In the shipbuilding and ship repairing industries between July 1923 and October 1926 the percentage of workers unemployed had varied from 30·6 to 61·3. At the beginning of this period the figure had stood at 59·4. Then it had gradually dropped to 30·6 in July 1924. From that date until October 1926 there had been a steep and steady rise to the horrible figure of 61·3. 'A bitter record,' commented the survey (55).[1] The situation in the collieries was no better. Miners working at the coal face could rarely earn £3 a week, and for that they were 'working longer hours than at any time during the last sixty years' (71). Most of the Tyneside coal, being hard steam coal, was exported. The general strike and the long coal strike which followed it had therefore been specially disastrous to Tyneside. Unemployment was heavy, but the poverty among those in full employment was scarcely less severe than among the unemployed, for at that date the unemployment insurance was not subject to the heavy depredations of the means test. Of all industries on Tyneside coal-mining seemed the most hopeless, and those belonging to it, both management and workers, had largely lost their faith in its future; and this failure of faith had been not allayed but rather exacerbated by the innumerable state commissions and reports which had been consistently unregarded. In coal-mining

the present situation is deplorable. Many collieries have closed down; the majority of others are working at a loss. Those men who have employment are working longer hours and earning less than for many years past. Many are unemployed, and there can be no doubt that there is considerable distress among them (74).

In housing the Tyneside situation was also menacing. The slums were as extensive as in most other industrial areas. The overcrowding was worse. In Newcastle itself, in 1921, 11·5 per cent. of all the families

---

[1] The figures given in brackets in the text refer to the relevant pages in the *Survey*.

were living in one room, and 25·3 per cent. in two rooms; and in Jarrow and Gateshead the figures were still worse. In England and Wales as a whole those two figures were 3·6 and 10·5. It meant that 33·6 per cent. of the families of Tyneside, or over 250,000 persons, were living in what by the official standards of the Ministry of Health were overcrowded conditions. This was a statistical distinction which Tyneside shared with Finsbury and Shoreditch in the County of London, but with nowhere else in England and Wales (79, 80).

The statistical consequences of Tyneside slums and overcrowding are set out in the tables of figures relating to infant mortality and the incidence of tuberculosis. As regards infant mortality the figures for the whole area of Tyneside were very high, but for Newcastle itself they had dropped between 1911 and 1925 from 120 to 96 per 1,000 live births, though this was 13 higher than the average of county boroughs in England and Wales (104). But the figures for tuberculosis on Tyneside were black indeed. Some of its towns ranked among the worst in the whole country. In Newcastle between 1921 and 1925, 1·525 out of every 1,000 deaths were due to this disease. The Survey gives the figures for twelve other towns in all parts of England and Scotland in the same period. They stretch from Dundee to Coventry and from Hull to Barrow, and among all these towns only Salford had a worse record than Newcastle. Newcastle itself paled by comparison with Hebburn and Jarrow, which had the horrifying totals of 1·812 and 2·387 (110).

The Survey covered nearly all the aspects of communal life in the area, and came at last to conclude that in spite of much that made the social life on Tyneside a hopeful experience the whole picture was 'very dark' (165). Dr. Mess had been forced to present the picture in terms of many rows of figures and statistical tables.

> But its real subject is the lives of men and women and of their children. . . . The overcrowding figures bring to mind homes so tiny and so crammed that they almost seem to protrude bedsteads as one passes along the street. . . . The health figures speak tragically to anyone who has sensibilities; they tell of house after house where there is some tuberculous member of the family, a child with swollen glands, a father in a sanatorium, or a daughter dying slowly in one of the two rooms which constitute a home. That violently fluctuating curve of unemployment (in the graph) corresponds to many hundreds of housewives who are trying to meet the ends of their households, with no assurance as to what money will be forthcoming on the morrow, or whether there will be any money at all (165).

And to set against all this in the opposite scale, Dr. Mess found but little. The voluntary social services, indeed, existed, and 'the great majority of social workers are members of Christian Churches' (142), but they were ill-organised, and there were many aspects of need they did not cover. Of the schools, he declared, 'One cannot believe that Newcastle will be content for ever to have its elementary schools so much worse staffed than those of Bradford and Nottingham, towns which it reckons as its peers' (167).

Such was the social situation in 1928. Bad as it was, it was presently to become even worse, for the world economic crisis was not yet in full swing, nor was the means test operating among the unemployed. But it was quite bad enough to be an intolerable burden to those on whom its weight fell, and an affront to the social conscience by which all Christians who really believe their religion are bound to be burdened. If therefore the people looked to the Churches for help and hope they looked to the place from which these graces ought to come. Dr. Mess's Survey was a highly important part of the Christian response to that unspoken cry. But it was inevitably the work of a very few highly gifted Christians. If the Churches were to work towards the remedying of the state of affairs which the Survey revealed, they must themselves be strong. What, in 1928 was their strength?

The Survey has a chapter on this, but its author began it by remarking that it was bound to be an unsatisfactory account. One cannot compute the health of Churches by counting heads, and yet this was the only way open to the author to use. Moreover it was not a scientifically satisfactory way in itself. Different Churches kept their statistics according to different methods, and none kept them fully or exactly. Even if the ecclesiastical statisticians had taken lessons from the Board of Trade and compiled their tables after the manner of Whitehall, nobody could possibly determine what the figures would signify in terms of spiritual energy. None the less the Survey did gather a number of interesting figures about the life and work of the Tyneside Churches. All of them relate to the year 1925.

The Anglican Church was baptising 70 per cent. and the Roman Catholic Church 18 per cent. of all the babies born. In the Sunday Schools of the Anglican Church were 19·5 per cent. of the children, as opposed to 4 per cent. for the Presbyterians and 8·4 per cent. for the Wesleyans. 16 per cent. of the children in the elementary schools were Roman Catholics. For Confirmations, Easter Communions, and Membership of the Electoral Rolls only the Anglican figures are given. They show that 3,519 adolescents were confirmed—about 20 per cent. of all who might have been; that 31,540 people made their communion on Easter Day and 2,016 during Easter week; and that there were 46,658 names on the electoral rolls, or 9 per cent. of the population over eighteen. The only comment the Survey makes on these figures is that it is impossible to measure whether the Anglican Church had been losing or gaining ground in the previous twenty years. On the other hand the Survey had no doubt that the Roman Catholics had gained ground, and that very quickly, until in 1925 they constituted one-eighth of the population.

In addition to compiling these statistics the organisers of the Survey called in volunteers and took two counts of people going to church on an average Sunday first in Wallsend and then in South Shields. The Wallsend census was taken on a first Sunday in February 1928. Only adults and adolescents over fourteen were counted, and the count was taken at every service in every church of whatever denomination. The total population over 14 years of age in Wallsend was 33,000. Of these, 7,698 went to church that day—that is, about one-fifth. Fifteen per cent. went to Anglican churches, 42 per cent. to Roman Catholic churches, and 43 per cent. to all the Free Churches put together. The census showed also that adolescents of every Church attended twice as well as adults.

The census in South Shields, which of course is in the diocese of Durham and ten miles from Newcastle, was taken on a dull and cold May Sunday in the same year. Here the Church of England had 30 per cent. of the attendances, the Roman Catholics 22 per cent., and the Free Churches 48 per cent. The attendances amounted to about an eighth of the population, and again adolescents attended better than adults.

The figures are certainly less depressing than one might expect. In these two sample townships there was no question of 'less than a tenth of the population having any connection with institutional religion.' But if one mentions this census to those who know Tyneside well, one is apt to be told that Wallsend is exceptional and that church life there has always been very strong. The local people would say that the South Shields figures would be nearer the average for all Tyneside. Suppose then that these South Shields figures be taken as representing Tyneside as a whole, it would mean that on an ordinary Sunday in May 1928, one-eighth of the whole population went to church and could be classed as habitual churchgoers. That would give a total of roughly 102,300 churchgoers on Tyneside, since the population at the 1921 census was 818,422. Of these 102,300 (and working still on the South Shields standards) the Church of England claimed 30 per cent., that is 30,690. Judging the city of Newcastle itself on the same standards the position would be that out of a population of 275,000, 34,375 were churchgoers, and of these 10,410 belonged to the Church of England. These figures are so rough and approximate that they would make a trained statistician blush, and the mere citing of them may cause the spiritual purist to utter his warning that spiritual strength must not be estimated by counting heads. But allowing for both these cautions, and allowing also for the further unknown factor that no one knows or can ever know what proportion of churchgoers are spiritual passengers, it remains true that the Church on Tyneside and in Newcastle could number its adherents in tens of thousands, and that among them there was sufficient force and to spare to make a great deal of difference to the quality of social life on Tyneside if it could be effectively harnessed and set in motion. It is also a significant indication of the health of the Church that throughout this period of great industrial depression and then of war the standard of missionary giving in the diocese remained relatively stable. Annual contributions to S.P.G. rose from £2,828 to £3,477 between 1919 and 1920, then fell slowly to £2,095 in 1935, and then gradually rose to £3,589 in 1944.

On Tyneside between the wars a number of men were serving who were quite capable of doing this marshalling of spiritual power, and were determined that it should be done. Canon Oliver Quick, one of the two or three most considerable theologians of his generation, was at the cathedral. Among his colleagues there was Archdeacon Leslie Hunter (now Bishop of Sheffield) a man who has always had more numerous contacts with more varied spheres of life than it seems possible for one man to sustain, and who has a genius for finding the exactly right man for a particular job and persuading him to do it. There was Ronald Hall at St. Luke's, Newcastle, and his curate William Greer, deep friends between whom life has now put half a world since the one is Bishop of Hong Kong and the other of Manchester. These two would be bound to make anything move that they touched. At St. John's, Newcastle, there was the present Bishop of the diocese, Dr. Noel Hudson, with a large and devoted congregation to form much of the backbone of any enterprise they espoused. At Gateshead, and later at Sunderland, Leonard Wilson reigned, and was heart and soul in the social movement. At Wallsend there was Canon Osborne, a disciple of Dolling, an erudite theologian, and a socialist. Behind all they did lay the work of Canon Newsom, Vicar of Newcastle, who had a perfect genius for friendship and for creating fellowship. These worked very closely together in those years. They secured the co-operation of the Free Churches, and were able to build in all sorts of ways the necessary bridges between the Churches, the agencies for social welfare, the trades union world, and the university.

Without this co-operation the whole effort must have been heavily handicapped, for the Free Churches were very strong. Much of the drive for social reform came from their ranks. The work done in this field by the Congregational Church of St. James was of a specially high order, and the Central Methodist Church seemed to supply a considerable part of the Town Council. For over thirty years one

H*

of the leading social workers of Newcastle was Miss Theresa Merz, a member of the Society of Friends, but she eventually made her pilgrimage into the Anglican Church. The support of the trades unionists was also very important, for the trade union leaders counted for much on Tyneside, and many of them were fine Christian men. They did not officially co-operate very much in the work of the Tyneside Council of Social Service, but unofficially they gave it both sympathy and much effective help. From the Anglican side there was a tradition of social consciousness which had been slowly built before and during the war by such men as Bishop Lloyd, Cyril Hepher of St. John's, Mole of St. Philip's, and others. All these were thoroughly in touch with the life of the Newcastle community as a whole, and their work helped to build the basis on which the Tyneside Council of Social Service could rest secure.

Certainly there were giants in the Church on Tyneside. But these giants were not only to be found among the clergy. Many laymen of all kinds supported all they did, and some did far more than support. And here again, as so often elsewhere in this book, one sample must stand for a host. It is safe to say that much that was done for our Lord on Tyneside in those years would not have been done, or would have been done differently, had James Andrew Halliday not been living. He had left school at the age of fourteen and given his working life to the municipal gasworks, where he eventually became a senior clerk. He was also a Plymouth Brother who became a Quaker, and a Quaker who became an Anglican, being drawn to take this last step, as are so many Free Churchmen, by his need of sacramental worship. A politician (in the Liberal interest) and a lifelong pacifist, he was also a man who valued and combined in a fruitful synthesis the things of mind and spirit. He was a very exact man, the born secretary of any organisation, tireless and persistent, and completely devoted to any cause he made his own. Perhaps the core of his insight was his belief that 'truth and light are best sought in the company of friends.'[1] All his life was given to the creation of that kind of friendship, and though he was an austere man, whose austerity was felt, he 'probably started more societies and study-groups than any other man in Newcastle.'[2] They ranged from the Economic Society to the Theological Society, of which the second was profoundly influential; and although not every society he began was successful, a high proportion were, and taken together they did much to demonstrate to the Tynesider that things are done best by friends, and that between men of very different tradition friendship is per-

---

[1] *James Andrew Halliday*, A Memorial Lecture by Leslie S. Hunter, Bishop of Sheffield (privately printed, 1932), p. 7.
[2] *Ibid.*, p. 16.

fectly possible if sought against a spiritual background. In any
society which he started 'his ambition was to do the heavy work of
planning, organising, and executing, and to leave for others the prestige of more honoured positions.'[1] Of such as he democracy is made,
and when the Hallidays all die and are not replaced democracy will
die with them.

Intellectually his three loves were political science, economics, and
theology, and it was his interest in and deep knowledge of theology,
eagerly encouraged by Oliver Quick, which brought him at last into
the Church of England, where he became a sidesman in the cathedral.
But more important by far than this was his starting of the Theological Society, ultimately the most influential of all his ventures.
The Christian social work on Tyneside in those years rested on two
pillars. One was the Tyneside Council of Social Service, which was
Dr. Mess's Survey Committee continued under another name. The
other was the Theological Society which Halliday founded.

It was not to be just a lecture society, still less one for debate, least of all
one for superficial interdenominational fraternities. It was to be a society
for the study of truth in the sincere and peaceable atmosphere of spiritual
fellowship.[2]

The last sentence has the typical Halliday hallmark. Quick was its
first chairman, and Canon Osborne succeeded him. Halliday was its
indispensable and indefatigable secretary. The 'Theological' quickly
became one of the best societies of its kind in the country. In some
ways it was unique. It had a membership of over two hundred, and
it was the heart and centre of interdenominational fellowship on
Tyneside, teaching Christians of different Churches to be together at
the levels of prayer and thought, and providing the best possible
basis for their fruitful co-operation in social work.

The Survey had noted that for most of the social service which was
being done at all Christians were responsible. The new Tyneside
Council of Social Service provided the leadership and organisation
and the Theological Society provided the experience of inter-denominational friendship and co-operation by which this social service was
informed, augmented, and made more effective than it had ever been.
The Churches therefore set to work with a will to do what they could
to help in the remedying of the social evils which the Survey had dis-
closed, and to demonstrate that a Christian Church must always
care as profoundly for the material as for the spiritual sufferings of
people. This charge they bore in a great variety of ways, of which
these three perhaps remain most vividly in memory after the passage
of the years.

[1] *Ibid.*, p. 16.   [2] *Ibid.*, p. 12.

It was on Christmas Day, 1927, that the first steps were taken which led to the foundation of the Newcastle Housing Improvement Trust. A few days before, Dr. Ronald Hall, then vicar of St. Luke's, had been handed the literature of the St. Pancras housing effort by a friend who remarked 'I have a little money in this,' and he knew that 'a little' was all she could have! On Christmas Day he preached on the subject of Homes, using the St. Pancras papers as examples. After the service a man said to him, 'Something must be done about this.' Something was, and that man is now Chairman of the Trust. Backing for the scheme came from many other churches and chapels, particularly from the parish of St. John, and the first share was bought by a missionary in China. This Trust reconditioned some sixty houses in the centre of the city, and turned them into model workers' flats, which are managed on the Octavia Hill plan; and the enterprise was copied by other Christian citizens in some other parts of Tyneside.

The blight of mass unemployment smote Tyneside with special severity, and the suffering here, as everywhere else in Britain, was made far worse than it need have been by the means test. To meet this challenge the Christians of Tyneside found they had to do just what other Christians from other 'distressed areas' were also doing, that is, feeding the undernourished and providing occupation for the enforced leisure of so many thousands. The feeding of the hungry was done in many different ways in different parishes, but nowhere more memorably than in St. Luke's.

The vicar and his curate found that it was on Wednesdays and Thursdays that people were hungriest, for by then the pitifully meagre benefit paid out on Fridays was often completely exhausted. At first they started a communal kitchen, but found that Tynesiders were too proudly independent to come to it. So they collected a cart, loaded it with soup, minced meat, and rice pudding, and the vicar pushed it round the parish while the curate walked in front ringing a bell. As they passed down the streets people came to their doors, paid the nominal sum of twopence so that it was not 'charity,' and were given heaped plates full of the hot, nourishing food. This piece of work opened the way to another which was far more difficult, the building of a bridge between the communists and the Christian congregation. The curate got into touch with the chairman of the local communists and asked for his co-operation in the planning of recreation for the unemployed. But the communist kept on insisting that it was food and not recreation that the unemployed people wanted. He hit his belt and said, 'It's here we need it.' The soup and minced meat cart proved to him that the Church too realised this need, and that it was actually doing what it could to supply the need. Thus when he was asked to come to the Saturday night group meetings of the congregation he felt unable to refuse, and agreed to come, 'If I'm not in gaol.'

The Christian citizens of Tyneside also at that time flung themselves into the task of providing occupational centres in many places for the unemployed, and this enterprise, started at first independently in a handful of parishes, was taken over by the Tyneside Council of Social Service, and greatly expanded and developed by that body, which was in effect the Christian Churches in social action. This sort of work was being done all over the country, wherever the presence of many unemployed workers made it necessary, and nearly always it was Christians, acting under the inspiration of their Christianity who did the bulk of it.

When, in 1939, the war began it was not long before the normal ways in which Christians express their sense of social responsibility were made impossible to follow. The building of houses and the succouring of physical and spiritual distress, these are the obvious paths for ordinary Christians to follow who believe that their Christianity must embrace the whole of life. Between 1919 and 1939 the feats of Christian social work which can be described in a narrative were nearly always to build houses and to help the unemployed. What Christians have done for hospitals, though probably greater in range and extent, cannot well be written because a work that is a matter of routine, performed steadily for generations, rarely affords any particular story to tell. After 1939 nobody, whether local authority or Christian body, could build houses. Very soon there were mercifully no hungry left to feed and no unemployed to succour. Nor does it now look as though within foreseeable time there will be much room for private enterprise by Christians in the meeting of social need, excepting in the really difficult and exacting work of moral welfare. The Welfare State is a particularly jealous and touchy institution which regards welfare attempted by anyone except its own officials as a particularly heinous form of impudence and lèse-majesté.

Inevitably, therefore, a Church as vital and alive as is the Church on Tyneside has had to find other forms of self-expression. A development which began in a small way in 1927 has pointed to the road which is now being followed and by now has brought Newcastle to its present distinction of being the diocese *par excellence* in which churchmanship has been given a remarkable power and vitality by the rapid growth of the institution of the Parish Communion, and all that flows from it. To-day out of forty parishes in the deanery of Newcastle seventeen have the Parish Communion every Sunday. In the deaneries of Bedlington and Tynemouth, sixteen and fourteen parishes respectively make it the feature of their Sunday morning worship. It is thus still largely an urban feature of the Church's life, but there are eight country parishes which have it too, and that number is increasing.

In 1927 the parish of St. John, Newcastle, in the heart of the city and within two minutes of the Central Station, decided that their Children's Eucharist at ten o'clock should become a Family Eucharist at 9.15. The clergy sent a letter to their people which said, 'The great ideal is that the whole family, father, mother, and children should all come together and worship God. The new hour (9.15) now makes this really possible. All can come to worship then, while those who are confirmed can also make their communion.' From the first whole families did come together, and special arrangements had to be made to help the little children to know what was being done at the altar and gradually to learn to take their share in the service. In the six years between 1927 and 1933 the communicants at this service grew from 60 to 170, and from the beginning the service has been followed by a breakfast for those who came. The parish has no hall or school building, so this breakfast has to be eaten in the vestry when it is wet or cold and in the churchyard overlooking the busy street when it is fine. As a result the clergy can write this paragraph in their parish magazine to-day:

'The NINE-FIFTEEN.' These words signify to us the most important event in our weekly life, when we come as a family to the Altar of our Church and find in the Parish Communion the source and strength of all our life and work. Many live their lives by the times of trains—the kick-off of a football match—the time of the first or second house at the pictures, or perhaps by the opening and closing time at the 'local,' or many regulate their watches by the chimes of Big Ben before the nine o'clock news; but still to us at St. John's and indeed in so many parishes where the Parish Communion is established, 'the 9.0' or 'the 9.15' or 'the 9.30' have become household words.

It is indeed true, and perhaps the best of it is that this way of observing Sunday morning is by no means confined to parishes of a strongly catholic tradition.

From this beginning there has grown something of a revolution in the worshipping habits of the Church of England in Newcastle. It is bound to be a profoundly influential revolution whether or no one can yet point to its precise effects, for it is ultimately the worship a Church offers which determines the quality of every single thing it does, and quickens it for the doing. To-day some eighteen or nineteen parish churches in Newcastle make the Parish Communion followed by the family breakfast, held at an hour when all can communicate, the chief and central service of the week. Moreover, it is the general testimony that this service quickens others. The vast amount of attention necessarily given to the details of the Parish Communion, has done much to establish the tradition that public worship is enjoyable and exciting for all and dull and boring for none. Where this lesson is taught by the Parish Communion it will very soon be reflected in the quality of worship at Evensong. When the choir-boys at Evensong walk to their places as though they had been care-fully drilled to do this small thing in a particular way, when the psalms are sung with clear and intelligent enunciation, and the whole congregation puts its heart into all it does in the worship, then worship lives. That in Newcastle this is an actual description of not a few parish churches on Sunday evenings is partly due to the fact that so many have the Parish Eucharist in the morning. For the Parish Eucharist is a service which is bound to die unless everyone who takes part in it is scrupulous in performing that part as well as he possibly can.

It is 8.45 on an ordinary Sunday morning, and already people are converging from all directions upon the cathedral, with its curious tower, so reminiscent of St. Giles', Edinburgh. As they enter the door for 'The Nine o'clock,' half a dozen boys and young men are quietly busy preparing the nave, altar and the sanctuary for worship. They move to and fro across the rose-pink of the altar frontal, and the two tall candles which one of them is lighting. The congregation comes in steadily and quietly until five minutes before the service begins, by which time nearly all are in their places: there are very few who arrive at the last minute and no late comers. We have therefore the few precious minutes of hushed silence in which to prepare for worship. Notice has plainly been taken of the tract *How to Enjoy our Services* which was written for the cathedral congregation, and which con-tains this paragraph in its suggestions for worshippers at 'The Nine o'clock.'

The sight of all these things (the altar, the reredos, and the cross) should fill us with wonder as we reverently kneel or sit and await the appearance of the ministers. It is quite essential to have this restful beginning; it sets the tone for the rest of the service. If our Sunday worship is to wash us clean from the week's worries and send us back empowered to battle again with sin and ugliness, there must be a complete absence of rush and bustle. Don't bother about *anything*; if by some accident you have forgotten your collection money just pass the plate on and think no more about it. We are to be absorbed in worship and adoration; nothing else matters. Sing the hymns and responses, if you feel like singing to-day; at other times you may prefer to worship silently, but no less fervently. And be comfortable in the posture you adopt; there is no point in going on kneeling upright if your back is aching, though ordinarily only the aged and infirm will need to sit—it looks lazy for young folks to do so. Only be sensible; worship is the thing—not correct attitudes. Eastern Christians stand most of the time.[1]

There are about 130 people in this congregation. It is its normal size. They are of every kind and type, of all ages, and of most levels of culture. Men and women are about even in number. Young clerks seem to predominate, but there are also several business men, a number of diocesan workers, and other people whom one cannot confidently label at a glance. There are also one or two visitors, staying for the week-end in one of the hotels, who have been invited to come to the Parish Communion at the cathedral rather than to the earlier communion and to stay for breakfast to meet the people afterwards with whom they shared the sacrament. There are no longer dwellings near the cathedral, and these people have all come from a distance, some of them as much as ten miles.

The choir and the celebrant come in and the service begins. The course of the service naturally needs no description, and even the less so because never once does it deviate from the Prayer Book. But it has features which at once strike a visitor. There may be a choir but if for any reason all its members were absent, it would not make much difference to the singing. For the service is sung to Merbecke, and everybody knows it, and everybody sings it. There are plenty of hymns but none are announced: their numbers are printed on a slip of paper containing details of the day's worship, and copies are in every pew. One of the canons gives a five-minute sermon on the New Life of the Community in Christ, and it really is five minutes and no longer, and is heard with attention. Every movement which the congregation makes in the course of the service it makes together, as one man. Through it all there is an atmosphere of deeply felt reality, of a steady and unstrained corporate devoutness; and this charges with a special meaning and resolve the last hymn, 'Just as I am,' the singing of which is most moving and remains long in the memory.

The service ends within the hour, and there is a short pause as the people make their thanksgivings, and then taking up small paper parcels, they move out of the church and into a hall with trestle tables across it. There are urns with tea and coffee, and everybody undoes his parcel and produces his breakfast from it—sandwiches, cake, bread and butter. They sit down in whatever order they happen to come in: no one seems to have a special place of his own which he claims by right. It is quickly obvious that everybody knows everybody else very well, and the talk and the jests fly, for these people are all friends. They are the Church, and all unconsciously they

---

[1] It was written by Verney Johnstone, canon of the cathedral, whose sudden death, almost as these words were written, was such a blow to the Church in Newcastle.

proclaim it. What they are making is the Beloved Community of Christ.

The characteristic cry of the earlier phase in the life of the Church in Newcastle is 'People Matter' and its authority is the Parable of Judgement. The characteristic cry of the later post-war phase is 'Let the Church be the Church,' and its authority is partly the Book of Common Prayer and partly, perhaps, the Epistle to the Ephesians. Yet there is no cast-iron separation between the phases. The second is implicit in the first, and the first in the second. It is a difference of emphasis, not of policy; and for this difference the inevitable and given circumstances of the time are at least as responsible as is the deliberate judgement of Church leaders. So it was too in the earlier phase. Given the terrible social conditions then existing, and the fact that it was then possible for Christians to be both active and effective in their relief, what else could anybody do but advance and act in such spheres as housing? The result is that any reasonably sensitive visitor to Newcastle gains three impressions, that the Church there is deeply respected by the whole city, that it is uncommonly alive and alert, and that it consists of a band of friends whose friendship is rooted in Christ.

Alton, Hampshire

No one who visits Alton to-day would guess from its buildings that it is an ancient place with a long history, which is mostly placid but has at least one moment of high dramatic excitement. Nor is there anything outward and visible to tell the visitor who comes to it by road from Winchester that from Ropley to Chawton he drives over what was once a dangerous stretch of road where a man was lucky if he did not fall among thieves, who burst upon him out of the woods. History has plenty to say about the highwaymen but nothing about any good Samaritans. Those woods to-day are full of jays and adders; one sees the former and the latter hide from sight. These things are in the books, but not scarred on the buildings; and Alton to-day looks just like what it is, a small country market town serving a wide rural area, and a Brewhouse-in-ordinary to village and town for many miles around. Those who know it well compare it with Basingstoke, or with a London suburb, and say that its development and the pace of its life is ten years behind the one and a hundred and fifty years behind the other. It is a placid, calm and gracious place; not externally a showpiece of any kind, but the very norm and type of what the English country town is traditionally supposed to be.

But it had its moment—a moment of high but strange and terrible dramatic excitement. This came to Alton, as to so many towns like it, in the Civil War. There is a brass in Winchester Cathedral which tells the outline of that story—how the royalist colonel Richard Boles defended Alton against the Cromwellians in 1643, and the last stand in the church itself:

his last Action, to omitt all Others was at Alton in this County of Southampton, was sirprised by five or six Thousand of the Rebells, which caused him there Quartered, to fly to the Church with neare Fourescore of his men who there Fought them six or seven Houers, and then the Rebell Breaking in upon him he Slew with his Sword six or seven of them and then was Slayne himself, with sixty of his men aboute him. His Gratious Soveraigne hearing of his Death gave him his high Commendation in this pationate Expression, Bring me a Moorning Scarffe, I have Lost one of the best Comanders in this Kingdome.

It was a desperate day and a forlorn hope. Waller had 6,000 trained soldiers, and Boles 500 undisciplined recruits from the wilds of Ireland and the Welsh mountains. They were slowly pressed back to the church hill, then into the churchyard, and then into the church itself. They locked and barricaded the doors, but

hand-grenades were thrown through the windows, bullets spit, split and scattered on to the grey walls, and riddled the stout oak door . . . The hinges gave and the angry troopers fought their way through into the church where the Cavaliers piled their dead horses in the aisles for breastworks. 'Charles! Charles!' rang the loyal battle-cry through the Norman arches under the belfry as man by man the defenders fell. 'No surrender!' and the Colonel swore his sword should slay any who cried for mercy. But his men, untrained, borne back by sheer weight of numbers, gave way, dropped their weapons, and yielded. Boles, fighting to the last, was slain.[1]

Those were the first, and up to the present the last desperate doings in Alton, which thereafter relapsed once more into a decent and seemly obscurity. The church was a charnel house, but they cleansed it and repaired the breaches of it, carefully preserving the marks of bullets on the walls, which remain to this day.

Alton may have made no further stir in the history books, but in some ways it has been remarkable, and chiefly for the uncommon variety of the work of the Church there. On the edge of the town stand the fine buildings of the Lord Mayor Treloar's Hospital. It was originally built by the Absent Minded Beggar Fund as a National Memorial Hospital, but was transferred by Parliament to Sir W. P. Treloar for his hospital for crippled children, and is one of the most famous orthopædic hospitals in the country. To staff and children the Anglican clergy of the town regularly minister. Up the hill beyond the great breweries is one of the houses of the Community of St. Mary the Virgin at Wantage, where the nuns look after some

[1] D. H. Moutray Read, *Highways and Byways in Hampshire* (Macmillan, 1932), p. 399.

forty homeless and feeble-minded girls. The sisters came to Alton in 1911. At first their only chapel was a room in the house, but by 1913 they had built on to it one of the loveliest domestic chapels in the country; and here too the clergy of Alton minister to the sisters. Near to it is Morland Hall, a well-known clinic for the curing of tubercular complaints of bone and skin. There are two or three private boarding schools, a large infirmary, and a cottage hospital. Once a year, in September, the district is invaded by hop-pickers, for in neighbouring villages like Selborne and Froyle they grow fine hops. In time past this visitation was something of an ordeal, for, as an ancient remarked, 'they carries on something chronic!'[1] But to-day night life in Alton is as tame in September as at any other time, largely because of the Church's ministration to the hoppers, in which the local clergy have taken a large part. To complete the list of the non-parochial institutions of Alton, there is Alton Abbey, inhabited by a small Order of Anglican monks and lay brethren, whose work in the world is that of ministering to the bodily and spiritual needs of retired merchant seamen.

All this work of pastoral ministry is borne by the clergy and people of the two parish churches of the town in addition to their normal round of parochial work. There is the church of St. Lawrence, the ancient parish church of the town, the same church which was once turned into a charnel house by the Parliament army. The second parish church, All Saints, stands on the main road at the western end of the town, and it has become the 'high' church of the two. But it was not so when it was first built 'principally for the Working Classes' in 1873. Just before the consecration a lady offered to present the new church with surplices for the choir, but the building committee refused to accept them, solemnly minuting that

considering the extreme sensitiveness of the majority of the population for whom the church is principally intended, it might prove prejudicial in debarring some of them from attending the Church, therefore it would be more likely to induce Peace and Goodwill to let the Choir attend in their usual dress.

It is often easiest to describe the essential character of a place by contrasting it with some other place which is its direct opposite. What, then, is the direct opposite of an ancient country town like Alton? There is no doubt of the answer. It is the recently built, ultra-modern, district or satellite township of a great city like London. There are some twenty thousand people living in housing estates, small detached villas, or large houses all built on an area of land which twenty years ago was all fields, heath, and woodlands. Everything is very hygienic, and all has been planned to emphasise the

[1] *Ibid.*, p. 403.

family's privacy, and does in fact emphasise its separation from other families. The people who live there are most of them rootless folk, with their interests in the Great Wen where they work, in the smaller and more historic towns in the neighbourhood where they go to school, or in the overcrowded and dingy districts from which they have escaped. It is a dormitory township, for people to sleep in and escape to—externally very pleasant and physically very healthy, but spiritually devastating. We may perhaps call it Sleepers' Hill, and anyone who knows Surrey will recognise it, for Surrey has many Sleepers' Hills.

In Sleepers' Hill nobody knows anybody; there is no pride of place; all are strangers. No sense of community exists. As a consequence there is much more unhappiness in Sleepers' Hill than in Bethnal Green or Lambeth. Those who have lived and worked in both Sleepers' Hill and Bethnal Green have no doubt that it is better to live in Bethnal Green. If one is ill in a slum, the fact is at once known and the neighbours are interested and try to do what they can to help. In Sleepers' Hill one could break one's leg and nobody would know. Disasters have to be shouldered alone. People would care if they knew, but life is patternless, and they are very unlikely to know. As we are meant to be members one of another we suffer when we are not, and in Sleepers' Hill the thoughtful and sensitive are often in despair. It is through this despair that community has to come; and the Church, through the parish priest, has to gather round him such of his people as are most evidently unhappy that Sleepers' Hill has no community life. They pray and talk together, and they try experiments, and most of them fail. Little by little they find that it is no use saying to Sleepers' Hill what one would naturally say in Bethnal Green, 'Let the heart of the community be the supernatural and let its focus be the altar.' One has to begin at the other end, and create a number of little societies and groups, scouts and guides, guilds, study circles, cells and the like. Then, in time, that association bears some communal fruit, and this can be offered at the altar. It is no use approaching the altar with nothing to bring.

Now Alton is in every way the precise opposite of Sleepers' Hill. In mentality it is fifty years behind it, and the pace of its life is far, far slower. But its enormous strength is that it is genuinely a community; and every man, woman and child has an authentic sense of belonging, and mattering. It is like a vast picture of a crowd, and everyone knows that if he looks he will find his own face somewhere on the canvas. If the butcher breaks his leg or the sweep has an unfortunate quarrel with a chimney and breaks his brushes, everybody knows about it and everybody is interested. In Alton it is not possible to have purely private joys or sorrows, blessings or disasters; and if it is not completely and universally true that the joy of one is the joy of all, and the hurt of one the hurt of all, at least these things are to a wide extent shared. In Alton, as in other towns of the same kind, people have a sense of security, for they live in a patterned life. They have their own place in it; and they know where it is, and how it fits into the whole picture.

Community of this power is dynamic, and dynamics, as Dean Bennett of Chester was fond of saying, are ambivalent. They tend to produce disconcerting, as well as splendid results. One of the inherent weaknesses of the Alton type of community is well known to anyone who has himself been the citizen of such a place. It is the sense of rivalry between the smaller communities within the larger. If a small town with strong traditions and a strong sense of community has two parish churches, and these churches are themselves strong communities, it is virtually certain that they will tend to measure themselves against each other and will find it harder to co-operate than they would if they were in two different towns. Similarly, there is likely to be some rivalry between the different denominations in the town.

The task of the Church in a town like Alton is therefore always the same, and always twofold. There is first the common pastoral and evangelistic task of all Churches everywhere, which in Alton is particularly exacting because of the unusual variety of institutions which the Church must serve. But beyond this lies the task of taking the community which exists as it were by the light of nature into the realm of the supernatural, that it may be purged of the distortions and excesses of internal rivalry. The history of the Church in Alton during the years 1919 to 1939 is primarily the history of its discharging of these two tasks.

First of all it had to be tackled and achieved as between the two parish churches. Both were and are strong Christian communities. Both churches are always full, and both have enjoyed a long succession of exceptionally devoted men as their vicars. But All Saints, in spite of its refusal of surplices for the choir in its earliest days, quickly became a catholic stronghold, while St. Lawrence remained what it had always been, broadly evangelical in its traditions. For many years the two communities had little to do with each other, and there was one famous occasion when the vicar of the parish church was invited to preach in the daughter church and began his sermon by saying earnestly, 'I stand before you in fear and trembling.' It was an urgent work of the Church to lay this suspicion to rest, and to put in its place a spirit of co-operation and fellowship. But to do this, some work had to be found in which both congregations could share, and big enough to tax the resources of each. This was found in the laying to rest of the other characteristic aberration of community, the isolation of the different Christian denominations from each other. This was tackled and achieved in two ways. First, all the clergy of the town were brought and held together in a fraternal; and though it was very difficult at first this fraternal gradually became true to its name, with the result that there is now a much closer co-operation and understanding between the Christian bodies in Alton. They found their common field of work in the town's Council of Social Service, which for some years has been operating with imagination and fruitfulness, and which has shouldered a multitude of burdens. Within twenty years the old spirit of suspicion between different Christian communities in the town has been done away, and a spirit of fellowship in Christ has taken its place, with real but incalculable consequences for the whole community of the town. It was a community of nature, and it is rapidly becoming a community of grace. This has perhaps been the particular thing which Christians in Alton were called to attempt for Christ in our time.

But side by side with it the ordinary work of evangelistic and pastoral ministry and of worship went steadily forward in both parishes. It was exacting and exhausting—more so in Alton than in many other places—and there is no town where clergy have to work harder. There are few indeed, if there are any, where the pastoral demand is so incessant, and none where it has been more splendidly met by all clergy over a long period of years. They have known their sheep, all of them, and been known of them. As a result the public worship of both churches is self-evidently the worship of a living community of Christ, a large and wholesomely varied community of young and old, rich and poor, one with another. But although all the clergy have been devoted men, one has been completely outstanding; and his life was so fully the sacrament of the whole Christian proclamation and witness in Alton that it must be briefly told.

The spiritual history of Alton during the first thirty years of the twentieth century is a story which revolves round a hero, for what Father Wainright was to London Docks that, and more besides, Charlie Bond was to Alton. He was born in the place, and he lived and served and died in it: in all his life he only left it for the three or four years while he was preparing for ordination. He was, and yet he was not, the typical parish priest—the sort of parish priest that all good men want to be and so few of us actually become. He was typical in the sense that he perfectly exemplified the characteristic virtue of the Anglican parish priest in every age, for he was before all else the faithful pastor who knew all his sheep and loved them, and was loved by them in turn, and who was wise and tireless in his care for them since he loved them in Christ, being a man of intense spirituality and humility. It is not for every Anglican priest that all this can be claimed, but it is the type of priestly excellence that every Anglican Christian best understands and most reveres, for our saints are always the pastors and George Herbert was the very type and image of Anglicanism at its best. His qualities reappear in every generation, and in the twentieth century not the least exemplar of them was Charlie Bond, vicar of All Saints, Alton.

His history was romantic indeed. He first appeared on the stage of memory in 1890, when he was a butcher's errand boy of fourteen years old. One day he was wandering up the High Street when a traction engine, towing two truck-loads of bricks, came in sight and drew near. Charlie could not resist it. He ran and leaped for the bar attaching the engine to the truck. He caught it, swung his leg over it, and then slipped and fell, and the wheels of the truck of bricks passed over his leg. It happened exactly outside All Saints Church to which he was to give all his life. He was at once taken to Alton hospital, his leg was amputated, and he lay there hovering between life and death for a long time. It was when this boy of fourteen was most gravely ill in the hospital that he had a strange and vivid experience. He was in the dream state of semi-consciousness when two doctors, thinking him unconscious, were standing by his bed and discussing his case. 'Of course he can't possibly live,' he heard one of them say. And then he heard another Voice, 'Yes, you *will* live, and then you shall work for me in this town.' Now Alton hospital in the nineties was a remarkable place with a remarkable matron. She was Miss Clark, a fine matron of gently commanding presence, who had a deep hold on the things of the Spirit. She interpreted her office as giving her a responsibility for her patients' souls as well as a charge over their bodies. There was a chapel in the hospital and the matron saw to it that it was used. Twice a day she gathered there all patients who could be moved and staff who could be spared, and she and they said together their morning and their evening prayers. Among them was young Bond, and everybody who knew him agreed that his time in Alton hospital was the turning point of his life.

But in the meantime there he was, short of one leg and no longer able to be an errand boy. Then it was that someone gave him a boy's set of carpenter's tools, and thereby solved the immediate problem and also gave him a joy which lasted his whole life. He was never so happy as when he was making things with bits of wood. It was his unfailing recreation, and he liked to think of himself as a carpenter-priest. For the present, however, it had to be his profession; and he started work again as a carpenter's apprentice. Soon he became a highly skilled craftsman, and when his artificial leg failed to give satisfaction he made himself another.

His hours of work at his new trade were very long, 6 A.M. to 5.30 P.M., and on Saturdays 6 A.M. to 4 P.M., and he was only fifteen years old. But while in the hospital he had been taken with a summons, a divine call, and his time was no longer his own. In the evenings he promptly started what came to be known as the Wash House Club. At the bottom of his mother's garden there was a little hut where she washed the family's clothes. There he gathered his friends, boys of his own age. They came together first as the expression of a piece of corporate hero worship for the men of the Alton Fire Brigade, which was famous throughout the county of Hampshire. The boys too were determined to have a fire brigade all of their own and emulate their elders, and under Bond they did it. But that was a summer game. When the long evenings began to darken early the boys still went regularly to the Bonds' washhouse, and there by the light of a few candles they held discussions on every problem under the visiting moon, they did some serious study, and Bond taught them to pray. After a year or two the Wash House Club outgrew the tiny hut, and the members transferred themselves to All Saints School, where Bond turned the club into a weeknight Bible class. He took it for years; and there are still people living who were in the Wash House Club and speak of it with great pride of belonging.

Thereafter his life followed the sequences which lead from carpentry to the priesthood. He became the Staff Sergeant of a huge Church Lads' Brigade, with a Bible class on his hands; then Sunday School Superintendent; then Lay Reader, with great men's services on Sunday afternoons and discussions of religion in the public houses at night; and all the time working at the bench for eleven hours a day. But that could not go on, and with a pang he withdrew from the carpentry and left Alton for the only time in his life to spend three years in Bournemouth performing prodigies of heroic study to get his A.K.C. degree, the condition of ordination. In 1914 he succeeded, and was ordained in Winchester Cathedral to serve the curacy of his beloved All Saints, Alton. He never left the town again.

He had at last come to the haven where he would be, and characteristically he spent the whole night before his ordination as priest in a vigil of prayer; and immediately after it, in a little room in the Royal Hotel in Winchester, he gave his first priestly blessing to his wife, who herself was a pearl among women and was always the sort of wife any priest might pray for. His Vicar, Father Carter, had also many qualities of the giant, but not in stature for he was a tiny man, while Bond was vast in every way. So they were called the Little Father and the Big Father. He was a bulky man who walked awkwardly. His amputation had not been completely a success, except that it had saved his life, for the stump gave him constant trouble and the pad which carried the weight of his heavy body on to his wooden leg chafed abominably no matter how often it was renewed and changed. His whole life was a life of pain, and he was never wholly free from it. Nevertheless one impression he left upon all who knew him was of a man who was always laughing. He laughed with the whole of his great frame, every part of him joining in, till he shook and quivered all over with merriment. Perhaps the best indication of the impression his appearance made was the spontaneous comment of a gipsy woman whose baby he was once baptising. As long as his mother held him the young Christian wept copiously, but when Bond took him his wailing was at once stilled as though by miracle. 'Ah,' commented the gipsy, not inaudibly, 'That be because you be fat and warrm.'

It was gipsy language for something more than a bulky frame and kindly face; and it pierced through to that quality of reassurance, of a bestowed sense of security, which flowed from him, and drew to him all conditions of men, women, and children to seek it. He seemed to them to carry about with him a sense of the Presence of God, an aura of bedrock spiritual reality; and it is of this that they still speak first when his name is mentioned. One felt safe with him, because he felt so safe with God. The unseen world was peopled for him, and was all about him. 'Do you know,' he said to a friend one day, 'that when I am at the Altar I am so thronged with the invisible host that I feel no thicker than a piece of paper.' Some years after Carter's death, when Bond was the Vicar, it was to him as though he was still in tutelage, for when he passed the pulpit 'he always saw the Little Father looking at the Crucifix as he used to do when he was alive.' Once a worshipper

was right at the back of the church on my knees. I had been there some time and was just getting up to go out when I saw an angel over the two men who were by the Altar Rail. I did not know till then that Charlie was hearing a confession. I looked at it again and it was still there, so I knelt down again. When I told Charlie what I had seen some days later he never doubted it but thought it was quite natural.

He had the inevitable difficulties of his position to overcome, for he was a man of the people, and though absolutely classless and fundamentally cultured, his education had been extremely sketchy, and everybody had known him as Charlie from the day of his birth. To become a Lay Reader was one thing, but to be raised to the priesthood and set to minister in Alton itself was quite another. At first it was difficult. There was, for instance, an old hot-gospeller, salvationist friend of his, who said bewilderingly, 'What I can never understand is Mr. Bond: he really was a converted man—everybody said so. He was saved and yet in spite of that he *still* stayed in the Church.'

But what might easily have defeated a less spiritually-minded man and a less Christian community was overcome by Bond and his people quickly and creatively. Thus when Father Carter died, and his successor, the Rev. K. McMaster, had retired, the parish petitioned the Bishop of Winchester for the appointment of Bond, and the Bishop had no doubt that it would be right to break his otherwise unbreakable rule, and appoint the curate to be vicar of the parish where he was serving his curacy. It is worth adding that before he made his decision the wise bishop interviewed Mrs. Bond—and had no more doubts. So Bond became vicar of All Saints in 1921, and life could hold no higher glory for him than that. He was of the same breed as the Curé d'Ars.

His incumbency of All Saints, Alton, is already a saga and will one day be a legend. It was fundamentally and tirelessly pastoral, for he was in the succession of traditional Anglican sanctity, which puts the pastoral ministry first and the prophetic a long way behind. But the pastor's life is made of a mass of detail, and the detail is composed of all the people who need help, encouragement, friendship, and comfort. It is an inchoate, privileged, and hidden ministry. It does not easily lend itself to become the material of a chronicler, for it is diffuse and unorganised, and most of it is confidential. The history of Charlie Bond's ministry will never be written. It had few high lights since it was simply a steady, persistent faithfulness which never flagged till death took him, worn out, at the early age of fifty-five. But there are momentary pictures of it which survive and have found their way into various kinds of written records, and they are the sacramental symbols of it all. They show him trudging rather painfully up the hill to St. Mary's Home, where the Wantage Sisters live, carrying to them the reserved Host, and the brewery men taking off their hats as he passed and they knew what he carried. There is the picture of him at the local hop-pickers' mission each year, driving out in a wagonette into the field at Selbourne and standing in it to preach to the hoppers, and after dark pinning a white sheet to a couple of trees for a lantern service. Or there is Charlie Bond as Chairman of the Board of Guardians, doing a great pastoral work in the Institution, where, after a meeting or many visits, 'he used to get thirsty and would go into the kitchen for a drink of water, and he liked it out of a jug.' And beside the parish priest there was the missioner, much in demand for children's missions; and the almoner who, with his wife, refused to sit down to their own Christmas dinner until they knew for certain that no single home in his parish would be without one. And then, finally, there was the confessor, to whom people came from near and far to open their grief and to find in him an epitome of wise understanding and kindly courage.

Such was the evangelical-catholic, as he called himself, and the carpenter priest. When he died he was buried in a coffin made by his own tools; and his body was robed in vestments, a chalice and paten in his hands, and his old set of carpenter's tools by his side. His funeral was a great triumph. Every shop was shut, and every soul in Alton, and many far away, mourned for him, yet rejoicing over the spirit of a brave and just man, made as near perfection as this world ever lets us come. His memorial was the building up of an authentic and genuine worshipping community of Christ, than which no priest could ask more, and it still stands.

Devotion of this order cannot fail of a response, particularly when there has been consistent loyalty to its standards shown both before and after Bond's life by predecessors and successors in both churches. It is in the power of this spirit that the Christians in Alton will now have to deal with their next challenges. For the world is now strongly challenging the immemorial community of the place. The plague of a purely nominal Christianity steadily seeps in, and only those who are active members of the supernatural community of the different churches seem to be armoured against it. The common disease of England, the triviality of interest engendered by the popular press, and the secularity of outlook upon life, batters at the doors of every house, and once admitted, quickly produces the dullness of a blinded sight. Already the temperament which is terrified of being thought religious is to be found among some who work in the breweries or in large offices. The greatest tasks of all lie still ahead, but nowhere is the Church more fully equipped to deal with them than in Alton.

III. *The Non-Parochial Ministries*

In the early twenties B. K. Cunningham complained that the Church of England had been too slow to welcome 'diversities of ministries' into its priesthood, and suggested that a greater flexibility might save us from the sort of priest who makes religion his God and not God his religion.[1] His words were prophetic, for one of the most striking features of the life of the Church during this period was the rapid development and the wide variety of the non-parochial ministries. For years past the student world had enjoyed chaplaincies of its own. They were provided by the deans and chaplains of the colleges in the universities, and by the innumerable ramifications of the Student Christian Movement. In Oxford, for example, the Oxford Pastorate, an evangelical organisation for the shepherding of undergraduates quickly resumed its great work after 1918 under

[1] Writing in *The Future of the Church of England*, edited by Sir James Marchant (Longmans, Green, 1926), p. 84.

Dr. Chavasse, now Bishop of Rochester. Its centre became the church of St. Aldate, and the work was steadily and imaginatively done by a number of very able and devoted clergy. This was matched on the Anglo-Catholic side by the pastoral work flowing from Pusey House. The needs of sick people in hospital had also been long recognised as reasonably lying outside the scope of the purely parochial ministry, and many hospitals had their own full-time chaplains, though these were still less in number than the hospitals which relied on the ministrations of the parochial clergy.

After 1918 the number of the clergy who were engaged in other non-parochial ministrations, or who became specialists in some single branch of the total ministry of the Church to the people steadily increased. The central boards and committees of the Church Assembly claimed a good many of them. Various works of healing—psychiatry, moral welfare, and spiritual healing—occupied others. The more research there was into the problem of how the Church might be made more effective the more clearly it was seen that though the work of the Church rested on the parochial system there were many people and many fields of life which the resources of the parish church could not be expected to do more than touch lightly in passing. The urban industrial proletariat as a class was showing itself more and more immune to the traditional methods of evangelism which the parish church could compass. Year by year it became clearer that the man in industry, whether worker, trade unionist, or manager, must be sought and won for Christ in his industrial milieu no less than in his own home. If this was to be done, then the parochial ministry must be heavily expanded or else supplemented. It was to meet this need that the modern system of sending specially trained clergy into the factories to act as chaplains was invented.

The need had been diagnosed years before, and the application of the remedy after 1919 was less of a novelty than it sounds. The scale on which it was then done was new, but not the enterprise in itself. The need had been foreseen by the old Guild of St. Matthew under Stewart Headlam, and it was one of his friends and disciples who appears to have done much of the pioneering. This was C. E. Escreet, a lifelong socialist priest, successively curate of Battersea, Vicar of St. Andrew's, Stockwell, Rector of Woolwich, and Archdeacon of Lewisham. Many of the enterprises which are commonplace now were already being done at Stockwell and at Woolwich under Escreet at the beginning of the century. His life was a saga, and his genius lay in awakening an enthusiasm for social work among very large numbers of men and women in his congregation. At Stockwell in 1889 he formed a parochial church council, the rules and constitution of which almost exactly foreshadowed those of every parochial church council to-day. At Woolwich he had more than a hundred people on the roll of his lay workers, and most of them were men. His clergy were voluntary factory chaplains and his people assisted them. There were regular meetings for prayer, worship, and religious teaching in a large drapery shop, in a dressmaker's workshop, and in a factory for the mass-production of pyjamas and shirts. All this naturally led to a great deal of welfare work; and as it all developed, the Free Churches joined in, and the whole enterprise was beautifully poised so as to lead from an undenominational basis to active membership of one or other of the churches taking part. Archdeacon Escreet is to-day largely forgotten, but he and his people, acting in perfect partnership, did much of the pioneering at Woolwich from 1900 onwards, and he has claims to be regarded as the patron saint of the whole modern enterprise of taking the Church into the factory.

A work at once so essential and so terribly difficult has naturally been tackled in many different ways. The vicar may occasionally go into the factory, perhaps to speak at a canteen service on some special occasion. There have been not a few Student Movement campaigns in factories. The Industrial Christian Fellowship has sent in its lay agents as a matter of regular routine, and has made many larger scale visitations of particular factories. But none of these enterprises can undertake the daily pastoral cares of a large factory, which are really more numerous and exacting than one full-time priest can discharge. One priest who is there all the time, however, has far more chance of discharging them than ten who come in sporadically on special occasions, since the difficult and confidential pastoral work is likely to be offered by those who need it only to a priest whom they have had time to know and to trust.

The need for specialised full-time factory chaplains was plain, and between the wars the Church began to provide them. The work of such a chaplain is largely undenominational. He recruits the congregations of all the local churches, not merely his own. By meetings, by private talks, by group discussions he teaches the Faith, and he breaks down the opposition between Church and factory. He makes all kinds of personal contacts, and he follows them through all the stages of welfare and remedial work. He restores, if he can, to modern industry the friendship that used to exist between the village church and the village craftsman, whether blacksmith or thatcher. His is a real ministry of reconciliation, and it is desperately difficult. One who has had much experience of these opportunities and the difficulties has written vividly of them:

The chaplain will set about his job in the factory in as workmanlike manner as possible. When others are working it will not do to give the

impression of lounging about with no particular business on hand . . . I
recall a sharp lesson taught me in a certain tool-room, where I was the
subject of a strong attack because I walked in with my hands in my
pockets, when people were engaged in 'honest work.' As a matter of fact
the chaplain's first introduction will probably be in a canteen lunch hour,
when he will be given an opportunity of explaining his intentions very
briefly. He will express a desire to be of service, a note that always meets
with a response. He will offer to put any people who may desire it in
touch with any particular church of whatever denomination . . . He will
say that it is not his intention to obtrude religion upon those who do not
wish it, but rather to answer any question put to him. After this short
speech he may retire altogether on the first occasion, since workers will
perhaps feel a little embarrassed at being the first to speak to him.[1]

Then he must win the confidence of the welfare department, and,
more important still, of the shop stewards; and thenceforward all
will depend on his inventiveness, his tact, his persistence, and his
courage. It is a lonely, difficult, but vitally important ministry, which
in the last thirty years has steadily grown, and is bound to grow still
further.

The great need to bridge the gulf between the Church and the
industrial worker carried a few priests into forms of ministry much
stranger than that of the factory chaplain. In the Church of England
Hugh Lister was perhaps the foremost example of these, just as his
contemporary, the Abbé Godin, was in France. For men like these
it was not enough to become chaplains in factories. They were
driven by an inner compulsion so strong that it was nothing less
than a divine vocation to become one in every sense with the men
of the industrial world whom they wished to win for Christ. They
must speak their language, think their thoughts, share their lives in
every detail, fight in their battles, live by their standards of comfort,
and in nothing be separated from them. Their ministry was characteristic of their tormented age, and their heroism deathless.

Hugh Lister, born in 1901, was a graduate of Trinity College,
Cambridge, with a pleasing passion for railways which carried him
into the service of the Great Western Railway, where it seemed he
was in the haven where he would be. But the experience of living in
railwaymen's dormitories in Cardiff awoke in him a tremendous
sense of compassion for the industrial worker, and made him clear
that he must express it not as a railwayman but in the ordained
ministry of the Church. At Cuddesdon he set himself to learn the
strength of asceticism in the ordering of the devotional life, and he
was ordained to serve a Poplar curacy. From there he went to
become one of the secretaries of the Student Christian Movement,
and he set himself to live and work on the standards allowed by un-

[1] C. H. Cleal, *The Chaplain in the Factory* (Student Christian Movement, 1945),
pp. 20, 21.

employment insurance. This experience temporarily broke his health
and permanently deepened his compassion. He was ill for two years,
and on his recovery he became a member of the staff of the Eton
Mission at Hackney Wick. He was then 34.

The church at Hackney Wick was flourishing but there seemed to
be few working men in the congregation—a fact which challenged
Lister. He determined that one way or another he would get hold of
them. He had no doubt of the path he must tread. It was the conditions which he saw in Hackney which, he believed, did more than
anything to foster secularism in working people; and it was the
Church's business, and his own as a priest of the Church, to change
the conditions. But he felt he could only work for this from within
the conditions to be changed; and he must use the only possible
instrument for change, the Trade Union Movement.

One of the most unusual things about him was his passion for
Trade Unions. He once wrote a letter to the employees of a factory
in Hackney which had no union:

> You and your mates have not got your rights as workers till you have a
> say in the wages and conditions under which you work. And you have no
> say whatever till you are organised in your Trade Union. An employer
> may be good: he may be bad. That is not the point. The point is that as
> long as he can deal with his employees one by one, as single individuals, he
> has all the say and they have none. And that is wrong. Is it not high time
> that you followed the example of your fellow-workers recently in other
> factories in and around the Wick and helped to make a Trades Union
> firm?[1]

When he knew what he must do, he did it with a single-minded and
thorough directness which made him extraordinarily effective.

He went with humility to working men who he knew cared that
conditions in Hackney were what they were. He set himself to be
taught by them, and he identified himself with them in every way,
living as they lived, and spending on himself no more than they spent.
At first they looked on him with tolerant amusement, and one told
him he was too 'pansy.' But soon he had built up a team of a dozen
working men determined to make Hackney a Trade Union centre,
and they saw nothing amiss in accepting his leadership. Together
they founded branches of the appropriate Union in one factory after
another, and when this involved the calling and running of a strike
neither Lister nor his friends shirked it. Between 1936 and 1939
Lister organised at least three strikes to win recognition for the
Union and to get better conditions for employees. It did not make
him popular with the local employers, at least one of whom pointedly
withdrew his firm's subscription to the Eton Mission. But it was

[1] Alice Cameron, *The Pursuit of Justice: The Story of Hugh Lister and his
Friends* (Student Christian Movement, 1946), p. 81.

before this that Lister himself had resigned from its whole-time and salaried service, and had used his savings to buy a house to serve as his own home and a centre for his Trade Union companions. He continued to take services in the church all Sundays, and early every morning he was there to worship at the Eucharist, himself celebrating in his turn.

All this he accomplished in three years, for when September 1939 came he joined the Welsh Guards, rose to become a major, and was killed in France in 1944. He joined the army because he was clear, as he had always been clear, that Fascism had to be fought, and he must take his chance with his mates in the firing line. In some ways the most considerable of all his feats was to win his friends to his views on conscription, and to issue jointly with them a manifesto commending it to the Trade Union world.

While doing the work of a Trade Union organiser Lister never forgot that he was a priest. He would have said that this was the way in which he was called to work out his priesthood. His habits of prayer and receiving of sacraments, in fact his whole rule of life was maintained in Hackney at the same level of austere intensity as they had reached at Cuddesdon, where his asceticism had caused anxiety to the college authorities. Nor did he ever forget that he was a fisher of men for Christ and His Church. But he would force religion on no man, nor would he make church membership any kind of condition of his friendship. Some of those most closely associated with him went to church with him, and others did not. But he was the devoted comrade of all alike and all equally. He used to hold weekly meetings for prayer and Bible study in the house, and between ten and thirty men usually came to them.

His experience led him to exactly the same conclusion that the Abbé Godin in Paris was to reach independently, that the way of evangelism among factory workers was *par excellence* the small dedicated group, and that it had this primacy by reason of the intensity of fellowship which its small numbers made possible. 'I find the value of that in my own (Trade Union) branch, where we have a little knot of men and boys who do pray together and preach at each other once a week. . . . What we have to attend to in the Church is community, not morals. Have a community which prays to Christ and morals can look after themselves.'[1]

Lister, then, had something to do with the initiation and development of another feature of the evangelistic ministry of the Church of his day, the small group or cell. So far as it can be traced back to its source the original impetus of the cell movement appears to have come from a London suburban parish, West Norwood, whose vicar,

[1] Cameron, *Op. cit.*, p. 128.

Sidney Ruscoe, took very seriously to heart the promise of our Lord, 'Wherever two or three are gathered together in my Name there am I in the midst of them.' He persuaded many of his lay people to organise themselves into little groups of not more than nine in number, who met regularly for prayer, study, and waiting upon God in each other's houses. Out of this shared experience there grew a very strong bond of fellowship, which is always the soil in which evangelism grows best. But at the same time many others were independently feeling their way towards the same idea, and among them was Hugh Lister. Thus the growth of these groups or cells was quite unorganised and spontaneous, and therefore it was untidy and ragged. All the more was this so because the motives which brought many different people independently to the judgement that the small dedicated and committed group of Christians was the best way of advance were very different. Some, like Lister, came to it gradually out of their own experience. Others saw in it the twentieth-century equivalent of the essential evangelistic method of the Early Church. There were some who saw that by their cellular expansion the Communists had spread their doctrine over the world, and believed that Christians should imitate them. The motive of yet others was that of impatient revolt against the ever increasing weight of organisation in the Church, and these saw in the essentially unorganised cell movement something which inspired them with fresh hope. Others again approached the matter more theologically, asked what was the basic pattern of spiritual energy in the Bible, and answered their own question by pointing to the small, disciplined group, corporately and expectantly waiting upon God. So it was that as the fatal year of 1939 drew near the idea of cellular expansion began to spread very rapidly, and cells came into existence in many parishes, and in some factories. Not until the war came did the great expansion of cellular work take place, for the conditions of war favoured its growth. In those years the method was developed into the different series of such cells or companies linked together in a living whole, such as the series which worked under the titles of 'The Nails,' and 'The Servants of Christ the King.' It was a new way of evangelism, radically biblical, and providing a body to implement the truth which pioneers like Lister had been teaching the Church, that the way of evangelising in secular spheres of life must be the winning of the larger community by the infection of the smaller community within itself; and that the heart of infection was fellowship. This whole movement is intensely alive to-day, and much of the hope of the future depends upon its development.

The same idea of unleashing the power of the laity, and persuading them to accept their charge of responsibility in Christ's name for all

I

the work of the Church, lay behind another development of lay evangelism. This became known as the Parish Meeting; and it was an attempt to do for the whole congregation what the cell did for a section of it. The heart of this enterprise was the periodical gathering together of the whole congregation (or as many as could or would come) in order that the whole body might talk over its problems and plan its witness and work together. It was in fact an effort to make it become in practice what it already was potentially, the Body of Christ in and for the area of its competence. Much of the pioneering of this work was done in a Sheffield parish, and though the Parish Meeting is much easier to start than to maintain, it has spread to many other parishes, and there seems no limit to the power it may one day become.

The common denominator of all these inter-war developments of specialised ministry is the emphasis they all laid on the laity. These ministries were not something done for the laity by the clergy. They were enterprises done by clergy and laity acting together for the sake of other laymen and women who remained untouched by religion; and their essence was the belief that the key to all modern evangelism is lay power. It was this emphasis which specially distinguished this from earlier periods in the history of the Church of England.

IV. *The Ministry of Architectural Suggestion*

If one of our Anglican ancestors of two hundred years ago came back from the grave to examine the modern Church, the most obvious change that he might remark is the great care now given to the cleanliness and decency of our parish churches and their decorations and furnishings. These changes, he would be bound to agree, are wholly for good since they constitute a perpetual ministry of suggestion. Most of them are to be placed to the credit of the Church of the last thirty years. Whatever modern Anglicans may have failed to learn, at least they have learned that labour or devotion given to the upkeep and seemliness of parish churches is never wasted. This labour they give, even if it is only in the matter—the exacting and expensive matter—of the altar flowers. Our churches are nearly always clean and obviously cared for, and their decorations and fittings increasingly betray an informed taste. Externally, it is the biggest change of the last thirty years.

The care of churches has been the subject of much informed regulation. One of the innumerable consequences of the Enabling Act was the setting up of Diocesan Advisory Committees before whom the authorities of every parish must justify any structural alterations, or any additions to fabric or to decorations they may be contemplating. Until the Advisory Committee is satisfied that the proposed scheme will enhance the beauty of the church, or at the least will do nothing to harm it, they do not advise the Chancellor of the diocese to issue the necessary faculty for the work. Gone are the days of irresponsible and ignorant alterations of churches, and no one may now choose ornaments or stained-glass windows by the simple criterion of his own fancy. This is no slight advance, as will be realised by anybody who recalls the ruination to the look of churches caused by the æsthetically ignorant zeal for renovation shown by so many of our forefathers.

But this regulation, and curbing of excessive local individualism, might have been burdensome if it had not come hand in hand with greatly improved artistic standards, and with an enhanced sense of responsibility to posterity for the maintenance of the beauty of the churches we inherit. Besides this, there has also grown up among us in the last thirty years a strong distaste for unseemliness in church. It has become a rare event to find altar linen which is less than scrupulously clean, or altar books which are mouldering or torn, or flowers which are withered and dropping. Most churches have some sort of guild of those whose business it is to keep the chancel and the sanctuary clean and fresh. When renewals are needed, or some scheme of decoration has to be put in hand, it is now easy to get expert advice. Societies like the Warham Guild have done an impressive work all over the country in preparing schemes of decoration, or lighting, or rearrangement of furniture, in which experienced knowledge and impeccable taste have been gladly placed at the disposal of parish churches, so that they may make the very best of the resources they have.

It is perhaps symbolical of the transformation which has come over the parish churches during the last thirty years that what many people think to be one of the finest carved representations in the world of Christ crucified should belong to these years. This is C. S. Jagger's bronze figure of our Lord on the Cross which crowns the great rood in the new chapel of the Society of the Sacred Mission at Kelham. The chapel was finished in 1928; and it is awe-inspiring in its beauty. The chancel is spanned by the great curved rood, and the wide space of the chapel itself carries the eye irresistibly to the Christ who crowns the rood. The great figure hangs on the cross, the hands nailed, and the arms and body manacled to the cross by a long rope, roughly and unevenly wound and tied. The weight of the body is taken by a rough saddle between the legs, and its effect seems to be the downward twisting of the feet at an unnatural angle. So the horror of Calvary must surely have been, for there is a sense of inevitability about this carving. But though the horror of it is emphasised by the angle of the feet, the real impression given is of another sort of inevitability—the sense of necessary triumph as the crown of suffering. The eye travels from feet to face, and in the face is the steady, strong expression of Him who, having experienced the real meaning of the opening words of Psalm 22, 'My God, My God, why hast thou forsaken me,' has followed the cycle of experience right through to the psalm's triumphant end, 'My seed shall come and the heaven shall declare his righteousness unto a people that shall be born, whom the Lord hath made.'

The arts of the sculptor and the architect are closely allied, and a veneration of the Christ of the Kelham rood of 1929 leads us naturally to the greatest and most significant gain of all in the ministry of ecclesiastical arts which the twenty years between the wars bestowed upon us. The gain was achieved in the building of new churches, and here we saw between 1919 and 1939 the first real touches of originality and inspiration since Christopher Wren.

The Church of Christ has always been the greatest of builders, and in the years between the wars the Church of England built a large number of new churches. But many, perhaps most of them, were built in an entirely new way and in accordance with a novel idiom; and at last there was a strong movement away from mediæval and Victorian Gothic. Most of these modern churches were built naturally enough to serve the new housing estates springing up all over the country. Among those designed as no churches in England had ever been designed before were St. Nicholas, Burnage, Manchester; St. Gabriel's, Blackburn; Testwood, in the diocese of Winchester; St. Saviour's, Eltham; John Keble Church, Mill Hill; and there were many others besides these. Externally they were various indeed. Some seemed at first to be merely bizarre, and bitter complaints were made that they looked more like factories than churches. Others, like St. Nicholas, Burnage, which somehow gave the impression by its curves and absence of angles of an immense ship, were immediately satisfying. But all were original, and none merely copied another of the same type. Their interiors, too, were novel—or they seemed it; and this novelty was immediately impressive and won almost universal admiration. The novelty lay not so much in the unusual placing of side chapels and lady chapels as in the sense of space and light. There was an unbroken vista with no pillars or screens to spoil it, and there was a glad welcome to all the light of heaven and no dark stained glass to dim it.

It was as though the architects and the builders of the Church had woken one day in the nineteen-twenties and determined to revolt against all the ecclesiastical conventions of church-building; and at the same time so to build as to enable the type of worship and the characteristic way of evangelism suggested by the Book of Common Prayer to come alive in the modern age. Church architects like N. F. Cachemaille-Day and his fellows had first of all to revolt if they were to do this successfully. Their revolt was against mediæval and nine-teenth-century Gothic, and not against the square box churches of the eighteenth century, for these set out to do what the Gothic churches deliberately avoided, the designing of churches in which every part could be seen from every other, and priest and people be so placed that in worship they were members one of another, a community.

It is the Prayer Book ideal of worship. But the Gothic churches had been precisely designed to make it as difficult as possible. As Canon G. W. O. Addleshaw and Mr. Frederick Etchells have demon-strated in their exhaustive *Architectural Setting of Anglican Worship*,[1] the mediæval builders exalted the principle of the Numinous over the principle of community, and believed England would be con-verted by a renewal of the sense of awe. To renew this sense, the architect must enhance the mystery of what was done in church by clothing it in 'dim religious light,' and by removing the priest at the altar far from the body of worshippers, who must only glimpse and never see him plainly. Hence the multiplication of pillars and rood screens, expressly designed to make the view of the altar fitful. Whatever may be said for this conception, and it is not the function of this book to argue the matter, it is certainly not the conception of the Prayer Book which undoubtedly expects that the dynamic force behind the processes of the conversion of England will be the strength and the outward-going of the community of the worshippers.

The fourteenth-century architects thought thus and their eigh-teenth-century successors thought otherwise. But the nineteenth century reversed the insight of the eighteenth and returned to Gothic. That it did so was the work of the early tractarians, largely expressed through the Cambridge Camden Society.

Few undergraduate societies have exercised such an influence as the Cambridge Camden Society (founded in 1839). By 1843 it had as its patrons two archbishops, sixteen bishops, thirty-one peers and members of Parliament, and a membership of no less than seven hundred. The society revolutionized the whole arrangement and appearance of our churches; and there is hardly a building in any part of the world, belonging to the Anglican communion, which does not betray the influences of its ideals. . . . The ecclesiologists started with the belief that there is a specifically Chris-tian style of church architecture in which every church must be built. The architecture was that of the Middle Ages, and its most perfect expression the Gothic of the fourteenth century. . . . They believed that a perfect plan of church was at hand; that it had been worked out in the fourteenth century; and that one had only to adopt the plan to restore the splendour

---

[1] Faber and Faber, 1948.

of mediæval worship. In designing a church it was all important to adopt this plan, and only then to think about the convenience of the congregation.[1]

Hence the font in the corner, where no one can see the baptism; and hence the altar far removed from the people, and pillars and screens to hide it from them.

The very uniformity with which this conception was applied to church-building for nearly a hundred years, and the rigidity of the plan, spelt tyranny, and this tyranny hid from the worshipper the splendour of Prayer Book communal ideals. It has been precisely in our time, between 1919 and 1939, that the Church's architects have revolted against it, and almost every new church built in England has repudiated it. If we are now learning again that the Prayer Book is right in its belief that the strength of the Church is the strength of its community, and that this community is engendered by a particular way of worshipping God, it is to the ministry of suggestion in the architecture and arrangement of the modern housing estate churches that we largely owe it.

[1] Addleshaw and Etchells, *Op. cit.*, pp. 203–5.

CHAPTER EIGHT

THE WITNESS OF THE CATHEDRALS

I. *Cathedrals Used and Abused*

In the life of the Church of England it is broadly true that the health of the cathedrals and the witness of the parish churches go hand in hand. In a thousand subtle ways they react upon each other and they feed each other. When cathedrals lapse into a state of dignified decay church life in the parishes grows 'poorer and thinner in default of their activity,' as Archbishop Benson observed in 1878;[1] and when vitality flows back into the veins of the one institution, the other is quickened.[2] Cathedrals and parish churches are mutually dependent. The renaissance of the English cathedrals during the two decades between the wars is one of the most hopeful features of the life of the Church in that most difficult period of her history; and this renewed vitality did much to enable and sustain the pastoral ministry of the parish churches, then as always the real centre of gravity of the whole witness of the Church.

It is chiefly because the parish churches find they cannot do without them that the cathedrals still stand. They are virtually the only mediæval buildings in the country which remain not as ruins but as glorious houses of God, not merely still in daily use, but more fully used and by more people than they have ever been before. To keep them standing, roofed, warmed, and equipped for worship through the centuries has cost enormous sums of money; and every cathedral has swallowed in repairs and maintenance an amount of money many times greater than the sum needed to build it in the first place. On Lincoln Cathedral alone £139,000[3] had to be spent between 1919 and 1939; and in the same period many thousands of pounds were spent on Chester and St. Paul's, and no doubt on other cathedrals as well. In the same period Liverpool Cathedral was steadily building and Guildford Cathedral had been begun. This money has mostly come directly or indirectly from the parishes, and if the parish priests had really disliked the cathedrals as much as in many generations they said they did, they could easily have prevented the money being

---

[1] E. W. Benson, *The Cathedral* (Murray, 1878), p. 4.
[2] Cf. Benson's testimony: 'No sooner had the cathedrals been crippled than the returning forces of church life reinvested them with significance.' *Op. cit.*, p. 4.
[3] *Crockford Prefaces*, pp. 140, 168.

found, and the cathedrals to-day would either be like Fountains Abbey or in the rather chilly custody of the Office of Works.

But cathedrals have been disliked as often as they have been loved. When Bishop Paget of Chester preached his farewell sermon in the cathedral he recalled how one day he had come across a large party of working men visitors from Sheffield standing before the rood and singing with reverence and devotion the hymn, 'When I survey the wondrous cross.' 'Such a thing as that,' he remarked, 'would have been absolutely incredible—the cathedral authorities would have made it quite impossible—fifty years ago.' His comment revealed one of the characteristic charges which have so often been made against cathedrals, a fussy archaic dignity which nursed only decay. Another charge was that they were the homes of exceedingly well-paid idleness; a third, that they were remote from ordinary people. The evidence for these charges was strong from Benson's day until our own; and the fact that of few if of any English cathedrals could such charges reasonably be brought to-day is evidence of the reality of the renaissance we have seen in the last thirty years. But they have had to travel a long way to lose their bad name. We are apt to forget how bad it was. Most people could quote Bishop Blomfield's angry comment about St. Paul's, but it was comfortably long ago (in 1836) that he said it. An anthology of similar remarks could, however, be easily continued well into modern times. No one believed more heartily in cathedrals than Archbishop Benson, yet he himself said of them in 1877:

Thirty years ago cathedral bodies were in the very depth of unpopularity. Nothing but some Heaven-born instinct in the English people then prevented their extinction. . . . The most far-reaching, the most effectively and beautifully constituted, the but-lately most influential Christian institutions of the country had been enervated, paralysed, devitalised until the basest appointments to their honours could injure them no further.

When Hensley Henson went to be Dean of Durham in 1913 he succeeded to the charge of a cathedral in which in quite recent times one dean

baffled by the Chapter in some effort of nepotism, sulked in such wise that he would no more attend the daily services in the cathedral. Annoyed by the ill behaviour of some students, he shut them out of the cathedral as a body.[1]

Again, when Dr. Lang, as Archbishop of York, went officially to visit Chester in 1925 and preached in the cathedral, he praised Dean Bennett's great work there by describing the low standards of cathedral life and worship which made that work so necessary:

[1] *Retrospect*, vol. i, p. 151.

Little more than fifty years ago (our English cathedrals) might have been described as the lost heritage of the Church of England. The glory of the former houses had passed away, and to the latter houses no glory had yet come. Their bodies, so to say, remained beautiful and imperishable, but the soul seemed to have gone. A strange blight seemed to fill their great spaces, and a smell as of death seemed often to pervade them.

And though much had been done to bring back their life, much more still remained to be done:

The cathedral, though once again the House of God, has still to win its place as the mother, the central church of the whole diocese to which the tribes of the Lord, the people from its towns and villages, go up with gladness. In many dioceses and in many parishes the cathedral is still a place remote and strange. Individuals may enter it sometimes, but it has little place of its own in the corporate life of the Church.

The purpose of Lang's sermon was to say how untrue this judgement was of Chester; yet by 1925 there were many other cathedrals of which it was becoming just as untrue, and there were probably none where the cathedral as an institution or the dean and chapter as a corporate body could have sat for their portraits to Hugh Walpole in his devastating novel, *The Cathedral*. Yet it was from an amalgam of that novel and their memories of Trollope's Barchester that many people drew their ideas of what the daily life of a cathedral was like.

To-day nobody who knows anything about them supposes that they, or the people who worship in them, are truly portrayed either by the satire of the novelists or by the strictures of the preachers of a generation ago. Their renaissance has been remarkable. 'The ancient cathedrals,' said the anonymous Editor of Crockford in 1943, 'are objects of more widespread interest than at any previous period. It is sometimes said that the present day is the Cathedral Age.'[1] Fourteen years before, he was saying the same thing still more strongly, 'There is hardly anything more noticeable in the life of the Church than the resurrection—that is not too strong a word to use—of Cathedral Churches.'[2] This anonymous writer is notoriously not given to bestowing praise lightly. The cathedral renaissance has indeed been one of the most striking features in the life of the Church, and a great deal of it has taken place before the eyes of those who are still living. But it is a story with two quite distinct phases. First the cathedrals had to be made useful. Then they had to be made lovable. The first phase has Archbishop Benson for its hero; the second revolves round the name of Bennett of Chester.

II. *Cathedrals Made Useful*

Benson was a man who thought on the grand scale, after the manner of the great Victorians. He had a vision which he held

[1] *Crockford Papers*, p. 275.   [2] *Ibid.*, p. 83.

I *

tenaciously throughout his life. It was that the Church of England was charged by the pressure of events with nothing less than the whole world's Christianity. This he wrote in a private letter to a friend, while he was still Canon and Chancellor of Lincoln Cathedral, and the rest of his life at Truro and at Lambeth showed that he meant exactly what he said. He believed also that the English cathedrals were the instruments of this dream, the divinely given institutions through which it could best be realised. If the Church of England was to lead the world's Christianity, the first thing to be done was to reform the cathedral system. 'With us,' he wrote, 'there are most important works not done now at all, nowhere likely to be done, nowhere capable of being done, unless cathedrals undertake them.' These 'important works' were five in number—the training of the clergy of the diocese in 'scientific theology and pastoral care, the inspection of religious education, the whole work of evangelism, the preparation and supervision of a new Order of Lay Readers, and the oversight of all the Sunday Schools,' which be believed were 'The catechetical institutions of the English Church.'[1] He therefore wanted in his ideal cathedral a dean and at least five canons. At Truro he was never able to achieve all these aims, though he went far towards them. But he did contrive to become the dean of his own cathedral. It was on principle that he did it, for he was certain, and in his book he said it over and over again that 'the breaking up of the cathedral system really took the form of the drawing apart of chapter and bishop.'[2] This unification of the two offices has, it may be added, been vigorously opposed by all the deans, and few, if any, of the bishops have desired it. Benson did great things for Truro, and through Truro for other cathedrals. He was the pioneer of the effort to think out again the question of what a cathedral is for in the modern world; and his reforms were copied elsewhere. When Bickersteth, for example, became Bishop of Exeter he had unusual luck in that all four canonries in the cathedral became vacant in the same year, so he had the chance to do completely what Benson could only do partially. He made one canon the diocesan missioner, a second had charge of all foreign missionary work, the third supervised the whole range of religious education, and the fourth he called his pastoral canon whom he appointed to look after the younger clergy. The only idea of Benson's he did not adopt was the identification of the offices of bishop and dean; the statutes of Exeter did not allow of it. The extent of Benson's influence on the English cathedrals is shown in the fact that ever since his day the enormous majority of canonries have been disposed of according to the principle he laid down. It is now firmly established that one of the first

[1] Benson, *op. cit.*, p. 110.   [2] *Op. cit.*, p. 81.

functions of residentiary canonries is to provide the diocese with men who can be useful to it. Nine canonries out of ten nowadays have far more diocesan than cathedral duties.

To his list of the functions to be assigned to the residentiary canons in his ideal cathedral Benson was careful to add this caution, 'But let their principle activity be corporate, conciliar.'[1] He realised well enough that his conception of the useful cathedral posed a dilemma. The dean and chapter is a corporate body; its members are to be a community of prayer and worship. If they are this they will also be a family of friends and colleagues. No one has ever doubted this, and certainly Benson did not. But to acknowledge the primacy of this aim is to be involved in a most difficult question. Ought the members of a capitular body to find the greater part of their work in the cathedral and in their studies? If so, can the cathedral give them enough work to do? Alternately, is Benson's conception that a canon should find the chief part of his work outside the cathedral the right one? That Benson did think this is certain, and the fact that he was prepared to amalgamate the offices of bishop and dean in one person shows it. A dean's is essentially a residential post and a bishop's is a travelling post: combine the two, and the traveller inevitably wins simply because he is the bishop and must perforce visit his parishes. If Benson was right, then the cathedral is certainly useful to the diocese, but it cannot be a home for the people. This is what Bennett of Chester felt so strongly. If he had had his way, he would have reduced the residentiary canonries to two, and he would have kept those two in the cathedral all the time.

It is a very ancient dilemma. Charlemagne had realised it and grappled with it, and solved it by anticipating Benson's conception. Residentiary canonries existed, he said, to provide teachers in the cathedral schools, diocesan servants, and historians. But they must also maintain a high quality of corporate life, and cement it by praying and working together. This idea of Charlemagne's of the cathedral as a community of diocesan workers has however often been challenged by the upholders of the other idea, that it should be a college of prayer and sacred study. No one ever admired Benson more than Hensley Henson. He was always quoting from him as from an unquestioned arbiter. But when Henson became Dean of Durham he was strongly critical of all Benson's theories of the true purpose of a cathedral, and he wrote in his diary:

Mostly my mind runs to the older (though too rarely accepted) ideal of the learned and studious dean, standing outside the practical work of the ecclesiastical administration. This ideal is now generally disregarded, and, in some powerful quarters, repudiated. It has been replaced by the

---

[1] *Op. cit.*, p. 111.

diocesan conception, which Benson formulated and pressed forward. I observe in the reports of Westcott's two visitations of this foundation how he was dominated by the notion that Deans and Chapters must find their justification in their *diocesan* service, whereas I apprehend that their true function in the system of a National Church is to correct the local influences and localising tendencies of the diocesan and parochial organisations. . . . Deans and Canons should remember that the interests specifically allotted to them, the maintenance of liturgical standards, and the pursuit of sacred studies—are not local but national in the loftiest sense. The attachment of canonries to diocesan services . . . means the appointment of canons with a view to such services, and this must sooner or later destroy the *raison d'être* of these foundations.[1]

If he had written this some years later, he would no doubt have used some other word than National; but before we dismiss his judgement as erring let us remember that Dean Bennett would have echoed every word in it, though he would also have added some even more significant words to it, as we shall presently see.

But Henson was bidding the wind to cease. To-day there are few cathedrals, except for the royal peculiars of Westminster and Windsor, in which most of the canonries are not attached to diocesan work, and it is in consequence true to say that most canons are now appointed with a view to performing those services. The process has in fact gone much further than Benson or Westcott would have approved, for in most cathedrals half the canonries are virtually reserved to provide the diocese with a suffragan bishop and an archdeacon. Nor could even the dean of Henson's dreams reasonably claim that this is all loss. Compared with the normal cathedral standards of fifty years ago it is gain, for cathedrals have now become so useful that it is hard to see how the dioceses could possibly do without them.

But a price has had to be paid. Cathedrals are not now renowned as centres of sacred learning. The canons rarely have the leisure to become real scholars. Striking and also amusing evidence that deep learning and diocesan usefulness can very rarely coexist in the same residentiary canon was given in a debate in the Convocation of Canterbury in 1925 on the motion 'That a Committee of this House be appointed to consider what practical steps can be taken to encourage the efficiency of Cathedral Chapters regarded as seats of learning.' This debate, like most others, had no observable consequences for the institutions discussed, but it drew from the Dean of Lincoln a sardonic description of what happened when the canons of a cathedral were appointed with a view to their diocesan usefulness :

The members of the Chapter of Lincoln go about as much as ever they can when they are asked. They are also put on every committee in the

---

[1] *Retrospect*, vol. i, pp. 151, 152.

diocese. As a consequence they hardly ever have any time left in which to open a book.

This provoked Canon T. A. Lacey of Worcester, a very eminent scholar himself, to add his testimony:

> It is no use talking about making cathedral chapters centres of learning. The members of chapters are far too busy. It is impossible and undesirable to make cathedral chapters centres of learning. Other places ought to be made centres of learning. Cathedrals are not the places for it.[1]

He did not say which places he would choose to be made centres of learning, but subsequent history suggests that it is to the monasteries that we must look. A very large part of the most original and influential work of scholarship during the last fifteen years has come out of the Anglican monasteries. Lacey was not a man whom anyone could accuse of caring too little for scholarship, but he was a realist and he rightly diagnosed the results of the modern development of cathedral life. A cathedral can uphold its high standards of worship, its chapter can be a genuine community of prayer, and neither of these is incompatible with the fulfilling of a great number of diocesan charges. But no chapter can add to all this the most exacting function of being a school of sacred learning and the producing of original work. The Church cannot have it both ways. It must choose which kind of cathedral it wants, and in fact it has already chosen to follow and develop the line laid down by Benson. He has thus left his impress on the life of the cathedrals for many years. Finding them useless, he showed them the way to become at first useful and later indispensable to the dioceses whose mother churches they are.

III. *Cathedrals made Lovable: Bennett of Chester*

When Frank Selwyn Macaulay Bennett was made Dean of Chester in 1920 one of the first facts he discovered gave him a shock, but it also helped to chart his course. It was that there were quite a number of people who had lived their whole lives under the very shadow of Chester Cathedral but had never once been inside it. The same lamentable fact would have been true of most other cathedrals, and it is still true of some. Those who live under the shadow of a cathedral are generally of two very distinct kinds. There are the dwellers in the close or the precincts, and there are those in the little tangles of dark and insanitary cottages which are so often to be found just round the corner within a few hundred yards of the cathedral walls. These are the people who are so apt to think that the cathedral is not for such as they. They do not become sightseers because they live

[1] *C.C.C.*, February 1925, pp. 29, 32.

so close to it that they take it for granted. They do not become worshippers because they suppose that everything inside it is all pomp
and solemnity, a ritual of class-consciousness, in which they can have
no part and which offers no place for them. In this they are mistaken,
but they do not come inside to be convinced of their error.

It takes a very long time to get rid of a general impression which
lives on long after the facts which once justified it have changed and
been reversed. For years, even for centuries, English cathedrals did
give the impression of a beautiful but a cold remoteness, and many
members of their congregations felt that they were there on suffer-
ance, and for fear of feeling it far more people never went inside.
There was indeed an occasion even as recently as during the war
when the dean of an English Cathedral informed the members of
the congregation in his Christmas Day sermon that they were allowed
to worship in the choir only by the grace of the dean and chapter,
who could at any time turn them out and keep them out.

In the nineteen-twenties a whole series of cathedral reforms were
undertaken in order to reverse the facts which had given rise to this
sad general impression. Time had shown that to make a cathedral a
centre of diocesan usefulness did very little to make it the spiritual
home of the people: to be useful was not the same thing as to be
lovable. In this second reforming movement, Chester cathedral
became the inspiration and the criterion for all the rest. It was
not alone in its pioneering work, but far more than any other at that
time it gained the public reputation of being determined to make
itself a spiritual home for all manner of people, and of giving the
warmest possible welcome to every soul that entered its doors. Its
brilliant success in this enterprise was due to the vision and the
personality of its dean, F. S. M. Bennett, who, more than any other
single figure, became the hero and the linchpin of the whole effort,
going on simultaneously in many cathedrals, to get a cathedral to be
used by all because everybody who came into it was made at once to
feel himself a welcome guest in his own home, and God's.

Bennett was a genius. But his genius is capable of analysis, and
the different threads which, woven together in synthesis, went to
form the unity which made him the greatest dean of his generation,
can be separated and identified. First and foremost he was a pastor,
and the Church of England has always known how to appreciate that.
He was interested in people, in all people just because they were
people. He liked all kinds of people, and he had no sense of class-
consciousness anywhere about him. Thus he had the power of inspiring their confidence. The cathedral he loved because people
came to it, and he undertook all his heavy work of renovation and
reform in order to make them want to come to it. When he had done

it and the cathedral was always full, he was always inside it. His pastoral opportunities came to him in the cathedral, so he stayed in it and sought no work outside it. He loved crowds not more and not less than he loved the separate individuals composing them. Whether he saw people in the mass or singly he was equally interested in them for he was a natural psychologist, to whom no crowd was an ordinary crowd and no person an ordinary person. All alike became to him an adventure in perception and understanding. Thus he came to have a most penetrating knowledge of how people's minds work; and he gave full recognition to the vast potency of the general impression that a place, or a political party, or a movement stamps upon the imagination. He knew that it takes a vast amount of reasoning to destroy a false general impression once given, and that suggestion is many times more powerful than argument or exhortation. More than that, he knew exactly how to create the general impression he wanted, and that in cathedrals, as he once remarked, 'The great thing is to arouse interest, and stately nothings won't do it.' He was certainly no enemy of stateliness in the right place: no dean ever took a more minute care than he over the marshalling of a procession, or over getting every detail of a Sung Eucharist exactly right. The eye, the ear, and the nose, he said, were the organs through which one received one's impressions—and particularly the nose, for he once said, 'The best preparation for a great crowd in a cathedral is to burn some incense.' He had, moveover, a strong sense of humour, a tremendous zest for life, for all living, breathing, and existing things, and a corresponding distaste for inertia, decay, and death. It gave him the power to quicken sloth into urgency, to take the inert and give it motion. The outburst of King Hezekiah might well have been his motto, 'The living, the living, he shall praise thee as I do this day'; and when he looked upon ancient buildings, he instinctively echoed the same monarch's earlier remark, 'The grave cannot praise thee, death cannot celebrate thee.'[1] Things that were dead he contemplated with no pleasure at all, especially when they were cathedrals, and about the sort of decay he found in parts of the building at Chester he once wrote, 'Some may think that ruins are pretty. This is a perverted taste. The ruin of a soul and the ruin of man's handiwork are both horrid. The only ruin that is nice is the ruin of something that was horrid to begin with, like a dungeon.' These quotations have made clear another of his native strengths, an eye for the effective choice and arrangement of words. In his book, *The Nature of a Cathedral*, there are any amount of unusually vivid phrases which catch the eye and linger in the memory—as, for example, this, 'Beauty is just the veil of thinnest lawn through which the

[1] *Isaiah*, xxxviii. 18, 19.

pure in heart may see God.' A man who could talk and write like
that was bound to attract attention towards whatever he was undertaking, and one of the reasons for the phenomenal speed of his success at Chester was his flair for the right kind of publicity. He could
not possibly help making other people aware of his dreams and con-
vincing them that they ought to be pursued until they became living
facts. Nor did he find much difficulty in persuading them to help,
which was important because every dream of his depended on the
previous raising of a very large sum of money. In Bennett, in fact, the
man, the need, and the opportunity all met, and the work done in
and for Chester cathedral in his time became one of the great episodes
and influences in the life of the Church in modern times.

To him a cathedral was no museum; museums are full of dead
things, so he disliked them. He had very little of the archæologist's
interest. The cathedral he dreamed of was a lovely living thing, and
the life in it—living people, living worship—was for him nine-tenths
of the loveliness. A great church was a place provided by God to be
a home of peace and beauty, of release and joy, a bit of Heaven lent
to the earth. There, more than anywhere, he thought, the work of
Heaven could be done on earth, for within a cathedral Heaven
should be able to communicate its own blessed spirit.

During the summer (he once wrote) extraordinarily good people organize
missions on the sands of Blackpool and elsewhere; but all the sea shore
sands of England are not a patch on the opportunity of its cathedrals on
Bank Holidays and summer Saturday afternoons.

But before anything like that could happen, people must be made to
want to come. The cathedral must be made interesting, and its
interest must be made known. When the people came, it must seem
to them as a home; so it must be obviously welcoming, both in atmosphere and in appearance. It could only have a welcoming atmosphere if all who worked there, dean, canons, vergers, choir, and
cleaners, were themselves a family, happy in the home. The abolition
of all tips to vergers was only a part, though an essential part, of this
process. In the welding of various grades of workers and differing
individualities into a team of single-minded enthusiasts Bennett
showed himself greatly skilled. If it was to be welcoming in appearance, there must be no fees of any sort, no forbidding or minatory
notices, free access everywhere and nothing locked but the safe.

I do not think myself that a Cathedral can even begin to do its proper
work until it has replaced visitors' fees by pilgrims' offerings. This being
my rooted conviction, I should have urged the abolition of fees in our
Cathedral at Chester, and should have stuck to the policy of a free Cathedral, even if we had lost money by the change. As a matter of fact we have
increased our receipts five-fold and each year they go on increasing.

The people who were to find it a home were broadly of three kinds, the casual visitors, the people who came on some diocesan occasion, and members of various vocational groups, as for example soldiers from the Cheshire Regiment. The need of the first required a priest to be generally on duty, if only to be available for those moved by the beauty of the place to open their grief. One of the reforms Bennett advocated but did not achieve was the reduction of the residentiary canons to two, but these two were to be full-time cathedral men. Moreover, he would have the full staff of cathedral clergy present at the Eucharist every morning, and at Compline every night. Those who came on a diocesan occasion would find it all the more a home if they could be fed and hold their meetings on the premises.

By a real cathedral (he wrote) I mean a great central, family house of God, through which, and through its many essential chapels, the diocese can express its manifold corporate life, under the shadow and in the inspiration of which it can do its rapidly increasing business, and in which or near which it can find refreshment for soul and body. At Chester we have just decided to move our diocesan offices into a house adjacent to our refectory and cloister, where we shall enjoy hereafter, and all under the same roof, a spaciousness and convenience that many a city might covet for its municipal buildings.[1]

Visitors who came as members of some vocational group would feel the cathedral was their home if they could say of one of its small chapels, 'This is ours.' Bennett was a great believer in making a full use of the chapels, and he once wrote:

A cathedral without chapels is like a gaunt, unfurnished house; a cathedral with chapels furnished, but used for no particular living purpose, is like a great house occupied by someone who does not know what to do with it.[2]

Such a man, tenaciously holding to just such visions, was Bennett when, one day in 1920, he surveyed Chester cathedral with the eyes and from the point of view of its new dean. There would, he saw, have to be many changes before any of his dreams could bear their fruit. Internally, it was far from welcoming, externally, parts of it were in bad disrepair. Two generations before Dean Howson had gathered, chiefly from America, £100,000 for its repair. This money had kept the cathedral standing erect. His successor, Dean Darby, had also done much to furnish the chapels, and had erected a rood over the entrance to the choir. Bennett did not therefore, as he himself was always saying, enter upon a wholly neglected heritage. Nevertheless there was much structural work left for him to do.

---

[1] *The Times*, August 5, 1924.   [2] *Ibid.*, August 5, 1924.

The north wall of the nave was unsound, the tower was shaky, the refectory was ruinous, the roof of the north transept needed over-hauling, and the north-west corner of the building was 'mouldy and tottering.' All this meant that he must first immerse himself in the raising of the £25,000 which would be needed for repairs. In the meantime he could make a start on the inside; and very soon every forbidding notice was taken down, fees and tips were abolished, and the cathedral was free and open for every hour of daylight on every day in the week. Chapels were gradually cleaned and furnished and then dedicated to the honouring of this society or that, of the Cheshire Regiment, of the Mothers' Union. Forty helpers were quickly enlisted and trained to show visitors round. The dean him-self was almost always to be found there, a tall figure in a cassock, with a welcoming manner, and an astonishing knack of making people want to talk with him, and, if need be, of piercing at once to the heart of their trouble. The fame of it quickly travelled, and the news spread far that at Chester something unusual and ex-citing in the life of cathedrals was happening. People came to see what it was, and went away to tell enthusiastically of what they had seen. Through this spreading process came much of the finance needed to save the building structurally, to rebuild its refectory, and to make its cloisters again usable and beautiful. The speed with which all was done can be illustrated by the dates of the rebuilding of the refectory. In 1920 it was a ruin, with neither windows nor roof. In 1922 it had been re-roofed, but inside it was still 'full of mess and out of gear.' In 1923 it was ready for use. It had four long tables and a high table, each with clean cloths and gleaming silver; and its high west window made the great room gloriously light. Pilgrims could be fed; and the diocese could and did use cathedral and re-fectory for a three-day convention of a hundred priests, who could find all they needed, beds alone excepted, without once leaving the precincts of the cathedral.

The impression which all this made was great and wide, and in due course it reached the London press. The accounts of it there pub-lished are perhaps the best of all the testimonies to the work Bennett did. First, there is *The Times*, of July 28, 1924.

A CATHEDRAL IN USE

New Methods at Chester

No traveller can enter Chester Cathedral to-day without feeling at once that it is different from other cathedrals. There seem to be a great many people in it; and they are all moving about, or sitting quiet, or unpreten-tiously on their knees, just as if they were very much at home there. If he is used to the ways of English cathedrals, he may even feel a little ill at ease when he can find no notices forbidding him to do this or that, no locked gates, and not a single official demanding 6d. He begins by wondering whether he has had the bad luck to be an intruder upon a specially invited party, and whether he ought not apologetically to slip out. A very little perseverance will show him that he, too, has been specially invited, and that all day and every day throughout the year the whole cathedral is open and free and his.

That is the first and most easily apprehended aspect of the great, the revolutionary change effected by Dean Bennett in his four years at Chester Cathedral.

. . . The ancient refectory of the monks, till very lately a ruin, is now a refectory once more, roofed, glazed, inviting, set with tables, and having a kitchen of its own (though it is no more than the passage way to the great kitchen of the monks), from which food, both cheap and good, is passed through the old buttery hatch, whether to the Chapter when it takes a meal there together in brotherhood, or to choir-treats, school-treats, parties of Cheshire soldiers, mothers' meetings, from any place in the diocese.

. . . and on the east side of this there are four chapels. One of them is specially devoted to the Church Lads' Brigade, the Boy Scouts, and boys in general. Another, the chapel of St. George, is the chapel of the Cheshire Regiment and its war memorial. Another is for the Church of England Men's Society and men in general; and in the fourth, which is for missions, stands a big globe so that you may find the very place where this or that missionary is working and say a prayer for him. There is also a chapel for the Navy (Chester Cathedral has the colours of H.M.S. Chester which flew at the battle of Jutland); the Lady Chapel is the women's chapel; there is a chapel for girls, and at the west-end, near the font, is the cheerful place where children come to look at pictures and books, and leave their little offerings of flowers and paintings, and say their prayers, and some times begin to play until they are gently shepherded into places fitter for play.

. . . One could multiply detail; but only a visit to Chester Cathedral can properly convey the unusual impression of a Cathedral that is in use and alive from end to end, a place where everyone is made to feel at home and where religion is made to seem quite natural. It is no small thing that this confidence in the public's honour and care has not once been abused; and it is interesting to learn that, since all fees were abolished, the receipts from visitors have been quadrupled.

Two years later, E. V. Knox, of *Punch* visited the cathedral, and wrote in the *Punch* of August 4, 1926, in his own charming style of what he found.

. . . Earlier in the summer, I was moved (also in Mr. Punch's pages) to criticise the authorities of a Midland Cathedral for their grudging policy of opening that building to visitors for only a brief hour-and-a-half each Sunday; and the time restrictions and sixpenny fees to be contended with in many other cathedrals have long been a source of provocative grief to this too feeble but persistent pen. Well, let me say roundly that Chester is a model. It is the most friendly and welcoming English cathedral that I have ever entered. Not a closed door; not a verger in sight; everything explained and made interesting by placards; picture-postcards on sale everywhere at twopence each, but no one to collect the twopences—you are put on your honour to drop them in a slot; and, more perhaps than all, there are garden seats *on which you may sit* around the fish-pond and fountains and among the flower-beds of the cloisters. I was never more pleased, more surprised.

At first it had seemed incredible. I stepped warily, at every turn wondering more and more what could have happened, why I was being given such latitude, why I was unmolested. In God's most beautiful and spacious houses we get so accustomed to importunity and warnings. Was there a verger's strike? Had there been a massacre of vergers? And then, at the entrance to the slype, I found one of the notices explaining the position. 'Free access to the whole cathedral,' it runs, 'both on Sundays and week-days, is given to visitors, in the confidence that they will in return—' and then follow the expectations, which are briefly, that they will behave themselves and remember that cathedrals are expensive to maintain.[1]

To-day, there is no cathedral in England where Mr. Knox would be 'molested,' as he calls it—none in which he need pay one penny which he does not gladly choose to give. This is one measure of the place Bennett has in the story of the twentieth-century Church.

But there is still another standard of measurement. One day a middle-aged woman was shopping in Chester. She had long been ill, and was facing much other trouble, and, being tired, thought she would go into the cathedral to rest for a little. She entered the nave and sat still and quiet, when suddenly a tall man in a cassock came and sat down beside her. She had never seen him before and had no idea that he was the dean. He smiled at her and said, 'You've had a lot of trouble in your life, haven't you?' 'Yes, but how did you know that?' Then he talked for five minutes, and left her. She never saw him again, but the memory and inspiration of that five-minute encounter remained with her all the rest of her life, and strengthened her at the moment of death. So it was for one woman, and for how many more? He had found cathedrals useful, and he made his own, and through his own so many others, lovable as well.

IV. *Cathedral Pilgrimage 1934*

If a cathedral is to claim in action its title of the Mother Church of a diocese, it must somehow make itself a place where the mass of Christian people are spiritually at home, and to do this it must show a concern for the strains and problems which help to determine the shape of life for the people it desires to welcome. In 1934 Britain was in the thick of the years of mass unemployment, and the agonies of it formed the first of all concerns in all minds, not only in those who were immediately its victims. At first sight it might seem that the grandeur and magnificence of cathedrals made one world and the anxious insecurity of the millions of unemployed workers made

---

[1] Reprinted by kind permission of the proprietors of *Punch*.

another, but nobody who had any vision of the cathedral as a mother of churches and people could be content with this separation. Thus when the suggestion came from a group of experienced social workers who were searching to find an answer to the chronic problem of the contradiction of widespread want in a world of plenty, that some good might come of mass pilgrimage to British cathedrals by people who would be pilgrims within the purposive context of the unemployment crisis, the idea was at once welcomed, first by the Dean of Canterbury, and then by all the other cathedral bodies in the British Isles. It would give them a chance to show once more that the Church cared deeply for the privations and anxieties of the millions who were out of work, and that the cathedrals, popularly supposed to be so remote from the cares of ordinary people, so superbly secure that they could not come alongside the minds of the insecure, were as concerned as the little parish church in the back street which had all its parishioners on the means test, and so could never escape from the problem by day or night.

Between July 1 and 14, 1934, this vast but scattered pilgrimage of Christian folk of all kinds took place. It was headed by the King and Queen who themselves became pilgrims to Westminster Abbey, joining in the opening pilgrimage service there, and wearing the pilgrimage badge. Everyone was asked to go on pilgrimage to at least one cathedral during the fortnight, and to pay the sum of half a crown for doing so, or if not half a crown then a shilling, and if even a shilling could not be afforded, then just a penny or two. The whole of the money offered was to be used for the good of the unemployed in those parts of the country where the burden was heaviest to be borne.

It was one of those spontaneous gestures which touched the chords of public imagination. The long pain of mass unemployment had left hardly any citizen untroubled in mind. But it was not in mind only that he was disturbed. His conscience also was affronted, and although no one could say just what effect upon the challenge of unemployment a great cathedral pilgrimage would have, and no one supposed that this would have power to put men back into work again, yet he dimly remembered that there was an ancient tradition that to go on pilgrimage was one of the classic ways of expiation. The ordinary citizen could not say *Mea Culpa Mea Maxima Culpa*, but it was in his conscience that unemployment most affronted him, and he could not divest himself of his own share in the guilt of it, so that the suggestion of a pilgrimage of expiation and sympathy was welcomed with an eagerness which those who first made it had hardly expected. The whole press fostered it, and in an article in the *Yorkshire Post* on July 7, 1934, Mr. Harold Nicolson spoke aptly for Church, press, and people when he praised the plan, because its originators had

shown much psychological ingenuity. The whole world is tired of impersonal travel, and this scheme provides the desired touch of romance, of individual service, of purpose. The pilgrim will have before him on every journey a sense of destination. He will enter the cathedral feeling that he has come from afar to perform this service.

The pilgrims were numbered in scores of thousands. They came by foot and by car, by water and by air. Some, as at Durham, were too poor to afford even a sixpenny badge; yet they thronged the great cathedral and offered their mites, and at the end *The Times*, on July 13, 1934, gravely commented on such as these, 'The pilgrimage has confirmed the popular saying, "It's the poor that helps the poor".' Travellers in Britain of many nationalities joined in; at Canterbury the pilgrims included Finns, Swedes, Hungarians, Indians, Africans, and many others. There were not a few who promptly improvised their own cheerful variations on the common theme. Two Cambridge undergraduates, for example, collected an elderly two-seater car and made pilgrimage to each one of the fifty-four cathedrals from Truro to Aberdeen; a number of people tramped the ancient Pilgrim's Way from Winchester to Canterbury; at Portsmouth, where the pilgrims were gathered each day on the Grand Parade to be led in procession by the bishop to the Cathedral, the long file was headed by two young men who had dressed themselves in the pilgrims' garb of the Middle Ages. All these with their judicious mixture of gaiety and purposefulness were in the pure Chaucer tradition, and afford an interesting example of how a tradition may linger for centuries unforgotten in the subconscious imagination of a nation, until an occasion comes which recalls it to memory.

In every cathedral there was a great pilgrimage on the Sunday, and every weekday pilgrims were met by the dean or provost, were conducted by him round the cathedral, and a service held for them. As the whole enterprise was connected with the unemployment challenge, this prayer was normally used at pilgrimage services:

O God of all wisdom and might by whose Spirit of truth man gains control of nature and makes her yield abundance of good things; give us, we pray thee, skill to speed our ploughs, to set our engines working, to pursue the path of science, to quicken enterprise and stimulate invention, and so to solve the problems of exchange and distribution that we be no longer tempted to destroy, or to restrict, or to withhold the things men lack, nor suffer needless want in a world where thy plenty abounds.

Apart from the services, each cathedral offered the pilgrims some special attraction of its own. At Derby the cathedral was decked with special banners and pictures. Durham opened its famous library and exhibited its historic manuscripts. At Manchester, true to the Lancashire tradition, they performed selections from *The Messiah*. At Winchester an historical play, *The Marriage of Henry IV*, was performed thrice daily in the Close, and at evensong 'the finest works of Wesley and other Winchester composers' were sung. At Exeter rest-rooms and meals were provided. In fact every cathedral did all it could, and nearly all found that they were crowded by pilgrims every day in the week.

It accomplished the raising of a large sum of money for the help of the unemployed, but something more than this, something intangible, indefinable, but real had been achieved. The cathedrals had taken one more step out of their old, fabled position of majestic aloofness from ordinary life and common folk; and the old tradition of Christendom that a pilgrimage was an event charged with spiritual potency had reasserted itself. It was left for an American observer to find the apt phrase of summary: 'Its dignity, purpose, and gentleness made a beautiful demonstration of a nation's sympathy for the unemployed, and its abiding interest in the leadership of the Church.'[1]

V. *The New Cathedrals*

The attention given in this account first to Truro and then to Chester may seem a little excessive and exclusive, and in truth practically all the cathedrals during this period concentrated much energy on making themselves more the homes of the people than they had ever been before. The fine work done in Manchester Cathedral first by Dean McCormick and then by Dean Hewlett Johnson to make that grim and black but still lovely building loved by the whole body of the citizens and a true home for the diocese was as symbolic as it was successful. At the same time the basis of cathedral finance was broadened and, in a way, democratised by the invention and rapid development of the institution called The Friends of the Cathedral, which is to-day an essential part of the financial resources of practically every cathedral in the country.

But the real testimony to the fact that the cathedral system was popularly believed to have a future as well as a past was the amount of building of new cathedrals which was being undertaken. Of these Liverpool is the most famous and the most nearly complete. The first portion of it was consecrated on July 19, 1924, in the presence of the King and Queen, in a ceremony perfectly organised and managed. Liverpool Cathedral has always attracted at least as many pilgrims and visitors as any other, and has always known how to

---

[1] *The Cathedral Age*, Washington, Autumn 1934.

make them welcome. Its services are usually packed. In the same period the new cathedral at Guildford was begun, and the work of enlarging the parish church cathedrals of the new dioceses of Blackburn and Sheffield was put in hand. The war temporarily ended these enterprises, but in time they will be completed. At no time since the Reformation has there been a tithe of the amount of cathedral building in England as we have seen in our own day; and no institution is dead when this can be said of it.

CHAPTER NINE

THE SEARCH FOR CHRISTIAN UNITY

I. *The Lambeth Appeal of 1920*

No Church passes through total war without being soiled in the process. It lives and works in all the warring nations, and on both sides of the barrier. It cannot be loftily superior to the miseries and glories of the nation in which it is set to witness, and it cannot avoid being itself compromised by every shift to which a nation fighting for its life is driven. Nor is a Church in any position to throw stones at the curse of nationalistic separations, for disunity is the immemorial occupational disease of every religion, and the Christian religion not less than others. Nevertheless great worldwide Churches do more easily think internationally than secular governments. Their faith and the inner springs of their being are cosmic in range. The diseases of separatism, though chronic, are for Churches also aberrations; and it is easier for Churches than for nations when a war has ended to come back again to their true course of seeking the unity of peoples and civilisations in a common loyalty to the King and Lord of all. Because both these characteristics lie deep in the situation of Churches, it is right and seemly, because it is good both for Church and State, that as soon as possible after a totalitarian war is ended a great international Church should gather its representative rulers from all over the world. Such a gathering reminds the world that in spite of all that has happened humanity is one and indivisible; and it offers to churchpeople an opportunity to express their sense of corporate repentance, and a chance to take up again their true mission of co-operation in creative fellowship in the proclamation of the Gospel in the changed world which a total war always makes.

It was this instinct which caused the Archbishop of Canterbury to determine to summon all the Anglican bishops to come together at the earliest possible moment after the war had ended for another Lambeth Conference, which was held in 1920. But those who looked only at the passing moment of history in 1919 and 1920 may well have doubted, as some did doubt, whether the time was ripe for it. Could the bishops do anything whatever to influence the calamitous course of political and economic fact? But they might even by the mere fact of their assembling, and apart from any wisdom which might come out of it, do something in the field of suggestion which would have the effect of changing the meaning and allaying the bitterness of the

249

facts. The background of the Conference could hardly have been more gloomy. Of the peacemaking at Versailles, J. M. Keynes had already delivered his judgement in *The Economic Consequences of the Peace*, a work of that highest journalism which is bound to be read, and which so describes facts and makes prophecies as to create universal moods. Half a dozen little wars were still being ferociously fought. Greeks and Turks were at each other's throats. Nearer home there was 'John Bull's Other Island' where Sinn Fein ruled. All the Russias were a sea of totalitarian cruelty. The infant League of Nations had already been virtually sabotaged by the refusal of the United States Congress to ratify the pledges of participation given by Woodrow Wilson. All content and all sense of great achievement had fled from the world, which oscillated feverishly between a false prosperity and a miserable destitution. Every democratic assembly of government was so behaving itself as to make a mock of genuine democratic principle. The realistic prophecy of Macaulay, 'Very few and very weary are those who are in at the death of the Blatant Beast' had come true with a vengeance; and the thoughtful among those weary few could not derive from current politics any reasonable hope that either their children or they themselves would be allowed to enter the kingdom of settled peace.

This lamentable catalogue had forced many people to realise that to build again upon spiritual foundations offered the only hope for hope. A conference of bishops, truly international in character and dedicated to just such an enterprise, might itself be an occasion of that hope, and therefore it was welcome. But all the more was it necessary that it should speak words with real meaning and deliver a message quick with spiritual power. To deliberate for weeks, and then to produce an encyclical letter and a crop of resolutions piously hopeful and platitudinously uninspired—if this were to be all, it would almost be better that the bishops should never be brought to Lambeth at all. Small wonder that the bishops came there heavy with responsibility. They knew better than anyone that the subjects which such a conference at such a time must consider were precisely those which most provoked platitudinous utterances. Some of them pressed their doubts on the Archbishop, Randall Davidson, who was indeed singularly well aware of them himself. But having taken full account of every possible danger, and having done his cautious utmost to be armoured against it, the sum of his judgement agreed with that of the hopeful, that the Conference ought to be held, and at that particular time, and that the holding of it would, in the providence of God, be a signpost for the tormented world pointing the way to the land of righteousness.

The members of the Conference themselves held very varied

opinions about the range of its influence. On the one hand there was Bishop Lawrence from America, who said, 'I doubt if there are a hundred persons in the United States who attach the smallest impor-tance to its decisions.'[1] On the other, there were the Bishops of Peter-borough, Hereford, and Zanzibar who joined forces to write a brief impression of the Conference and who were sure that 'whole churches and congregations were on the qui vive, watching in tense expect-ancy for any signal which might be hoisted at Lambeth.' The truth no doubt lay midway between these judgements. No conference is ever as important as its enthusiasts or as uninfluential as its pessimists suppose; and this Lambeth Conference, as things turned out, was perhaps the most influential of the whole series. What made it so was the work done by its committee on Reunion, for the Lambeth Appeal for Unity which the committee drafted and the Conference issued was certainly not the least important of the documents in the long history of Christendom. Its influence lay in the catholicity of experience of the bishops who issued it, in the circumstances of the moment in history when it was proclaimed, and in the actual phrasing and arrangement of its contents. The year 1920 was certainly a land-mark in Christian history, and the bishops whose work made it so have been described in the published diary of one of their number, Henson of Durham, who was certainly no uncritical admirer either of them or of the Conference, in words which are well worth quoting:

The bishops themselves impressed me as a body of men intensely earnest, not (with few exceptions) either learned or men of marked intellec-tual powers, but devoted to their work. It is no exaggeration to say that the Conference had something of the range and largeness of a truly Catholic assembly. Some of the missionary bishops are ecclesiastical statesmen of no mean quality. Several men struck me as genuinely apostles, e.g. Brent, now Bishop of Western New York. The prevailing spirit of the Conference was neo-Tractarian, though there were a good many bishops who would call themselves Evangelical. . . . There is a real desire for union with non-episcopalians, but no adequate perception of the difficulty.[2]

Thus even Henson, who also wrote, 'I count the days till this precious Conference is over,'[3] paid testimony to the universal faithfulness of the Anglican episcopate; and because they brought that quality to Lambeth with them the Conference was undoubtedly used by God.

The Conference gave its mind to many subjects but it lives in history for its handling of only one of them, and that by far the thorn-iest, the reunion of the Churches of Christendom. To end an ancient outrage upon the last prayer of Christ[4] had for centuries been the dream of all who cared that this prayer of His had not yet been

---

[1] Hensley Henson, *Retrospect*, vol. ii, p. 17.   [2] *Ibid.*, pp. 22, 23.
[3] *Ibid.*, p. 15.   [4] *St. John*, xvii. 20, 23.

granted. But the history of the efforts to give unity for division had not been encouraging, and reunion is always an alarming subject to discuss. It is so easy to utter vague platitudes of aspiration which have no life in them, but in avoiding the platitudinous it is even easier to exacerbate the divisions, and even to add new schisms to old ones. In hardly any field of human thought and action is it harder to avoid doing more harm than good. That is true of reunion generally and always. But it was so to speak even truer than usual in the circumstances of 1918. Every great war is an example of the judgement which overtakes disunity in the political sphere; and the end of each one causes a deep longing for international unity among all ordinary folk. So it was in 1918. But by 1920 it was already clear that the ordinary instruments of state diplomacy could not bring it. Here at Lambeth were the bishops of a great supra-national Communion of Churches, meeting in the Name of Christ and praying for the inspiration of the Holy Spirit. The erring statesmen had claimed no such authority and offered no such credentials. Might it not be possible for such a body of men at such a moment of history to show a new road to the unity of mankind by taking the unity of Christendom many steps towards realisation? If it was impossible to give unity to people who worshipped the same God and recited the same creeds and read the same scriptures, how could it be possible ever to unite all mankind politically in fruitful co-operation? So many pondered and watched, and the bishops who were appointed to serve on the reunion committee of the Conference knew it. It made them solemn with burdens.

When Gore wrote apprehensively in January 1920 to the Archbishop:

> I hope that Divine Providence intends the Church of England to exist over the next year or two without a schism which would separate off the Catholic section, but I dread the Lambeth Conference and its consequences.

he was thinking of the modernist and the reunion issues, and the latter he judged especially dangerous because reunionists were people 'who yield themselves to their amiable impulses and do no clear thinking.'[1] But he wrote before he knew the composition of the reunion committee. It contained no doubt some men justly described in Gore's words. But those who carried most weight in it were famous for being awkwardly honest, for being *difficile*, not for any sort of amiable muddle-headedness. These were such men as Henson of Durham, Weston of Zanzibar, Gibson of Gloucester, and the Archbishop of Rupertsland, ready to pounce upon and correct

---

[1] Bell, vol. ii, p. 1004.

any tendency to put sentimentality before principle: and it had the Archbishop of York (Lang) for its chairman, who led and guided the committee with a skill, a tact, and a vision which was quite incomparable. His chairmanship of it was perhaps the most perfect single piece of work he ever did. The amiability which is impatient with principle and tends to breed schism is, moreover, a fruit of too much optimism in the approach to a task. But there was very little anterior optimism among the bishops who composed the committee. Rather they laboured under a sense of foreboding and even dread.

I had some conversation (noted Henson) with the Archbishop of Rupertsland on the prospect of 'Reunion' in the Conference. He said he was not hopeful: for he found a change for the worse in the feeling of the bishops. He said that the Archbishop of Melbourne (Dr. Lowther Clarke) was as depressed at the prospect as himself. I had a few words with D'Arcy, now Archbishop of Armagh, and he also seemed rather disheartened.[1]

These men, in their several ways, were all on the side of those who put first reunion with non-episcopal Churches of the English-speaking peoples. The strongest among them, Henson, was especially determined to bring about union between Anglicans and Presbyterians. In his diary of the Conference he wrote almost as if only the Presbyterians mattered to him. 'I drew a distinction between Presbyterians and other non-Episcopalians. . . . My demand was that we should acknowledge frankly the validity of Presbyterian Orders and Sacraments.'[2] But other bishops, like Weston, who would naturally see everything from a strictly catholic point of view, were themselves just as apprehensive. After the Conference was over Weston joined with Woods of Peterborough and Linton-Smith of Hereford in the writing of an account of the Conference,[3] which reveals clearly how at first the difficulties were much more clear to them than the opportunities.

Every account of the proceedings of the committee lays emphasis on the sense of frustration and stalemate which made the first half of its course a weary, apprehensive business. Every time Weston of Zanzibar rose to speak—and he was pertinaciously eloquent—the other bishops, having memories of Kikuyu, eyed him warily. They had to listen to a good deal of denigration of the Conference from him, and to acidly humorous suggestions that the bishops would do better to go and live in the slums and ask to dinner the people they found there. In the first days of the committee he sketched an outline of the shape which he believed the great united Church of the

---

[1] *Retrospect*, vol. ii, p. 3.   [2] *Ibid.*, pp. 4, 5.
[3] The Bishops of Peterborough, Zanzibar and Hereford, *Lambeth and Reunion* (S.P.C.K., 1921).

future would take, and suggested that the way to it might well be through federated groupings of Churches, in which the non-episcopal denominations might well form one such group. But this suggestion seemed to get nowhere, and for day after day the committee sat in uncreative perplexity. Especially was this true of that part of the committee charged with the relations with non-episcopal Churches. It reached deadlock, and came near to breaking up; and Henson noted that 'there is a bad spirit among many members.' The context makes it clear that the stand made by some bishops against any approach to non-episcopalians was what provoked his charge.[1]

This frustration was due to the continuous effort of the bishops to move along paths which at that time could lead nowhere, and which were littered with the corpses of earlier optimistic travellers. They wanted to produce a scheme for reunion, a sketch of a united Church, a plan for definite action. But all the time they knew in their hearts that the great mass of worshippers of all Churches had even still but little realisation of the evils of disunity, and less desire to end them. It was when they faced the fact that the first thing they had to do to promote reunion was to convert their constituents to desire it that they began at last to make progress. Their earlier discussions, their interviews with nonconformist leaders, and the reviews they had made of previous reunion movements provided them with a mass of useful material. The question was how it might best be used. Then, on Sunday, July 18, the answer was given to a little group of the bishops sitting on the lawn of Lambeth Palace. The Archbishop of York was there, and the Bishop of Peterborough (Theodore Woods), and two American bishops, Rhinelander and Brent. The Archbishop of Canterbury joined them, and for an hour or more they went through the material they had collected, and the various resolutions they had suggested. The trouble was that it all left them cold, and would be bound to leave others cold. Conference resolutions are invariably chilly, and have no power to warm; and what was wanted was something the mere reading of which would set the blood moving and quicken the desire. To which bishop it was that the inspiration came history does not say, but the suggestion that all the material should be used to inform the theme of a great appeal made history. The party on the lawn considered and approved it, and little by little the rest of the committee were brought to the point where they could say of the project, 'It seemed good to the Holy Ghost and to us.' Bishop Palmer of Bombay, a master of good English, wrote most of it; and eventually the whole Conference accepted it and sang the Doxology over it. Thus the document known to history as the Lambeth Appeal was born. It proved to be the act which gave that

---

[1] *Retrospect*, vol. ii, p. 10.

Lambeth Conference its fame, and the issuing of the Appeal was a landmark in the history of reunion.

> We, Archbishops, Bishops Metropolitan, and other Bishops of the Holy Catholic Church in full communion with the Church of England . . . make this appeal to all Christian people. We acknowledge all those who believe in our Lord Jesus Christ, and have been baptised into the name of the Holy Trinity, as sharing with us membership of the universal Church of Christ, which is His Body. We believe that the Holy Spirit has called us in a very solemn and special manner to associate ourselves in penitence and prayer with all those who deplore the divisions of Christian people, and are inspired by the vision and hope of a visible unity of the whole Church.

Thus the Appeal began, stressing the fact of fellowship and striking the note of penitence. It was deliberately made, be it noted, to people, not to Churches, recognising that the only power which can give us back our unity is the passionate desire of the ordinary people of Christendom for it. The letter was an appeal, and appeals must always be addressed to the heart and conscience; but it was also a realistic document, which asked people to face the facts and to think about them in the light of quickened emotion and an awakened conscience. First of all it was necessary to define the Church into which all Christians should be able to come. It is a sacrament of God's general will for fellowship.

> We believe that it is God's purpose to manifest this fellowship, so far as this world is concerned in an outward, visible and united society, holding one faith, having its own recognised officers, using God-given means of grace, and inspiring all its members to the world-wide service of the Kingdom of God. That is what we mean by the Catholic Church.

This Catholic Church can be built only on the 'whole-hearted acceptance of' the points of the old Lambeth Quadrilateral, the Scriptures, Creeds, Sacraments, and 'a ministry acknowledged by every part of the Church as possessing not only the inward call of the Spirit, but also the commission of Christ and the authority of the whole Body.' The last of these points had always been the difficulty and would continue to be so. But the Appeal bracketed the statement it was bound to make of the Anglican principle of the ministry with a prior acknowledgement of the Anglican share in the sin of which this difficulty was the consequence, and with an anterior offer of a concession which went further than the Church had ever gone before. The first arm of the bracket was drawn in these words:

> We acknowledge the condition of broken fellowship to be contrary to God's will, and we desire frankly to confess our share in the guilt of thus crippling the Body of Christ and hindering the activity of His Spirit.

Because the Appeal had said that, it could go on to say the more creatively that the Lambeth Quadrilateral was still a basic condition of union. But even this irreducible minimum was more qualified than it had ever been, and in such a way as not to weaken any principle in it:

> We, who send forth this appeal would say that if the authorities of other Communions should so desire, we are persuaded that, terms of union having been otherwise satisfactorily adjusted, Bishops and clergy of our Communion would willingly accept from these authorities a form of commission or recognition which would commend our ministry to their congregation, as having its place in the one family life. We can only say that we offer it in all sincerity as a token of our longing that all ministries of grace, theirs and ours, shall be available for the service of our Lord in a united Church.

That was a big step forward. It offered to non-episcopal Churches that Anglican priests would accept, say, Methodist commission if Methodist clergy would accept the Anglican commission by episcopal ordination. It asked nobody to repudiate his previous ministry.

> God forbid that any man should repudiate a past experience rich in spiritual blessings for himself and others. Nor would any of us be dishonouring the Holy Spirit of God, whose call led us to our several ministries, and whose power enabled us to perform them. We shall be publicly and formally seeking additional recognition of a new call to wider service in a reunited Church.

The Anglican Church thus made it clear once and for all that it neither expected nor desired reunion by piecemeal submission.

The Appeal was made to all Christendom by the Church most fitted to make it; and this act, just because it was done in this particular way, made the Lambeth Conference of 1920 the most important of the whole series.

II. *Report of Progress*

The bishops ended the Conference by solemnly and spontaneously singing the Doxology when the Appeal was accepted. The Bishop of Durham remarked in his diary, 'Everybody was delighted at having reached the end of the Conference, but whether the effort has been worth while may be questioned.'[1] The Archbishop of Canterbury knew that what had been done was profoundly right and of historic importance, but he was not carried away by it, and he forgot none of the difficulties ahead.

He knew that the non-episcopalians would urge that, important as episcopacy might be for future ordinations, it was not important enough to render it necessary for Anglicans to ask those who were already Ministers to receive episcopal ordination: and that the non-episcopalians would almost certainly propose that Anglicans should simply recognise their ministry as it is.[2]

---

[1] *Retrospect*, vol. ii, p. 21.   [2] Bell, vol. ii, pp. 1014, 1015.

This he knew would cost a grave and deep schism in the Church and make confusion worse confounded.

The Appeal was sent to the heads of all the Churches, and each of them returned courteous and encouraging replies. The bishops at the Conference were asked to do all they could to bring it to the notice of people of all denominations in their own dioceses, and to do all they could to encourage discussions between representatives of the different Churches. In a very short time discussions and negotiations of every kind, both official and private, were proceeding in most parts of the world. The years between 1920 and 1930 were the delight of the reunionist and the embarrassment of the historian, for every month that passed added to the variety and complication of the story he would one day have to tell. Not only were these discussions proceeding between dozens of different Churches, but the pattern was made still more complicated and involved by the several world conferences of Churches under the ægis of the Ecumenical Movement, each of which, directly or indirectly, contributed its own quota to the mass of reunion material which the Lambeth Appeal created. Dr. George Bell's *Documents on Christian Unity* deals only with the first consequences of the Lambeth Appeal during the years 1920–1924, and it includes only the more important of the available documents. There are ninety of them, printed in a book of 382 pages, and there are few parts of the world, from Hungary to New Zealand and the West Indies, which did not contribute at least one document to Dr. Bell's collection.

The bewilderment of the modern student who is looking for the wood and cannot find it because of the trees was, however, not shared by Dr. Randall Davidson who kept his finger on all these discussions in a masterly way, and knew at any given moment just how far each discussion had gone, where it stood, and whither it was tending. At Christmas 1923 he sent out a pastoral letter to all the bishops of the Anglican Communion to give them a picture of the whole reunion scene as he saw it a little more than three years after the issuing of the Appeal. This letter shows that the Appeal really did have the effect intended. It was meant to provide a fresh start and to set things in motion, and this it certainly did. 'That Appeal has in all cases formed the background to what has been done and said.'[1]

'Done and said'—inevitably there had been far more saying than doing, but then the saying, the discussions and negotiations, must naturally come first. Nevertheless talk and the composition and exchange of learned documents had in fact brought about solid and

---

[1] G. K. A. Bell, Bishop of Chichester, *Documents on Christian Unity*, 1920–4 (Oxford University Press, 1924), p. 339.

impressive practical results so far as the Orthodox Church of the East was concerned. The Patriarchates of Constantinople and Jerusalem had recognised the validity of Anglican Orders, and the Church of Cyprus had followed their example; and a measure of guarded inter-communion was in fair prospect. The conversations at Malines between Roman Catholics and Anglicans, with which the next section of this chapter deals, were in full swing. A whole series of discussions between Anglicans and the non-episcopal Churches in many parts of the world had been begun and were proceeding in an atmosphere of cordiality and friendship. It looked at that moment as though they might really lead at last and in time to the healing of that breach, and the Archbishop, never at any time given to extravagant optimism, wrote of them:

> It seems to me that we have a right, with thankfulness to Almighty God, to regard the position in Great Britain itself as fraught with hope. There can be no question that the leaders upon all sides, and through them the officers, clerical and lay, of the respective Churches are disposed in quite a novel degree to appreciate one another's position and to look forward to a yet nearer approach.[1]

Of three years' work this was indeed an impressive balance sheet, and in every case the Anglican Church, having issued the Appeal, had maintained the initiative in asking for the discussions.

Nevertheless these high hopes were not maintained as the years went by. By the next Lambeth Conference in 1930, there was but little more progress to report than the Archbishop's letter of 1923 had registered. The difficult mountain of episcopal and non-episcopal orders had resisted every attempt to scale it. The Appeal had undoubtedly done much to produce friendly relations between the Churches, and had been worth the issuing for that alone. But actual reunion seemed no nearer than it had been, except for the Orthodox Church. The difficulties are vaster by far than most people realise, and as an illustration of them this account turns now to describe three typical sets of reunion discussions, with the Roman Catholics, the Orthodox, and the non-episcopal Churches. These three form a fair sample of the course of many others.

III. *Malines*

The largest branch of the Church is of the Roman obedience, and in thinking of reunion it is impossible to ignore Rome for long. To do so is to indulge in unrealistic dreaming. It is particularly true of the Anglican Church that she may not forget Rome, for she claims to be catholic in history and in temper, and she has maintained intact

[1] *Op. cit.*, p. 340.

all the visible insignia of catholicism. But it is also true that the Anglican Church claims to be reformed, and has ties of loyalty and debts of gratitude to the Reformation. She can therefore no more forget her duty to the several protestant Churches of the world than she can forget Rome. This uniquely central position in Christendom may offer Anglicanism special opportunities in the work of Christian unity, and it was this position which made it apt and meet for the bishops of the Anglican Communion to address to the whole of Christendom an appeal for unity. But this centrality means that any effort to seek for unity made by the Anglican Church must be difficult and complicated beyond the ordinary because it is impossible for her to move so far in one direction as to lose touch with other Churches. It is inevitable that the Anglican course in matters of re-union is always specially tortuous and involved, and that its history should always take on the air of highly complicated diplomacy. This initial difficulty of having to face two ways at the same time makes discussions and negotiations with any one Church far more delicate and exacting than they would otherwise be, but it is part of the *data* of Anglicanism and it has to be accepted.

From the time of the Reformation until 1920 there had been few negotiations with other Churches, but among them was one serious approach to the Roman Catholics. The conversations conducted by Lord Halifax and others in 1894 and 1895 may have been unofficial but they were serious. But they ended discouragingly with a slamming of the door by the Pope with his promulgation of the papal bull *Apostolicæ Curæ* in 1896 which declared Anglican Orders invalid. This wrecking of all hopes had been in part engineered by the English Roman Catholics; and it was greeted by Cardinal Vaughan with public acclamations of joy, and remarks to the effect that the 'Erastian and Protestant Church of England rejects all idea of a sacrificing priesthood,' and finds itself 'shivering in insular isolation.' To this he added his considered opinion that the dream of the reunion of the Churches was 'a snare of the Evil One.'[1] The ground of scholarship in these polemics was cut from under the feet of the Roman Catholic controversialists by the devastating reply to the bull *Apostolicæ Curæ* which the Archbishops of Canterbury and York composed and despatched. But the polemics continued for a time.

As long as the papal bull *Apostolicæ Curæ* remained the unalterable policy of the Holy See not even the limitless optimism of Lord Halifax could suppose that discussions between the two Churches could lead anywhere. Thus from 1896 to 1920 no attempts to resume them were made. But the Lambeth Appeal for unity was sent to Cardinal Mercier of Malines, and produced from him a most

---

[1] J. G. Lockhart, *Viscount Halifax* (Bles, 1936), vol. ii, p. 79.

friendly reply. Here at any rate was a cardinal who did not think that Satan prompted all talk of reunion. The Lambeth Appeal, moreover, contained an offer so worded as to suggest a possible way round the impasse of the papal declaration on the validity of Anglican Orders, for it declared the readiness of Anglican bishops and clergy to accept from other Churches 'a form of commission or recognition which would commend our ministry to their congregations, as having its place in the one family life.'[1] This phrasing seemed both to Halifax and to the Abbé Portal, the survivors of the earlier discussions, to offer fresh hope, and they resolved to seize it. They went to see Cardinal Mercier, Halifax carrying with him letters of introduction from the Archbishops of Canterbury and York, and finding Mercier more than agreeable to the opening of a fresh series of discussions under his own chairmanship if Halifax would bring two Anglican friends with him, the first of the Malines conversations was arranged. Halifax was to take Walter Frere, superior of the Mirfield Community and Armitage Robinson, Dean of Wells, with him—a choice not made by Randall Davidson, Archbishop of Canterbury, but pleasing to him because the absolute self-control of the one and the deep scholarship of the other would do much to keep the exuberance of Halifax in check, while his enthusiasm would act as a goad to their caution.

There have been many accounts of the series of conversations at Malines which began on December 6, 1921, and continued intermittently until October 12, 1926. These accounts are chiefly concerned with the matter of the discussions, and the effect they had upon ecclesiastical politics at Lambeth and at Rome. But they all make it clear that the story of Malines is a drama of personalities. Had the men who met at Malines been other than the particular individuals who took the matter in hand, the talks would certainly have taken a different course and probably dealt with different subjects. They might indeed never have been held at all, and must have ended far sooner than they did. They constituted an heroic effort of a handful of individuals to find a basis upon which it might some day be possible for Rome and Lambeth to talk on terms of equality with an honest and good intent to find the way to end the centuries of separation. All who took part in them were painfully conscious that although they had the blessing of the highest authority on both sides, they were not delegates, they could commit nobody, and whatever conclusions they might come to might very well be at once repudiated by the two Churches. Thus it was that all of them were perpetually struggling to persuade the ecclesiastical authorities to give them more authority by publicly appointing them to do this work, while both

[1] *Op. cit.*, vol. ii, p. 267.

Pope and Archbishop were determined not to be drawn into any committal which would make difficult the loyalty of the Christian souls for whom they spoke.

The whole episode turned upon the personality of Cardinal Mercier, and when he died the talks died with him. He was a fearless saint, a great ruler, and man of heroic humility. During the first world war the faith of the Belgians and their capacity for resistance under foreign occupation was symbolised in the eyes of the outside world by two men. One was King Albert and other was Cardinal Mercier, Archbishop of Malines. His outspoken courage in resisting and denouncing the evil the Germans were wreaking was one of the beacons of Europe in the darkness of those years, and when the war ended he had a prestige throughout the continent which no other ecclesiastic enjoyed. But this courage and this capacity to flame suddenly into righteous anger, and to express it in searing words, was superimposed upon a universal charm and a grave courtesy. If one wanted an example to show that the common phrase, a Prince of the Church, is not necessarily in contrast with the spirit of the Head of the Church as shown in the Gospels, then Cardinal Mercier would be as good an example as history can offer. If there was to be any hope that the conversations would lead anywhere, Mercier was not only the best man that could be found to represent the Roman side, he was also the only man of all those who took part who could possibly have maintained the part of chairman. He had a passion for reunion, and, rare among Roman Catholics, sufficient understanding of the Church of England to know that it could not come either by individual conversions or by absorption. He preached union with, not absorption in or submission to the Roman Church. How near union was to his heart is shown by the spirit of the pastoral letter he wrote to his clergy to reprove such of them as had questioned his welcome to the conversations:

A great nation was, for more than eight centuries, our beloved sister; this nation gave the Church a phalanx of saints whom to this day we honour in our liturgy; it has preserved astonishing resources of Christian life within its vast empire; from it numberless missions have gone out; but a gaping wound is in its side. We Catholics, kept safe, by the grace of God in the whole truth, we lament the criminal sundering which tore it away, four centuries ago, from the Church our Mother; and there are Catholics who, like the Levite and the Priest of the old Law, reproved by our divine Saviour in the parable of the Samaritan, would have a Catholic bishop pass by, proudly indifferent, refusing to pour a drop of oil in this gaping wound, to tend it, and try to lead the sick man to God's house whither God's mercy calls him. I should have judged myself guilty, if I had been so cowardly.[1]

[1] Lockhart, vol. ii, p. 309.

Roman Catholics who can so honour from their hearts another Church are the right people to take the initial steps which might lead some day to a restored unity. At the same time there was a sense in which Mercier was the most thorough-going of all Romans. He held the full doctrine of the papal supremacy with a deep conviction from which he never wavered, and never could have done. More than this, he went even further in his devotion to the Blessed Virgin than his co-religionists would have been ready to go. He wanted the Church to bestow upon her a new title—Mediatrix; and he worked and prayed for the day when the Church would lay it down as an article of dog-matic faith that divine grace came to men and women only through her intercession. With that doctrine no Anglican could have had anything to do. But it seems that none of the Anglicans who took part in the conversations knew at the time that Mercier had this in his mind.

The three men on the Anglican side who took part in the first three of the five series of conversations were Lord Halifax, Fr. Walter Frere, and Armitage Robinson. For the last two conversations the Archbishop of Canterbury officially delegated Bishop Gore and Dr. Kidd, Warden of Keble College, Oxford, to join the original trio. In his diary, Hensley Henson put his finger on the real weakness of their position:

Can anyone who knows the men and knows the Churches pretend to think that Anglicanism is fairly represented by a distinguished mediævalist (Armitage Robinson) and four Anglo-Catholic leaders?[1]

And what he had written privately, he soon said publicly in a letter to *The Times:*

In these conferences the English delegates are not the men whom English Churchmen would naturally regard as champions of 'the historical Anglican position and claims' . . . All of them, with one doubtful exception, are prominent Anglo-Catholics, and one of them, Lord Halifax, is so Roman that the Archbishop has thought it necessary to repudiate his opinions in a special note.[2]

The 'one doubtful exception' was presumably Gore. But having found a handy label which fitted them all, Henson tied it round their necks much too summarily, forgetting that no trio or quintette of men is disposed of or sufficiently docketed by being called Anglo-Catholics or Protestants and left at that. They were in fact as fully different men as could be found in the Church. No one ever believed more sincerely in the catholicity of the Anglican Church than Gore or Frere, but they did not believe it in the same way, and they ex-pressed it very differently. Halifax refused to include Gore in the

[1] *Retrospect*, vol. ii, p. 146.   [2] *Ibid.*, p. 147.

original party, thinking that for this he would be 'impossible.'
Armitage Robinson, the most learned theologian among them, seems
to have played but a little part. It consisted mostly of mislaying important papers at the moment when they were most needed. When
he arrived at Lambeth to report to Davidson, he found he had lost
the papers he needed, a circumstance which did nothing to inspire a
thoroughly uneasy archbishop with confidence in the negotiators.

Just as Mercier was essential to the whole enterprise and the only
possible chairman of it, so on the English side everything hinged on
Lord Halifax, without whom there would have been no conversations. It was his second chance to further the dream of his life, and
as he was now a very old man it was bound to be his last. He was an
extremist in all he did, and these facts set in violent motion the whole
of his latent capacity for single minded enthusiasm. No one was ever
more selfless, and yet, unconsciously, he saw this effort dramatically
as a personal challenge, a chance to vindicate the cause he had ever
made his own, and his own life with it, since his cause and his life
were to him one and the same. He had neither reserve nor detach-
ment. His faith so burned within him that it created in him a credulity at which others marvelled or blasphemed, and made him impatient with relevant facts. When, for instance, the Roman Catholics
so insisted that the papal primacy was given by the very appointment
of Christ Himself as to shock all the other Anglicans, Halifax was not
shocked at all, and was quite prepared to accept it as the price to be
paid for keeping the talks in being, magnificently disregarding the
vital fact that no Anglicans could possibly accept it. Knowing his
Halifax very well (and loving him dearly) the Archbishop had expressly to warn him:

Don't detract from the importance of the XXXIX Articles. Don't
budge an inch as to the necessity of carrying the East with us in ultimate
Reunion steps. Bear constantly in mind that in any admission made as to
what Roman leadership or 'primacy' may mean, we have to make quite
clear too that which it must not mean.[1]

The warning was certainly necessary. But the intensity of faith which
Halifax brought to the task held him firmly cleaving to his purpose,
and no amount of delays, set-backs, and extreme caution from
authority proved able to deter him. They bewildered him for the
moment, but they were quite powerless to dim even for a moment
the light he saw. The last years of his life were strenuous indeed, and
by all medical rules he should have collapsed and died under the
strain, but his faith gave him these extra years, and his inflexible
determination carried him through them to the last bitter moment

[1] Bell, vol. ii, pp. 1260, 1261.

when Mercier died, and the Roman authorities ordered the talks to end.

On December 5, 1921, the Anglican travellers, Halifax, Frere, Armitage Robinson, arrived at Malines, and their hope was reinforced by the courtesy of Cardinal Mercier who sent his secretary to meet them at the station. In the great drawing-room of the Cardinal's palace Mercier, a tall and grave figure who was always the very flower of courtesy, welcomed his guests. The next morning the conversations began. They nearly always followed much the same course. There was Mass in the domestic chapel at seven. Coffee, rolls, and butter were served at nine; and at ten o'clock the Abbé Portal took the Anglican party into the drawing-room, and the vicar-general, Monsignor van Roey, and the Cardinal entered. They all sat round a small circular table, Mercier invoked the blessing of the Holy Spirit upon them, and they began. The talk went on till lunch-time, and after that there was a break until four, when they met again and continued the discussion until dinner at seven. At nine o'clock the guests were expected to go to their own rooms, where they read or wrote until bedtime. The talks generally lasted for two days, so the programme did not seem to be exhausting; and although disagreements must perforce be expressed and explained most of the time, Mercier's personal charm made it easy to speak the truth as one sees it in love. When, at a later stage, Gore came, he thought it his duty to speak of Anglican convictions with all his own ruggedness, but such was the atmosphere of loving kindness which Mercier had created among them that he knew well he might do so without giving any offence. When Gore went back to London, and thought again over what had passed, it was Mercier's goodness which was uppermost in his mind; and he took pen and paper and wrote to his host:

I can hardly express, because it is almost inexpressible, the sense of your goodness towards we Anglicans at Malines. It is not only that you have been so generous a host, but also that you have succeeded in making we heretics feel so completely at home in your house that we felt able to speak with perfect freedom even about the most disagreeable topics. I was touched to the quick by your most persevering tolerance, and I ask your forgiveness if I have said one single word more than was necessary to make clear our position.[1]

But whereas Gore found that in his host, others, and notably Frere, found something else to add to it. This was so ingrained and insuperable a failure to understand the Anglican position that it might be called a blind spot:

[1] Prestige, *Life of Charles Gore*, p. 483.

The largeness of his heart embraced us all but his head did not seem to take in our position. . . . Naughty children we were, but we must be treated with the utmost patience and generosity.[1]

That may be true of his attitude during the first part of the conversations. But as they proceeded the Anglicans found that it gradually became less true, and before the end they saw him tentatively grasping for a position where he at last began to think of the Anglican Church as an inexorably corporate body, and to see that the hope of reunion turned on Rome being willing to treat with her as a partner in Christendom, and to talk of incorporation rather than submission. Even while Frere sensed that the Cardinal's patience and generosity were qualities deliberately willed in him, he knew well the contrast between Mercier and the English Roman Catholics, who would have individual submission or nothing, and realised that never have conversations between Anglicans and Roman Catholics been carried on in so thoroughly Christian an atmosphere.

There were five sets of talks in all, but the last was concerned only with producing an agreed record of the results of the first four—an attempt to tidy up an episode which all knew could go no further. The first discussion began in October 1921 and the last in October 1926. They had all agreed to begin with a point by point comparison of the Thirty-Nine Articles with the formularies of the Council of Trent. Pusey had said once of these two documents that they seemed to him potentially reconcilable. But the comparison of these formularies led them very quickly into a discussion of the processes by which a truth becomes a matter of faith in the Roman Church, and from there it was not a long step to a consideration of all the really vital questions at issue between the two Churches. This first series of talks was not more than a trial run or a preliminary skirmish, but all the major points which were to come up again and again were produced and given a preliminary airing. Of these, two haunted them all the time. They were the position of the Papacy in Roman theology and in a fully reunited Christendom, and the relationship of the Anglican Communion to Rome if full communion were restored between them. Under these two main heads of fundamental disagreement all other sources of division, the Roman additions to scriptural doctrine and the validity of Anglican Orders, could be comprehended. Once settle the difficulties of the Roman doctrine of the Papacy and the terms on which the tradition and self-respect of a local Church could be kept inviolate even when that Church was united to Rome and all the other difficulties would very quickly settle themselves.

It was the primacy of the Pope over the whole of Christendom rather than his infallibility when he speaks *ex cathedra* on matters of

[1] Frere. Quoted in Lockhart, vol. ii, pp. 305, 306.

K*

faith and morals that formed the staple of the Malines conversations.
On this matter Mercier was completely unyielding. It was for him
not a logical necessity but a dogma full of emotional power. When,
in the course of the conversations, a new Pope, Pius XI, was elected,
Mercier at once wrote to his diocese that three hundred million
people paid their homage to the new Holy Father.

> In the intimacy of their conscience and in their full personal independence they paid him the complete homage of their faith, and the submission of their intellect, will, and filial affection, ready to accept death if need be, rather than to infringe, I do not say one of his commands, but the least of his wishes.[1]

To this extravagance of language even Halifax demurred, specially
as Mercier had thoughtfully provided an English translation that it
might be read here. 'I am afraid it won't do us much good. Let us
only hope it won't do harm. Foreigners never can understand the
English mind.'[2] From the beginning to the end of the talks the
Romans never yielded one inch on the necessary supremacy of the
Pope. All Christians whatsoever owed him allegiance and unquestioning obedience. He was not among other bishops *primus inter
pares*, but supreme and unique in his own right, and all forms of
ministry were derived from Christ and through the Pope, and the
Pope alone. This the Romans would state as often as might be required. They did not tire of it. They might vary the words they
chose to state it, and the tone of voice in which they uttered them.
But the doctrinal position never changed in the least. The only real
discussion they would permit about it was over the question of
whether the Pope had this position by the ordering of the Church or
by the divine and direct appointment of God in Christ. The Romans
were sure that it was by divine appointment, and so was Halifax who
held it our Anglican duty 'to recognise a Primacy not merely *jure
ecclesiastico* but *jure divino*.'[3] None of the other Anglicans would
follow him thus far, but the Romans, perceiving that Halifax was
willing, and overestimating his influence on the Church of England,
were prepared to listen to Frere, Gore, and Armitage Robinson
while they argued learnedly and at length on the real meaning of the
scriptural text, 'Thou art Peter and upon this rock I will build my
Church.' They found the Romans both naïve and uninformed about
the ordinary processes of biblical criticism. Frere also commented,
'One of the texts concerning St. Peter had hypnotised the Roman
Catholics in their outlook, to the exclusion of the scriptural description of the Church itself.'[4] Their attitude on this vital dogmatic
issue was well summarised by Gore in a letter to Halifax, 'The R.C.'s

[1] Bell, vol. ii, p. 1261.
[2] Lockhart, vol. ii, p. 280.
[3] *Ibid.*, p. 292.
[4] *Ibid.*, p. 319.

showed themselves quite unrelenting on the dogmatic issue. . . .
They did even more—they made the discussion on the grounds of
Scripture and antiquity more hopeless than ever.'[1]

The shadow of this doctrinal impasse was seen in the first of the
conversations. In the hope of preventing the shadow from becoming
the too solid flesh in other conversations the Anglicans suggested that
the doctrinal issue should be dropped, and instead that they should
talk of the methods whereby the Anglican Communion might one
day be brought into union with the Holy See. When they heard of
this request the Archbishop of Canterbury was doubtful of its wisdom and the Cardinal was surprised. Nevertheless he agreed. The
event showed that Halifax was wiser than either of them at this
juncture. As long as the conversations were held to this one point
they did achieve something. It was not union: it could never be that
as long as there was a fundamental cleavage on doctrine. But the
Romans showed themselves ready to make, and even themselves to
suggest real concessions. In the future it may prove really important
to have it recorded on paper that a group of responsible Roman
Catholic clergy were prepared to make suggestions as to how the
Anglican Communion could be reunited to Rome by methods other
than individual submission, and on terms neither humiliating to
Anglicans nor at variance with their whole tradition.

Two main points were involved here. The first was that in the
Papal Bull *Apostolicæ Curæ* Rome had pronounced Anglican
Orders invalid. Was there any way round or over that? The wording
of one of the clauses of the Lambeth Appeal for Unity suggested to
the Abbé Portal that there might be. The Anglican bishops had
written:

> We are persuaded that, terms of union having been otherwise satis-
> factorily adjusted, Bishops and clergy of our Communion would willingly
> accept from these authorities a form of commission or recognition which
> would commend our ministry to their congregations, as having its place in
> the one family life.

Portal said that in this clause the Anglican bishops had set a great
example of Christian humility. But Mercier, reading it aloud, was
then silent a moment and spoke with hesitation, saying that even so
some form of supplementary ordination would probably still be
required.

The second point also involved the validity of Anglican Orders,
but more indirectly because it was concerned with the attempt to
persuade Rome to agree that the only way to treat with the Anglican
Church was to treat with her as an equal. In the time of Queen

[1] Lockhart, vol. ii, p. 302.

Elizabeth, Anglicanism was established only in a miniature isolated outpost of Christendom, in the provinces of Canterbury and York. But now the Anglican Communion was a worldwide family of Churches, and constantly growing, second in size and in political importance only to Rome herself. On this point Mercier and his friends were far more conciliatory. They were prepared to recognise the special position which the Anglican Communion must occupy in a united Christendom, and provided her bishops would agree that their authority was derived from the Pope, they could agree to the continuance of particular Anglican traditions, such as use of the Book of Common Prayer and the marriage of the clergy. At a later stage Mercier himself said the Roman Church must not attempt to absorb the Anglican. They must work, on the other hand, for a union of the Churches. He then quoted with approval the opinion of a canonist whom he had consulted, and who had said that there should be a new patriarchate of Canterbury, with its own liturgy and canon law, and that when this had been done the Roman Catholic sees in England should be suppressed. This canonist, though highly respected for his learning, was naturally speaking for himself, but Mercier would not have quoted him to the gathering had he not himself approved his opinion.

This concessiveness was naturally academic, but it was still concessiveness. It led nowhere: it could not, for it was based upon the supposition that the doctrinal issues were solved. Halifax was delighted, but both the Archbishop and Gore were perturbed lest the Anglicans should be conceding too much, and Gore wrote:

The concessiveness of our delegation to Malines, apparently at the first Conference and certainly at the second, seems to me more disastrous and perilous the more I think of it. It astonishes me to hear from the Dean (Armitage Robinson) what he was prepared to admit as to Roman supremacy.[1]

The Archbishop, though expressing himself less forcefully, was just as disturbed, especially over the suggestion that Anglican bishops should accept the *Pallium* from the Pope. He wrote to Mercier, as well as to Halifax and his friends, to insist that it was useless to discuss administrative terms of union while the doctrinal issues were still unsettled.

These were the points with which the five conversations were chiefly concerned. But running through the conversations like a single thread may run through a complicated pattern of weaving and yet be always noticeable was the search by both sides for official authorisation. Without this the talks must remain no more than

[1] Bell, vol. ii, p. 1267.

academic discussions which could not lead to where all alike wished
to go, and which might even lie under the condemnation of wasting
the time of busy men. Mercier's hopes were raised by the election of a
new Pope (Pius XI) in 1922, for he was known to have reunion much
at heart. Soon afterwards Mercier was assured 'by an authorised but
confidential voice'[1] that papal authority looked favourably on their
enterprise and hoped it would continue. He reported this to the
Archbishop himself, and wrote to Halifax to say how he hoped that
'the Anglicans with whom we should be conversing next time would
be "Anglicans named by the Archbishop of Canterbury in order to
consider etc." ' [2]

But the Archbishop of Canterbury was in a most difficult position.
Having sponsored the Lambeth Appeal he could not, even had he
wished, withhold some form of recognition from the Malines conversations. But at the same time he could not forget the negotiations even
then in progress with the Orthodox Churches, the Old Catholics,
and various protestant Churches, and could take no step towards the
Roman Catholics which would be likely to make such negotiations
more difficult for they were after all so much more promising. Nor
could he go further officially than his fellow churchmen were prepared to follow him, and it was obvious that hardly any of them
were ready to submit to any form of reordination or to admit the
doctrine of the supremacy of the papacy if it meant conceding that
the whole priesthood of the Church derived its validity from the
Pope. Besides, he was himself completely loyal in his own heart to
the Anglican position, and he wrote his considered judgement upon
the conversations in these words:

> It ought to be made clear on the Anglican side, beyond possibility of
> doubt, that the great principles upon which the Reformation turned are our
> principles still. . . . It would be unfair to our Roman Catholic friends to
> leave them in any doubt as to our adherence, on large questions of con-
> troversy, to the main principles for which men like Hooker or Andrews or
> Cosin contended. . . . What those men stood for we stand for still.[3]

He well understood the many Anglicans who were not prepared to
go one inch of the journey towards reunion with Rome on any terms;
and these were not powerless by any means. While the Malines conversations were going on the chief preoccupation of the Archbishop
was the revision of the Prayer Book, and every passing day made it
more evident that he could not hope it would be easy to pilot it
through the Church Assembly, the Convocations and Parliament.
If the protestants were to be made more suspicious than they already
were it might well be impossible, and the bishops, to whom Davidson
early reported what was going on, were emphatic in their warnings

---

[1] Lockhart, vol. ii, p. 281.   [2] *Ibid.*   [3] *Ibid.*, p. 299.

of trouble ahead. Moreover, while he, like everyone else, held Halifax in love and veneration, he did not trust his judgement and he almost dreaded his exuberance. Nor did he think that either Armitage Robinson or Frere could be a sufficient brake on any car which Halifax was driving.

Accordingly he was inflexible in maintaining the distinction between recognition and authorisation. He would openly and officially recognise that the conversations were proceeding with his knowledge and approval. This he did by including some account of them in his pastoral to the bishops on the progress of all reunion negotiations; and also by officially appointing Gore and Kidd to join the original team. He also maintained a close connection between Mercier and himself by correspondence. But beyond that he would never go, for indeed he could not.

Gradually it became apparent that the conversations were not to have anything more than this by way of official recognition on either side, and that the majority of Anglican churchmen profoundly distrusted them. It was clear, too, that at least some continental Roman Catholics were also hostile to them, for Mercier had publicly to rebuke them for their lack of charity. This knowledge became the signal for the English Roman Catholics, who one and all disliked them intensely, to go openly into action against them.

Halifax remembered only too clearly the fate of the earlier series of discussions, and so he had begun this time by going to see the Cardinal Archbishop of Westminster and asking for his 'good services to help in every possible way to bring about such conferences as Leo XIII discussed in 1894.' Cardinal Bourne received him graciously:

Ah! Cardinal Mercier! (he said) I know him well and have a great regard for him; we were at Louvain together. He is a great man, a most distinguished personality with a strong influence. I am *very glad* that you have seen him.

'My visit,' added Halifax, 'was a great success.'[1] Was it? Even at that early date Bourne had not gone one inch beyond a courteous sympathy. Before the course of the conversations was half run Fr. Woodlock was writing in the Anglican papers to express his hostility, and his belief that nothing could come of them because

With us the infallibility and supremacy of the Pope is a dogma which rests exactly on the same authority as does that of the Godhead of Christ.[2]

Later still, when it was clear that the conversations were not to be in any way official, he went much further and wrote continuously to the

---

[1] Lockhart, vol. ii, p. 273.   [2] *Ibid.,* p. 294.

newspapers in the most intransigently Roman style, in which he was fully supported by the English Roman Catholic press. In the midst of this controversial activity of his he was firmly rebuked by Mercier for misrepresenting Halifax and misquoting Portal, but more than that, because he was

> Attacking the Conversations and making it a grievance that his own experience and advice had not been sought. Mercier rejected assistance from such a quarter and dissociated himself from such methods of controversy. He and his Catholic colleagues were as familiar as was Fr. Woodlock with the doctrine of the Church and had no intention of betraying it. He ended by charging Fr. Woodlock with ignoring the plainly expressed wishes of the Pope himself.[1]

Mercier asked Halifax to have this letter published in *The Times* but Bourne managed to prevent it, and then himself publicly attacked the Church of England at York. By then Mercier was dead, and Rome sent word to his successor that the talks must cease, and the report about them must not be published. The *coup de grâce* was given on January 6, 1928, when the Pope issued the encyclical *Mortalium Animos*. The doctrine of the Papal Supremacy was restated in the extremest language, and certain unidentified movements towards reunion were condemned. A fortnight later the *Osservatore Romano* announced that the Malines Conversations were ended, and would not be resumed.

The English Romans had once more triumphed. But what gave them the victory was the death of Mercier. As he had been in life so he was in death. The doctors told him he had incurable cancer. 'To-night I have something to offer to the Holy Virgin. It is something quite out of the ordinary,' he replied. Halifax realised at once that this would be the end of his dream. He heard that Mercier would like to see him, and, a very old man though he was, he at once made the journey to Malines. There he saw once more the great prince of the Church who had become his friend. Mercier was very weak and his life was fast flowing away. But he found strength to beg Halifax to persevere with the talks, and he dictated a last message to the Archbishop of Canterbury:

> *Ut unum Sint*: it is the supreme wish of Christ, the wish of the Sovereign Pontiff: it is mine, it is yours. May it be realised in its fulness.[2]

Then he took from his finger the ring he always wore, his gold episcopal ring which his family had given him at his consecration, and he insisted on giving it to Halifax, and then he blessed him and let him go.

[1] *Ibid.*, p. 321.   [2] *Ibid.*, p. 327.

The end of the story concerns this ring. Halifax wore it on a chain round his neck until he died. Then it was welded to a chalice, above its base, which the present Lord Halifax presented to York Minster. In that great church this chalice, with Mercier's episcopal ring set in it, has been used ever since on three occasions in the year, on St. Peter's Day, and on the anniversaries of the deaths of Mercier and Halifax. It is the one solid outcome of the great effort they had made together, and the ring may still be a portent.

IV. *Kikuyu*

Kikuyu, in East Africa, is a name which matters in Anglican history, for it was in successive conferences held there that one of the most persevering attempts to find a basis for union between Anglican and Nonconformist Churches was made. This effort was spread over eighteen years. It began in 1908—but at Maseno, not Kikuyu—and it continued at intervals until 1926 when the third and last Kikuyu conference ended and it was lamentably clear that nothing could be gained by calling another. Efforts were still made, however, to stave off the confession of failure. It was not until 1937 that it became finally clear that one more effort to find the way to a union of separated Churches had failed and no one could deny it.

In 1908 representatives of most of the reformed Churches at work in the area met at Maseno in order to reach sufficient agreement to form a federation of missionary Churches in East Africa. The Anglican dioceses of Mombasa and Uganda, the Church of Scotland, the Methodist Church, and the interdenominational Africa Inland Mission all took part. But in 1911 this effort ended in deadlock. Then in 1913 they tried again at the first Kikuyu conference, and this time they did produce a basis of federation. They agreed to assign to each mission its own geographical sphere of influence, and to a system whereby a convert who moved from one area to another would be welcomed and shepherded wherever he went. A limited degree of safeguarded intercommunion was established, and an interchange of pulpits between ministers of the different Churches was agreed. On the vital question of ordinations the conference decided that all candidates should be trained according to an approved system, and then 'be duly set apart by lawful authority, and by the laying on of hands.'[1] It was at the end of this conference that the united Holy Communion was celebrated by the Bishop of Mombasa in the Presbyterian church at Kikuyu which brought the Bishop of Zanzibar into the field in tempestuous denunciation and involved the

[1] Rt. Rev. J. J. Willis and Rev. J. W. Arthur, *Towards a United Church*, 1913–1947, Part I, *Kikuyu and after* (Edinburgh House Press, 1947), p. 31.

whole Anglican Communion in bitter controversy, which only the opening of the first world war stilled.[1]

That made two failures, of which the second had been sensational. The persistence with which they decided in 1918 to try yet again is therefore especially praiseworthy, especially as Frank Weston, whose intervention and charges of heresy had wrecked all the hopes of 1913, was still Bishop of Zanzibar. He was a formidable figure to have in any reunion discussions, but there could be none without him. It was the sincerity of their missionary zeal which made them try yet once more, for the transference of European sources and causes of division to East Africa, where the Moslems were so strong, was doing great damage to the native converts, and seriously weakening the influence of Christians with the colonial government in matters of education.

The third conference at Kikuyu met in July 1918, and was composed of members of the four Churches which had suggested federation in 1913. Again the dioceses of Mombasa and Uganda were represented by their bishops. But on this occasion Dr. Frank Weston and a priest from the Universities' Mission to Central Africa were present as guests. Whether guest or member he was bound to dominate the conference, and this nettle was at once grasped. Before any discussions about terms of union were even begun, the delegates asked Weston to tell them where he stood. He had definite proposals to make, and he outlined them in a speech the whole tone of which showed how absolutely he was with them all in longing for unity. His proposals were nine in number, and of these only three were controversial, for they involved a declaration about episcopacy. He asked acceptance of the facts about episcopacy, that it has always existed and that it ruled the greater part of Christendom. But he said, too, that it need not be a monarchical or even a diocesan institution, and he advocated the democratic election of bishops. 'Nor,' he added, 'is it essential that we hold any one view of episcopacy on the doctrinal side provided the fact of its existence and continuance be admitted.' But he did demand that all the Churches must 'consent to some episcopal consecration and ordination' without which it would not be possible for members of non-episcopal Churches to minister in Anglican churches. But if they would do that, he himself would 'gladly come before any of their congregations, and accept any form of popular recognition.' By these proposals the delegates were surprised, which is strange, for they were the utmost that a bishop holding Weston's views could offer. After a period of reflection the Free Church missions rejected them, giving various reasons, of which this weighed most:

[1] *Op. cit.* See also vol. i, pp. 97–9.

We feel that no basis which places the Church above the Word of God, no ritual which would take the place of personal communion, and no ecclesiastical control which limits personal liberty in vital things, or fails to honour authority conferred by our own Churches, is possible.[1]

It was therefore evident that the diocese of Zanzibar could not be a partner in the federation. But there were other Anglican dioceses in the area, Mombasa and Uganda; and these were prepared to go further than Zanzibar. The conference therefore proceeded to write a constitution for what is called 'The Alliance of Missionary Societies (Protestant) in British East Africa,' in which it was first of all made plain that this was a federation of Missionary societies and not of the Churches through which the Societies worked. A united Church they hoped one day to see. Their immediate purpose was an alliance of missions. This constitution was signed and endorsed by the two Anglican bishops, and it was eventually ratified by the home authorities of all the missions concerned in it.

Although this Alliance was based on a common acceptance of Bible, Creeds, and the dominical Sacraments, it was at first limited in its range to matters of organisation and administration, and it left the thorny questions of intercommunion and ordination alone. If it worked satisfactorily in these easier fields, these questions were bound to be raised sooner or later, but they could be left until they clamoured for solution. In the meantime there was exceedingly important work the Alliance could do in that field which was becoming more significant for missionary expansion than any other, the relationship of missions to government. All the missions in the area could now speak to the government with a single voice through the Alliance, and this they did. They took up with the government every question which affected the welfare of the natives, and they dealt with the educational and medical government departments with a new and enhanced effectiveness. The power of their new administrative unity was such that no government could ignore them, and missionaries became members of various legislative and executive committees of the government. It was a notable example of how greatly the power of Christians over the organisation of society is increased if there is unity and co-operation between them.

The full conference of the missions which had formed this Alliance met once more at Kikuyu in 1922. Since the previous conference of 1918, the Lambeth Conference had met and had placed its famous appeal for union before the whole of Christendom. The bishops at Lambeth had, however, expressly declared against intercommunion and exchange of pulpits. The new Kikuyu conference warmly welcomed the Lambeth appeal, but, moved by their own experience of

---

[1] *Op. cit.*, pp. 56–8.

harmonious co-operation and by the bewilderment of African natives over the ecclesiastical divisions of the Churches of Europe, they demanded more than the bishops at Lambeth had been prepared to grant. The missions in the Alliance resolved to ask the home Churches to which they owed obedience for the following concessions:

1. That at all future ordinations of African ministers the various Churches accepting the basis of the Alliance should be represented by those authorised to ordain in the various Churches, who should participate in the actual ordination so that all African ministers so ordained would be freely recognised as ministers in all the Churches concerned.
2. That all fresh missionaries be ordained in the same way.
3. That ordained foreign missionaries already at work in the country should at once be given the power of mutual recognition.
4. That eventually communicants of any branch of the Church become communicants of all the others without the requirement of a special religious ceremony.

The last request meant that the alliance was now prepared to go further than it had gone before, and to remove the idea of a United African Church from the status of a dream to that of an immediate object of policy. The Church of England could not of course grant their requests, but it was sympathetic towards their formulation. The Church of Scotland called their proposals exceedingly attractive.

The Alliance then set up a Committee on Reunion in order to prepare the way for the United African Church, which it believed to be so nearly a matter of practical politics that in its documents it always referred to it by its initials, U.A.C. The Committee defined the aim as an autonomously governed united Church, regulating its acts 'by the necessity of maintaining fellowship with the Church universal,' and that after union all members of the uniting Churches would be equally full members of the U.A.C. But all this was dependent upon agreement between the Churches in the difficult matter of the ministry, and the sacraments which depended upon it. This could no longer be shirked, and it is remarkable that the committee found itself agreed on these proposals:

1. That all ministers of the uniting Churches ordained before union be fully recognised as ministers in the United African Church.
2. That all future ordinations to the Presbyterate (Ministry) be performed by the laying-on of hands of at least one Bishop and two Presbyters (Ministers).
3. That without accepting any theory as to its reasons the ancient practice of presenting Bishops Elect to three Bishops for consecration be agreed to.

But before any man can be ordained in any Church he must be trained, and to ask for a unified, universal ministry in a single limited Africa Church must be to ask also for a single Theological School for the whole Alliance in which the African priests of the future might be trained. The committee proposed therefore to set up an Alliance Theological College in which all ordination candidates should be required to reside for at least the final part of their training. But this college never came into being.

On paper it might well have seemed to the committee that this last part of their plan might have been the easier to carry into effect. It was logical that a single theological college should precede the unification of the ministry. Moreover the Alliance had by now become experienced and successful in the building and management of schools. Their Alliance High School at Kikuyu quickly became the most famous institution for the higher education of Africans in East Africa, and it is so to-day.

A result of the third Kikuyu Conference, held in 1926, was that

> Communion services, at which all communicants partook were regularly held and conducted by ministers from the various Churches; and in 1935 an *Order of Service for Holy Communion*, approved by the Churches of the Alliance, came into use.[1]

Moreover, the Representative Council of the Alliance agreed in 1929 that visitors from any Church in the Alliance to a district where another Church was in possession of the field, should be freely admitted to communion in that Church without having to conform to its special discipline.

But in 1929 eight Africans of the Kikuyu people were ordained to the Church of Scotland, three at Kikuyu and five at Tumutumu. At Kikuyu a Baptist, a Methodist, and an Anglican priest took part in the laying on of hands; and at Tumutumu two Anglicans joined with the ministers of the Church of Scotland in the act of ordaining. For this action the Anglicans had no episcopal authority. They had not sought it. It was a spontaneous act on their part. Nine years later, in 1935, an Anglican bishop (Dr. Heywood of Mombasa) and three Anglican priests were present when three more Africans were ordained in the Church of Scotland, but though the bishop gave the address, the Anglicans took no part in the actual ordination. Between those two dates, various Africans were ordained in the Anglican Church, but the ministers of the other Churches were not invited to take part in it, for the decisions of the Lambeth Conference had made it impossible to give such invitations.

Thereafter the story is a sad one. The United African Church has receded ever farther into the distance, and denominational rigidity has advanced into the foreground. It has been suggested that the decision of the eight Anglican dioceses of East Africa, meeting at

[1] *Op. cit.*, p. 71.

Kampala in 1937, to ask for the formation of an Anglican Province of East Africa, was responsible. The charge is made on the ground that this involves an Anglican type of organisational administration which cannot be squared with the very different system adopted by the Church of Scotland.[1] Thus on the long series of attempts associated with Kikuyu to unite the Christian Churches in East Africa an epitaph and not a prothalamium has to be written. This epitaph has been justly and charitably phrased by the Rev. J. W. Arthur, of the Church of Scotland.

These movements have undeniably led to that denominational rigidity which was foreseen in the early days and which the Alliance worked so hard to prevent. Doubtless there has been, and is, a great deal of working into one another between the Churches, but it would be true to say that the spirit of denominationalism has become a part of African Church life in Kenya to-day. In spite of this, however, we may thank God for the movement through the years towards a united Church in Kenya, and for all the deepened fellowship between mission and mission, missionary and missionary, and, later, Church and Church, which it fostered.[2]

V. *The Fellowship of St. Alban and St. Sergius*

In the negotiations at Malines and at Kikuyu we have seen the failure of the direct effort to find a basis for reunion between Anglicans and Roman Catholics on the one hand and Free Churchmen on the other. What we have now to witness is a different approach to the same problem, this time involving a part of the Orthodox Church, in which Anglican and Orthodox Christians came together to pursue fellowship and mutual study and understanding, and at a later stage unexpectedly found themselves face to face with a problem of reunion, which both sides felt they must grapple with and pursue.

The expulsion and exile of many Russian priests by the Bolshevists had had at least one effect which had benefited Christendom as a whole. These priests had established themselves in Paris, and had there set up a thriving theological academy, where they prepared for ordination an average of forty students a year, and from which a great deal of first-rate and original theological work came and was available to all the Churches of the Western world. Nicholas Berdyaev was one of these exiles, and all his greatest work was done in Paris. He became one of the unofficial theological tutors of every Church in Christendom, a man whose books one had to read because of the immense distinction of his mind and the depth of his learning. Writing in exile he had a far wider range of influence than would ever have been his had he not suffered the deep pain of exile from his

[1] *Op. cit.*, p. 73.   [2] *Op. cit.*, p. 74.

beloved Russia. With him at the Paris Academy were men of the stature of Bulgakov, Bezobraxov and Florovsky, and many others.

In this Russian Academy in Paris the Student Christian Movement was soon at work, and it was under its auspices that the Fellowship of St. Alban and St. Sergius was begun. Its purpose was to provide a mould in which Anglican and Russian-Orthodox clergy and students could seize the chance of this proximity and come together regularly. As with most things the Student Christian Movement undertook, so with this: 'let there be a conference, and then see what would come of it.' The first conference took place at St. Albans in 1927; and this was so successful that a second was held a year later, and the decision to create the Fellowship of St. Alban and St. Sergius was taken.

It consisted of Anglican and Orthodox members, clergy, laity, and students, and there were a few Free Churchmen, who were associates rather than members, and who held a sort of watching brief. The members had to accept the declared aims of the Fellowship, must observe the rule of regular prayer for the reunion of Christendom, and 'must have the experience of eucharistic worship in the Orthodox and Anglican Church.' The society was one for prayer and spiritual intimacy; it was not, as its members said again and again, any kind of negotiating body between the two Churches.

Its valuable work was for the most part done by the annual conferences. The quality of fellowship achieved was of a high and impressive order, and these conferences gave hundreds of Anglicans a new understanding of the Orthodox liturgy and methods of worship. There was a regular interchange of liturgies at the daily Eucharist; one morning it was celebrated according to the Orthodox use, and the next according to the Anglican use. Members of each Church attended every day, but they made their communions only on those days when their own liturgy celebrated by their own priesthood was in use. The same alternative order was followed every evening when the Anglican Compline alternated with the Russian Vespers. During the day the members prayed, ate and studied together; and it was arranged that the two sides should have an equal share, again in strict alternation, in the reading of the papers to be discussed. It is impossible for sincere men and women to share thus in all the springs of devotion without in the process gaining a vast amount of understanding of each other, or that they can fail to carry fellowship and comradeship over the bridge which divides both from community. There were many who learned at these conferences at St. Albans and, later, at High Leigh, what the Russian word *sobornost* or catholicity really means, and they learned it in the only way they could, that is by actually living in the context of these conferences. Those who were regularly present found that the Russian liturgy spoke to the deepest things in them, and drew from them a haunting sense of unity with their Russian friends. Among the Anglicans Evelyn Underhill was often found. She was then writing her great book *Worship*, and she came to soak herself in the liturgy of the Eastern Church, and found it the more satisfying because she was sharing the experience of it with both Anglicans and Orthodox. The day was to come when there would be much strain and tension within the Fellowship, as is presently to be told; and in those days members were always referring to the experience of the Fellowship at High Leigh as 'a spiritual fact of the first order,' and as something giving them all an authority which 'it is impossible to escape.'

This was a remarkable achievement for there were real difficulties to be overcome. They were mostly due to the inherent difference between the two nationalities, and between men who were exiles and others who were at home and free. The Anglicans found the Russian habit of taking as long as possible over everything both trying and exhausting. Russian services seemed very protracted, and their speeches interminable, and often unintelligible. Once Russian speakers were fairly launched, nothing on earth, certainly not the dinner gong or the signal for morning coffee, would stop them. They would start with some fairly clear and obvious statements, and then delve steadily deeper and deeper, uncovering one fundamental basis after another, with an ever increasing air of being in the sorest travail. Soon they had left their Anglican listeners far behind, and the chairman—not a coveted post—had to decide whether to stop the Russians in mid-course and seem rude, or whether to ignore the refreshment bell and let everyone's lunch or coffee get cold. There is a real truth in P. G. Wodehouse's casual remark about Russian fiction: 'A Russian novel is one in which nothing whatever happens until page 394 when the moujik decides to commit suicide,' and there is a sense in which it applies also to Russian theology. Then the Russians, in their turn, found themselves both bewildered and shocked by the Anglican habit of assuming as beyond argument the agreed results of biblical criticism. Even the book of *Genesis* they refused to regard as allegory, as the Anglicans did, but always spoke of it as 'metaphysically true in what they called the realm of meta-history,'[1] a phrase which did not notably lighten counsel. This in turn brought out the Anglican sense of superiority, and it was a Russian member who wrote:

When the very possibility of critical research in connection with the Scriptures was denied, when beforehand there was prejudiced rejection of

---

[1] *Report of the Second Anglo-Russian Student Conference* (S.C.M., 1928), p. 8.

the last results of criticism, which was sometimes shown by some of the Orthodox members of the Conference, then the English seemed troubled, and often, on seeing such an attitude, became deaf to our arguments, and affirmed that we were simply scientifically behind them, and not therefore competent in these questions.[1]

When Bishop Gore, taking for granted the Christian social attitude, insisted on the translation, 'The Kingdom of God is *among* you,' the Russians were distressed when he would not change it to '*within* you,' since it seemed to them to undervalue the mystical interpretation of the Faith. Someone who was present said that the two sides started with a simple formula, Orthodox equals mysticism and Anglicanism equals social reform, and it was hard to get away from it. Again, 'a phrase used by the Bishop, "Christianity is a life to be lived before it is a doctrine to be believed" puzzled at least one group.'[2] Moreover it was found that the 'Western ethical emphasis' was apt to clash with the 'Eastern eschatological expectation' even over such unexpected matters as the value of the conversion of Constantine.[3] Finally, it was discovered that the word Truth did not mean the same things to the two groups, which is not to say that the Russians valued it less highly than the Anglicans. One who was present at all the conferences defined the difference thus, 'We must remember that two conceptions of Truth are at stake. To the Orthodox Truth practically equals unanimity. In the Western tradition Truth is something outside and beyond the Church: there is an element of exclusiveness about it.' These differences were never overcome in the sense of being charmed out of existence. They remained, and indeed became increasingly evident when a definite uniting action was proposed. But they were made to seem unimportant when set beside the reality and depth of the communion of spirit enjoyed by the two sides of the Fellowship. That in itself was no small achievement, and it still goes on.

From 1927 to 1933 the Fellowship placidly followed the course it had charted. Every day at successive conferences the Orthodox and the Anglican members prayed together, became friends, and tried to understand each other more and more. Each shared in the other's liturgy and the daily eucharist, but they did not attempt to communicate together. But to one of the Russian members, Father Sergius Bulgakov, this seemed an intolerable deprivation. They had done so much together for so long that they had become a unity. Why, then, must they stop short at the sharing of the sacrament of unity? Was it not spiritually dangerous to continue for too long in a mere discussion of differences? Was it to be for ever true that discussion in prayer and fellowship lead only to more discussion? But he was too

[1] *Report*, p. 11.   [2] *Report*, p. 22.   [3] *Report*, p. 23.

much of a realist and had too strong a sense of Church order to suggest that they should simply defy it by communicating together forth-
with. These things he had long been pondering, and at last, at the
conference at High Leigh in June 1933, he thought he saw a possible
compromise, and he suddenly laid it before the Fellowship. It was
that the Fellowship should take what he called 'molecular action,'
and proceed with a plan of intercommunion for its own members,
without waiting for the two Churches as a whole to act officially.
But in order to safeguard the principle of Church order, he asked
that the first communion together should be inaugurated by a special
sacramental blessing to be bestowed upon the Anglicans by an Orthodox hierarch, and that the Anglicans should submit to it and accept
it as 'an act of sacrifice.'

The great difficulties of reuniting two Churches which have once
been separated, even though they have a common dogmatic basis of
belief, are illustrated by the long negotiations which followed this
proposal and the tensions to which they exposed the Fellowship. If
it had not been worthy of its title, they would have broken it to pieces.
Here were a body of men the reality of whose devotion to the cause
of reunion could not be questioned, men who had spent seven years
in learning to test, to know, and to trust each other, men who interpreted their membership of the Fellowship as involving a charge to
set forward the union of their Churches. If reunion were the easy
thing which the unwary think it, such men as they could have accepted Bulgakov's proposal at once. They could not do that, and Bulgakov had not supposed they could. But being what they were, they
could not summarily reject it. Inevitably there had to be much discussion, examination, definition, and negotiation; not less inevitably
the long process smothered the germ of the idea, and to read the
papers which tell the story is to wrestle with what has every air of a
peculiarly involved and tortuous piece of international diplomacy,
in which complication silenced simplicity, and all the actors
knew perfectly well that it was doing so, and yet were helpless to
stop it.

First of all, what was a sacramental blessing, and what in this context did it imply? Bulgakov had said that it must be given by an
Orthodox hierarch, and had asked the Anglicans to accept it as 'an
act of sacrifice.' Did that mean that the Anglicans were in any way
submitting to the judgement of the Orthodox hierarch on the validity
of their orders, and were thus admitting to any doubt about them?
No, replied Bulgakov, that was not so. The sacramental blessing

is not to be confused with re-ordination or conditional ordination, or any
other sacrament of the Church. It is to be related to the purpose of partial
intercommunion, and is defined as expressing the need of sacramental

action in an effort towards restoring the violated sacramental unity of the Church. It would be conferred on both clergy and laity taking part.

Nor was the sacramental blessing to be thought of as itself a sacrament. It was, on the other hand, something belonging to the indefinite field of possible *sacramentalia*, which existed in the Orthodox Church.

What we want is the Sacrament of Union—a new Sacrament. Such a Sacrament does not yet exist, but the possibility of such sacramental development for special cases exists. . . . My personal dream is that some time the Church will bless the work of artists or scholars by a special Sacramental Blessing, which would express the exclusive importance of such work.

But the work done by artists and scholars was not more important than that being attempted by the Fellowship. It needed now a measure of intercommunion to set it loose and free, and that in turn needed a sacramental blessing to inaugurate it. Thus he argued, and as time passed he was persuaded to add to his first suggestion the considerable addition that the Orthodox members too must be sacramentally blessed by an Anglican bishop. Two years later (the negotiations were still going on) Bulgakov was persuaded to give a more detailed picture of this sacramental blessing. It is

a solemn blessing bestowed by the appropriate episcopal authority for the purpose of establishing Eucharistic intercommunion. It is bestowed from the Orthodox side by the bishop prior to the celebration of the Liturgy during Prime . . . through the laying-on of the hands of the bishop on the Anglican priest with the words of the prayer from the ordaining of priests, with the words changed in an appropriate manner. 'The grace divine cleaveth through the laying-on of hands on the priest N. for inter-communion with the Orthodox members of the Fellowship of St. Alban and St. Sergius, wherefore let us pray for him that the grace of the all-Holy Spirit may come upon him.' The corresponding blessing is bestowed from the Anglican side by the Anglican bishop on the Orthodox priest for the same purpose of intercommunion in the Eucharist.

Such was Bulgakov's proposal. He knew he must make it, but perhaps he was secretly uneasy about its outcome, for he added a warning, 'We shall be held responsible if we have not the daring to try this new Sacramental Blessing.'

The executive of the Fellowship devoted its next meeting to Bulgakov's proposal. Its chairman, the Bishop of Truro, Dr. Frere, was cautiously welcoming, and said that the remoteness of full sacramental union was not so great as was sometimes supposed, but he was also very technical and full of words like Economy, of distinctions between praying and negotiating bodies, and of questions about how far such a Fellowship as theirs could be regarded as a canonical body. This meeting set in motion a series of negotiations of great complexity and length, which need only the briefest description here.

In November 1933 Bulgakov and the Bishop of Truro met. Dr. Frere was still welcoming in manner, but in substance was even more cautious than he had been before. He counselled 'careful discussion proceeding over a period of years,' to which Bulgakov replied rather pathetically, 'The plan of the Bishop of Truro is to go on discussing it at five or six conferences, and I myself (as well as the Bishop of Truro I imagine) cannot be at all sure that we shall both be in this world for these five or six conferences.' These conversations were reported to another meeting of the executive in February 1934. Bulgakov showed himself increasingly apprehensive over the unexpected opposition of many Russians to his idea, and yet persisted with it because, he said, 'I am sure that a reunion of the Churches by the official and diplomatic way will never be achieved.' However, the Fellowship as a whole was sure that the conversations must still go on, and at the conference in June 1934 the Bishop of Truro, as chairman, consented to their continuance on three conditions. They were that the corporate thinking must be clear and accurate, that any action taken must be disciplined and unhasty, and that the Fellowship must definitely state its readiness to make this task its own. This decision was taken privately to Dr. William Temple, who approved of it but added:

With regard to the proposals of Bulgakov you will remember that the recent decisions of both Convocations would approve inter-communion at gatherings of the Fellowship in a case of this sort. I confess I do not think that the Convocations will go further and specify certain Fellowships or Societies as those which may most reasonably avail themselves of the permission then given in general terms.

But by the end of the year (1934) it was clear to most of the members that there was really no chance of a unanimous acceptance of the sacramental blessing, nor of the intercommunion which it was designed to inaugurate. For on December 16, Mr. A. F. Dobbie-Bateman, a layman who was the convener of the executive, wrote a note in sad terms:

The first question is: is the proposal for Intercommunion between the Orthodox and Anglicans still alive? I do not mean: is it still on the agenda? but has it within itself any further power to move and inspire our thought? My own impression, for what it is worth, is that, at any rate in its present form, this proposal cannot now be considered alive . . . The plain fact is that the proposal has scarcely moved one step forward during the discussion of the past year.

He gave a summary of the reasons for this deadlock, and then added, 'I certainly must admit a considerable degree of disillusionment,' and asked pertinently, 'If the Fellowship is actively to pursue the cause of Reunion, what kinds of activity are open to us?' But he did not attempt to answer his own question. He had accurately sensed the hitherto unspoken judgement of his fellow-members. They had given the proposal every chance, and it was clear that it could not work. In May 1935 Bulgakov made a last desperate attempt to keep it alive, but vainly, and after that it slowly petered out.

Instead of nurturing Bulgakov's proposal the discussions had smothered it. Yet they were carried on by men of goodwill, who were friends, and who had known each other at the deep levels in Christ. If these men failed, no others in the same circumstances could have succeeded. The blame, if blame there be, falls on the circumstances, not on the men. At the time when Bulgakov made his proposal the circumstances which made it impossible from the beginning of course existed, but they were not then seen clearly. Nor could they have been, for only by the kind of discussion which followed could they be displayed in a clear light.

What, then, were the circumstances which doomed all hope of the sacramental blessing and intercommunion within the Fellowship? Take the Russian side first. It was soon made clear that the Russians were themselves divided about it. Bulgakov knew from the beginning that he would find opposition from his own side, but he had not realised how strong the opposition would be. Florovsky, for example, spoke for many of the Russians when he said that the sacramental blessing could not absolve schismatics from the duty and obligation of submitting to the sacrament of penance before admission to the Church, for this was the essential rite for the reception of schismatics 'in their existing orders.' It seemed to him that under the proposals intercommunion was to be had too cheaply by the Anglicans; and this naturally strengthened the convictions of those among the Anglicans who were against it. When Bulgakov said on many occasions that his proposal had nothing to do with the question of the validity of Anglican orders, many of the Russians promptly made it clear that they believed the exact opposite. Bulgakov, in fact, was in a minority among the Russian exiles, while they themselves were not in harmony either with the Church of White Russia or with the Patriarch of Moscow. The Russian members of the Fellowship were quite uninfluential in the counsels of Orthodoxy as a whole. In addition to this, Bulgakov had to further his proposal in the Fellowship with one hand while with the other he was defending himself before his Metropolitan on charges of doctrinal heresy. These charges had nothing to do with his proposal, but were concerned with something he had written about the Orthodox doctrine of sophiology which had caused him to be accused of 'pagan-gnosticism.' He had little difficulty in defending himself, but the mere fact that the charge could be made weakened his authority.

The Anglicans were just as divided about the wisdom of Bulgakov's proposals, but with them the division was more even. They were very conscious that more of the Russians opposed it than welcomed it, and that the exiles as a whole certainly could not count on being supported by the rest of the Orthodox Church. As negotiations between the Anglican and the Orthodox Church were at that time being officially conducted by the highest authorities of both Churches, the Anglican members of the Fellowship were particularly anxious not to do anything, however well-meaning, which might damage the official negotiations. At that very moment the negotiations with the Orthodox Church in Rumania had reached a most important stage; and if the hierarchy in Rumania decided to commend a measure of inter-Church communion, it was most likely that the Church in Yugoslavia would follow suit. Thus Tissington Tatlow spoke the real mind of the Anglicans when he said in a letter to Nicholas Zernov:

> I am not convinced that we should concentrate our attention on achieving Intercommunion between a very small group of members of the Anglican and Orthodox Churches. I think we should aim at something bigger. . . . Those of us who hesitate about Intercommunion on the limited scale proposed are not to be thought of as people who wish to do nothing. . . . Whatever we do must have a far larger objective than that. If Intercommunion of the type suggested were likely to lead on to Intercommunion on the wider scale (i.e. between the two Churches) I should feel differently about the proposal.

That thought was certainly present in the minds of the Anglicans and that it should be voiced by so doughty a champion of Christian unity as Tissington Tatlow underlined and deepened it. There was, moreover, another hesitation. Each Church of the Anglican Communion was constitutionally free, and if the diocesan bishop gave his approval there would be nothing ecclesiastically illegal in the measure of intercommunion proposed. But it was commonly understood by every part of the Anglican Communion that the different Churches composing it do not act independently in matters of high importance without having first laid the issue before the Lambeth Conference. That conference had laid upon the individual diocesan bishop the duty of deciding upon such an issue as this. But it was still true that what one Church did affected all the others, and the Anglicans feared to take an action which might compromise the sister Churches before they could be consulted. So it was that the conclusion of Tissington Tatlow's letter laid bare the true reason for the Anglican hesitation:

> I think that if we go in for limited Intercommunion at this stage, we shall do two things: (1) Isolate the Fellowship from influence which in the Providence of God I believe it is meant to have in the Orthodox world. (2) We shall make relations between the Church of England and several of

the Orthodox Churches very difficult at a time when everyone ought to be praying that conditions may not arise from within any of the Churches . . . making difficulties.

But though there were the deeply felt difficulties among the Anglicans, they seem to have been seldom mentioned in the actual discussions. They were strong in desire to communicate with their Russian friends, for all alike had been honestly and deeply moved by the experience of praying and studying together. Thus they felt bound to keep the discussions going long after there was any hope left that they could succeed. Thus the discussions proceeded to take the simple and obvious and to complicate it almost beyond recognition by a very free use of technical jargon. And the Russians were always being reminded of the Anglican responsibilities as a 'Bridge Church,' holding out hands to all other Churches, and this was used again and again as a reason for refusing to be so far committed to one Church as to make more difficult the approach to the others. But experience has shown clearly that if one stands in the centre of a circle offering to shake hands all round or not at all, the result is that nobody at all takes one's hand.

So the proposal had failed, and the limited intercommunion had proved impossible, and the Fellowship was gradually brought back to the path which it had made its own, and in which it still beneficently continues.

VI. *Estimate of Progress*

The stories of Malines, Kikuyu, and the Fellowship of St. Alban and St. Sergius are all disappointing. Yet to the high hopes with which each began the Lambeth Appeal contributed much. That was the great merit of the Appeal: it did quicken hopes which before it were rather moribund, and it did cause all sorts of people in every Church to take fresh heart and a deep breath, and to start out once more to tread the old and weary road. But the journey became weary again as it always had done before. The fault of this was certainly not in the Appeal. It aroused hope. It even offered a way round the old Hill Difficulty of different conceptions of the ministry by which no Church was asked to surrender anything but only to add to what it already possessed. It set things moving which had previously run down into a dejected quiescence. It succeeded in what it set out to do. The consequences were indeed disappointing, but the fault was not in the Appeal. Where, then, was it?

The three examples of reunion activities inspired by the Lambeth Appeal suggest some part of the answer. Malines showed that reunion is never possible where the parties disagree on vital doctrine,

where one party demands surrender as the price, and where the negotiators have no real backing from their Churches in the shape of a
widely felt desire to be reunited. Kikuyu shows that nothing permanent is to be had from attempts simply to by-pass the crucial difficulty of Orders and impatiently to treat it as the idiosyncracy of a few
theological pedants. The Fellowship of St. Alban and St. Sergius
shows that intercommunion is the fruit of reunion and not a means
to it, and that when it is treated as a means it does the aim of reunion
no good, and comes near to breaking what measure of unity in
the spirit has already been achieved. These three examples, taken
together with the other discussions and negotiations which the
Lambeth Appeal set in motion suggest also that a clear line of demar-
cation must be drawn between the action of small, private and unofficial groups within the Churches, and that of the action of Churches
as a whole through their officially appointed leaders who negotiate
in the name of the whole body. Both kinds of action are necessary.
Each is essential to the other. The function of the small unofficial
group of members of two separated Churches, such as the Fellowship
of St. Alban and St. Sergius, is to create a desire for unity and the
spiritual atmosphere of friendship, understanding, and trust in which
it can be pursued. If it goes beyond that it jeopardises the good it
has done and runs the risk of creating positive harm, and for small
groups to run independently ahead of the Churches to which they
belong hinders the cause. Negotiation is the function of Churches
as a whole, carried on by their appointed officials. The solid achievements in the field of reunion between 1920 and to-day have always
been the fruit of officially conducted negotiations between Churches.
They include the recognition of the validity of Anglican Orders by
most of the various Patriarchates of the Orthodox Church, the
achievement of full communion between the Old Catholic Church in
Europe and ourselves, and the setting up of the South India United
Church.

In the whole field of Church history there are very few negotiations
more tortuous, more prolonged, and more complicated than those
which resulted in the most notable act of reunion of this century, the
setting up of the new South Indian United Church in 1947. It is composed of the Presbyterians and Congregationalists, who had already
united to form the Old South India United Church, the Methodists,
and, at last, the Anglicans of the South Indian Dioceses. The story
is so long and complicated that it would be wholly disproportionate
to the scheme and purpose of this book even to summarise it here.
Indeed, a bare summary would need a whole book of its own, for not
only did each Church have constantly to consult its own home
authority, but in India the Methodist Church had to obtain the

sanction of five, the Anglican Church of sixteen, the old South Indian United Church of nine separate bodies for every draft put forward and every step taken. The whole process, too, was subjected to a great barrage of advice and warning, of encouragements and forebodings from home; and was still further complicated by the fact that the Anglicans had to keep the missionary societies as well as the Lambeth Conference and its permanent consultative body informed of all they proposed. The difficulties were so many that it is hardly short of a miracle that agreement was ever reached at all. Yet it was, and there the united Church stands to-day, not indeed part of the Anglican Communion for thirty years until the different ministries have been unified by time, but an autonomous Indian Church, with Anglican bishops and priests serving in it. The achievement is a testimony to the enduring strength of the original impulse of 1919, when thirty-three ministers, almost all of them Indians, met at Tranquebar, and solemnly stated:

We face together the titanic task of the winning of India for Christ—one-fifth of the human race. Yet, confronted by such an overwhelming responsibility, we find ourselves rendered weak and relatively impotent by our unhappy divisions—divisions for which we were not responsible, and which have been, as it were, imposed upon us from without; divisions which we did not create, and which we do not desire to perpetuate.

The misgivings from within and without which these reuniting Churches have had to face were many, and they still are. But the simple and moving words of those thirty-three Indian clergy of Tranquebar have proved to be the most potent of all the forces engaged.

Such are the visible results of the Lambeth Appeal. Its invisible results may well be ultimately still more influential. There is to-day an honest and consistent desire for real friendship between the Churches, and in very many towns that desire has become a realised fact. Fraternal associations between Anglican clergy and Free Church ministers are not only more numerous but also far more fruitful than they used to be; and in many places they have led to regular co-operation in the proclamation of and witness to the Gospel through councils of Christian congregations, united missions, and even, here and there, regular weekly chapter meetings of all the clergy and ministers in a district, at which the whole routine work of the Churches in the district is planned and dovetailed. We have all come, too, to the point where the very name of religious and sectarian controversy is hated, and even the most bitter partisan hesitates for longer than once he did to stir the ashes of dead quarrels or to raise new fires.

As these words are written the Lambeth Conference of 1948 is about to meet, and once more it will be devoting much of its prayer and discussion to furthering the long process of reunion. The bishops to-day are at the very least in a far better and more Christian position over this most imperious need of Christendom than they would have been if their predecessors of 1920 had not issued the Lambeth Appeal.

CHAPTER TEN

MISSIONS AND CHRISTIAN COMMUNITY

I. *'One of the Greatest Eras'*

This title is in inverted commas because it is a quotation: but what gives this fact significance is the source from which the quotation comes. It is from the seventh and last volume of Professor Kenneth Scott Latourette's, *A History of the Expansion of Christianity*[1]—a work fully as authoritative as it is monumental. This last volume covers the thirty years 1914–1944, which, at first sight, most people would promptly classify as one of the most discouraging eras the Church of Christ has ever experienced. But Professor Latourette does not think so. Over and over again he calls these thirty years 'one of the greatest eras of Christianity.'[2] However grievously Christianity suffered in some lands, its gains over the whole field were greater than its losses, and in 1944 it was exercising a more potent influence over the world than in 1914.

When the last volume of Professor Latourette's work was published in 1945 some reviewers in secular journals rubbed their eyes over the author's optimism, as though it was somehow a sin for a Christian writer to display the unfashionable but Christian virtue of hope. But the really significant fact about this judgement that ours has been one of the greatest of all the eras of Christian expansion is that it was made, and reiterated again and again, by the man who quite probably knows more of the detail of missionary work than anybody else in the whole world. As he surveys the world, region by region and country by country, he gives ample documentation for his estimate. At last no serious doubt has been left in the reader's mind because the Professor has forced him to keep his eye on the big maps.

In 1944 there were more Christians than in 1914; they counted for more in world politics, and they were more evenly spread over the world. No one could reasonably hope to say which of the various Churches of the world had done most to make this era great, but the Professor states emphatically that it was due more to the non-Roman than to the Roman Catholic Church.[3] In any case ecclesiastical competitiveness in Christian expansion is both unseemly in itself and foreign to the modern spirit of co-operation between nearly all non-Roman Churches, which has done more than anything to make the

---

[1] Published by Eyre and Spottiswoode, vol. vii, 1945.
[2] E.g., pp. 3, 65, 410.   [3] *Op. cit.*, pp. 16, 17.

expansion possible. But in the whole endeavour it is quite certain that the Churches of the Anglican Communion have borne a very large share, though no one will ever know how large a share. Indeed, it would not be possible even for the most rigid and exclusive Anglican to survey the whole field, isolate a portion of it, and say, This is solely the work of the Anglican Church. To write of Christian expansion between the wars (the really fruitful twenty years) is quite impossible unless one is prepared to think internationally, inter-racially, and in interdenominational terms. It cannot be otherwise done, because the thing happened in that way, and not in any other. The expansion has been both a cause and a consequence of the steadily increasing co-operation between the Churches, while this co-operation in its turn has been throughout soundly based upon the evangelistic motive. The movement towards co-operation between the Churches and the missionary cause have been in our time inextricably inter-twined, and everything which has happened in the missionary sphere since the Edinburgh Interdenominational Missionary Conference of 1910 proves that it really was the portent which at the time it seemed to be. 'Hang on to co-operation like grim death,' ran the cable from the Chinese Christians to the new International Missionary Committee set up after the Edinburgh Conference. The Churches have done so, and the expansion was made possible. There is therefore no separating for the purposes of literary convenience the cause of Christian unity from that of worldwide evangelism, and the two stories must be told together. Far from separating them, there is yet another to be added. This is the story of how the Churches perceived with steadily growing vividness that their evangelistic task was the bringing of the saving power of the Gospel not only to separate in-dividuals all over the world but also to the total culture, the social order, the systems of getting and spending of these individuals. This is the story of the Churches' growing sense of responsibility for the life and work of people as much as for the people themselves.

This width of co-operation forms what is known as the Ecumenical Movement; and this in turn is like a rope woven out of three strands. They are the movement towards unity, which came to be called Faith and Order; the movement towards the re-creation of the sys-tems which support society as well as of the people who compose it, called Life and Work; and the whole world cause of missions. But the Ecumenical Movement, though made out of the plaiting of these threads, is nevertheless more than their sum. It has been a steady drawing together of non-Roman Christendom, and of the Churches which compose it. This movement has reversed in our own time the universal trend of Christendom for more than fifteen hundred years towards the ever wider separation of the Christian Bodies. By

L*

A.D. 500 nearly all Christians were united in a single Church. From then until our own time the spirit of independent separatism had triumphed over the spirit of unity. But from 1910 onwards, and especially after 1918, the spirit of unity began to triumph over the spirit of separation, and that at a time when the pressures of secularism were driving the nations of the world further apart than ever before. Moreover, the new unity of co-operation is not, as the unity of A.D. 500 was, the triumph of any one Church over its rivals. It is a unity of spirit, not of absorption. Its aim precludes any possibility of unity by absorption, for it is a drawing together of Christians of different ecclesiastical loyalties who bring precisely their differences as well as their points of agreement into the larger fellowship, and who welcome each other in Christ's name as bringing different experiences of Church life, which by their differences enhance the richness of the common pool of experience to be explored and shared. Thus while 'Faith and Order' is concerned with reunion, and missions with evangelism, the Ecumenical Movement has been concerned with both but not exclusively with either. It hopes indeed to pave the way to reunion, but 'it is wholly to misread the history of the ecumenical movement to suppose that it is simply concerned with reunion.'[1] It is indeed concerned with evangelism, for it grew out of an evangelistic and missionary soil and has always been tied to the soil which nourishes it. But all the great conferences of the movement have laid their stress on the renewal of the Church, and therefore the movement has recently been thus defined, 'Essentially the ecumenical movement stands for the recognition that evangelism, unity and responsibility for society, entwined under the Cross, are the indispensable marks of a Church which would be renewed into the likeness of its Lord.'[2]

The movement began in a conference—Edinburgh 1910—and during the years between the wars it marked its growth by periodic conferences—Stockholm 1925, Lausanne 1927, Jerusalem 1928, Oxford 1937, Edinburgh 1937, Utrecht 1937, Madras 1938, and Amsterdam 1939. It was indeed an era of great interdenominational conferences. But until 1937 each of them was organised under the ægis of one of the supporting movements out of which the Ecumenical Movement was made. Thus Lausanne and Edinburgh were concerned with Faith and Order, Stockholm and Oxford with Life and Work, Jerusalem and Madras with missions. The title made a real difference, but the membership of these conferences seemed to be often much the same, as did the technique of organisation. The same great figures of the Ecumenical Movement were to be seen at most of them, whatever their theme, 'not simply (or even partly) because they

---

[1] Oliver Tomkins, *Reunion from Above or Below?* in *Theology*, 1948, p. 284.
[2] *Ibid.*, p. 285.

liked conferences, but because they realised that the conferences were ultimately all about the same thing'[1]—the renewal of the Church. They found, too, that they were all about the same thing in another sense. However complex the world scene, and however multitudinous and various the problems of Christendom laid before the conferences by the delegates, it was realised that every speech was talking of the same war. From the Arctic to the Falkland Islands and from California westwards round the globe to Formosa it was one war— Christianity versus Secularism, or God versus Mammon. It is undoubtedly true that in this period the several Churches did very much to renew their life by a full use of the conference as an instrument; and this tendency seems certain to continue. The interdenominational and international Christian conference has been doing for modern times much that the General Council of the Church did in ancient times. It is the invention of twentieth-century Christendom, and the primary instrument of whatever community it has achieved.

II. *The Great Conferences*

There seems in retrospect to be no doubt at all of the great power for righteousness which the long succession of conferences exercised. Nor is there any doubt that they were always exacting and exhausting. It took months of work to organise them, and the achievements of one in the series had to be tied to the hope for the next by the labours of continuation committees. While they were in being every account which has been written of them agrees that they laid the delegates under heavy strains of more than one kind. These strains bore most heavily on those who had the leadership. There was, to begin with, the inevitability of physical fatigue. The long sessions of the conference must be attended, and the still longer sessions of its subordinate committees. At these every speech, every interjection must be hearkened to with sympathy and concentration. Without this it would be impossible to draft the reports and messages, and other documents by which alone every conference clarifies its own collective mind, and makes the world outside aware of its judgement. Every conference therefore had an enormous amount of paper work to be done against time, during its course. It could only be done by working far into the night. At Edinburgh, for instance, Archbishop Temple wrote home, 'I was writing till 1.15 last night; I wrote continuously for $4\frac{1}{2}$ hours, and so finished a draft of the Message.'[2] It was quite a commonplace sentence for him to write during any of

[1] Oliver Tomkins, *loc. cit.*, p. 285.
[2] F. A. Iremonger, *William Temple: His Life and Letters* (Oxford University Press, 1948), p. 410.

these conferences—and he was present at most of them. On another occasion, at Jerusalem, he sat all morning in his committee, and then

after lunch I attended a small Committee because I am to be joint-chairman on the Christian Message in relation to other religions. . . . We shall have two mornings on that subject in full conference, and two afternoons on it in groups—Hinduism, Buddhism, Islam, Confucianism, Secularism. Then a committee made of the chairmen and secretaries of those groups with Speer and myself, will settle down to draft 'findings,' to report to the full conference, and go on till we have done.[1]

Nor was it only Temple who was thus driven. Everybody who bore office in such conferences, and had a share in the interminable drafting of documents which had to be done, was bound to emerge at the end a very tired man.

Sometimes, too, the physical conditions under which the delegates lived were not such as to ease the burden. At Jerusalem, the only way Temple could get a bath was to walk over to the Bishop of Jerusalem's house and get one there. Where he was put to live no such luxury existed. It was a hut in a long building

with a corridor right through the middle, and doors along it into compartments five yards long and three yards wide. The furniture is a small but comfortable bedstead, and a table carrying basin, jug, etc. There is no sort of cupboard or drawer. We are partitioned to the roof on the corridor side but only as high as the angle of the outside wall and roof between the compartments. The whole thing is made of board and sounds travel. Consequently I knew all about the unfortunate man in the same row who had violent sick attacks at 1.0, 3.0, and 5.0 A.M.!! . . . There is a draught in the hut this evening for some reason so my own candle is hopeless on the table. I have had to put it on the floor and write lying on the boards on my tummy.[2]

But perhaps the most exhausting thing of all was the struggle for understanding between delegates of so many different nations and races, and such widely differing Church traditions. This naturally came out most clearly at the conferences on Faith and Order. At Edinburgh it proved alarmingly difficult to combine in any agreed statement the Protestant anxiety for intercommunion before formal unity, and as a means to it, and the Anglican insistence that unity must be achieved first and intercommunion would then crown it. In fact, the two views were not (and still are not) reconciled: it was hard enough for each party to understand the other's point of view. At Lausanne, on a rather more doctrinal level, the discovery that while the Lutherans and the Orthodox both demanded a statement that the Church is both visible and invisible they put precisely opposite interpretations on the terms they both used, caused a real increase in the

---

[1] Iremonger, *op. cit.*, p. 395.   [2] *Ibid.*, pp. 394, 396.

strain all the delegates were bearing. Nevertheless there was hardly a soul at these conferences who hesitated to say that the strain of attending them was much more than worth while, and history certainly supports them. A new thing, the 'great new fact of our time,' was being born, and it was not likely to be without travail.

This 'new thing' was of such a nature that though it was conceived in the matrix of faithfulness to the missionary cause, it could only be brought to birth in the setting of the great international conference. If one looks at the actual achievements of these conferences in the particular spheres they set themselves to occupy, it is easy to be despondent about them. Lausanne and Edinburgh were exploring the path which might lead to the formal union of the Churches. They revealed a surprisingly large element of agreement among them. But reunion has not yet come. Stockholm and Oxford were concerned with the processes by which the 'kingdoms of this world,' the actual social order in which all Churches are set, become the kingdoms of our Lord. A terrific amount of work went into them and a whole series of volumes of analysis came out of them, but to all appearances the twentieth century plunged unimpressed along the road to perdition. A cynic might easily say that the time and the energy of many good men, and the money of the faithful, were wasted because they did not produce immediately solutions to all the problems considered. But the giants who inspired the conferences, Bishop Brent of the Episcopal Church of America, whose episcopate of the Philippines was one of the special glories of the Anglican Communion, Archbishop Sodorblom of Upsala, and, in the next generation, Archbishop William Temple, all of them busier and far more realistically minded than any cynic, did not judge their time wasted, and never doubted the value of what was being done.

The value was in the meeting, in the fact that at Edinburgh, for example, in 1937, 414 delegates from 122 Christian Churches in 43 different countries prayed, lived, and worked together, speaking in love the truth as they saw it precisely about matters of high sensitiveness, which were life and death to all of them, and by which they were divided almost as often as they were united, and yet went away not only friends for life, but with an awareness of unity stronger by far than any awareness of separation. This they did in different contexts again and again in those twenty years in centres as far apart as Madras, Jerusalem, and Stockholm. At last the ground was prepared to give this new-found unity of friends in Christ a more formal and permanent shape, and in the summer of 1937, at Utrecht, the three strands, Missions, Life and Work, and Faith and Order, were ready to be woven into a single rope, and the constitution of the World Council of Churches was worked out by the delegates of more than 70 Churches, under the chairmanship of Temple. Even in the war of 1939 that rope did not break, and in 1948 the World Council of Churches had its first conference at Amsterdam. Much had in fact been done by these conferences which without them could not have been done at all for the reunion of Christendom, for the Christianising of twentieth-century social and international order, for the whole missionary cause. But if nothing whatever had been done to further any of them, the whole series of conferences would still have been amply worth while, for through them nation and Church did speak peace to nation and Church. While governments split into fragments, dragging their hapless citizens with them, the unity in joy and co-operation in love of the Christian Churches remained a strong and enduring fact, on which, and as it seems on which alone, the nations of mankind in their search for peace can count.

III. *The Missionary Seed Bed*

The separate endeavours and accomplishments of all these conferences have been estimated a dozen times, and stand on record in the voluminous reports which their committees published. There is already a considerable literature about the formative years of the Ecumenical Movement and any worth-while addition to it would require not less than the space of a whole book. No attempt need therefore be made here to enumerate what each conference did. We turn instead to a broad outline of the general development of the missionary adventure during the period, in which the Church of England played a part of hardly less importance, and shouldered a burden quite as heavy, as she had done in the half century before.

Before 1918 it was becoming evident that the days of missionary pioneering pure and simple were over. Geographically speaking, the Gospel had been taken to the whole world. Just as there were no more large tracts of land left for explorers to discover for the first time, so there was no considerable part of the world where some kind of an organised Christian Church did not exist. There could be no new Columbus and no new Livingstone. This does not mean that the need for Christian expansion had passed. But in future the expansion would have to be spiritual rather than geographical, and the new ground would have to be won not by isolated Christian adventurers, however heroic, but through the work and prayer of organised Churches. The missionary's would have to be a controlled activity, for wherever in the whole mission field he might work he would be in some diocese, with a bishop set over him and some kind of diocesan organisation, however rudimentary, behind him. The nineteenth-century pioneers had done their work for they had planted the visible Church in every land; and the conversion of souls, as of the forms of civilisation which nourished these souls, had become, as it always must, the function of the organised Church.

Now all these missionary Churches had been founded by one or other of the older Churches in the British Empire or in the United States. They had sent them their missionaries, their bishops and clergy, and provided much of their finance. These Younger Churches as they came to be called, were thus tied by many cords to the Older Churches at home. This state of affairs plainly could not and should not continue for very long, more particularly in view of the increasingly passionate political nationalism of the countries of the East. It was therefore inevitable that the universal theme of missionary discussion after 1918 should be the way in which these cords could best be severed, or at least slackened, and the Church in Africa or in China become genuinely and authentically African or Chinese while yet remaining Anglican. To use the technical term, how could a young Church become indigenous, a Church completely native in soil of its own national and racial culture?

To this problem the missionary conference at Jerusalem returned again and again. No one doubted that the Church of Christ in any land must become native to that land, but how was it to be done? The stage of growth reached in 1928 was that practically every Anglican Church had become what the members of the conference called autonomous. They were all Churches, that is, in the words of one of the delegates, whose growth has resulted 'in the transfer to these national Churches of ecclesiastical government, and the independent control by themselves of all their own ecclesiastical affairs. The adoption of credal statements, the ordination of their clergy, the admission and discipline of their members, the question of union with other Churches are wholly within the governing authority of these Churches.'[1] To have got so far from the leading strings of ecclesiastical paternalism was no slight feat. But still it was not enough to be autonomous in the sense defined above: a Church must advance towards becoming indigenous, just as the Church of England centuries ago had to advance to the fully indigenous state in which it now is. Two years before, the famous missionary statesman, John R. Mott, had suggested a definition of what the word 'Indigenous' should mean. An indigenous Church, he said, was one which fulfilled these four conditions:

1. It must be natural, homelike, and belonging to the country.
2. The 'Church edifice must be planted right in the heart of the people wherever they are.'

---

[1] *Record of Jerusalem Meeting of the International Missionary Council* (Oxford University Press, 1928), vol. iii, p. 78.

3. Its architecture and every art it uses in worship must be native architecture and native art.
4. It must be self-supporting, self-governing, and self-propagating.[1]

But the conference was sure that 'there is not to-day in any mission field in the world a national Church which is either completely self-supporting or adequately self-propagating.'[2] That indeed was true, for all alike had to receive considerable grants in money from one or another of the missionary societies at home, as they still do. Eventually the conference adopted this formal statement of what an indigenous Church is:

The Secret of a Living Indigenous Church

A Church, deeply rooted in God through Jesus Christ, an integral part of the Church Universal, may be said to be living and indigenous when

1. Its interpretation of Christ and its expression in worship and service, in custom, art, and architecture incorporate the worthy characteristics of the people, while conserving at the same time the heritage of the Church in all lands and in all ages.
2. When through it the Spirit of Jesus Christ influences all phases of life, bringing to His service the potentialities of both men and women.
3. When it actively shares its life with the nation in which it finds itself.
4. When it is alert to the problems of the times and as a spiritual force in the community it courageously and sympathetically makes its contribution to their solution.
5. When it is kindled with missionary ardour and the pioneering spirit.[3]

This definition, though in some ways still vague, does point clearly to the two essential marks of an indigenous Church. These are that if in Africa it must become as authentically African as the Church of England is English, and to that end must work towards the day when it can provide the whole of its ministry from among its own people.

It required action on many lines. One step was the asserting of equality of status as between older and younger Churches. Here the actual composition of the delegates to the great missionary conferences, which became steadily less and less dominated by Europeans, helped impalpably but enormously. At Edinburgh in 1910 the coloured Christians were a bare dozen out of some 1,200 members of the conference. At Jerusalem in 1928 more than a third, and at Madras in 1938 more than half the delegates came from the younger Churches. On a lesser scale the same thing had been true in China. In 1907 the centenary celebrations of the beginning of the mission to China were not graced by a Chinese speaker, and not a single Chinese sat on the platform. In 1913 the Shanghai conference of missions in China was nearly dominated by the Chinese. In 1921 the President

[1] *Record*, vol. iii, p. 46.   [2] *Ibid.*, p. 44.   [3] *Ibid.*, pp. 208, 209.

and the Chairman of the Business Committee of the National Christian Conference of China were Chinese, as also were more than half of the members of the National Christian Council which the conference set up.

The road to the independence of the Anglican Church in China was greatly smoothed by the vision and perspicacity of Archbishop Randall Davidson. When the first Chinese national was appointed a bishop in 1917 it was Davidson who insisted that he should make his oath of canonical obedience to the Anglican Church in China, the Chung Hua Sheng Kung Hui, and not, as hitherto the English bishops in China had done, to the diocesan authorities at home. Furthermore, when in 1928 Bishop Molony of Chekiang wished to resign, Davidson not only made him offer his resignation to the Presiding Bishop of the Chung Hua Sheng Kung Hui, but he saw to it that Bishop Molony's successor was chosen by the Chinese House of Bishops, and consecrated in China, not in England.

They chose an Englishman, Bishop Curtis. A few years later they would probably have chosen a Chinese. For the road towards the status of becoming an indigenous Church has its outward and visible milestones, and these are reached when the young Church not only chooses its own bishops, but begins to choose its own nationals to be bishops. Before 1939 this had begun to happen in China, Japan, India, and Africa; and their record in the desperate years to come showed their fitness for rule and responsibility.

The growth to indigenous maturity of the younger Churches was also aided by the immemorial instinct of the pioneer missionaries of all Churches to add works of healing and education to their directly evangelistic work. In unbroken succession from Pentecost onwards the Church has always regarded the healing of the body as of hardly less importance than the healing of the soul, and one of the very first acts of all missions had been to provide hospitals, doctors, and nurses. This work went on steadily, and it was harder than it otherwise would have been for even the most embittered nationalist agitator to gain credence for his charge that a European mission which thus served the people at the point of their acutest need was secretly determined to exploit them in the interests of European spiritual domination. Another form of the same realisation that European missionaries were in Africa or China in order to build up an authentically African or Chinese Anglican Church, and not just a new province of the Church of England, was the new missionary policy to bring into the Church whole families or villages, and to make them the unit of conversion, rather than individual converts one at a time. The great developments in missionary educational policy whereby for the first time there was close co-operation in many lands between mission and

L**

government in the whole range of public education, of which the
college at Achimota is perhaps the most celebrated of many such
symbols, all told the same tale. To look at the work of Anglican
missions as a whole in the years 1919 to 1939 is to be convinced that
the whole adventure was governed by the clear aim to lead the
younger Churches as quickly as possible to the stage of development
in which they could be rightly left free of all kinds of tutelage, and so
become fully indigenous.

The home base in England of all this missionary activity was as
alert and as energetic as it had ever been in the past. The great
societies, S.P.G., C.M.S., and the others were served by men of
particular distinction and ability. They carried most of the routine
burden of maintaining financially the various missions which they had
founded years before, and they worked in almost perfect co-operation with each other. Behind them was the International Missionary
Council, in which was concentrated a great deal of the necessary
work of missionary research, and which was served by men of the
calibre of Dr. J. H. Oldham and William Paton—names which stand
high on the long roll of missionary heroes. There was, however, one
new feature of the landscape of the home base of Anglican missions,
the Missionary Council of the Church Assembly. This body was not
quite the novelty which to many people it seemed to be, and it had
quite a long pedigree. In 1884 two provincial Boards of Missions
were set up for Canterbury and York, and within a few years these
Boards sat together instead of separately. In 1908 they became the
Central Board of Missions. Nevertheless the Missionary Council,
which began in 1921, though a lineal successor of these, had a much
more official existence because it was a Council of the Church
Assembly, and therefore an organ of a statutory body. Archbishop
St. Clair Donaldson of Brisbane was brought back to England as
Bishop of Salisbury with the intent that he should also become the
first chairman of the Missionary Council, and, while neither sup-
planting nor attempting to supplant the traditional missionary
societies, under him it became a body of great importance. Before
he died he had made it an essential part of the missionary organisation of the Church. Its purpose, as its first chairman saw it, was to
'cement the relationship of the Missionary Societies to each other
and to the Church at large,'[1] and also to be the organ of the missionary education of the Church at home. The second purpose has been
splendidly achieved, but the first has caused, and still causes, a certain amount of tension.

[1] C. T. Dimont and F. de Witt Batty, *St. Clair Donaldson* (Faber and Faber,
1939), p. 143.

The heart of the difficulty came over the slogan which the devotees of the Missionary Council were fond of using—the Church is its own Missionary Society. But in days gone by the societies had done the work of the Church because the Church, as a corporate body, was content to leave it to the voluntary societies. These reflected the different ecclesiastical traditions of the Church's history, and in the passage of time had attracted a great mass of loyalty to themselves through the fellowship in missionary and evangelistic work which they had provided. They had also contracted all kinds of financial obligations of the most sacred kind, and they doubted, probably with justice, whether the Missionary Council would be able to command even a quarter of the financial support which they enjoyed. Their policy throughout has been to aid the advance of ecclesiastical independence through the growth of a proper Church structure of the missions they had founded, and they all took ceaseless pains to ensure that the relationship between them would be one of co-operation and not of competition. The Missionary Council in its turn has never claimed that it ought to supersede the societies, but has from time to time claimed through its annual reports that missionary Churches ought to be able to speak direct to the Church of England, as one Church to another, but that in fact they have to speak as 'Church with Missionary Society.'[1] This in turn is denied by the societies. The heart of the tension has been most neatly laid bare by the present secretary of C.M.S., Canon Max Warren, in his pamphlet *Iona and Rome*, which he begins by pointing out that

the terms 'Iona' and 'Rome' are used to symbolise two creative and contrasting ideas as to how the missionary task of the Church in the world can be fulfilled. . . . The one lays stress on inspired spontaneity working through voluntary associations, believing this method best calculated to break new ground. The other emphasises the need for centralised direction.[2]

This tension has never, however, developed into anything which could be called a quarrel; and the record of missionary work suggests that it is the sort of tension which gives health to the whole body which contains it. Certainly the Missionary Council is here to stay, for it has done so many necessary things which could not have been done without it. Just as certainly, the voluntary societies, affectionately known by their initials, are permanently an essential part of the missionary picture of England.

In the fulfilling of the Missionary Council's educational charge the name of St. Clair Donaldson, Bishop of Salisbury, is of the greatest importance. When he came back from Australia he was very impressed by the fact that far too many churchpeople at home took

---

[1] Quoted in *Iona and Rome*, p. 10.   [2] *Iona and Rome*, p. 2.

no interest in missions and had no knowledge of them. The burden was being borne by the few, and the many were too engrossed by the affairs of the Church at home to have any attention left to spare for the Church overseas. But this, he believed, was due to ignorance, not to a fundamental weakening of imaginative sympathy. He was therefore sure that the first work of the Missionary Council must be to present the facts to the whole body of churchpeople in such a way that only the blindly insensitive could fail to hearken. He therefore persuaded the Missionary Council to set in simultaneous motion two enterprises whereby prayer might be so fruitfully wedded to knowledge as to ensure response.

The first part of the task was the creation of the Jerusalem Chamber Fellowship of Prayer. In 1925 Donaldson gathered a group of men and women round him in the Jerusalem Chamber at Westminster Abbey. They asked why the Church seemed to be relatively unimpressed by the fact of the greatest Christian opportunity in history, and they answered that it was due to poverty of prayer as well as to poverty of knowledge. They decided therefore to begin a circle of intercession to pray systematically for the extension of Christ's kingdom. Such circles have been started many times, but this, the Jerusalem Chamber Fellowship of Prayer, was unusual in that, without advertisement or publicity it quickly numbered its members by thousands in many parts of the world. They issued to their members suggestions for intercession, and rules of sacrificial self-discipline in prayer—and these were of a conspicuously high spiritual quality. Few more moving or searching acts of prayer and praise have been written than the set of prayers based on the seven objectives of the Jerusalem Fellowship, which are printed as an appendix to Donaldson's biography. The effect of all this widespread work of prayer, which amounted to something not far short of a prayer revival in the Church, was of course incalculable—hid with Christ in God. But occasional pieces of evidence cropped up to show a little of the power for righteousness set loose by this great enterprise. There were, for example, the undergraduates, who, inspired by their prayer through the Jerusalem Fellowship, persuaded their friends to join them in giving up the whole of a summer vacation to touring the dioceses in order to spread knowledge of the missionary situation. They offered themselves to the Missionary Council, who prepared them, sent them out in groups around the country, with quite remarkable results. This was only one of the tangible results of this Fellowship of prayer, and there must be hundreds of others of which no record exists.

The other enterprise of the Missionary Council under Donaldson's chairmanship arose out of his resolve to 'provide the Church with a

considered policy for its work overseas.'[1] This was the World Call
to the Church. The mission field was divided into six great sections,
the Far East, Africa, India, the Moslem World, the Jews, and our
own people overseas. The first four volumes were published in 1925,
and the last two in 1928. They were prepared and written by commissions of people who had knowledge of the facts of each area. But
an unusual feature was that churchpeople in each diocese were asked
to take a hand in the necessary preliminary study. Donaldson's own
diocese of Salisbury was asked to study the needs of India, and study
groups met regularly in many parts of the diocese. The reports were
highly knowledgeable and expert documents, and their publication
formed a new chapter in missionary history. The editor of Crockford, than whom no one was ever less given to uncritical enthusiasm,
noted of them:

> It may be doubted whether any Church has ever possessed so complete a
> summary of its foreign work and opportunities. The collection of the
> necessary statistics alone must have been a very laborious undertaking.
> Yet no one could possibly call any of the reports dull. The first impression
> they produce on the reader's mind is not far removed from bewilderment
> at the kaleidoscopic changes which are taking place in every part of the
> world, not least in what have been for centuries the three great citadels of
> immutable conservatism, India, China, and the House of Islam. The
> second, astonishment (if it is not profane to use the word in this con-
> nexion) that so much has been accomplished with such slender resources.[2]

To write and publish a series of reports so comprehensive and
authoritative would have been impossible without making heavy
draughts upon the specialised funds of knowledge which only the
missionary societies possessed. The societies enthusiastically took
their full share in preparing them, so that the most notable piece of
missionary enterprise in England after 1919 was the result of willing,
fruitful co-operation between the old societies and the new Missionary Council.

By 1925 the first four reports of the World Call were ready, and it
remained to present them to the Church as a whole. Donaldson was
quite prepared for either success or failure, and he explicitly said so
in his preface. 'It may be that the facts when known will themselves
act with awakening power upon the Church. . . . On the other hand
it may be that the Church will turn a deaf ear, that the seductive influences of comfort, and the zest of domestic controversy may have
paralysed her spirit.' In the event, the more hopeful guess turned out
to be the true one, and the World Call was certainly heeded. But this
was due not only to the informed excellence of the reports. Even
more the response was due to the fact that the reports constituted a

---

[1] Dimont, *op. cit.*, p. 148.   [2] *Crockford Prefaces*, p. 61.

call, the World Call, and the trumpet uttering the call was sounded loudly and skilfully. Few bishops have shrunk from publicity more than Donaldson, and few could use it more fully and pertinaciously when it was necessary. The sounding of the call was admirably managed. The first blast of the trumpet was sounded at the opening conference in London in January 1925 in the ears of three thousand delegates, representing every diocese in England, every kind of churchmanship, and every missionary society. One after another the call to the home Church from its daughter Churches in China, Japan, Africa, India, and the Near East was brought home to those present. It was clinched in one of the most eloquent speeches that even Dr. Lang, then Archbishop of York, ever made, who was always at his best—and *what* a best that was!—on a missionary occasion. The peroration was the theme, Now or Never:

> It may be, for all I know, a real crisis, when the Church will stand at God's bar, and the issue will be whether at this moment in the world's history it accepts or shirks its primary trust. Read these Reports quickly and you will hear behind you all the time a voice sounding like a bell, with most impressive persistency—Now or Never. The chance is here, it may be seized, or lost for ever.[1]

In the dioceses there were similar scenes, and everywhere crowds of churchpeople were gathered to hear the reports interpreted. One immediate result was a large and swift increase in the membership of the Jerusalem Fellowship of Prayer. Other results were seen in the increase of volunteers for missionary work and in augmented giving of money.

It may perhaps be also laid, at least partly, to the credit of the World Call that throughout the period there was a steady increase in the attractiveness of missionary literature which ranged from the twopenny pamphlet to the long and serious book, such as Dr. J. H. Oldham's *Christianity and the Race Problem*, which is one of the classics of missionary scholarship. The Church was blessed in those years by the possession of an unusual number of men and women who could write of missions with great vividness, and force the ordinary reader to see both the immensity of the issues at stake, and also how missions really were making history in changing the face of large portions of the earth. There was Basil Matthews, whose book, *The Clash of Colour*, must be one of the most widely circulated of all missionary books; and in our own time his mantle has been donned by Canon McLeod Campbell, who, in successive annual surveys of the total missionary scene, has enriched the Church by presenting his wide and scholarly knowledge in language no less vivid

[1] Dimont, *op. cit.*, p. 151.

and forceful. Churchpeople in these two decades had less excuse than ever before if they paid no heed to the missionary challenge.

Out in the mission field itself, which was so vast that it stretched over half the world and took in whole continents, conditions were so varied that but little experience was common to every part of it. Nevertheless there was some common ground. The missionaries in places so far apart as West Africa, Korea, India, or China did find that some of their experiences and problems, however differently dressed, were basically the same. The militantly secular conception of life, with its concomitant doctrine of individual man as the slave of the collective state, was the universal and ubiquitous enemy which all had to fight. The English missionary everywhere found that his special work was more institutional than pioneering. For the most part he was wanted to man the schools, the hospitals, or the theological colleges. He had to learn to be something of an administrator as well as a pastor, and it was but seldom that he could depart into the blue to villages and settlements where they had never heard the name of Christ. The great days of the individualistic adventures in evangelism were inexorably passed.

Dom Bernard Clements may serve as an example. Few priests have ever been more evangelistically minded than he. But when his abbey at Pershore (the Benedictine community of monks now at Nashdom) sent him to take charge of their work at Kumasi in West Africa, he found that he had first of all to become a mixture of architect, diplomatist, and contractor, and that success in his real business of teaching absolutely depended on his first achieving some measure of success in these other and, to him, rather alien fields.

New college buildings had to be started, endless 'contracts' achieved, some kind of domestic economy established, means of transport found. . . . In January 1928 the new buildings were started. The gathering in of the necessary funds must have been an excruciating business, even though Dom Bernard excelled in the art of begging for the needs of the church. 'This is the ninth day of building,' he wrote to his mother, 'and the walls of the chapel are two feet above the ground, and the foundations of the lecture-room block are in.'[1]

By April the college was ready to be ceremonially opened; but the work was not finished. In May the builders were still busy, shouting so loud to each other that Dom Bernard's lectures on moral theology could not be given because no one could possibly hear his voice above the din. Then a tornado came, and the college was flooded, and carpeted all over with warm mud. When that had laboriously

[1] E. M. Almedingen, *Dom Bernard Clements* (John Lane, 1945), p. 73.

been cleaned, the planting of the garden had to be carefully planned and carried through. Thereafter he would have to

spend an arduous morning, struggling with accounts and incomprehensible balance sheets, and be defeated in the struggle. Then dry-minded business men came out to Kumasi and tried to argue with him, and on some occasions he lost his temper, retorting that he was a priest and not a bank clerk, and then turn to quick and hot repentance, and once again wage war on the demoniac ranks of figures which seemed to him so stubborn, incomprehensible, and idiotic.[1]

Such were the external conditions in which one of the greatest missionaries of the day, and thousands of others, had to labour. Success or failure in these things governed the possibility of their being able to do the real work for which they had been sent out. Nor, on the other hand, could a man hope to do the one job only. Bernard Clements was sent to be the head of the Kumasi Theological College—much more than a whole-time occupation in itself. But he was also responsible for the work of the Church in the town of Kumasi, and in an area as large as Wales, with sixteen out-stations. Much time, therefore, had to be spent in travelling; and often enough there were no roads. So it was with most missions. The letter from the bishop in the mission's periodical which circulated at home among its supporters was often composed chiefly of vivid accounts of his journeys, and their difficulties.

Anglican Churches overseas were educators, healers, builders, and evangelists. They received, taught, and cared for vast mass movements of converts, as in South India and the Philippine Islands, with resources of men and money quite ludicrously insufficient. But it was perhaps in their attitude to quite another institution, the institution of the colour bar, that Anglican missions in this period became most famous. The constant and outspoken condemnation of the general attitude of white settlers and of governments in South Africa towards the African nationals by all the South African bishops was most courageous. It did not make them very popular with governmental authority, but the Church in South Africa became known as meaning exactly what it said when it spoke of the equality of all human beings in Christ, and in it the coloured peoples knew they had a champion and a friend. Much the same story was repeated farther north, in Zanzibar and in Kenya, where Archdeacon Owen, among others, wrote a grand page of missionary history. So it was, too, on the other side of the continent with Bernard Clements who refused to allow the accidents of colour to make even the least difference to his relationships, and heartily rebuked such white people as did. 'May I tell you,' wrote to his mother one African he had brought

[1] Almedingen, *op. cit.*, p. 75.

close to Christ, 'that we Africans love your son very much. In fact there is nothing adequate to say about him than "a black man born white." '[1]

All this may seem a catalogue of comparative trivialities when set against the immensity of the storm of evil so soon to rage over the world. But in that storm the work was tested, and in the test it was shown that it was good. Of the heroes and heroines of the mission field during the second world war, and particularly in those parts of the world occupied by the Japanese, this is not the place to speak. That great story of martyred Papuan and Karen nurses, of the discovery that Christian missions could turn cannibals into saints in two generations, of the bravery, faithfulness, and privations of missionaries of every kind, has now been told many times—and these men and women have become at once our pride and our accusation. To read it is to live again in the magic of the language of *Hebrews* xi 35: they 'were tortured not accepting deliverance.' One single indication of the proven greatness of the work when tested shall suffice. No one has ever yet put the essential spirit of missions more grandly than Bishop Strong of New Guinea in his now classical broadcast to his people while the Japanese were landing in their islands.

I have from the first felt that we must endeavour to carry on our work in all circumstances, no matter what the cost may ultimately be to any of us individually. God expects this of us. The Universal Church expects it. The tradition and history of missions requires it of us. Missionaries who have been faithful to the uttermost and are now at rest are surely expecting it of us. The people whom we serve expect it of us. Our own consciences expect it of us. We could never hold up our faces again if, for our own safety, we all forsook Him and fled when the shadows of the Passion began to gather round Him in His Spiritual and Mystical Body, the Church in Papua. Our life in the future would be burdened with shame and we could not come back here and face our people again; and we would be conscious always of rejected opportunities. The history of the Church tells us that missionaries do not think of themselves in the hour of danger and crisis, but of the Master who called them to give their all, and of the people whom He trusts them to serve and to love to the uttermost, even as He has served and loved to the uttermost. . . .

No! my brothers and sisters, fellow workers in Christ, whatever others may do, we cannot leave. We shall not leave. We shall stay by our trust. We shall stand by our vocation. We do not know what it may mean to us. Many already think us fools and mad. What does that matter? If we are fools, 'We are fools for Christ's sake.' I cannot foretell the future. I cannot guarantee that all will be well—that we shall all come through unscathed. One thing only I can guarantee is that if we do not forsake Christ here in Papua in His Body, the Church, He will not forsake us. He will uphold us; He will sustain us; He will strengthen us, and He will guide and keep us through the days that lie ahead. If we all left, it would take

---

[1] Almedingen, *op. cit.*, p. 79.

years for the Church here to recover from our betrayal of our trust. If we remain—and even if the worst came to the worst and we all were to perish in remaining—the Church will not perish, for there would have been no breach of trust in its walls, but its foundation and structure would have received added strength for the future building by or faithfulness unto death.[1]

By this missionary faithfulness history was made. But even this was not an isolated instance of faithfulness. It was, in a sense, a dramatic climax, a sacrament of many generations of faithfulness on the part of thousands of entirely obscure and unknown men and women of the Anglican Church, who knew that they must take the Gospel to the ends of the world, and continue to serve their people to the ends of time. They have created far more than they could ever have dreamed. The existence of the Anglican Communion can be credited to them. The Ecumenical Movement was embedded in their work. The hope of millions of the underprivileged in all parts of the world was and is built of their fidelity. The missionary enterprise has changed history for good and bettered destiny in every land where it has penetrated, and the vision of old John Donne of St. Paul's, declared in a sermon to the Virginia Company in 1622, has come true:

And you that are young may live to see your friends, yea children, as well accommodated in that place as any other. You shall have made this island which is but as the suburbs of the old world, a bridge, a gallery to the new, to join all to that world that shall never grow old—the kingdom of heaven, and add names to the books of our chronicles, and to the book of life.

[1] Ruth Henrich, *South Sea Epic* (S.P.G., 1944), pp. 22, 23.

EPILOGUE

For good or ill the task begun ten years ago is now completed. It was to describe the life of the Church of England in the first forty years of the twentieth century. The intertwining themes of its history in this period are so complex that only by an almost harsh selectiveness has it been possible to impose upon material so confused and so embarrassingly plentiful any ordered pattern. No one is more conscious than the author of all the themes which might have been treated in these volumes and yet are not to be found in them. But however ill performed such a task may be, no one could possibly devote to it ten years of reading, thought, and writing without reaching certain fundamental convictions about the true meaning of the whole story. What, basically, is the story all about? What has the Church of England been really trying to do in these forty years? And is that what God has wanted of her, and still wants? The answers to such questions are the morals of the story; and the Duchess in *Alice in Wonderland* was after all perfectly right when she demanded to be told the moral of every episode, for the history which yields no moral must be a confused and insignificant noise. Many morals could no doubt be justly drawn. But in the author's mind during the last ten years two have emerged from all the others as of quite crucial importance, and have grown until they are to-day basic convictions of the true meaning of the whole of the history of the Church of England in this century.

The first of these convictions is that the whole story of the Church of England in our time has been fundamentally about the re-founding of the Christian doctrine of man in twentieth-century society, and that in this whole enterprise the Church of England is peculiarly well-equipped—is even better equipped than any other Church—to play the leading part. If this is so, our Church is in the heart of the real battlefield of the century, and not skirmishing aimlessly on the outskirts of it. For there can be no doubt left now that the historian of five hundred years hence will write about the twentieth century as primarily the era in which the idea of man as a free, sacred, and infinitely precious personality was lost or won. It is as certain as anything can be that within the next fifty years the ordinary citizen will be delivered for centuries to come into slavery or else delivered from the slavery which now threatens him. The twentieth century is all about the freedom or slavery of man. There is no need to produce arguments to justify the starkness of this view. Hundreds of diagnoses have already proclaimed it, and even if they had never been written, every new day's events make it abundantly plain. In any case, the purpose of this epilogue is rather to state convictions than to argue for them.

It is no less clear that the freedom and dignity of man, and every chance he has of reaching the right relationship with the state, the class, or any other collective group, is inextricably tied to Christianity. We can claim freedom and denounce slavery for man because God loves him, made him in His image, Himself became man and died to save him, and, in Christ, taught him the infinite value of his soul and sacredness of his personality. In the last analysis there are no other grounds than these for claiming human freedom, and the idea of personality as sacred is embedded in the truth of the Gospel— there, and nowhere else. It follows that in a century where the truth of this view of the purpose of man's life and of his status is under an attack more violent, more universal, and more determined than ever before in history, the Church's battlefield is automatically decided. The prize of the twentieth-century battle is the soul of man, and therefore the freedom of man.

Every Church in the world is involved in this battle, which cannot be won if any Church retires from it. But though the battlefield is one and indivisible the Churches are not, and therefore each Church has to bring to the fight its own characteristic and distinctive strength. This is the only conceivable excuse for the fact that there are many Churches rather than one Church. Throughout history, and especially in this century, it almost seems as though God had been preparing the Church of England and the Anglican Communion to which it gave birth for such a moment as this. Our whole Anglican tradition, which the Book of Common Prayer enshrines more completely than any other document, seems to be equipping us for this historic hour. The tradition exalts freedom above all other goods. It places this freedom in a context of order, but in any clash between these two freedom is invariably preferred. It rates the average far above the exceptional. The tradition is deeply pastoral, and its characteristic speech is not that of impersonal leadership exhorting and managing an equally impersonal and amorphous mass of discipleship, but of person with person, and friend with friend. The whole relationship thus rests upon that sensitive courtesy which regards a man as himself uniquely, and not as a mere representative of some class or group. Its steadfast refusal of the dual standard of morality or holiness as between priest and layman, saint and sinner, sets on a sure foundation the dignity of being human.

The swing of Anglican history in the last forty years has steadily

underlined all this. The emphasis of what is called the Christian
Social Movement in the Church from Maurice to the Malvern Conference and the famous Summer Schools of Christian Sociology has
been consistently on the need to claim man's dignity and to set him
free in the household his work creates. It is this simple and single
insight which unites men so various as Charles Kingsley, Stewart
Headlam, Samuel Barnett, Charles Gore, and Basil Jellicoe. Whether
this social movement has expressed itself in denouncing financial
tyrannies, in building houses, in espousing guild or some other kind
of socialism, in driving to the roots of the matter in a new statement
of the doctrine of creation, it has been held together and its history
made a consistent whole by its passionate belief in human dignity.
Exactly the same emphasis links the pioneer missionaries to the
policy of the present indigenous Churches they founded. The Church
overseas has consistently stood, stands now, and is widely known to
stand as the defender of the full human rights and dignities of
coloured peoples and the enemy of all who would deny them.

At home the same trend has been apparent. The creation of the
Church Assembly made an end, and was intended to make an end,
of the old superstition that in the affairs of Church government the
laity had less competence than the clergy. The leaders of the Church
who have made most mark on the consciousness of the people were
precisely those who were known to care for the common man, and
that it mattered intensely to them that he should be set free to grow
to his full stature. Our theology, written more and more often by
laymen, has been steadily popularised, and become less and less of
an esoteric mystery for the few. At the same time, because it is in
theological understanding that the moral justification of freedom is
embedded, theological writing has become ever more definite, more
ineradicably supernatural in emphasis, more dogmatic, more 'from
God to Man.' Nothing has been more significant in these forty years
than the decline and fall of that theological spirit called modernism.
It has fallen for two reasons. Its exponents seemed always to be so
much more conscious of what they did not believe than of what they
did, and its exposition was generally far beyond the understanding of
ordinary people. It never became popular because it disdained to
popularise itself. In the first ten years of the period it seemed to be
carrying all before it, and by 1940 it was already an irrelevant back-
number, because it was seen to offer nothing firm on which the
common man, standing the siege of all the world's thieves of his
freedom, could stand.

No one who knows the Church could possibly say that it had yet
become the fully secure, central bulwark of human freedom in our
age. But it has consistently tried to be the champion of freedom and

of the Christian doctrine of man in which alone this freedom is grounded; and it has been this consistency of effort which has given unity to the diversity of its history in the last forty years.

The second conviction concerns the condition under which this championing of the dignity of personality and human freedom in the name of Christ can be done. We best stand for freedom when we stand together: we weaken it when we stand alone. This condition of togetherness is part and parcel of our Christian discipleship. Rugged individualism on the part of Churches considered corporately, or on the part of any of their members, always springs from a desire for freedom. But this desire of the unteachable individualist is more for freedom for himself than for others. It is quite evident that those of our Anglican leaders during this century who have been most notable for their independent individualism are those who have made the least contribution to the mission of the universal Church to set man free to restore to him his dignity as a person. The lesson of the experience of all the Churches in those years has been that the condition of the phrase 'Set man free in the name of Christ' is the other and now famous phrase, 'Let the Church be the Church.' Let it be the Church, not for the Church's sake but for the people's sake.

As we look back and survey the broad trends of Anglican history since 1919, and try to discover the essential meaning of the whole story, it is important that we should ask the right question. This is, What has God been doing with the Church?—a differently formulated question from, What has the Church been doing? For Christians the Godward phrasing of the question is always the right one. There is but little doubt of the answer. The facts compel it. It is that God has been steadily drawing us closer together, giving us the spirit of fellowship and exorcising the demon of separatism. It is as though He had said to us, using, as He so often seems to do, the eloquence of facts, 'In your togetherness lies your strength and your use.' This general tendency to substitute the spirit of togetherness or fellowship (it is *not* the same thing as unity) for that of separateness or independence has moved simultaneously on two fronts, both within the Church of England itself, and also within the whole of the non-Roman Christian world.

Suppose an English churchman who died in 1918 returned to life in 1939. Though he would at once resume his churchmanship he would soon find he had lost some of his bearings. There would be many changes he would notice, and some would delight him. But the greatest change of all would be that by 1939 the heart had gone out of ecclesiastical partisanship. In the Church he had known that heart was beating all too strongly. The delight in controversy which

was so marked a feature of Church life in England from 1900 to 1914 ·
had changed by 1939 to an utter detestation of it. The first volume
of this work, which told the story from 1900 to 1918, had of necessity
to give much space to examining the hostility which the Anglo-
Catholics excited, and to tracing the processes by which they at last
won their case, and the Church accepted what they offered. The
second volume rarely uses the titles of Anglo-Catholic and Evangelical, and there is hardly a word in it about the 'High Church' and
'Low Church' quarrels which loomed so large before, and indeed
during the war of 1914. Ecclesiastical partisanship was no longer in
the air, and the parties to whom it had once seemed the breath of life
were rapidly ceasing to be relevant. They had done their work, their
undoubtedly necessary work. After 1918 there was little or nothing
worth doing which could be done through ecclesiastical partisanship.
The flare of the old quarrel at the time of the revision of the Prayer
Book was fierce while it lasted, but it was the bright flicker of a dying
flame. Sectarian partisanship in the Church is not of course completely silenced, but it has become no more than languid and routine
slogan-mongering, and none but the really violent extremists ever
listen to it. The general consciousness of churchpeople has become
that of membership of *Ecclesia Anglicana*, not of membership of the
Anglo-Catholics or the Evangelicals.

Another striking development may well be a consequence of the
first, for it is a steady widening of the consciousness of belonging to
something far bigger than the Church of England. More and more
we are all becoming aware of our membership of a worldwide family
of Churches, the Anglican Communion. This consciousness was not
so widespread by 1939 as it has become since 1945. But whereas our
disinterred and reanimated churchman of 1900 to 1918 would, to
judge by the records, have thought but seldom of his membership
in the same communion with Americans, Chinese, or Indians, he
would now be reminded of it almost every day, and some reference
to it would be made in quite a third of the sermons he hears. A very
real sense first of partnership, then of fellowship, and now of brotherhood between the various Churches of the Anglican Communion
has not only been created, but actually felt by steadily increasing
numbers of rank and file churchpeople.

For all this increase of the sense of togetherness the theologians
have been steadily working. Their emphases have naturally been very
different in many ways, but one emphasis has been consistent and
not far from unanimous. It is the stress Anglican theology of the last
thirty years has laid on the mystery of the Church as the Body of
Christ, called forth by God Himself to be a supernatural association
of man with God and man with man whilst still in the world of space-

time. In many ways the theologians have been struggling to instruct
us all what such a churchmanship means, and to give to the common
phrase, Members one of another, a richer meaning than it has had
for centuries. The historians have been hammering at a different
aspect of the same truth in their constant reminder that we are called
to live in the heart of the biblical drama, and that our closest kin in
all the history of Christendom are the Christians of the first three
centuries.

This steady search for the togetherness of Christians, beginning
within the Church of England itself, and then widening to the Anglican Communion, has been stretching further still to cover and enrich
Anglican relationships with many other Churches. Here again the
inevitable differences between these two volumes are instructive and
significant. In the first it was possible to write about the Church of
England and almost to ignore the other Churches, except of course
for the Student Christian Movement and the Edinburgh Conference
of 1910. But in the second volume so rigid a concentration upon the
title, the Church of England, has been quite impossible. However
hard one might try, after 1918 (actually the dividing line is 1910)
there is no possibility of writing about the Church of England without bringing members of other Churches into the tale again and
again. For one thing, the Ecumenical Movement becomes steadily
more crucial for Anglicanism. For another, the heroes of one Church
become more and more the common property of all. Men like John
R. Mott and William Paton seem to belong to Anglicans almost as
fully as to the members of their own communions, and William
Temple was thought of as 'Our Archbishop' by thousands of good
nonconformists. In theology, too, we Anglicans have learned almost
as much from writers like Berdyaev, Maritain, and Niebuhr as from
our own Hoskyns and Quick. It is not merely that on the human
plane Christians of all non-Roman Churches have been driven by a
common apprehension of the power of the universal enemy of militant godlessness to see that they must 'hang together if they are not to
hang separately.' What has moved us all is not so much 'the great
dangers we are in by our unhappy divisions,' but something much
more positive and disinterested. It is the steadily growing conviction
that the togetherness of Christians in the Church is the will of God,
a thing lovely and pleasant for its own sake, quite apart from what
can be done with it and that could not be done without it.

The growth of the spirit of community is both the real achievement and the real lesson of Christian history in this century; and in
this the Church of England has played no unworthy part. The
belief is steadily growing among perfectly ordinary churchpeople in
the parishes that in the achievement of Christian Community our

hope lies. A group of schoolgirls in their summary of the fruit of a long discussion on the needs of the Church to-day admirably expressed it: 'the answer to Communism is found in the exercise of Charity from within Christian Community'. The growth in parish after parish of the Parish Communion and the steady spread of the cell movement in all its ramifications, alike testify to it. Deliverance is in the hands of a Christian community, whose members know that because they are in the Church, they belong to a divine society which is part of the Body of Christ.

We have far, very far, to go; but we have also gone very far. In forty years the distance we have travelled is really astonishing. The Church of England is not yet without spot or wrinkle, but it is a glorious Church, and for his membership no one need be apologetic. It is well able to bring many sons and daughters to glory if they serve it with love and loyalty, and to be not the least of the guardians of the freedom and the dignity of twentieth-century man.

INDEX TO VOLUME TWO

Gore, C., Bishop of Oxford, 51, 52, 83,
85, 93, 102, 252, 262, 264, 266, 268,
270, 280, 311
Greenwood, Arthur, 132
Greer, W., Bishop of Manchester, 201
Guild of St. Matthew, 82–4
Guildford Cathedral, 231

H

HALIFAX, Lord, 2nd Viscount, 36,
259–72
Hall, R., Bishop of Hong Kong, 201
Halliday, James Andrew, 202, 203
Hamilton, General Sir Ian, 121
Hamilton, I., 118
Headlam, A. C., Bishop of Gloucester,
45, 46
Headlam, Stuart, 82, 92, 311
Hebert, A. G., 49, 58, *The Parish Com-
munion*, 72–5, *Liturgy and Society*,
108
Henson, H., Bishop of Durham, 36,
37, 39, 168, 169, 196, 232, 235, 236,
251–4, 256, 262
Hepher, Cyril, 202
Herbert, George, 23
Heywood, R. S., Bishop of Mombasa,
276
Hill, Miss I. N., 118
Hill, Octavia, 126, 139, 204
Hodgson, Canon L., 204
Holland, H. Scott, 83, 98
Hopkinson, A., 191
Hoskyns, Sir Edwyn, 16, 26, 48–57, 58,
59, 314, *The Riddle of the New
Testament*, 57
Hough, Bishop, Bishop of Woolwich,
98
Housing and the Church, 112–40, in
Newcastle, 197–8, 204
Housing Act (1930), 126
Howson, J. S., Dean of Chester, 241
Hubbard, F., 118
Hudson, N., Bishop of Newcastle,
201
Hügel, Baron F. von, 43
Hume, David, 79
Hunter, L., Bishop of Sheffield, 151,
201
Huxley, Aldous, 171
Huxley, Thomas, 29

I

INCUMBENT, trials of the, 148–52
Industrial Christian Fellowship, 15,
96–8, 221
Indkip, T. W. H., 6
International Missionary Council,
300–5

J

JACKSON, Dr. Foakes, 39, 40
Jagger, C. S., 227
Jellicoe, Admiral Lord, 121
Jellicoe, Basil, 13, 16, 113, 114–26, 131,
311
Jenkinson, C., 16, 131–7
Jerusalem Chamber Fellowship of
Prayer, 302
Jerusalem Missionary Conference
(1928), 166, 167, 292, 294, 298
John Kebel Church (Mill Hill), 228
Johnson, Hewlett, Dean of Manchester,
subsequently Dean of Canterbury,
245, 247
Jones, Prof. Henry, 41
Jones, Rufus M., 166

K

KEATS, John, 115
Kelham Rood, 227–8
Kempthorne, J. A., Bishop of Lich-
field, 96
Kennet, Lord, 133
Keynes, Lord, *The Economic Conse-
quences of the Peace*, 250
Kidd, Benjamin, *Science of Power*, 81
Kidd, B. J., 262, 270
Kikuyu Conferences, 272–7, 286
Kingsley, Charles, 82, 86, 88, 92, 311
Kirk, P. T. R., 96
Knox, E. V., 243, 244
Knox, John, 28
Knutsford, Test School for Ordina-
tion Candidates, 8, 143, 146
Kumasi Theological College, 305, 306

L

LACEY, Canon T. R., 237
Lake, Dr. Kirsopp, *Landmarks of
Early Christianity*, 39, 40
Lambeth Appeal (1920), 249–56, 259,
267, 286–9
Lambeth Conference (1920), 8, 249–56,
(1948), 289
Lambeth Quadrilateral, 255
Lang, Cosmo Gordon, Archbishop of
Canterbury, 12, 13, 138, 160–3, 191,
232, 233, 245
Latourette, K. S., *A History of the Ex-
pansion of Christianity*, 39, 40
Laud, Archbishop, 23
Lawrence, D. H., 171
Lawrence, T. E., 1, 5, *Seven Pillars of
Wisdom*, 2